Population and development projects in Africa

Population and development projects in Africa

edited by **John I. Clarke**
Mustafa Khogali
Leszek A. Kosiński

for **International Geographical Union**
Commission on Population Geography

The right of the
University of Cambridge
to print and sell
all manner of books
was granted by
Henry VIII in 1534.
The University has printed
and published continuously
since 1584.

Cambridge University Press

Cambridge
London   New York   New Rochelle
Melbourne   Sydney

Published by the Press Syndicate of the University of Cambridge
The Pitt Building, Trumpington Street, Cambridge CB2 1RP
32 East 57th Street, New York, NY 10022, USA
10 Stamford Road, Oakleigh, Melbourne 3166, Australia

First published 1985

Printed in Great Britain at the University Press, Cambridge

Library of Congress catalogue card number: 84–29323

British Library cataloguing in publication data
Population and development projects in Africa.
1. Population geography
2. Economic development projects
3. Africa, Sub-Saharan – Population
I. Clarke, John I.   II. Khogali, Mustafa
III. Kosiński, Leszek A.   IV. International
Geographical Union Commission on Population Geography
304.6'0967   HB2121

ISBN 0 521 30527 6

SE

Contents

Tables

Figures

Contributors

Mohamed el-Hadi Abusin: Dept. of Geography, University of Khartoum, Sudan

Aderanti Adepoju: Dept. of Demography and Social Statistics, University of Ife, Ile-Ife, Nigeria

Manuel G.M. De Araújo: Dept. of Geography, Eduardo Mondlane University, Maputo, Mozambique

George Benneh: Dept. of Geography, University of Ghana, Legon, Accra, Ghana

John I. Clarke: Dept. of Geography, University of Durham, U.K.

Lufti A. Desougi: Faculty of Education, University of Khartoum, Sudan

Zeinab B. El Bakri: Dept. of Anthropology and Sociology, University of Khartoum, Sudan

Mohammed Osman El Sammani: Dept. of Geography, University of Khartoum, Sudan

Galal el-Din el-Tayeb: Dept. of Geography, University of Khartoum, Sudan

Abdul-Aziz M. Farah: Census and Statistics Dept., Khartoum, Sudan

Mahgoub O. Gaafar: Census and Statistics Dept., Khartoum, Sudan

Amna Beshir Homoudi: Faculty of Arts, University of Khartoum, Sudan Sudan

John B. Kabera: Dept. of Geography, Makerere University, Kampala, Uganda

El Watig Mohamed Kameir: Dept. of Anthropology and Sociology, University of Khartoum, Sudan

Mustafa Khogali: Dept. of Geography, University of Khartoum, Sudan

Leszek A. Kosiński: Dept. of Geography, University of Alberta, Edmonton, Canada

E.M. Letsoalo: Dept. of Geography, University of Witwatersrand, Johannesburg, South Africa

Anne M. Lewandowski: Institute of Environmental Studies, University of Khartoum, Sudan

Michael McCall: Technology and Development Group, Twente University of Technology, Enschede, Netherlands

L.R. Mills: Population Studies Centre, University of Gezira, Wad Medani, Sudan

Yagoub Abdalla Mohamed: Dept. of Geography, University of Khartoum, Sudan

Babiker Abdalla Abdel Rahman: Faculty of Education, University of Khartoum, Sudan

K.V. Ramachandran: Population Division, Economic Commission for Africa, Addis Ababa, Ethiopia

C.M. Rogerson: Dept. of Geography, University of Witwatersrand, Johannesburg, South Africa

John R. Rogge: Dept. of Geography, University of Manitoba, Winnipeg, Canada

Hassan Mohamed Salih: Dept. of Sociology, University of Khartoum, Sudan

Ian Thomas: School of Development Studies, University of East Anglia, Norwich, U.K.

Adrian P. Wood: Dept. of Geography, University of Zambia, Lusaka, Zambia

Preface

One of the most suitable countries for witnessing the impact of development projects upon population redistribution is Sudan. The largest country in Africa, it possesses what appears to be almost limitless space, ranging from arid desert in the north to tropical rainforest in the south, across which flows one of the world's greatest water resources, the Nile and its two great tributaries, the White Nile and the Blue Nile. The utilization of these waters has involved a long series of development projects, large and small, which have not only greatly affected the economic development of Sudan, but also its population distribution and growth. For each project involves the displacement and changed life styles of people, both local and remote, as it attracts people from far and wide. And the localization of projects is necessarily uneven, and so also is the accompanying urbanization. Consequently, development involves major movements of people.

It follows that government policies for economic and social development must give careful attention to the effects of development projects upon population redistribution, and over the last decade or so there has been growing awareness of the significance of this phenomenon. Among the interested international organizations, the International Geographical Union's (I.G.U.) Commission on Population Geography has played a role in holding symposia in different parts of the world, bringing together not only geographers but economists, anthropologists, sociologists, demographers, planners and others to discuss the problem.

Khartoum was therefore a most appropriate venue for an international symposium upon 'the impact of development projects upon population redistribution'. It was locally organized in 1982 on behalf of the I.G.U. Commission on Population Geography and the Department of Geography in the University of Khartoum by Mustafa M. Khogali, who is a member of both. The other co-editors are the present and past Commission chairmen, John I. Clarke and Leszek A. Kosiński. There were 43 other participants at the symposium, from Canada, Ethiopia, Saudi Arabia, Sudan, Tanzania, Turkey, U.K., U.S.A., Uganda and Zambia, who presented 28 papers, many of which provide a nucleus for this volume. Some other papers were solicited from non-participants, in Ghana, Nigeria, Mozambique and South Africa, in order to provide a wider scope for the volume. Obviously, it is impossible to provide case studies from the whole of the fragmented continent of Africa or to examine all the implications of development projects upon population redistribution, but it is felt that this volume provides a useful contribution to the literature.

It would not have seen the light of day without the generous support of the British Overseas Development Administration, the International Geographical Union and the University of Khartoum, particularly the Faculty of Arts and the Department of Geography.

Inevitably, with widespread co-editors and authors, much of the labour of editorial work has rested in the University of Durham, where the Chairman of the I.G.U. Commission on Population Geography is especially grateful to his secretary, Joan Dresser, for dealing with manuscripts from many countries, and to the Department of Geography's cartographers (Arthur Corner, George Brown, David Cowton and David Hume), photographers (Derek Hudspeth, Linda Dodds and Andrew Hudspeth) and printers (John Normile and Marlene Crichton). To all we extend most sincere thanks.

John I. Clarke

Durham
October, 1984

1 The demographic background to development in Africa

Aderanti Adepoju and
John I. Clarke

Introduction

Development in Africa is not nearly as rapid as hoped for, and development projects are sporadic but not numerous, yet population growth is faster than anywhere else in the world and population redistribution is accelerating more than most countries would wish. The relationships between development and development projects on the one hand and rapid population growth and redistribution on the other are far from simple or stable in a continent with such strong spatial unevenness and heterogeneity of population geography and such remarkable diversity and fragmentation of political geography. Thus, in order to understand these relationships, and how Africa's many countries deal with them or think about them, it is important to consider the demographic background to development.

The bare facts are that with 513 million people (1983) Africa contains about 11 per cent of the world's inhabitants on 22 per cent of its land area and that the number of inhabitants is increasing by about 3 per cent each year – well above the world average of 1.8 per cent – owing to high fertility (the average birth rate is 46 per thousand) and relatively high but declining mortality (about 16 per thousand). The urban population, however, is growing much more quickly (about 7 per cent per annum), sustained by migration from rural areas and small towns to the major cities (Adepoju, 1982). Other pertinent characteristics common to Africa are under-development, polarized development and regional inequality, the inheritance of various forms of colonial domination which have shaped and continue to influence greatly the strategy and patterns of economic development as well as migration and spatial population distribution.

Behind these broad generalizations, however, there is considerable diversity in the size and spatial distribution of population, resource endowment, colonial experience, political systems, culture and level of development. The 53 countries and islands listed in Table 1.1 exhibit important variations in land area, population numbers, population density, level of urbanization and the rate of growth of both national and urban populations.

A very significant feature is the small population size of a large number of African countries (Clarke and Kosiński, 1982); in 1983, nearly one-quarter of

1

Table 1.1. *Selected characteristics of the population of Africa*

Region/country	Area (000 km²)	Population estimate Mid-1983 (millions)	Crude birth rate	Crude death rate	Rate of natural increase (annual, %)	Infant mortality rate	Urban population (%)	Persons per km² of arable land
World		4,677	29	11	1.8	84	39	98
More developed		1,158	15	10	0.6	19	70	59
Less developed		3,519	33	12	2.1	93	29	128
Africa	30,319	513	46	16	3.0	120	27	50
Northern Africa		120	44	13	3.1	109	42	95
Algeria	2,382	20.7	46	14	3.2	116	52	44
Egypt	1,001	45.9	43	12	3.1	102	44	1,533
Libya	1,760	3.3	47	13	3.4	99	52	33
Morocco	447	22.9	44	13	3.1	106	41	107
Sudan	2,506	20.6	47	17	3.0	123	25	62
Tunisia	164	6.8	35	10	2.5	98	52	87
Western Africa		155	49	18	3.1	139	22	74
Benin	113	3.8	49	19	3.0	153	14	372
Cape Verde	4	0.4	28	9	1.8	81	20	526
Gambia	11	0.6	49	28	2.1	197	18	105
Ghana	239	13.9	48	16	3.2	102	36	90
Guinea	246	5.4	46	21	2.5	164	19	72
Guinea Bissau	36	0.8	40	21	1.9	147	24	52
Ivory Coast	322	8.9	47	18	2.9	126	38	72
Liberia	111	2.1	47	15	3.2	153	33	315
Mali	1,240	7.3	47	21	2.6	153	17	21
Mauritania	1,030	1.8	50	22	2.8	142	23	4
Niger	1,267	6.1	51	22	2.9	145	13	46
Nigeria	924	84.2	50	17	3.3	134	20	178
Senegal	196	6.1	48	22	2.6	146	33	72
Sierra Leone	72	3.8	45	19	2.6	206	25	129
Togo	56	2.8	48	18	3.0	108	17	162
Upper Volta	274	6.8	48	22	2.6	210	9	37

Eastern Africa		146	48	17	3.1	111	14	45
Burundi	28	4.5	46	22	2.4	121	2	245
Comoros	2	0.4	46	17	2.9	92	19	357
Djibouti	22	0.3	49	23	2.7	—	74	185
Ethiopia	1,222	31.3	48	23	2.5	146	14	43
Kenya	583	18.6	54	13	4.1	86	13	273
Madagascar	587	9.5	46	16	3.0	70	18	24
Malawi	118	6.8	51	18	3.3	171	9	150
Mauritius	2	1.0	26	7	1.9	35	43	829
Mozambique	783	13.1	45	18	2.7	114	9	23
Reunion	3	0.5	23	6	1.7	16	41	912
Rwanda	26	5.6	49	18	3.1	106	4	361
Seychelles	3	0.1	29	7	2.2	24.0	25	1,320
Somalia	638	5.3	46	21	2.6	146	30	13
Tanzania	945	20.5	46	14	3.2	102	13	38
Uganda	236	13.8	46	15	3.1	96	7	132
Zambia	753	6.2	48	16	3.2	105	43	17
Zimbabwe	389	8.4	47	13	3.4	73	20	104
Middle Africa		58	45	19	2.7	121	30	37
Angola	1,247	7.6	47	22	2.5	153	21	22
Cameroon	475	9.1	44	18	2.7	108	35	55
Central African Rep.	623	2.5	45	20	2.5	147	41	40
Chad	1,254	4.7	45	23	2.1	147	18	10
Congo	343	1.7	44	18	2.6	128	37	11
Equatorial Guinea	28	0.3	42	18	2.5	142	54	76
Gabon	268	0.7	35	20	1.5	116	36	13
Sao Tome & Principe	1	0.1	39	10	2.9	72	33	230
Zaire	2,345	31.3	46	18	2.8	111	30	97
Southern Africa		34	37	11	2.6	97	46	17
Botswana	606	0.9	51	17	3.4	82	29	2
Lesotho	30	1.4	41	13	2.9	114	5	59
Namibia	824	1.1	43	14	2.9	119	45	2
South Africa	1,221	30.2	36	10	2.6	95	50	30
Swaziland	17	0.6	49	16	3.3	134	15	40

Source: 1983 World Population Data Sheet of the Population Reference Bureau Inc., Washington D.C.

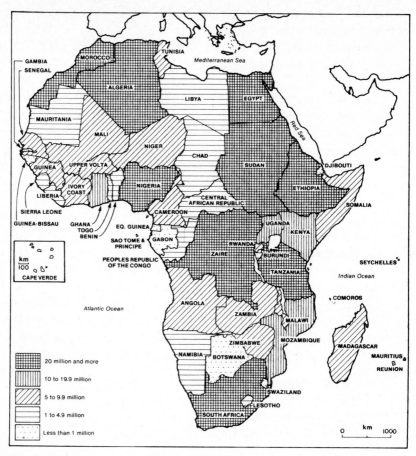

Fig. 1.1 Population sizes of African countries, 1983

them had less than one million inhabitants each (Fig. 1.1). In contrast, the combined populations of Nigeria and Egypt, the two largest in Africa, account for about one-quarter of the total population of the continent. Moreover, in terms of areal size Sudan is at one extreme with about 1 million square miles whereas countries like Cape Verde, Djibouti, Gambia, Mauritius, Reunion and Swaziland have less than 10,000 square miles. Obviously, the population/area relationships of countries greatly influence population redistribution within the continent, and there are marked contrasts between the macro- and micro-states, however defined. In general, the smaller countries, in area and population, have not only greater demographic volatility through more rapidly changing vital rates and a greater impact of external migration, but also pose quite different problems for economic development. With smaller resource bases, less complex spatial patterns and more limited economies, they are generally less viable and are more vulnerable to external pressures than the larger countries of Africa. The latter, however, have their own difficulties of internal heterogeneity, especially of multifarious ethnic groups, and a major problem in maintaining national unity. They are also perhaps fortunate (though some might dispute this) in that many of the development strategies implemented in developing countries, including those of Africa, have had the meso- and macro-states in mind, rather than the micro-states with which Africa abounds.

But size is not everything. Sharp contrasts also exist between on the one hand the relatively prosperous and less precarious coastal countries, where cash cropping and commercial economies evolved, and on the other the mainly poorer countries of the interior, where subsistence economies have often prevailed. These broad coastal/interior contrasts are reflected in the distribution of main cities, which, with the exception of a few land-locked countries in West Africa, are mostly located in coastal countries (E.C.A., 1972; Udo, 1979).

The 14 land-locked countries, of course, suffer particular problems of access and distance to the sea, high levels of contiguity with other states and political vulnerability to stronger neighbours. It is not surprising that of the 31 countries designated least developed (L.L.D.C.s) or 'poorest of the poor' by the United Nations, 21 are in Africa, and that 10 of these are land-locked (Fig. 1.2). Indeed, Mali has been designated as the poorest country in the world. Furthermore, 33 of the 53 countries in the world that the United Nations Fund for Population Activities (U.N.F.P.A.) has selected as priority countries are in Africa; selection being on the basis of GNP *per capita* of US\$ 500 or less, and two of the following:

> annual increase of at least 100,000 inhabitants;
> gross reproduction rate of 2.5 or more;
> infant mortality rate of 160 or more;
> density of agricultural population per hectare of arable land of 2 or more.

The priority group had a population of 223 million in 1980, almost 48 per cent of the African population, and excluded most of the countries of Northern and Southern Africa.

Few African countries find themselves at the other end of the economic scale, but a diverse group of oil- or mineral-rich countries including Libya, Gabon, South Africa and Algeria are much more fortunate (Fig. 1.2), although such economies have their own particular problems, in particular the reliance upon immigrant labour.

So there is much diversity within the unity of population geography in Africa, and generalizations usually require qualification.

Spatial population distribution

A mere glance at a map of population distribution of Africa reveals a marked patchiness at the macro- and micro-levels. At the macro-level there are massive contrasts, as between the oppressive densities in the Nile delta and the virtual absence of population in the neighbouring Sahara desert, but equally at the micro-

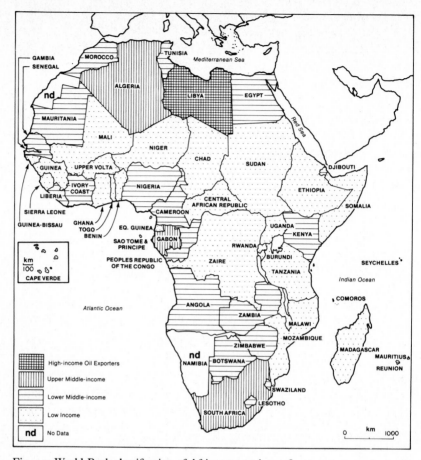

Fig. 1.2 World Bank classification of African countries, 1983

level there are also great contrasts, as between the concentrations in mining centres or irrigation projects and the sparse densities of nomadic grazing areas (Clarke, 1975).

The details of the pattern of population distribution need not concern us here, but the most important recent change has been the growing concentration in towns and cities. Compared with other major world regions, Africa has one of the lowest proportions of population (27 per cent) living in urban areas, a little ahead of South Asia, where about one-quarter of the population is classified as urban. On the other hand, since the second half of this century, the level of urbanization in Africa has shown a consistently upward trend (U.N., 1980). The rate of growth of the urban population in Africa is by far the highest among the world regions; the growth rate of 5 per cent per year during the 1960–70 decade increased to 7 per cent during the 1970–75 period. The rapid urban growth results from a combination of high natural increase and accelerated in-migration to towns. In 1950, only 15 per cent, or about 32 million, of Africa's population lived in urban

Table 1.2. *Percentage of population living in urban areas:
Africa and other regions, 1950–2000*

Region	Year						
	1950	1960	1970	1975	1980	1990	2000
World total	28.9	33.9	37.5	39.3	41.3	45.9	51.3
Africa	14.5	18.2	22.9	25.7	28.9	35.7	42.3
Eastern Africa	5.5	7.5	10.7	13.2	16.1	22.7	29.4
Middle Africa	14.6	18.1	25.2	29.7	34.4	43.7	51.6
Northern Africa	24.5	29.8	36.6	40.1	43.8	51.4	58.3
Southern Africa	37.3	41.7	43.8	44.8	46.5	51.5	57.9
Western Africa	10.2	13.5	17.3	19.6	22.3	28.6	35.9
Other regions							
Latin America	41.2	49.4	57.4	61.2	64.7	70.7	75.2
Northern America	63.8	67.1	70.4	72.0	73.7	77.2	80.8
East Asia	16.7	24.7	28.6	30.7	33.0	38.6	45.4
Southern Asia	15.6	17.8	20.4	22.0	23.9	29.1	36.1
Europe	53.7	58.4	63.9	66.4	68.8	73.2	77.1
Oceania	61.2	66.2	70.8	73.3	75.9	80.4	83.0
U.S.S.R.	39.3	48.8	56.7	60.9	64.8	71.3	76.1

Source: U.N. (1980)

areas. By 1980 this percentage had nearly doubled and about 133 million lived in towns; but by the end of this century there may be 350 million urban dwellers, about 42 per cent of the total population. Even then Africa will still be one of the least urbanized of world regions, although there is a remarkable variation between African regions (1980), ranging from only 16 per cent in Eastern Africa and 22 per cent in Western Africa to 47 per cent in Southern Africa and 44 per cent in Northern Africa (Table 1.2). The non-tropical areas distinguished themselves in this respect, as in many other ways (Fig. 1.3).

In spite of this high growth rate of the urban centres, Africa's rural population has been increasing steadily at close to 2 per cent per annum, making it the fastest growing after that of South Asia among the world regions. This is in spite of the increasing rural exodus of youths at the prime of both reproductive and productive periods, and, in particular, the dislocating effects of out-migration on marriage patterns and family organization in rural areas.

Explanations of population distribution

The prevailing patterns of population distribution and migration in Africa have been greatly influenced by historical and demographic factors, physical and ecological conditions and the process of economic development, including the impact of imported technology on the African society (Udo, 1979; Gosling, 1979).

Historical factors such as slavery have laid bold and, some argue, long-term

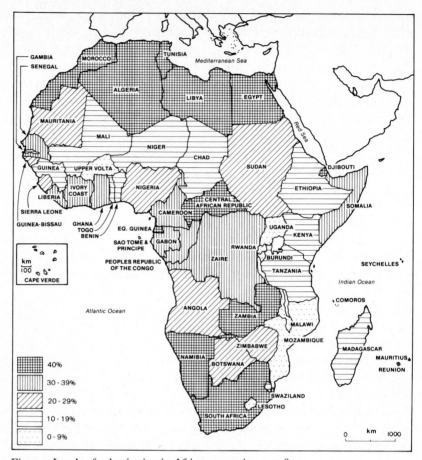

Fig. 1.3 Levels of urbanization in African countries, *c.* 1980

imprints on the spatial distribution and population growth in various parts of the continent. According to Udo (1979: 67), 'The sparse population of parts of sub-Saharan Africa has often been attributed to the loss of population during the period of the slave trade.' The demographic effects of the slave trade in the source areas are apparent in the relative stagnation of the population during the slave trade, implying that the slave trade 'pulled off enough people, and disrupted the lives of enough others, to essentially stop population growth for about 200 years' (Franke, 1981: 18). This is especially the case of the 'middle belt' countries of West Africa, as well as Gabon, Angola and northern Sudan.

Without entering into details, we may also point to the influence of the immense profusion of African ethnic groups upon population distribution, notably in the zone of cultural fragmentation stretching across the tropical zone from Senegal to Ethiopia. Their bewildering diversity of numbers, customs, settlement forms and economies has long imposed a strong influence upon the overall and local patterns of population, and the ethnic heterogeneity of countries like Nigeria, Ethiopia and Uganda have had centrifugal effects which have been difficult to resist.

Population distribution in Africa also results from demographic factors. In spite of the rapid population growth rate, pockets of infertility are found in the countries of Central Africa (Zaire, Gabon, Congo, Central African Republic, northern Cameroon), parts of West Africa (Upper Volta, Senegal), as well as Sudan, Tanzania and Uganda, where the low fertility and low rates of population growth have been factors in low population density. This, according to Franke (1981: 13–14) is 'one of the mysteries of African demography; the existence, on a continent with otherwise very high fertility, of a belt of very low fertility'. The low fertility is usually attributed to high incidence of venereal disease (Adadevoh, 1979); it is also possible that poor nutrition is a contributory factor. In any case, the high fertility/infertility phenomenon has resulted in varying levels of population growth.

The high degree of population concentration in Africa's cities has been fostered by the rapidly increasing migration from rural areas and small urban places as well as the prevailing high fertility. The former results from both economic and political factors. The location of economic opportunities (Mortimore, 1982) and especially the development of trade along coastal areas has usually exerted a strong impact on migration and population distribution. As Hoover (1972: 653) noted, 'policies involving the location of investment and employment affect the geographical distribution of different labour market destinations for migrants'. The economic factors are primary; both incomes and living conditions are higher in urban than in rural areas. Urban areas have become industrial, commercial and administrative centres; these have, in turn, attracted migrants from the poor rural areas. The result is the primacy of major cities in Africa and their growing supremacy over the numerical size and importance of small and medium-sized towns (Gugler and Flanagan, 1978). The high degree of population concentration in Africa's cities is especially noticeable in Malawi, Kenya, Zimbabwe, Guinea and Sierra Leone, where over 80 per cent of the urban population live in the major cities; in countries like Mauritius, Tanzania, Tunisia, Sudan, Upper Volta and Mozambique, however, 50 per cent or less of the urban population live in the main cities.

The colonial development strategy in African countries was systematically geared towards the exploitation of the local resources for the use of the metropolitan countries, the link between them being the many city-ports around the coasts. As a result, the strategy of selective development of areas of abundant resources – mines, cash cropping areas, plantations, etc. – was adopted and rigorously pursued. In Zambia, for instance, the line of rail became the zone of major population settlement (Ohadike, 1981), as in the case of the development of the Lagos/Port Harcourt/Kano axes in Nigeria. The strong urban bias pursued in the planning strategies of independent African governments was also influential in provoking primate cities, such as Dakar, Freetown, Abidjan and Nairobi, to emerge as dominant in their urban hierarchies, serving as administrative, political, commercial and educational centres. Consequently, the absence or relative unimportance of medium-sized towns is characteristic of the urban population scene in Africa, though in small countries like Gambia, Swaziland, Djibouti and Gabon one such town performs the function of capital.

Environmental and ecological conditions also contribute to the prevailing population distribution in Africa, but they have been variously utilized and modified during colonial and post-colonial times. For example, widespread diseases and pests occur. Hence, 'vast areas of Africa, especially Zaire, West Africa, Gabon and Zambia, are infested with tsetse fly and other diseases which lead to depopulation in the affected areas' (Udo, 1979: 66). The same observation applies to the Volta Basin in Ghana, and to parts of Benin, Togo, Niger, Upper Volta, Ivory Coast and Mali infested by river blindness. However, the impact of imported technology on population distribution in Africa is seen in the transformation of hitherto uninhabitable land into areas suitable for human habitation, as in the areas formerly infested with tsetse fly, river blindness, trypanosomiasis and other diseases.

It is also evident that the dry savanna and desert zones of the interior are usually sparsely populated and are invariably uninhabitable for the greater part of the year (E.C.A., 1972). Most of the Sahelian regions of Mauritania, Mali, Niger, Chad and Sudan are in this situation. As Udo (1979) asserted, 'aridity is the single most important environmental factor which has made vast areas of West Africa, East Africa and South Africa unsuitable for human settlement'.

Somalia and Sudan are examples of countries with large nomadic populations which roam the widespread but sparsely inhabited semi-arid and arid lands. It is estimated, for instance, that over two-thirds of the population of Somalia are nomads (I.L.O./J.A.S.P.A., 1977). In general, nomadic, animal-herding societies have lower fertility than settled, agrarian ones (Franke, 1981), a factor which further limits population density.

In Swaziland, as in Somalia, both the cattle and the human population share the limited agricultural land. Indeed, the national average for cattle holding, of 34 head per sq km, in Swaziland is the highest cattle density in Africa, and is even higher on Swazi land (51 per sq km) on which 83 per cent of the total cattle are found and where there is over-grazing and considerable soil erosion (Government of Swaziland, 1978: 6). At the time of independence in 1968, 45 per cent of the land was owned by foreigners, mostly white settlers. The prevailing large-scale farming of cash crops for export resulted in low population density on these farms. Even by 1978, up to 17 per cent of the land was still owned by expatriates.

Similarly, during the colonial era in Kenya population density was lowest in the 'scheduled areas' and 'white highlands' where most of the white settlers lived, and highest among the African settlements. Comparable situations prevailed in Zambia and Zimbabwe prior to independence, and continue to exist in South Africa, where the policy of separate development involves the creation of 'homelands' in various parts of the country, resulting in the arbitrary allocation of 70 per cent of the population to 13 per cent of its territory, which includes the poorest areas of land.

The end of colonial rule was to drastically alter the spatial distribution in some of these colonized countries. In Eastern and Southern Africa, where movements of population had been restricted, 'clearly one of the dominant features of twentieth century African history has been the migration of Africans to urban enclaves established by Europeans, with consequent striking changes in population distribution patterns' (U.N., 1979). This movement has been associated with the relaxation of rules and conditions hitherto inhibiting the movement of Africans to 'prohibited' areas.

The post-colonial period has also witnessed a considerable increase in international labour migration. The profusion of political units in Africa, with over 50,000 miles of boundaries, has internationalized much migration that occurred formerly between parts of colonial empires, as for example the movements out of poorer countries like Upper Volta, Swaziland and Malawi and into richer countries like Ivory Coast, South Africa and Zambia. Those countries benefiting from mineral wealth, like Libya, Nigeria and Gabon, are most attractive to migrant workers from poorer countries, which sometimes become very dependent upon remittances, as in Egypt, Lesotho and Upper Volta. Some African countries have been anxious to stem or control these movements through the development of visa and passport regulations, customs controls, work permits and restrictions upon the movement of currency (E.C.A., 1981). Some, like Ghana, Zambia and Sierra Leone, have at one time or another expelled other Africans (Addo, 1982) in order to offer greater employment to their own national workforces. But border controls are not easy, and Africa now has millions of illegal migrants, a fact emphasized when Nigeria expelled vast numbers of them in 1983.

Tropical Africa has also many millions of refugees, and it constitutes one of the major crisis areas in the world, especially as many of the receiving countries, like Somalia, Sudan and Zaire, are low-income countries ill-equipped by themselves to cope with large numbers of extra people in their rural frontier zones, where they become a volatile and special problem.

Attitudes and policies

As Gosling (1979: 408) stated, 'economic development, especially higher standards of living for the population, is both the objective and the determinant of population distribution. There is no optimum distribution pattern outside of the economic context, hence no population redistribution policy is relevant or effective unless it is conducted within the framework of general economic development in a comprehensive national planning effort.' In line with this view, the following discussion posits the prevailing population redistribution and migration policies in a developmental context.

The high primacy of capital cities, the rapid growth rate of urban areas and the extreme dispersion of population distribution in general and in rural areas in particular have been identified as major spatial distribution problems in Africa.

For a long time, both the perception of the problem and the formulation of policies designed to alter the undesirable patterns have been conditioned, in part, by the inadequate data base, the limited manpower and financial resources and the lack of strong political will to provide the necessary support for the success of policies so formulated.

Before the 1980 round of censuses, very few African countries had reliable and comprehensive population data. This shortcoming had adversely influenced planning and the perception of policy makers regarding key population issues, especially the growth, distribution and structure of population. Equally important, the interrelations between population and development have not been clearly articulated by planners in Africa; moreover, few countries have integrated, concretely, population variables in the planning process. While very few countries have explicit policies relating to fertility and rate of population growth, a great concern has been expressed by virtually all countries about population distribution and the role of migration in the process. This is predicated on the increasing realization that migration, among the major demographic variables, exerts a quick impact on other planning sectors. In fact, it has been indicated that 'from the population inquiries conducted by the United Nations secretariat in 1976 and in 1978, statements made at the World Population Conference and subsequent meetings, national development plans and so on, it became evident that more of a consensus existed at world level with respect to spatial distribution and internal migration than on any other demographic topic' (U.N. 1980: 40).

The prevailing population distribution in Africa – between and within subregions and countries – poses tremendous planning problems. It has become increasingly difficult, for instance, to provide adequate social services to the widely-scattered settlements, as is the situation in Sudan, Mozambique, Zambia and Libya, while the few and grossly inadequate services in the major cities, such as Kinshasa, Maputo and Lagos, have been stretched to the limit because of rapidly-increasing population. It is therefore not surprising that no African country considered the prevailing spatial population distribution acceptable, and only 27 per cent considered it partly appropriate. Indeed, a high proportion of countries in Middle Africa (80 per cent) and Western Africa (81 per cent) considered the spatial distribution of their population inappropriate (Table 1.3).

In spite of the above perception, 27 per cent of the countries did not intend to modify the existing configuration of settlements. This is not surprising, as few development plans include objectives and policy measures for implementing such redistributive strategies (Adepoju, 1982). Besides, the enormous manpower and financial resources required to translate plans into concrete, feasible projects are generally in short supply. However, a few countries, notably Tanzania, Mozambique and Zambia (see chapters 9–12), are vigorously pursuing policies of village regrouping in order, in part, to facilitate the provision of social services to the hitherto scattered communities.

With regard to internal migration, nearly two-thirds of African countries have policies designed to decelerate prevailing trends. Few countries (14 per cent) plan to reverse the trend, while over one-fifth (22 per cent) have no interventionist policies to influence migration trends. However, no single country has a policy to accelerate trends in internal migration which, in the majority of the countries, takes the form of both rural-to-rural and rural-to-urban movements (Table 1.3).

The various policies designed to alter migration trends and, where this is not possible, to accommodate them, are rarely executed. A few such policies have been tried over the years, and these vary by political system and the performance of the economy of the countries concerned. In socialist-oriented countries, like Zambia, Mozambique, Tanzania and Somalia, a series of programmes including rural development, agricultural projects, youth camps and clustering of villages or village regrouping have been undertaken in order to encourage youths and adults to remain in or return to the rural areas. Sometimes as a result of the prevailing congenial political system, such policies have achieved partial success. In countries with free market economies where individuals are guaranteed freedom of movement, policies that have direct and indirect effects on population redistributions are sometimes geared at stimulating the development of secondary towns by providing economic incentives like low-cost housing and job opportunities to attract migrants there, as is currently being attempted in Nigeria.

Urban renewal programmes are sometimes designed to expand the economic and social base of the towns to accommodate the influx of migrants. A related policy involves making jobs more labour-intensive, and improving social infrastructure. In other countries where migrants are disproportionately concentrated in capital cities, governments have, for strategic and political reasons, diverted population to new areas of low population concentration, or even moved the capital cities to the interior, as in Dodoma (Tanzania) and Abuja (Nigeria).

A few countries that experience high urban unemployment, particularly among young (migrant) school leavers, have established special youth camps as in Somalia and Zambia, or farm settlement schemes as in Nigeria and Ghana, to absorb the young migrants. Virtually all the countries preach the doctrine of 'return to the land' to the young migrants. However, it has become apparent that, except where adequate employment and social infrastructure and amenities are provided in rural areas and both the structure and content of rural education are reviewed by vocationalizing or making education more relevant to farming, moral persuasion is doomed to become an empty campaign.

Finally, high fertility (and, in some countries, infertility) is a salient factor in the prevailing population distribution, hence the need to examine the perception of planners and types of policy measures usually advocated to alter the level of fertility. With respect to growth of population, 7 per cent of the countries desired higher rates of growth while 33 per cent desired lower rates. The majority – 60 per cent – considered the prevailing rates to be acceptable (U.N., 1980: 10). Regarding fertility, prevailing rates were satisfactory for 50 per cent of governments in Africa, 12 per cent regarded them as too low, while 38 per cent felt that their rate was too

Table 1.3. *Government perceptions and policies regarding population distribution, Africa, 1980*

Sub-regions and countries	Perception of over-all acceptability of spatial distribution			Policies regarding basic trends in internal migration				Policies regarding modification of rural and urban configuration of settlement			
	Appropriate	Partly appropriate	Inappropriate	Accelerate	No intervention	Decelerate	Reverse	No modification	Rural configuration	Urban configuration	Rural and urban configuration
Northern Africa											
Algeria	—	—	x	—	—	x	—	—	—	—	x
Egypt	—	—	x	—	—	x	—	—	—	—	x
Libya	—	x	—	—	—	x	—	—	—	—	x
Morocco	—	—	x	—	—	x	—	x	—	—	—
Sudan	—	—	x	—	—	x	—	—	x	—	—
Tunisia	—	x	—	—	—	x	—	—	—	—	x
Western Africa											
Cape Verde	—	—	x	—	x	—	—	x	—	—	—
Benin	—	—	x	—	x	—	—	—	x	—	—
Gambia	—	x	—	—	—	x	—	x	—	—	—
Ghana	—	—	x	—	—	x	—	—	—	—	x
Guinea	—	x	—	—	x	—	—	x	—	—	—
Guinea-Bissau	—	—	x	—	—	—	x	x	—	—	—
Ivory Coast	—	—	x	—	—	x	—	—	—	—	x
Liberia	—	—	x	—	—	x	—	—	—	—	x
Mali	—	—	x	—	—	x	—	x	—	—	—
Mauritania	—	—	x	—	—	x	—	—	x	—	—
Niger	—	—	x	—	x	—	—	x	—	—	—
Nigeria	—	—	x	—	—	x	—	x	—	—	—
Senegal	—	—	x	—	—	x	—	—	—	—	x
Sierra Leone	—	x	—	—	x	—	—	x	—	—	—
Togo	—	—	x	—	x	—	—	—	—	—	x
Upper Volta	—	—	x	—	—	x	—	—	x	—	—

Eastern Africa												
Burundi	—	x	—	—	x	—	—	—	x	—	—
Comoros	—	x	—	—	x	—	—	—	—	—	—
Djibouti	—	x	—	—	—	—	x	—	x	—	—
Ethiopia	—	—	x	—	—	x	—	—	x	—	x
Kenya	—	—	x	—	—	x	—	—	—	—	—
Madagascar	—	x	x	—	—	x	—	—	x	—	x
Malawi	—	—	x	—	—	x	—	—	—	—	—
Mauritius	—	—	—	—	—	x	x	—	—	—	x
Mozambique	—	x	x	—	x	x	x	—	—	—	x
Rwanda	—	—	x	—	—	—	—	—	—	—	x
Seychelles	—	—	—	—	—	x	—	—	x	—	—
Somalia	—	x	x	—	—	x	—	x	x	—	—
Uganda	—	—	x	—	—	x	—	—	—	—	—
Tanzania	—	x	x	—	x	x	x	—	x	—	x
Zambia	—	—	x	—	—	x	x	—	x	—	—
Zimbabwe	—	x	—	—	—	x	—	—	x	—	—
Middle Africa												
Angola	—	x	x	—	x	—	x	—	—	—	x
Central African Republic	—	—	—	—	—	—	—	—	—	—	—
Chad	—	x	x	—	x	—	x	—	x	—	—
Congo	—	—	x	—	x	x	—	x	x	—	—
Equatorial Guinea	—	—	—	—	—	—	—	—	—	—	—
Gabon	—	x	x	—	—	x	x	—	x	—	x
Sao Tome and Principe	—	—	—	—	—	—	—	—	—	—	—
Cameroon	—	x	x	—	x	x	—	—	x	—	x
Zaire	—	x	x	—	x	x	—	—	—	—	x
Southern Africa												
Botswana	—	—	x	—	x	x	—	—	—	—	x
Lesotho	—	x	—	—	x	—	x	x	—	—	—
South Africa	—	x	x	—	—	x	—	x	—	—	x
Swaziland	—	—	x	—	—	x	x	x	x	—	x
Total	0	14	37	0	11	33	7	14	16	0	21
			51			51					51

Source: U.N., 1980: 412–13.

high. Also, 94 per cent considered the level of life expectancy at birth unacceptable; the African average is only 50, about the same as in South Asia. In fact, the poor health and low life-expectancy are regarded as the most serious population problem in Africa (U.N., 1980: 23).

The 'irrational distribution' of the population is thus regarded as a crucial demographic problem, next to morbidity and mortality. It must be stressed, however, that spatial distribution of population is interrelated with population growth, which in turn is determined by both fertility and mortality. Efforts to modify the configuration of population distribution should also embrace policies on fertility. That this is not the case at the moment is a major shortcoming of existing policies to alter the prevailing distribution of population in Africa.

Unfortunately, too many past policies for population redistribution have been uni-dimensional and have addressed themselves to a few aspects of population mobility, such as rural–urban migration, and have neglected well known migrational characteristics such as the gravity rule, information flows and selectivity. It is now realized that to be successful population redistribution policies should be multi-dimensional, taking into consideration all redistributional processes and broadly reflecting overall national policies (U.N., 1981). Indeed, the programmes which are most effective are usually those for which there is a strong political will. One thinks of the case of Nigeria, faced with immense ethnic complexity, firm distrust of centralized control, and strong demands for devolution of political power and socio-economic development. Not only has Nigeria created 19 state capitals, but it is now building a new federal capital at Abuja, in the centre of the country. Political decentralization is here a key force in population redistribution. Equally, Tanzania's programme of agro-industrial villagization was only accomplished by a strong political volition. In short, although population redistribution is not controlled by governments it is greatly affected by political decision-making, and the more governments that take this fully into account the better. One concurs with Mabogunje (1981) that government intervention in African population redistribution is inevitable and vital to the thrust of development.

It is encouraging that the Nairobi Parliamentary Conference on Population and Development in Africa recognized the importance of population in development programmes and that it recommended the following measures to develop rural areas and reduce the high rates of urbanization (Population and Development Review, 1981):

1. creation of jobs in rural areas through provision of water supplies, subsidized farm inputs and agricultural support services, and in small towns through the establishment of agro-based industries;
2. resettlement schemes to move people from infertile and rugged mountainous districts to more fertile ones;
3. change of educational emphasis towards agriculture in primary and secondary schools;

4. creation of more middle-sized towns, especially through political decentralization and by increasing the number of administrative units; and

5. increased research into causes and consequences of the changes in geographical distribution of population.

Better data

Research requires better data than are at present generally available in African countries. African mobility eludes simplistic enumeration, for not only are its movements variable and complex but its participants are not easily counted or even identified on a locational basis (i.e. place or area of residence or birth). The problem of political boundaries means that border-crossing data are rare, except at ports, so our knowledge of international migration is notoriously inaccurate (E.C.A., 1981). Most migration data in Africa have been derived from censuses, though censuses have not had a record of conspicuous success, being highly variable in universality, content, accuracy and acceptance. Generally speaking, migration data from censuses are largely inadequate because they are retrospective (and therefore reflect past rather than present movements) and because their periodic snapshot technique may do little to elucidate important circulatory movements of, for example, a seasonal nature. For the most common relevant question is place of birth by region, territory or country, a question which reveals nothing about time of migration, and is preferably supplemented by questions concerning residence at a fixed past date, say one year or five years previously. However, neither of these time periods is wholly satisfactory, though more useful than a question on previous residence, which may have been a few months or many decades ago. Equally, data on duration of residence are valuable supplementary evidence but have limitations as sole evidence of migration, as they do not indicate either sources of origin or numbers of out-movements, so net migration cannot be determined. On the other hand, data on nationality may not coincide with country-of-birth data, and can therefore enable differentiation of (a) immigrants, (b) returnees,.(c) persons born abroad but holding the nationality of the country of enumeration, and (d) persons born in the same country but holding foreign nationality (E.C.A., 1981). In all these circumstances it is inevitable that periodic sample surveys of a longitudinal character have become important, though their objectives have varied and they have focused more on areas of in-migration than out-migration. In most cases the lack of an adequate sampling frame is a major problem.

It follows that cooperation is vital between researchers and government statistical services in order that government planners and policy-makers may be fully appraised of the processes and patterns of population redistribution taking place within their countries. Their task is extremely difficult, for population redistribution is merely one aspect of social and economic development (Goslin, 1979). It is, however, a neglected aspect, and one which is of great importance to the people of this continent. Given the political complexity of Africa, there are no simple formulae, but there can be much greater understanding.

REFERENCES

Adadevoh, B.K. (ed.) (1979) *Sub-fertility and Infertility in Africa*. Ibadan, Caxton Press.

Addo, N.O. (1982) Government-induced transfers of foreign nationals, in J.I. Clarke and L.A. Kosiński (eds.), *Redistribution of Population in Africa*, London, Heinemann, pp. 31–8.

Adepoju, A. (1982) Population redistribution in tropical Africa. A review of governmental policies, in J.I. Clarke and L.A. Kosiński (eds.), *Redistribution of Population in Africa*, London, Heinemann, pp. 58–65.

Adepoju, A. (1983) Issues in the study of migration and urbanization in Africa south of the Sahara, in P. Morrison (ed.), *Population Movements: Their Form and Functions in Urbanization and Development*, Liège, International Union for the Scientific Study of Population.

Clarke, J.I. (1975) Population geography, in J.I. Clarke *et al.*, *Advanced Geography of Africa*, London, Hulton Educational Publications, pp. 217–303.

Clarke, J.I. and Kosiński, L.A. (eds.) (1982) *Redistribution of Population in Africa*, London, Heinemann.

Economic Commission for Africa (E.C.A.) (1972) Distribution of population in Africa and review of governmental policies affecting population distribution. Document No. F/CN14/POP 189, paper read at *Seminar on Statistics and Studies of Migration and Urbanization*, 11–12 September, Moscow.

Economic Commission for Africa (E.C.A.) (1978) *Demographic Handbook for Africa, 1978*, Addis Ababa.

Economic Commission for Africa (E.C.A.) (1981) International migration in Africa: past, present and future prospects, unpublished memo, ECA/PD/WF/1982/2.

Franke, R.W. (1981) Land, labour and people, in *POPULI: Journal of the United Nations Fund for Population Activities*, 8, 8–31.

Gosling, L.A.P. (1979) Population redistribution: patterns, policies and prospects, in P.M. Hauser (ed.), *World Population and Development: Challenges and Prospects*, Syracuse University Press, pp. 403–39.

Government of Swaziland (1978) *Third National Development Plan 1978/79, 1982/83*, Mbabane.

Gugler, J. and Flanagan, W.G. (1978) *Urbanization and Social Change in West Africa*, Cambridge, Cambridge University Press.

Hoover, E.M. (1972) Policy objectives for population distribution, in S.M. Maize (ed.), *Population Distribution and Policy*, vol. 5, Washington, D.C., The Commission on Population Growth and the American Future, pp. 649–64.

International Labour Office/Jobs and Skills Programme for Africa (I.L.O./J.A.S.P.A.), (1977) *Economic Transformation in a Socialist Framework: An Employment and Basic Needs Oriented Development Strategy for Somalia*, Addis Ababa.

Mabogunje, A.L. (1981) Objectives and rationales for regional population redistribution in developing countries, in U.N., *Population Distribution Policies in Development*

Planning, Dept. of International Economic and Social Affairs, Population Studies, no. 75, pp. 19–29.

Maro, P.S. and Mlay, W.F.I. (1979) Decentralization and the organization of space in Tanzania, *Africa*, 49, 291–301.

Mortimore, M. (1982) Framework for population mobility: the perception of opportunities in Nigeria, in J.I. Clarke and L.A. Kosiński (eds.), *Redistribution of Population in Africa*, London, Heinemann, pp. 50–7.

Ohadike, P. (1981) *Demographic Perspectives in Zambia: Rural–Urban Growth and Social Change*, Zambian Papers no. 15, Manchester University Press.

Population and Development Review (1981), vol. 7, no. 4, The Parliamentary Conference on Population and Development in Africa: Conclusions and Recommendations, 719–25.

Udo, R.K. (1979) Size, distribution and characteristics of population in Africa, in R.K. Udo (ed.), *Population Education Source Book for Sub-Saharan Africa*. Nairobi, Heinemann Educational Books, pp. 62–74.

United Nations (U.N.) (1979) *Report on Monitoring of Population Policies* (Document ESA/PWP 69), New York.

United Nations (U.N.) (1980) *World Population Trends and Policies; 1979 Monitoring Report, Vol. 2: Population Policies*, New York.

United Nations (U.N.) (1981) *Population Redistribution Policies in Development Planning*, Dept. of International Economic and Social Affairs, Population Studies, no. 75.

2   Development projects and their demographic impact

Leszek A. Kosiński

Introduction

The existence of a close mutual interrelationship between population trends and patterns on one hand, and economic and social development on the other, has long been acknowledged in the literature. The writings of Malthus in the late eighteenth century provide an early example of this preoccupation, and since that time economists and social scientists have studied the problem and politicians have attempted to make use of theoretical and predictive formulations postulated by researchers and analysts. The literature is still growing at an impressive rate (U.N., 1971; Tabah, 1976; Hauser, 1979; Easterlin, 1980).

In this essay an attempt is made to discuss briefly various relevant concepts and to suggest possible relationships between the two basic sets of variables – one pertaining to development projects and the other to demographic behaviour. The author is aware that even if the discussion starts at a fairly general level (national), it must inevitably focus on a regional or even local scene, where geographers have often made relevant detailed studies (Webb, 1976: 15).

Development processes and policies

The concept of development and its objectives have been variously defined in the past. The earlier narrowly-conceived economic definition, whereby development was considered synonymous with increasing *per capita* income or gross national product (G.N.P.), was gradually replaced by a broader concept including various measures – economic, social and structural (Hoselitz, 1960; Kuznets, 1966; Todaro, 1977). The contemporary geographical literature opts for a broad definition (Johnson, 1981: 78).

Operationalization of such complex definitions is obviously rather difficult. An innovative if somewhat problematic proposal by the U.N. Research Institute for Social Development involved the use of 18 indicators of development, integrated into one synthetic index (McGranahan *et al.*, 1972). The annual World Development Reports published by the World Bank contain a similar variety of development indicators (World Bank, 1978). Any discussion of development must inevitably take account of interrelationships which produce negative as well as positive effects as emphasized by the terms 'interdependent development' (Brookfield, 1975) or, even more starkly, 'underdevelopment' (Frank, 1969; Roxborough, 1979; Bagchi, 1982).

The development process may be conceived of as an economic and social transformation of a society, resulting in the reduction of the role of the primary (and later also the secondary) sector, increasing urbanization and changing aspirations, attitudes and behaviour.

Usually development is perceived by both the public and the government as a desirable goal. Consequently, any measures which may accelerate it are considered worthy of attention and application. This places the government in a special position since it is the public sector which is usually expected to take the initiative and see to it that the results are acceptable.

In a 1979 seminar held in Bangkok and sponsored by the U.N. Fund for Population Activities, two authors were invited to summarize arguments for and against government interventions to modify national population characteristics. Since the seminar was devoted to questions of the territorial distribution of population, the focus of debate was obviously close to geographers' preoccupations (U.N., 1981b).

Mabogunje suggested five groups of factors justifying government intervention:

> Economic – greater efficiency of resource utilization;
> Ecological – avoidance of disequilibria which inevitably develop in a
> spontaneous process of development;
> Social – assuring equity or reasonable fairness in the distribution of
> income;
> Administrative – assuring viability of services;
> Political – fostering nation building.

On the other hand, Stöhr proposed the following counter-arguments, divided into two major categories:

(i) Practical/political, concerning both adaptive and normative intervention

(a) In the case of adaptive measures to environmental modifications, the policies reacting to abrupt changes, such as earthquakes or floods, are generally acceptable but those reacting to long-term alterations, even if acceptable, are usually very difficult, both because such changes are hard to predict and because there are often conflicts between short-term and long-term considerations.

(b) In the case of adaptive measures to functional changes in socio-economic structures, the controversy might depend upon whether their results rapidly benefit small elites only or, in the long run, society as a whole.

(c) The normative measures facilitating desired changes are usually pursued in countries with a high degree of nationalistic and/or ideological mobilization and a highly centralized decision-making system. Therefore any alternative views have a very low probability of articulation and the enforced policies, even if beneficial at national level, might result in considerable hardship for the individual and at the local level.

(d) The normative measures aimed at restricting possible disruptive effects of functional changes may often lead to conflicts between the interests of territorial communities and large-scale functional organizations (national or supranational).

(ii) Theoretical arguments

(a) Restrictions on freedom of movement and residence.

(b) Possible disturbance of an automatic equilibrium mechanism.

(c) Ineffectiveness of such interventions due to the great complexity of the factors involved.

As mentioned before, regardless of the weight of all counter-arguments, developmental policies are being pursued by governments and encouraged by international agencies. These policies, aimed at accelerating development on a national scale, are usually sectorally (or inter-sectorally) orientated, have a distant horizon, and rarely have an explicit spatial dimension, though often they do have spatial connotations. Their relevance for development can be either direct and specific or indirect and facilitating. Attitudinal and behavioural changes related to educational reforms, building up of physical or social infrastructure – these are examples of pervasive development which may affect millions, by contrast with the often localized impact of discrete development projects.

Development projects

However, in the context of this volume we are less interested in the overall process of development and much more interested in specific development projects, which can be defined as schemes with clearly-defined developmental goals, temporally and territorially restricted. These are frequently government-sponsored but may also result from the activities of non-governmental organizations (e.g. the churches) or international agencies. They might represent steps in long-term development planning or they might also be *ad hoc* solutions to problems requiring immediate and specific attention.

Development schemes can be classified according to different criteria (Table 2.1). In fact several of them can be applied to an individual project, which can be conceived of as a cell in a multi-dimensional classificatory system. For instance, opening new lands related to a great irrigation scheme will probably be a long-term national enterprise with a regional impact, requiring very substantial financial inputs from both national and international sources. Its location will probably be peripheral rather than central and its degree of integration with the national economy rather limited since some sectoral interests only will be involved. The areal extent may be influenced by ecological factors (e.g. river drainage area) and

Table 2.1. *Methods of classification of development projects*

Criteria of classification	Types of projects
Hierarchical level of the sponsoring agency	Local, regional, national
Time scale involved	Short, medium, long-term
Spatial impact of the project	Local, regional, national, international
Size of financial inputs	Modest, substantial, very large
Method of financing	Non-government, regional or national government, international
Sector of economy	Agriculture, forestry, fishing, recreation, defence, manufacturing, mining, administration, culture, comprehensive
Areal basis	Administrative, ecological (e.g. river basin), planning zone
Location	Central, peripheral
Degree of integration	Fully integrated, limited linkage, isolated
Decisions and degree of popular participation	Central and imposed, joint, based on local initiative.

Table 2.2. *Examples of policies and programmes aimed at population redistribution*

Urban-orientated	Rural-orientated
Closed-city programmes	Land settlement programmes
City growth limiting programmes	Rural development programmes (including service centre development, villagization)
Slum and squatter settlement	Water projects (dams, irrigation etc.) Relocation from disaster/war areas
Dormitory towns and satellite-city programmes	Natural resource conservation programmes
Growth-centre strategies	Squatter relocation

Source: U.N., 1981b.

the decisions can be taken centrally with limited participation of the local population.

Development planners have at their disposal a limited number of policy instruments for redistributing population, which in the U.N. study have been divided into urban-directed and rural-directed, depending on the emphasis of the planning process. Examples mentioned in Table 2.2 are related to those policies and programmes which cause or prevent population redistribution. Most of them are normative (active) rather than adaptive (passive) policies and as such are by definition rather controversial.

Population and development

Growing literature on the subject reflects increasing awareness that the set of demographic variables has to be placed at the centre of attention, not only because the variables influence development and are influenced by it, but also because man is after all the chief agent and benefactor (or victim) of development (Pitchford, 1974; King, 1974; Ridker, 1976; Robinson, 1975; Hawthorne, 1978; I.L.O., 1982).

Major international agencies, including those belonging to the U.N. family, are involved in the development field and they are increasingly interested in the population-development interface. Within the U.N. an Interagency Task Force on Inter-Relationships between Population and Development was established in 1977 with participation from the U.N. Headquarters, the U.N. Economic Commission for Latin America, the U.N. Economic and Social Commission for Asia and the Pacific, the International Labour Office, the Food and Agriculture Organization, U.N.E.S.C.O., the World Health Organization and the World Bank (U.N., 1981c). Following the 1974 World Population Conference and in response to the World Population Plan of Action adopted by this conference, the U.N. Population Division undertakes and compiles periodic reports on world population trends and policies in which governments' perceptions, attitudes and policies related to population and development are monitored (U.N., 1980). The United Nations Fund for Population Activities (U.N.F.P.A.) has been instrumental in funding and sponsoring research, conferences and publications on the subject (Hauser, 1979; U.N., 1981a, b). Also important are the initiatives of non-governmental organizations such as the Population Council (Robinson, 1975; Stamper, 1977) or the International Union for the Scientific Study of Population (Tabah, 1976).

It is clear from this brief review that the topic is recognized as very important and there is certainly abundant research interest and resulting literature, including a specialized periodical of very high calibre, *Population and Development Review*, published by the Population Council.

There is obviously a great variety of approaches, including those that are policy-orientated. Among them one should mention attempts to develop models which could be used not only to study past and present trends but also to try and analyse possible future scenarios (U.N., 1981 a, c). Reports on the U.N.-sponsored work on population and development modelling identify a large number of mutually-related variables which are incorporated in these models. In fact, the 'map of interaction' which presents in summary form the conceptual framework used by the Interagency Task Force identified the following determinants, which can also be perceived as dependent variables since the relations are often reversed: 15 objectives of development, 10 population variables, and 36 other variables (Table 2.3).

Development projects and population

The focus of this paper is not on general relationships between development and population but rather on a specific category of development efforts, defined earlier as development projects, and its demographic ramifications. It is assumed that

Table 2.3. *List of variables used in U.N. models of population–development interrelationships*

Objectives of development (O)
O1:   Communications
O2:   Consumption
O3:   Education
O4:   Employment and working conditions
O5:   Health
O6:   Income/output
O7:   Individual security and status
O8:   National or group prestige or status
O9:   Popular participation
O10: Quality of environment
O11: Equality
O12: Science and technology
O13: Self-reliance and self-sufficiency
O14: Spatial population distribution
O15: Options and freedom of choice

Population variables (P)
P1:   Population size
P2:   Population density
P3:   Population growth
P4:   General mortality
P5:   Fertility
P6:   Migration
P7:   Nuptiality
P8:   Sex/age structure
P9:   Family type
P10: Family and household composition and size

Other variables (Q)

Economic factors
Q1:   Capital stock
Q2:   Land utilization and ownership patterns
Q3:   Investment
Q4:   Production and industrial structure
Q5:   Rate of development
Q6:   Relative prices (interval)
Q7:   Inflation
Q8:   International trade
Q9:   International terms of trade
Q10: Labour force participation rates
Q11: Wage, wage structure, other earnings
Q12: Savings
Q13: National wealth/heritage and human capital
Q14: Multinationals

Instruments
Q15: Educational infrastructure
Q16: Health care delivery system
Q17: Research and development
Q18: Family planning programmes
Q19: Public finance
Q20: International aid and capital flows
Q21: Legislation, economic inducements

Table 2.3. (*cont.*)

Socio-cultural and exogenous factors
Q22: Fertility regulation
Q 23: Child-rearing practices
Q 24: Opportunity cost of child-rearing
Q 25: Marriage institutions
Q 26: Respect for the individual
Q 27: Group structure
Q 28: Distribution of power
Q 29: Institutional constraints
Q 30: Language
Q 31: Other socio-cultural factors
Q 32: Administrative practices
Q 33: Political stability
Q 34: Political system
Q 35: Natural resources
Q 36: War

Source: U.N., 1981c: 7

such projects are often undertaken in order to meet specified social or economic objectives (for instance, to increase basic food supplies and to enhance the export capability of the country); to fulfil political aims (for instance, to build up support in certain categories of population); or to satisfy regional aspirations. Consequently, the success or otherwise of these projects will be measured by attainment of predetermined goals. However, demographic trends and patterns (as well as environmental factors) will undoubtedly both influence these projects and result from them and as such should always be considered by the planners (Fig. 2.1).

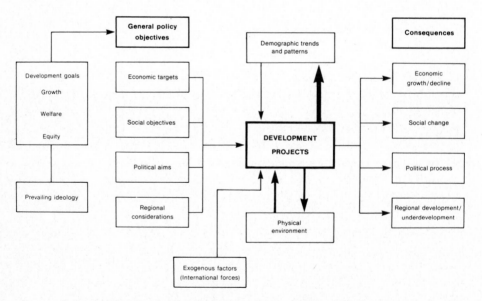

Fig. 2.1 Determinants and consequences of development projects

Table 2.4. *Demographic consequences of development projects: ways of classification*

Expected or not
Direct or indirect
Long or short-term
Lasting or transitory
Local – regional – national – international
Types of impact
    – size and density of population
    – characteristics/structure of population
    – fertility and mortality
    – migration

Table 2.5. *Short-term demographic consequences of selected development projects*

Examples of development projects	Population variables			
	Size and density	Characteristics of population	Fertility mortality	Migration patterns
Restrictions on urban growth	+	o	o	+
Inter-city relocations	#	o	o	+
New towns and growth centres	#	+	o	#
Land settlement	#	+	+	#
Irrigation projects	+	+	o	#
Resource protection	+	+	+	+

o   Negligible impact
+   Some impact
#   Strong impact
Source: This table is partly based on Thomas, 1978: 21–2.

Demographic consequences might vary considerably (Table 2.4). Some projects may be deliberately aimed at altering population patterns; others may produce unexpected and unintended changes. Some demographic changes at both national and local level may result from overall social or economic policies rather than from specific development projects. However, if we limit our attention to those projects in which demographic consequences are expected and/or deliberately induced, it might be suggested that the effects can be quite varied (Table 2.5). One should also keep in mind that short-term effects may differ from long-term results and even be mutually contradictory.

Various questions related to policies of population distribution in relation to development planning were extensively discussed at a U.N.F.P.A.-sponsored seminar held in Bangkok in 1979 (U.N., 1981b). It was pointed out that population distribution policies have in most countries been dominated by urban-orientated policies, although there were also examples of rural-focused programmes (Table

2.2). The overall success of the programmes adopted in various developing countries was rather limited. It seems that the probable reasons for these limited accomplishments are as follows:

> incomplete knowledge of the redistribution processes;
> conflicts between the effects of explicit policies and hidden (stronger) effects of implicit policies;
> conflicts between planned changes and spontaneous processes;
> use of inappropriate measures (U.N., 1981b: 3)

Regardless of whether or not these policies eventually succeeded in their stated aim, they did produce tangible results, demographic as well as others. This volume brings together several case studies from various African countries, in which changes in population distribution and dynamics are discussed in greater detail.

ACKNOWLEDGEMENT

The early draft of this paper was seen by Ian Thomas who offered a number of valuable comments. His help is greatly appreciated.

REFERENCES

Bagchi, A.K. (1982) *The Political Economy of Underdevelopment*, Cambridge, Cambridge University Press.

Brookfield, H. (1975) *Interdependent Development*, London, Methuen, and Pittsburgh, University of Pittsburgh Press.

Du Guerny, J. (1978) *Migration and Rural Development: Selected Topics for Teaching and Research*, Food and Agricultural Organization, Economic and Social Development Paper 3, Rome.

Easterlin, R.A. (ed.) (1980) *Population and Economic Change in Developing Countries*, Chicago, University of Chicago Press.

Frank, A.G. (1969) *Latin America: Underdevelopment or Revolution*, New York/London, Monthly Review Press.

Hauser, P.M. (ed.) (1979) *World Population and Development: Challenges and Prospects*, Syracuse, Syracuse University Press.

Hawthorne, G. (ed.) (1978) *Population and Development*, London, Totowa, Frank Cass; originally in *Journal of Development Studies*, 14, 4.

Hoselitz, B.F. (ed.) (1960) *Theories of Economic Growth*, New York, Free Press.

I.L.O. (1982) *Population and Development*, A progress report on I.L.O. Research on population, labour, employment and income distribution, Geneva, International Labour Office.

Johnson, R.J. (ed.) (1981) *The Dictionary of Human Geography*, Oxford, Blackwell.

King, T. (1974) *Population Policies and Economic Development*, Baltimore, John Hopkins University Press.

Kuznets, S. (1966) *Modern Economic Growth: Rate, Structure and Spread*, New Haven, Yale University Press.

McGranahan, D.V. *et al.* (1972) *Contents and Measurement of Socio-economic Development*, New York, Praeger.

Pitchford, J.D. (1974) *Population in Economic Growth*, New York, American Elsevier Co.

Pryor, R.J. (ed.) (1979) *Migration and Development in South-East Asia: A Demographic Perspective*, New York, Oxford University Press.

Ridker, R. (ed.) (1976) *Population and Development: The Search for Selective Interventions*, Baltimore, John Hopkins University Press.

Robinson, W.C. (ed.) (1975) *Population and Development Planning*, New York, Population Council.

Roxborough, I. (1979) *Theories of Underdevelopment*, London, Macmillan and Atlantic Highlands, Humanities Press.

Salvatore, D. (1981) *Internal Migration and Economic Development*, Lanham, University Press of America.

Stamper, M.B. (1977) *Population and Planning in Developing Nations: A Review of Sixty Development Plans for the 1970s*, New York, Population Council.

Tabah, L. (ed.) (1976) *Population Growth and Economic Development in the Third World*, Dolhain, Ordina Editions.

Thomas, I. (1978) *Population Policy in Tanzania*, Development Studies Discussion Paper 41, Norwich, University of East Anglia.

Todaro, M. (1977) *Economic Development in the Third World: An Introduction to Problems and Policies and Global Perspectives*, New York, Langwan.

United Nations (U.N.) (1971) *Determinants and Consequences of Population Trends*, 2 vols., Population Studies no. 50, New York.

United Nations (U.N.) (1980) *World Population Trends and Policies: 1979 Monitoring Report*, 2 vols., Population Studies no. 70, New York.

United Nations (U.N.) (1981a) *Population and Development Modelling*. Proceedings of the U.N./U.N.F.P.A. Export Group Meeting Geneva, 24–28 September 1979, Population Studies no. 73, New York.

United Nations (U.N.) (1981b) *Population Distribution Policies in Development Planning*. Papers of the U.N./U.N.F.P.A. Workshop on Population Distribution Policies in Development Planning Bangkok, 4–13 September 1979, Population Studies no. 75, New York.

United Nations (U.N.) (1981c) *The Work of the Task Force on Inter-Relationships between Population and Development*, Population Division Working Paper, New York ESA/P/WP.76 (revised and updated version of an earlier report POP/SC/WP/96).

Webb, J.W. (1976) Geographers and scales, in J.W. Webb and L.A. Kosiński, (eds.) *Population and Microscale*, Christchurch, New Zealand Geographical Society for I.G.U. Commission on Population Geography, pp. 13–19.

World Bank (1978) *World Development Report*, annual. New York, Oxford University Press, for the International Bank for Reconstruction and Development.

World Bank (1980) *Poverty and Human Development*. New York, Oxford University Press, for the International Bank for Reconstruction and Development.

3 Conceptualization of the impacts of rural development projects on population redistribution

Abdul-Aziz M. Farah, Lufti A. Desougi and Anne M. Lewandowski

Since the second world war, many developing nations have been experiencing rapid economic growth. However, the benefits of such growth have been unjustifiably distributed to a few localities, with large sectors of the population remaining peripheral to these benefits. The necessary structural change for a more balanced distribution of benefits is still in its infant stage.

Among a number of factors which contribute to the unbalanced distribution of economic benefits in developing nations, such as their colonial past and the need to earn foreign exchange and to get quick returns, two may be singled out. First, there is a large subsistence sector in the population, with a low productivity level, low income and little access to innovation and modernization. Facing limited resources, developing nations tend to locate development projects in a few urban and commercial crop-producing areas (e.g. cotton in the Gezira area of Sudan, tea in Kenya), thereby introducing a dualist structure into the economy.

Secondly, due to previously unbalanced growth, the subsistence population sector lags behind, in development, the rapidly-growing urban and commercial crop-producing areas. Due to lack of opportunities and facilities, people in the subsistence sector tend to migrate to these growth centres to improve their living conditions; but although the centres have grown fast during recent decades they do not offer sufficient opportunities for the migrants, and consequently there are high unemployment rates in urban areas.

Due to the two factors just mentioned, urban and crop-producing areas increased rapidly, causing concentration of population, and in an effort to improve the standard of living governments superimposed development schemes, mainly agricultural, in these high growth areas.

At this stage of development, enough is known about the dynamics of these schemes to enable planners and administrators to foresee problems and restructure national policy to avert them. A conceptual framework, such as the one developed in this paper, provides policy-makers with a tool for planning future development based on past experience. This conceptualization lays the foundation for empirically testing the various hypotheses incorporated in the framework. Hopefully the results will demonstrate the empirical relationship between the individual, socio-economic and environmental variables and the dynamics of population redistribution.

The framework introduced in this paper examines the impact of agro-industrial development schemes on the redistribution of rural population in developing nations. The intricacy of this issue has led scholars to emphasize certain aspects of the whole problem rather than to formulate a comprehensive framework. This framework, though it makes an attempt at being comprehensive, is designed specifically to evaluate development impacts on rural areas.

A theoretical framework

To be useful to planners and administrators, any framework should specify channels or links between variables that are based on a hypothesis or on certain postulates. The approach taken here is an attempt to explain, interpret and synthesize an empirical set of relationships underlying the following hypothesis: development projects have an impact on population redistribution through a set of intermediate factors. Specifically, a development project in a rural subsistence setting activates multiple individual, socio-economic and environmental factors that have latent effects on population dynamics. These effects, in turn, shape population growth in that rural area.

Figure 3.1 (page 37) which depicts the conceptual framework, is based on the following premises and components:

1. the development scheme is superimposed on a rural setting (Box I);
2. there are direct positive and negative effects on individuals and the surrounding environment (Box II);
3. the individuals and the environment have multiple effects on population dynamics (Box III);
4. a change in population dynamics has an impact on the population distribution at a specific point in time (Box IV);
5. a change in distribution, during the initial period of the project, has consequences for new development impulses (Box V).

The nature of development projects

Governments of developing nations have some difficult choices to make when it comes to selecting a site for a development project. Limited by their financial resources, the existing infrastructure and other constraints, they look for sites that have the highest development potential. Physical conditions such as climate, surface contours, soil fertility, availability of water and spatial proximity to other market areas and ports also have an important influence on the choice of the site. Once the site is selected, certain fundamental inputs must be supplied to begin the process of implementing the scheme: labour; natural resources (land, water, minerals); capital (machines, chemicals, support equipment, cash); administration and basic infrastructure (housing, roads, schools, canals, etc). Some inputs are present, some are absent; some involve local improvements, some can be directed as needed.

The immediate impact of such a scheme is to generate certain positive outputs (cash crops, subsistence foods, industrial products, etc.), which are reflected, for example, in an increased standard of living for the people. However, the scheme also generates negative outputs, such as a potentially negative impact on the environment. The overall success of the scheme, then, depends on whether the positive impacts outweigh the negative ones.

Individual, socio-economic and environmental factors

So far we have seen that implementing a project in the assumed setting is an inducing factor for both positive and negative effects on the population in the scheme. These effects cause concomitant changes on health, social, economic, housing, infrastructural and environmental conditions of the project region.

Health conditions

Human health status is largely influenced by various acquired and innate factors. Among the acquired factors, nutrition and immunization are important candidates for increasing human resistance to disease.

The relationship between health and proper nourishment has been well documented. McKeown (1976) demonstrated that common infectious diseases such as measles, dysentery and tuberculosis, which are less serious in well-fed societies, often prove fatal in malnourished populations. Nutritional status, however, is not only a function of nutritional intake but also of nutritional practices.

The direct or indirect impact of a development scheme should be to raise the health of the people in the scheme. Since the primary function of the scheme is to produce cash crops or products, the health of individuals may actually deteriorate. Basic food intake can become nutritionally unbalanced as the tenant feels more pressure to raise cash crops over subsistence food.

Prevailing diseases are those which are infectious (cholera, bronchitis, tuberculosis, etc.). The change in mode of production from subsistence to modern practices is associated with certain types of diseases. It has been contended that schistosomiasis increases as irrigation canals are built to increase agricultural production, since the canals provide a suitable habitat for the snail hosts of schistosomes, and the chain of transmission is completed by humans working and voiding in them. Expansion of agricultural production is also associated with the increased incidence of malaria through expanding water reservoirs, which also may indirectly reduce the adequacy of the tenants' nutritional intake by allowing for the expansion of cash crop production at the expense of subsistence food production. Hence, a synergistic effect is introduced when resistance is lowered due to malnutrition, leaving the individual more vulnerable to other invading diseases. Apparently, in the populous area of the Gezira the malaria prevalence rate in children rose from 3 per cent in 1962 to 20 per cent in 1971, when it reached epidemic proportions. According to Farah (1981), the increase was partially explained by the expansion and intensification of irrigation, the same author indicating that bilharzia increased by one-third during the same period (1962–74), for the same reason.

A scheme which focuses on manufacturing also has unintended side-effects on the health of the people involved, such as accidents, or increased risk of cancer, tuberculosis and pneumonia.

Providing basic housing is a fundamental condition of any development scheme. Good housing conditions are judged by the quality of a dwelling unit, the availability and quality of water within the house, toilet facilities, ventilation, electricity and the availability of consumer durables, such as a refrigerator, television, car, radio, record player, stove, air cooler, etc. Many infectious diseases are water-borne. Thus, the purer the water, the less likely it is that diseases will be transmitted than when hygienic toilet facilities are not available. The expectation is that households with water closets are likely to control transmission of certain contractable diseases (e.g. typhoid, cholera, schistosomiasis) that persist in cases where households use fields for faecal disposal. Use of a refrigerator to store food is an important practice that may prevent contamination. The presence of radio and television in the dwelling quarter may influence and modify the feeding and nutritional habits. In sum, there is a direct causal relationship between housing conditions and disease factors.

Economic factors

Another basic premise of a successful development scheme is to increase employment opportunities for the people in and around the region of the scheme. Employment opportunities in the scheme are markedly different from those of a subsistence economy. The scheme introduces a new element of specialization of jobs and diversification of activities, as well as cash- and market-oriented thinking for people who previously relied on a barter system. Moreover the scheme links tenants with commercial and agricultural mechanisms both within the country and abroad.

As a result of modernizing agriculture, average productivity increases, which in turn augments *per capita* income and *per capita* consumption. However, in the absence of land and social reforms, the mode of transformation is likely to deepen the capitalistic character of the production system by increasing the concentration of wealth among a few large tenants. Therefore the problems of economic diversification should not be overlooked in evaluating the performance of such a scheme.

With respect to consumption, a development scheme is likely to produce a tendency on the part of the tenant to over-indulge in conspicuous consumption.

Infrastructure
Implementing a development scheme necessitates concurrent development of an infrastructure, such as power supplies, communications networks, transportation facilities, administrative services and schools. A well-developed infrastructure facilitates migration of population to the scheme, and is thus both a prerequisite for siting the scheme and a necessary condition for linking the scheme to its markets.

Education
The establishment of a development scheme attracts and supports an increased, broad-based level of education in the scheme area. As a result of a higher concentration of people, government planners will tend to provide more schools and educational institutions for the area. Moreover, scheme administrations support the establishment of educational systems because of their need for skilled labour.

 Education is one of the most effective modernization variables; it impinges on the potential supply of labour, increases efficiency and productivity, improves health and hygiene habits, and transforms traditional constrained behaviour to one that is more emancipated. Therefore education generates both social and economic benefits for the society in the scheme area. Hence, the introduction of a development scheme and subsequent expansion of educational opportunities sets the society in the scheme on the path of social evolution.

 However, because the curriculum may not be suited to the needs of the people in the scheme, education can create a gap between reality and the expectation of the educated community. To accrue maximum benefits, the curriculum should be related to the functional conditions of the area, introducing new lessons that deal, for example, with the local physical environment, home economics, child care, health and nutrition and the role of women.

Family structure and social interaction
In a subsistence economy, the primary relationship of the extended family is the glue that holds society together; in a modernized, sub-urbanized setting, such as that of a development scheme, the primary familial relationship is transformed and secondary relationships begin to emerge.

 Due to the input of new variables (commercialization, education, mechanization) the traditional norm of social interaction, characterized by a communal form of living, begins to change. This generates conflict between the traditional form of living and a new more individualistic pattern of interaction which is beginning to take shape. The society itself can be described as an evolving one, with various degrees of traditional and modern structure.

 In a subsistence economy, husband and wife work in their field together. But as the scheme begins to shake the roots of traditional relationships, men tend to protect their families from new elements (human, mechanical, social) being introduced in the scheme. Women become secluded and revert back to traditional, conservative roles.

After an adaptation period, the situation favours the participation of women in the field or in the industrial process because of the increased demand for labour and the new values being adopted. The effect of increased education, socialization, mass media and outside contacts helps to loosen constraints on women. Consequently, the distance between husband and wife is reduced, so that responsibilities and decisions are more equally shared. If women are respected in the family, they tend to be of more value in society.

An unexpected side-effect of this social transition has been the emergence of class stratification in agricultural schemes. Tenant farmers have begun adopting the habits of their predecessors (pre-scheme period). As stated in a case study of the Gezira Scheme (Al-Arifi, 1975), the tenants have begun to view themselves as landowners, rejecting their role as farmers and hiring labourers to do the farm work. Because the tenant farmers' financial standing has improved substantially and labour is easily available, the farmers have begun to think of themselves as the leisure class. Hence a stratification of classes begins.

Thus the scheme-induced evolution from traditional to more modern societal relations has both positive and negative effects on the population of the scheme. It shakes the old values of extended family relations, and introduces new relations and new, more complicated social problems.

Contraceptive behaviour

The development scheme may introduce the concept of having larger families because of an increased demand for labour. Therefore, contraceptive behaviour is almost non-existent in a scheme setting. Parents view children as an economic asset, and so are reluctant to accept any methods of contraception. Traditional patterns of having children will persist until a threshold point is reached, in which sufficient modernity factors (i.e. urban life, higher education, widely-available public health measures, mass media influence, higher income, etc.) prevail. At that time, individual couples will be motivated to control the number of children they want.

Environmental factors

The World Bank in its 1979 publication on environment and development (Wall, 1979) attributes environmental problems in developing nations to poverty and economic development. As a result of poverty, the environment shows the signs of many years of overgrazing, erosion, deforestation and surface water pollution. Economic growth, in the form of agricultural and industrial development, brings its own set of environmental problems.

Agricultural development transforms subsistence food production to a modern, high productive system. In the process of this change, cultivation practices improve, the infrastructure of facilities and services for production is expanded and new lands are brought under cultivation through irrigation and river basin development. Although crucial to development, this can produce negative environmental side effects. Irrigation can cause leaching of nutrients and salinization of the soil, effectively reducing the productive life of a farm field. Expanding agriculture to relatively infertile soils can lead to soil depletion and erosion. The use of chemicals to control weeds and pests may have negative side-effects on the population of a scheme. There is already preliminary evidence that D.D.T. is accumulating in the tissue of fish in the Upper Nile and in the breast milk of mothers residing in the Gezira Scheme area; both are believed to be related to crop-dusting practices at Gezira.

The expansion of water reservoirs and irrigation canals increases the habitat of water-related diseases, e.g. malaria and schistosomiasis. The use of irrigation canals for drinking, bathing, etc., can spread further highly communicable diseases such as dysentery.

Industrial development often results in the discharge of pollutants into the air, water and or onto land. Workers may be adversely affected by poor working conditions and exposure to dangerous processes or substances. This additional stress encountered in the workplace can lead to an increased risk of cancer and other diseases associated with industrialization (heart attacks, high blood pressure, etc.).

Yet not all changes in the environment resulting from a development scheme are adverse in nature. One cost-effective way of eradicating a disease such as malaria or dysentery is to spray the area with pesticides. By spraying, health officials not only cover a large area, but also get at the root of the disease. This method, compared to treating the symptoms of a disease in a hospital setting, is very cost-effective. For example, spraying D.D.T. to eradicate malaria increased the life expectancy of the citizens of Sri Lanka by ten years.

Unfortunately, during the planning and implementation of a development scheme, potential environmental changes are usually overlooked.

Population dynamics

The structure of any population at a given point in time in a given area is defined in terms of its past trend of fertility, mortality and migration. It has been recognized that each of these population dynamics affects and is affected by prevailing individual, socio-economic environmental factors. Therefore the intermediate state of population dynamics in the proposed framework (Box III in Fig. 3.1), between individual, socio-economic and environmental factors (Box II) and population growth (Box IV), can be conceived.

Fertility
There is increasing evidence and realization that the economic process *per se* (increasing income) does not by itself stimulate changes in fertility. The changes in

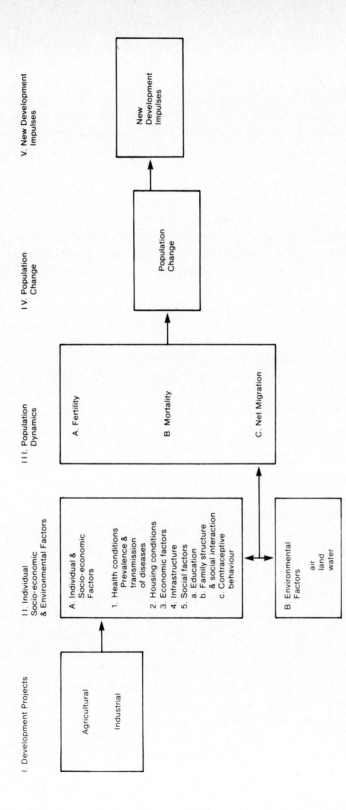

Fig. 3.1 Conceptual framework of the impacts of development projects on population redistribution

income and fertility empirically observed by many economists do not reflect the true line of causation between increase in income and decreased fertility. There are many variables for which income has become a proxy. It has been indicated by many that fertility in the traditional stage is positively correlated to income.

According to Easterlin (1975) actual fertility in the pre-modern stage of development is below the potential supply of children for newly-married couples. This phase is called the deficit situation. Factors such as high sterility, stillbirths, fecundability impairment in females, impotency and diseases due to the presence of poverty and malnutrition constrain the actual fertility in this phase. In similar conditions any economic improvement is postulated to generate a rising trend in fertility. With the superimposition of a development scheme, positive effects, such as improved health conditions, increased income, better housing, etc., interactively free the above-mentioned fertility constraints and thereby raise fertility. Hence it can be assumed that the development-related variables (increased income, health, education) are positively correlated with fertility.

In the initial stage of a development scheme, however, the growth of income working by itself, or being a proxy for other factors, stimulates and increases fertility by reducing the biological and non-biological constraints in the natural fertility regime. On the other hand, the unintended environmental effects produced by the scheme on the individuals in the area may even slow down the increasing trend of fertility in the initial stage. Hence the line of causation between the environment and fertility (Box II to Box III in Fig. 3.1).

Mortality

Death, as an individual phenomenon, has biological determinants and these determinants are predominantly influenced by social, economic and environmental conditions, changes in which generate impacts in two directions: (a) to influence the individual's bodily defensive attributes (innate or acquired) through nutrition, health and hygiene behaviour, etc., and thus his resistance to disease; and (b) to influence the prevalence, virulence and transmission of disease. The clinical outcome of these two processes is determined by the extent to which one or both of these processes are activated.

The advent of a development scheme that generates positive and negative effects on the intervening variables (arrayed in Box II) has certain implications on the resistance and exposure factors. First, there is a causal relationship between the scheme and the health of individuals. The socio-economic progress generated by the implementation of the scheme introduces new health ingredients in the society by making food commodities available, changing health and hygiene habits, increasing education and providing better housing. All these factors and others which have not been mentioned are positive impacts on people's general resistance to disease. On the other hand, as stated earlier, the establishment of a scheme may be associated with unintended ecological changes that enlarge disease vectors.

Migration
Many agricultural scheme areas have become points of attraction for labour from economically less-privileged areas. However, as contended by El-Tayeb in chapter 4, by introducing capitalism the project generates social differentiation into categories of landowners and landless tenants, eventually leading to out-migration of less privileged groups.

By the nature of the scheme, in-migrants are automatically pre-selected according to its labour requirements. They are more prone to be productive, adult and male. On the other hand, the out-migrants are generally of two types: (a) people who generally have less capability to adjust to the scheme and are therefore displaced, and (b) second- or third-generation tenant farmers who have reaped the benefits of increased education and increased income and are now seeking greater fortunes outside the scheme, especially in urban centres.

The influx of migration creates social conflicts between the original people of the area and those who migrate to the scheme. In the absence of social reform, the scheme generates some social inequity. Although in-migration has a labour input, its side-effects should not be overlooked. Besides the social conflict just mentioned, there are a host of factors that can be detrimental to the area; for example, people coming from different environments are likely to bring with them a variety of contractable diseases to which the original population of the area may not have been exposed.

In terms of volume of net migration, the decisive factor will be the likely surplus of net in-migrants over net out-migrants, especially in the initial phase of the scheme. If this contention is true, the scheme then draws population from outside to the benefit of the scheme.

In an attempt to formulate the 'push–pull' theory of migration, in the scheme setting, the following equation is proposed for the relationships between the scheme area and the subsistence area:

$$NM(i) = f(y/p)(i) - (y/p)(s), \text{ where}$$

NM = net migration
i = scheme area
y/p = average index of increased health services, education, income etc.
s = subsistence area outside the scheme

although, of course, other areas may be related to the scheme.

Population growth
According to our analysis, fertility should increase in the pre-modern phase of a scheme, mortality is likely to decrease, and net migration will tend to be positive. Hence the population of the scheme will increase faster relative to the subsistence sector, and thereby gain significance in terms of population redistribution over time.

The relative effects of differential population growth between the population of the scheme area and that of the subsistence sector can be exemplified using the following geometric progression formula:

$P_{(1)} = P_{(2)}e^{rt}$, where

$P_{(1)}$ = initial population

$P_{(2)}$ = population at a point in time (after the establishment of the scheme)

r = population growth rate

t = time span between the time of establishment and the time being considered.

In the absence of a scheme, if we assume that the population, which has a growth rate (r), doubles in X years, and if the r doubles due to the advent of a scheme, then the doubling period will be $\frac{1}{2}X$. Therefore the ratio of scheme population to subsistence population will grow exponentially, every doubling period, thereby creating an imbalance in population distribution. The upper limit of this exponential growth is reached when the carrying capacity of the area is saturated.

New development impulses

We have traced the effects of development projects on population dynamics and distribution, and now we consider the effects of this process on new development impulses. By impulse, we mean the point in the project at which society begins to stabilize. There is little, if any, in-migration because the scheme has reached maximum operating capacity. Fertility deflects downwards as modernizing factors become accepted and couples are motivated to regulate fertility. Out-migration increases slightly, especially from the recently-formed upper class who wish to join the urban elite. At this stage, what is expected is a class struggle within the scheme, and a society clearly differentiated on a social class basis.

If the scheme meets the standards set for it, the experience gained by the project will send waves of influence to be replicated in other areas.

REFERENCES

Al-Arifi, S.A. (1975) Landlordism among small farmers: the case of the Gezira tenant in the Sudan, *Sudan Journal of Economics and Social Studies*, 2.

Easterlin, R.A. (1975) An economic framework for fertility analysis, *Studies in Family Planning*, 6 (3), 54–63.

Farah, Abdul-Aziz (1981) Child mortality and its correlates in Sudan, Ph.D. thesis, University of Pennsylvania.

International Labour Office (1976) *Growth, Employment and Equity: A Comprehensive Strategy for the Sudan*, Geneva, Imprimeries Populaires.

McKeown, T. (1976) *The Modern Rise of Population*, London, Arnold.

Wall, A. (1979) *Environment and Development*, Washington, World Bank.

4   Capitalism and the population landscape

Galal el-Din el-Tayeb

This chapter seeks to provide a very modest contribution to the theoretical conceptualization of population studies by suggesting the incorporation of a social dimension in any population theory. It therefore looks past the superficial spatial and sectoral appearance of population movements at the inner essence and the social nature of these movements. Using some empirical evidence from the Sudan, it looks into the hypothesis that under capitalism the major spatial and sectoral population movements emanate from deep and multiple, but dialectically interrelated, social processes, and that the population landscape is determined mostly by the needs of capital. The distinction between private and public capital is immaterial when both are guided by the same laws of accumulation.

Theoretical framework

Classical theories of population are only an integral constituent of the whole body of bourgeois social science, popularizing the same concepts and perpetuating the same mode of thought and ideology. Bourgeois social science, including population theories, equates ideological validation with scientific verification through the segmentation of total reality, distortion of rational knowledge, and presentation of ideological concepts as universal truth. Most models of man presented by these population theories are examples of abstract man; likewise, populations are projected as isolated, competitive individuals or, at best, aggregations of individuals. 'Average' man and abstraction of population are used as *concrete* categories. These theories, and, indeed, all bourgeois social science, are ideological postulations and a conscious mystification of the social forces at work in society and of the class division of population.

An alternative, but equally ideological, theory of population emphasizes that: 'An abstract law of population exists only for plants and animals and even then only in the absence of any historical intervention by man' (Marx, 1977: 784); and that: 'The population is an abstraction if I leave out, for example, the classes of which it is composed. These classes in turn are an empty phrase if I am not familiar with the elements on which they rest, e.g. wage labour, capital, etc . . .' (Marx, 1973: 100). Nowhere do people exist as abstract, isolated individuals who confront each other and society to satisfy universal human needs. There are only historically-bound men – in time and place – existing and producing within particular social formations or societies; man can only individuate himself in the midst of society. Social beings get involved in social processes, dealing mainly with the production and reproduction of the material bases of life. Different social processes under different historical epochs produce different social and economic landscapes (Peet, 1977: 21); these landscapes produce, in turn, different population landscapes. The organizational patterns of the population landscape, population growth and population movements vary from one historical epoch to another. As society develops the means to control and manage its environment in a more effective manner and its forces of production, the growth, movement and distribution of population tend to be determined more and more by the social relations of production. As society becomes socially divided, these social relations of production become antagonistic and involve the production by some and the appropriation by others of surplus value (i.e. the value of labour-time over and above what is necessary for the reproduction (subsistence) of labour power) which is the source of rent, interest and profit. Thus, an appropriate theory of population should stem from the labour theory of value (Harvey, 1977: 229–30).

With the advent and development of the capitalist mode of production, an historically-specific law of population has come into play, one which is bound up with the prevailing capitalist relations of production. The development of capitalism gives rise to, among other things, the individualization of society and the enhancement of the individual's ability to have, and need for, 'free movement' through the breaking down of the economic and social factors inhibiting such 'free movement'. Processes to enhance people's 'free movement' over space and between sectors would include the divorce of an ever bigger proportion of the population from the ownership of the means of production, the destruction of the traditional or pre-capitalist methods of production, mechanization, and the destruction or transformation of tribal and family structures and relations. Through these processes and the concomitant transformations a 'relative surplus population' or 'an industrial reserve army' is produced and reproduced; and the apparent 'over-population' and 'resource scarcity' (forcing people to move) which then arise are relative not to natural conditions and the resource-base, but to the needs of capital accumulation, because capital requires a reserve army of labour power on which it can draw quickly and easily in case of a sudden expansion of capitalist production, and which acts to hold the pretensions of the working class in check (Perelman, 1979: 83).

Urbanization and the population landscape

Changes in the distributional pattern of population are brought about by the disequilibrating effect of capital. In its quest for above-average profits, capitalism creates and intensifies a geographical differentiation in labour productivity, rates of profit, organic composition of capital and cost of variable capital or wage rates

(Soja, 1978: 21). The development of the urban process and the concentration of economic activity, particularly industry, in major cities have resulted in a higher degree of the socialization of the forces of production, a higher rate of profit and a higher wage rate than in other areas. The cumulative nature of such geographical concentration of capital and the increasing need of industrial capital for wage labour, together with the simultaneous impoverishment of the countryside and the repelling conditions arising therefrom determine the pattern and magnitude of rural–urban population movements.

In the Sudan, for example, the geographically-varying degrees of the development of capitalist commodity production and of the urban process have differentiated wage rates for workers and rates of profit for capital over the various provinces (Table 4.1). The wage differential represents the driving force on the part of labour to move from where wages are low to where they are higher; the differentiated rates of profit express the degree to which capital is attracted as well as its increasing demand for labour.

Table 4.2 shows the high degree of concentration of capital in Khartoum Province, particularly in terms of labour force and surplus value which is the origin of profit. Khartoum Province is followed, but far behind, by the provinces of Blue Nile and Kassala, the three of which comprise almost all industrial locations. These three relatively more urbanized and industrialized provinces have wages and rates of profit higher than the national averages while all other provinces have less-than-average figures (Table 4.1). As anticipated, these three provinces have annual rates of population growth higher than the national average, all attracting population from the more rural provinces. Khartoum Province had been growing during the intercensal period (1955–73) by more than twice the national rate, whereas the two provinces of Upper Nile and Equatoria, with the lowest wage rates and rates of profit, had shown a decline in population attributable partly to the 18-year-long war in the south. Moreover, within all provinces the rate of population growth was higher for urban centres than for rural areas. This is causally related to the fact that within all provinces industrial capital is almost completely confined to a few urban centres. For example, in the Blue Nile Province, the three centres of Wad Medani-Maringan, El-Hasaheisa-Qoz Kabaru and Rabak accounted in 1971 for 87 per cent of the total number of plants, 94 per cent of industrial capital investment and 91 per cent of the total value added in industry in the province; and in Kassala Province the three figures for the two towns of Khashm el-Girba and Port Sudan were 75, 82 and 83 per cent of the provincial totals, respectively (El-Tayeb, 1980: 22).

Consisting of Khartoum City, Khartoum North and Omdurman, Greater Khartoum is the primate city and capital, and has a high population growth and concentration. Its dramatic growth is indicated by its twenty-fold population increase from 50,000 in 1900 to about one million in 1975. During 1965–75 Khartoum City grew in population by over 100 per cent, Khartoum North by over 85 per cent and Omdurman by more than 60 per cent (El-Bushra, 1976: 75). The

Table 4.1. *Industrial wages, rates of profit and rate of population growth, early 1970s*

Province	Wages (Sudanese pounds)	Rate of profit	Rate of population growth (%) 1956–73
Khartoum	435	0.11	4.85
Blue Nile	326	0.07	3.50
Kassala	395	0.06	3.00
Northern	291	0.03	0.65
Kordofan	207	0.04	1.28
Darfur	104	0.04	2.85
Bahr el-Ghazal	102	0.01	1.99
Upper Nile	93	0.01	−0.62
Equatoria	91	0.01	−0.04
Sudan (average)	301	0.05	2.14

Source: Compiled from Industrial Development Centre for Arab States, *A Report on the Industrial Survey and Opportunities for Industrial Development in the Democratic Republic of Sudan*, Department of Statistics, Khartoum, 1970; Department of Statistics, *Industrial Survey 1970–71 for Plants Employing less than 25 Workers*, Khartoum, 1976; *Preliminary Report on the 1973 census*; other reports on the Southern Region. All 1,291 industrial plants are considered.

Table 4.2. *Geographical concentration of industrial activity in three provinces of Sudan, 1971*

Province	Number of plants (%)	Labour force (%)	Wages (%)	Investment (%)	Surplus value (%)
Khartoum	44.6	62.6	65.6	48.7	66.2
Blue Nile	25.7	20.8	15.9	24.0	16.5
Kassala	10.0	9.5	12.9	19.2	13.7
% of whole of Sudan	80.3	92.9	94.4	91.9	96.4

Source: Galal el-Din el-Tayeb, *Industry and Peripheral Capitalism in the Sudan: A Geographical Analysis*, Ph.D. thesis, University of California, Los Angeles, 1980: 165, 168, 173, 183 and 239. All 1,291 plants are considered.

fact that the current annual rate of population growth for Greater Khartoum stands close to 5 per cent indicates that the natural population growth rate is inflated by the continued influx of migrants from other parts of the country. A survey conducted by the International Labour Organization (I.L.O., 1976: 351–8) reveals that population movement into the capital city is basically a function of geographical differentiation in job availability and wage level. Considering former employment, the survey finds that of all in-migrants, only 37 per cent were previously working, of whom 73 per cent were in agriculture. Regarding their occupational status, it was found that 18 per cent of them were private employees, 6 per cent government employees and the remaining 76 per cent were either self-employed or unpaid family workers. Among the self-employed and unpaid family workers, 82 and 97 per cent respectively were in agriculture. The fact that 89 per cent of those who were working before migrating have come to seek employment suggests that either they did not have adequate work on the family farm or else their earnings were low enough, compared to the expected earnings, to initiate the move to Greater Khartoum.

Of the total number of in-migrants, 36 per cent remained unemployed, feeding into the 'industrial reserve army'. Those who were employed provided cheap labour mainly for industrial capital since of all employed in-migrants manufacturing industry absorbed 25 per cent as production workers and about 17 per cent as unskilled labourers; others were employed in various activities, particularly services. For all occupations, in-migrant labour is cheaper than resident labour. Table 4.3 shows that in 1974 the average annual wage of an in-migrant was about 36 per cent below that of the average resident production worker and the resident 'unidentified' worker; and about 25 per cent below that of the resident worker in all other occupations.

Table 4.3. *Average annual earnings of in-migrants, Khartoum, 1974*

| Occupation | Resident (Sudanese pounds) | In-migrant | |
		Sudanese pounds	As % of resident
Tradesman	553	412	74.5
Clerical	639	472	73.9
Service worker	291	217	74.6
Production worker	425	273	64.2
Unskilled worker	327	251	76.8
Unidentified	655	424	64.7

Source: International Labour Office, *Growth, Employment and Equity: A Comprehensive Strategy for the Sudan*, Geneva, 1976: 359.

Such population movements, which are mainly rural–urban, suggest the following major features:

1. Redistribution of population is largely a function of the accumulation process, which produces and reproduces the conditions necessary for population movements. The accumulation process may not necessarily be local but it may be operating at distant centres within the social formation and, indeed, well beyond the national boundaries. On the one hand, the needs of capital in Greater Khartoum have initiated population movements from as far away as Darfur Province and the Southern Region. On the other hand, the international division of labour and the needs of British industrial capital enforced the restructuration of the population landscape in the Gezira area during the third decade of this century, when the colonial administration established the Gezira Scheme to secure an adequate supply of cheap, long-staple cotton for the British textile industry, which was suffering from mounting competition (mainly from

Japan and the United States of America) for, and from the concomitant inflated prices of, this type of cotton (Abdel Rahim, 1968: 49).

2. These population movements are not only spatial in nature, involving physical movement from a rural area to an urban centre; they are also sectoral, with labour moving out of traditional agriculture into manufacturing industry and services; but of more significance is the simultaneous social nature of these movements which are initiated by social processes to consolidate the social power of capital, and which have far-reaching social connotations on those who move. It is not a random sample of the people who move, but the least-privileged and the poor, whether unemployed, underemployed or low paid, who are forced to migrate (I.L.O., 1976: 351–8). In the urban centres, in-migrants either remain unemployed or get employment at low wage rates, both to the advantage of capital; they live alienated and under subhuman conditions on the urban fringes, as around Greater Khartoum. Being subjected to all economic, social and psychological vices of capitalism, in-migrants increasingly resort to crime and drug addiction. Initially induced by capital to move in search of more decent and human living conditions, it is, paradoxically, capital itself which subjugates and dehumanizes them after they migrate. It is one of the built-in contradictions of capitalist urbanization.

3. The rate of population movement from rural areas to urban centres would have been higher had it not been for some forces at work in the rural part of the national territory. Significant among these forces is the dominance of pre-capitalist and petty forms of commodity production as well as tribal and extended family structures and relations. The manner and magnitude of the change in the distributional pattern of population depends on, among other things, the nature and extent of the penetration of capital in the form of the so-called 'developmental projects' into these pre-capitalist formations, and on the nature and depth of transformations brought about by such penetration.

It seems in order, at this point, to look at the other side of the coin, the countryside or the origin of migration, to see the impact of 'developmental projects' on the changing pattern of the distribution of population.

Capital and pre-capitalist societies

In the Sudan, as well as in all peripheral societies, most rural populations were or are use-value and petty-commodity producers, combining in various proportions pastoralism and traditional forms of agriculture; these societies were self-sufficient and producing basically for subsistence, using family labour. The right to use land was communally arranged, and the production process was largely collective. The basic producing unit was the family or a part of a tribe. With the penetration of capital, these societies were significantly transformed.

The geographical expansion of capital into pre-capitalist formations is to enhance the process of accumulation, the historic mission of capital. This process of accumulation is guided by the fundamental law of motion of capital which derives from the dialectical unity between production and circulation as the two processes which together sustain the development of capital (de Janvry and Garramon, 1977: 29). In order to realize surplus value embodied in the value of commodities, and thus let capital grow, commodities must circulate. The capacity of the economy to consume has to grow continuously in order to expand the capacity to produce, to reap more surplus value, and to secure sustained capital accumulation.

The penetration by capital of these pre-capitalist societies is to establish large areas of labour reserve and complementary markets able to respond quickly and easily to the spasmodic, unequal and contradictory development of capitalist production (Mandel, 1968: 373). To expand the market for capitalist production, capitalism has to forcibly break the self-sufficiency of pre-capitalist communities, to monetize the economy to allow for and enhance the circulation of value through the commercialization of production, to introduce new life styles, and to create new social needs. Through the incorporation, capitalization and transformation of pre-capitalist communities, capitalism progressively divorces larger and larger segments of use-value producers and petty-commodity producers from the ownership of the means of production, converting them into 'free workers'. This proletarianization process is crucial for the survival and development of capitalism because, as Mandel (1976: 43) argues: 'If in order to survive, all of the working population found jobs in the region where they lived, there would no longer be reserves of wage labour free for the sudden expansion of industrial production.'

The effects of 'developmental projects' on the distribution of population may vary, but the social processes conditioning population landscapes remain basically the same. The geographical transfer of labour in response to the needs of 'developmental projects' was recorded in the Sudan as early as the beginning of this century. The colonial administration initiated in the 1910s the production of cotton in the Baraka and Gash deltas in eastern Sudan, and thus created the need for labour. The permanent population of the Baraka area was only 2,000 in 1910, or about 20 per cent of the agricultural labour force required during the busy seasons; thus, the administration encouraged both permanent and seasonal migration to the area. The immigrant wage labour in 1910 numbered about 8,000 persons (i.e. four times the total number of the local population), most of whom were Eritrean Habad, Sudanese Beja and West African Hausa, Takruni and Falata (McLoughlin, 1970: 112). A similar shortage in wage labour was encountered in the Gash area into which agricultural workers were encouraged to move from Eritrea and the Gedaref area; in 1907 and 1912, 400 Abyssinians and 1,000 West Africans, respectively, were settled in Kassala to augment the existing agricultural wage labour needed by the Gash Scheme (McLoughlin, 1970: 112 and 114).

The erection of agricultural schemes has meant to some people a reduction in the grazing land and an equivalent decrease in the magnitude of their seasonal movements; for those nomads who used the Nile water and riverine pasture, developmental schemes along the Blue and White Niles have meant a loss of an invaluable source of animal life, and an increased movement generally southward. Schemes like the Gezira and Rahad have transformed almost all local population from agro-pastoralists to tenants, bringing to an end their former movements, but the schemes also attracted people from other parts of the country as tenants and as agricultural workers. The restructuring of the Gezira and Rahad population landscape has been accompanied by a host of social changes: the communal use of land has been replaced by individually operated tenancies; the customary rights to the use of land have been legalized; the decision-making process as to what, where, when and how to cultivate, which was formerly vested in the people themselves, has now been given to the bureaucracy, and the tenants have to adhere strictly to a detailed, predetermined schedule of agricultural operations. But the greatest social change is that, whereas the former community was differentiated quantitatively by size of land and livestock, the present community exhibits a qualitative differentiation by ownership of means of production.

The social processes which give rise to population movements and thus condition the population landscape are summarized in Figure 4.1. This scheme is an oversimplification of these processes, and is intended to show the degree to which capital creates, through various interrelated processes, the conditions which would necessitate migration. It is not conclusive, and does not apply to all community members for, as mentioned earlier, only some are forced to migrate. It should also be noted that the partial or total applicability depends on the degree of the development of capitalist production. Nonetheless, the relation between capital and population or labour movement in the agro-pastoral societies of the periphery can be analysed within the general framework of the scheme, which suggests the following:

1. When modern agricultural schemes are established on fertile land previously used for grazing and traditional subsistence farming depending on natural factors, grazing and cultivated land will be decreased, as in central Blue Nile Province, or the agro-pastoral society will be pushed into marginal land (e.g. the nomads along the White Nile north and south of Ed Dueim). In both cases cultivated crops and pasture will decrease, provoking the need for additional animal feed, and with it the need for cash. Thus capital has created the initial conditions to transform the economy and society.

2. To obtain cash to buy fodder crops some people will sell part of their crop and, later, some of their animals and animal products to commercial and industrial capital, while some – usually the most active members of society – will seek employment in industry and modern agriculture; other members will start borrowing. At this juncture, the self-sufficiency of the

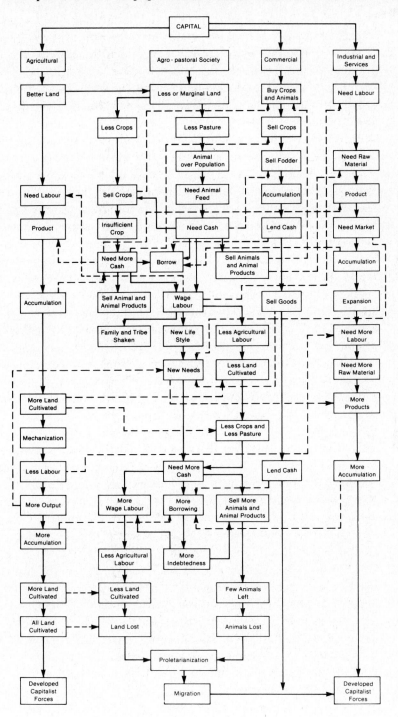

Fig. 4.1 Capital and labour migration

community is broken, mainly through reducing the dependence of the community on nature; rendering the community more dependent on, and responsive to, conditions created by capital; commercialization of production and circulation of money; and the development of wage labour. The former producing unit starts to change, and the tribal and family bases of community organization and relations start to shake and to disintegrate.

3. With the development of the forces of production and the expanded reproduction of capital the following transformational processes will be reinforced and intensified: the sale of crops and animal products, especially milk which is an important component of the society's diet; the reduction of agricultural family labour as a result of some members of the family, usually active males, leaving the farm to seek employment for cash; the reduction in cultivated land resulting from shortage of family labour and the geographical expansion of modern agriculture; the fall in the production of food crops to levels below the subsistence needs of the families; all these processes intensify the need for food crops and for cash. This situation is usually aggravated by the emergence of new demands and new social needs as industrial production, modern agriculture and commercial activities expand and develop, and as the society is transformed and incorporated into a market economy. The search by the people to satisfy the ever-increasing need for money pushes borrowing and indebtedness, the sale of animals and animal products, and the sale of labour power to progressively higher levels.

4. When capitalist production takes hold of agriculture, the demand for agricultural labour begins to decrease absolutely while the accumulation of agricultural capital increases steadily. So, at every stage of the development and capitalization of modern agriculture and at every corresponding stage of the destruction of traditional subsistence farming, part of the agricultural population is on the point of moving out of the agricultural sector to non-agricultural activities, mainly industry and services.

5. The accumulation process requires that property and means of production be concentrated in fewer hands, thus 'freeing' an increasing number of people to move and concentrate in urban centres. The development of capital presupposes, initiates and intensifies the underdevelopment of the lower social stratum of the population, converting them into 'free' workers. The poorer segments of the agro-pastoral community continually lose their means of production and subsistence in cultivated land and livestock, and become, in the end, totally dependent for their subsistence on the sale of their labour power. After being thus proletarianized, this part of the population is forced to migrate to seek employment, mainly in urban centres where capital is most concentrated.

Conclusion

Theories confined only to the spatial and sectoral population movements neglect the grassroot forces which govern these population movements. A more powerful and explanatory theory of population is the one which is founded on the social and changing nature of society, and on the dynamics of the production process, particularly the social relations of production. Population landscapes arising therefrom are, therefore, not static, but are changing with changes in the mode of production and with the evolution of the productive forces. Historically, population movements and distribution were largely governed by the natural environment; but with the advent and development of capitalism, the organization and reorganization of population landscapes have increasingly become a function of the accumulation process.

In its quest to expand the capacity of the economy to consume and to maximize accumulation, capital penetrates and transforms pre-capitalist societies, and concentrates production and population (labour reserve) in urban centres and the means of production in fewer hands. This is achieved through the destruction of former structures and relations, the capitalization of agricultural production, and the total divorce of ever larger segments of the population from the ownership of the means of production, thus forcing them to move. Such population movements are, therefore, socially selective since it is the marginalized and proletarianized strata of the population which are forced to move and migrate to where capital needs them. Under capitalism, population landscapes arise out of the dialectical relationship between the development of capital and the underdevelopment of people, between the overpopulation of urban centres and the underpopulation of the countryside.

REFERENCES

Abdel Wahab Abdel Rahim, (1968) *An Economic History of the Gezira Scheme 1900–1956*, Ph.D. thesis, University of Manchester.
De Janvry, A. and Garramon, C. (1977) Laws of motion of capital in the center-periphery structure, *The Review of Radical Political Economies*, 9, 29–38.
El-Sayed El-Bushra (1976) *An Atlas of Khartoum Conurbation*, Khartoum, Khartoum University Press.
Galal el-Din El-Tayeb, (1980) Industry and peripheral capitalism in the Sudan: a geographical analysis, Ph.D. thesis, University of California, Los Angeles.
Harvey, D. (1977) Population, resources and the ideology of science, in R. Peet (ed.), *Radical Geography: Alternative Viewpoints on Contemporary Social Issues*, Chicago, Maaroufa Press, pp. 213–42.
International Labour Office (I.L.O.) (1976) *Growth, Employment and Equity: A Comprehensive Strategy for the Sudan*, Geneva, Imprimeries Populaires.
Mandel, E. (1968) *Marxist Economic Theory*, New York, Monthly Review Press.
Mandel, E. (1976) Capitalism and regional disparities, *Southwest Economy and Society*, 1.
Marx, K. (1973) *Grundrisse*, Harmondsworth, Penguin.

Marx, K. (1977) *Capital*, New York, Vintage.

McLoughlin, P. F. M. (1970) Labour market conditions and wages in the Three Towns, 1900–1950, *Sudan Notes and Records*, 51, 105–18.

Peet, R. (1977) The development of radical geography in the United States, in R. Peet (ed.), *Radical Geography: Alternative Viewpoints on Contemporary Social Issues*, Chicago, Maaroufa Press, pp. 6–30.

Perelman, M. (1979) Marx, Malthus and the concept of natural resources' scarcity, *Antipode*, 11, 80–91.

Soja, E. W. (1978) 'Topian' Marxism and spatial praxis: a reconstruction of the political economy of space, paper presented at the annual meeting of the Association of American Geographers, April, New Orleans.

5   Unequal participation of migrant labour in wage employment

El Watig Mohamed Kameir and
Zeinab B. El Bakri

Introduction

Various traditional conceptions within different disciplines have presented a certain image of population movements generally and of the labour migration of specific groups in particular. Geographers generally describe the movement of groups of people as a geographic or spatial phenomenon, and also describe its potential consequences for changing urbanization rates and levels, the growth of cities in a spatial sense, demographic characteristics of migrants, etc. Meanwhile, economists dwell on the advantages and disadvantages (or costs and benefits) of population movements for the individuals concerned, concentrating in particular on the economic 'rationality' of such movements for individual migrants. Arrighi and Saul (1973: 183) have been especially critical of the latter types of analyses, particularly pointing out their unfounded concentration on the 'spontaneity' of the market forces (i.e. the free and 'rational' choice of individuals in the market place) with little or no role given to open or concealed forms of compulsion.

The point remains that both these traditional conceptions tend to neglect crucial aspects of the reality of population movements, notably:

1. That population movements are much more than simple spatial or economic phenomena ultimately produced and shaped by the specific historical developments and changes in the systems of economic production in the areas where they occur.
2. Population movements relate to the differential position of groups within the entire social formation, and are, consequently, a factor of these differential placings rather than being subject to the prerogatives of individual choice or principles of economically rational behaviour, as the latter is defined within the capitalist system. Rather, such movements are intimately related to the very expansion of that system and the element of compulsion involved in the spread of its relations of production, especially under the hegemony of the colonial state.
3. This means therefore that a viable analysis of population movements of whatever kind requires resorting to the use of an alternative approach that goes beyond narrowly-set economic and geographical/spatial perspec-

53

tives. It is necessary to examine the phenomenon of population movement from all angles and at different levels of analysis, singling out the differential historical position of the groups involved within the scope of the specific social formation under concern. It is therefore proposed to undertake an alternative analysis of the population movements of one particular group within the Sudanese social formation: the Nuer, and their circulatory pattern of labour migration to the Three Towns (Khartoum, Omdurman and Khartoum North). It becomes imperative to analyse this phenomenon at three different levels, corresponding to the different sections of this paper:

First: The processes underlying the development of a class of mobile wage labourers in Sudan under colonialism and the continued reproduction of these processes since independence. The consideration of these processes is especially crucial because in our view they constitute the roots of most population movements in Sudan during the twentieth century.

Second: The development of 'urban' wage employment within the context of the specific process of Sudanese urbanization, particularly given the latter's unequal and dependent nature.

Third: The differential participation of diverse groups of urban migrants in wage employment through utilizing a particular type of population movement. This is a reflection of regional developmental disparities and the uneven penetration of capitalist relations in the areas of origin of the population under concern.

Therefore, the first analysis attempts to explain such movements within the context of colonial policies at the national level, aiming at the creation of a class of wage labourers that would facilitate colonial attempts for access to cheap raw materials and expansion of its markets. The second level of analysis is more specific and concentrates on the character of urbanization, urban economies, and how these have shaped the growth of a migrant urban wage-earning class, especially in the Three Towns. Finally, the particular patterns of population movement undertaken by specific groups (e.g. the Nuer) and their differential participation in the urban labour market is explained by referring to the disparities between their region of origin and the rest of the country.

The development of a class of wage labourers and its effect on population movements

The first large-scale population movements whether within rural areas or from rural to urban areas during this century were to a large extent a consequence of colonial policies aimed at the creation of a class of wage labourers to serve the colonial state. In order to understand these initial and also subsequent population movements, it becomes necessary to analyse colonial policies carefully within the context of the expanding capitalist system.

Certain forms of wage labour had existed to some extent in pre-colonial Sudan, as in other parts of Africa. 'Wages' were sometimes paid by chiefs and kings to those who produced weapons, garments, etc.; farmers hired artisans for certain tasks, and traders paid for assistance in the transportation of goods. Such labour consisted basically of the exchange of services for certain goods. Services were offered either within an overall system of social obligations and reciprocities based on kinship relations, or as aspects of permanent agreements based on the mutual consent of the parties involved. But although such exchanges were negotiated, there was no market in which labour power was bought or sold. The creation and development of categories of wage earners who offered their labour power as a commodity on an open market was essentially initiated by colonial society and the British colonial state.

With the final establishment of the colonial state under British rule in 1898, colonial policy was largely dictated by a concern to provide privileged British access to cheap raw materials, coupled with the aim of developing and protecting markets for commodities produced in Britain. For ecological reasons, the exploitation of these resources was not sought through the development of plantations or the imposition of European settler farmers employing local labour, as in many other African colonies, notably Kenya, Rhodesia, and some parts of Uganda and Tanzania. Instead, the production of raw materials, cotton especially, was encouraged in Sudan, through turning Sudanese subsistence farmers into cultivators producing for the export market. As expressed by Abdel Muhsin Mustafa (1975):

The colonial policy exerted its farthest reaching impact on the evolving structure of the economy through the link it established between the Sudanese economy and the British economy. The link was effected through assigning to the former the role of supplying the British market, and later the Western European market, but through Britain, with a very narrow range of primary products in which cotton comprised 80–90% of the total. In exchange, the Sudanese economy was opened to products from Britain.

In pursuit of this objective the British embarked through the colonial state on a plan for various forms of primitive capital accumulation:

1. The imposition of different kinds of taxes, such as bull and hut taxes.
2. In certain areas, particularly in the south where many people refused to cooperate, the state used political coercion, through tribal chiefs, to drive people to work in construction activities such as the building of roads and dams and water carrying. Among certain Nuer clans in Southern Sudan, the Gawer clan for example, young men were required by the administrative authorities of the province to labour on public works like roads, banks and *tukls* (workers' huts).
3. Economic pressures on local populations were developed through the importation of consumer goods such as textiles, sugar and tea that could only be purchased with cash. The cash 'needs' thus stimulated became a decisive force in attracting people to wage-employment, even if only on a

temporary basis, during the early phases of colonial rule. The aim of developing cash needs led to the application of various measures by the colonial regime for recruiting labour in different regions of Sudan. The Nuer of the Upper Nile Province, for instance, were in some areas compelled to grow cotton for cash. The introduction of cotton growing stimulated the money economy and thus enabled the collection of tribute in cash from individual able-bodied men instead of collecting dues in the form of animals, fish or game. In this respect, it is interesting to note the following comment made by the Governor of the Upper Nile Province to the Civil Secretary in Khartoum in 1927 (Sudan Archives, Durham, 212/11): 'The introduction of money and the means of making money have no doubt had a great effect in bringing these Nuer into line. Their one desire is cattle, and they find that by growing cotton they can buy cows, and so much is in fact appreciated that a chief can and does fine a tribesman who refuses to grow cotton.'

4. The most important type of capital accumulation was developed by inducing subsistence farmers to bring their own land and tools into production for export at prices that did not even cover the costs incurred by the cultivators and their families, i.e. of labour power reproduction. This is because the latter were expected to satisfy most of their needs through subsistence activities bringing mainly their surplus labour into the production of marketable crops.

5. Private ownership of land was stimulated and protected by the introduction of land laws such as the *Titles to Land Ordinance*, 1898 and the *Land Settlement Ordinance*, 1905. As noted by Collins (1976): 'although these laws did not immediately transfer land tenure, they laid the foundation for the lucrative agricultural schemes that became the basis of the Sudanese colonial economy'.

Apart from the above, however, the main arena where capitalist activities penetrated pre-colonial structures and which further accelerated the creation of a class of wage labourers was the market. At the time of the colonial conquest, market relationships played no more than a marginal role in most parts of the Sudan (Abdel Muhsin Mustafa, 1975: 9–10). Despite the long-established trade relations within the Sudan and with the outside world, and despite the connections created by the slave trade since the nineteenth century, most people in the country were still relatively self-sufficient for most of their daily needs (O'Fahey and Spaulding, 1974). After the imposition of the colonial state, a wider range of consumer goods, such as textiles, household utensils, soap and matches, was introduced. To meet these new demands people had to learn how to produce low-priced and labour-intensive export commodities through the development on a capitalist basis of irrigated agriculture and mechanized farming.

The stimulation of capital accumulation by the colonial system thus led to the emergence of classes of landlords, tenants and wage labourers. Furthermore, the development of export/import activities eventually led to the emergence of merchant capitalists trading locally as well as in export commodities such as livestock, meat, oil seeds, cotton, sesame and dura.

These processes of capital accumulation disrupted the former essentially subsistence economies. All those who remained in villages became increasingly dependent on cash earnings to cover their daily needs. In some parts of Northern and Western Sudan, it was possible for farmers to turn themselves into export producing cultivators. However, for those who failed to meet their needs as export producing cultivators, migration seeking wage labour in agricultural schemes or urban centres became the only viable alternative.

Thus, the essential point in the first section is that initial large-scale population movements were directly related to colonial attempts, using various strategies, to create a class of wage labourers which would facilitate the accomplishment of certain aims. These strategies included large-scale imposition of taxes and stimulation of cash needs to purchase newly-available commodities, which soon became necessities. However, due to the very features of production systems in various areas of Sudan, there was only a limited opportunity for continual provision of the necessary cash without resorting to migration to large agricultural schemes and urban centres, both being areas of heavy colonial investment, which depended totally on the existence of a class of wage labourers. The process whereby the peasants have been progressively alienated from their means of production has continued in the post-independence period. The capitalist choice of development by the state in this period has enhanced this process.

In the coming section, we arrive at the second level of analysis delineated in the introduction. This relates to population movements from rural to urban areas, which we maintain can be explained by examining features of urbanization and industrialization and the structures of urban economies in Sudan.

Rural–urban population movements, the emergence of urban wage labourers and patterns of urbanization and industrial development in Sudan

As has been stressed by Magubane (1979), urban economies in Africa exist and operate within a system which is geared to extracting raw materials for metropolitan industry. Thus industrialization did not develop together with urbanization (as was the case in Western Europe) because that would have resulted in a large-scale local accumulation of capital that might have posed a challenge to colonial monopolies. In effect then the urbanization of the population was not accompanied by diversification of the urban economy and alteration in urban–rural economic relations. This very fact, the intimate relation between urban patterns and colonial objectives and policies, meant that urbanization in Africa and by extension, Sudan, came to exhibit three specific features:

1. Extreme inequalities and disparities exist, whether between rural and urban areas, between urban areas or within specific urban areas. The effect of these inequalities has been wide discrepancies between over-urbanized sub-regions and underdeveloped backlands. Furthermore, there is the pattern of primate city dominance where the largest city contains an extremely high percentage of both the total and urban populations, in addition to controlling the processes of decision-making, communications and other facilities. Even within major cities the co-existence of fragmented sets of ecologically distinctive areas is witnessed where different classes lead lives relatively isolated from those of other classes (Abu Lughod, 1976).

2. Problems of employment are, therefore, intimately connected to the above types of inequalities but also to the labour laws enacted by the colonial state. These aimed to admit into urban areas only those whose labour power was needed, others being uprooted to create a floating workforce that could be used to undermine and depress the wages of those employed in colonial industries (Magubane, 1979).

3. Industrial development itself had specific features, which had a direct impact on the workings of the urban economy, and notably, employment.

How the above three points feature in the case of Sudan and their effect on rural–urban population movements is the subject of analysis below.

The first major tasks urban migrants were expected to perform for the colonial government were porterage and labour infrastructural projects. Although labourers received wages for their services, few people were attracted to labouring, as the work was considered arduous, and the need for money was not yet widely felt. Since the spontaneous supply of workers was insufficient in some parts of the country, the colonial authorities often resorted to recruitment of labour through political pressures by directing 'tribal' chiefs to supply specific numbers of men for certain projects.

Another strategy employed by the colonial state to supply the required labour was capitalizing on Nigerian immigration, especially since the Sudanese population, to a large extent, was not yet socialized in the direction of a large-scale and full dependence on wage labour. Thus according to Duffield (forthcoming): 'Nigerian immigration into Sudan which gathered momentum soon after colonization was quickly recognized as being a solution to the labour problem and a means of reducing its high cost.'

Within the Three Towns, the need for a substantial labour force for various projects was felt by the colonial authorities since the earlier years of this century. Up to the Second World War labourers were recruited by several government departments for the construction of large and permanent office buildings, warehouses and other extensive public works like roads, transportation and the Khartoum river wall built in 1905. As early as 1900, large construction projects had started to rebuild Khartoum. Over 5,000 men were directly employed in brickmaking, quarrying and the burning of lime. Railway construction and the establishment of the dockyards and of the Mechanical Transport Department in Khartoum North soon called for yet further labour (El-Sayed El-Bushra, 1971 and 1972a, b; Barbour, 1961; McLoughlin, 1970; Mohammed El-Awad Galal El Din, 1975).

Important facts to be noted here concern the composition of the labour force, the nature of recruitment and the pattern of migration that developed. By far the greater influx to the Three Towns consisted of Northern Sudanese and people of Darfurian origin, especially after the annexation of the Darfur Sultanate in 1916. The majority of migrant labourers in that period were either domestic slaves or runaway ex-slaves (El Din, 1975). Most of the Northern Sudanese migrants were circulating rather than permanent labourers. They moved back and forth between the towns and their farms. This was due to short-period work contracts, to low wages, and the continuing need for cultivation for the subsistence of members of their household. Many seasonal agricultural workers, particularly in the Gezira Scheme, first took employment for some time in the Three Towns, before moving to the Gezira area. However, the demand for labourers while the government continued to rebuild Khartoum as the capital led the colonial authorities to establish the Labour Bureau in 1907. The main function of this office was to regulate the flow of migrant workers to the town in accordance with demand.

The temporary nature of such migrations to the urban areas was reflected in fluctuations in the size of the urban population. According to McLoughlin (1970) the 1903 population was approximately 83,680, but this had dropped to 81,880 in 1904. The general characteristics of this migration remained much the same up to the Second World War. However, the urban population grew from 81,880 in 1904 to 202,281 in 1931. In that year, the world-wide depression hit the economy of the Sudan and the net consequence was a sharp fall in urban employment. By then the Labour Bureau was involved in trying to reverse the flow of migrants by sending unemployed persons back to their home areas. By the mid-1930s, conditions had started to improve again and a fresh demand for labour became acute, especially for the building industry.

An exodus from the Three Towns then developed with the Second World War, as the general demand for food rose. Large numbers of migrants moved to the Gezira area to produce food for the Armed Forces in Sudan, as well as in the Middle East, India and North Africa. Notwithstanding this outflow, the number of migrants to the Three Towns accelerated during and especially after the war period. Thus the *Annual Report, Khartoum Province* (1950) states: 'There is a constant movement from the provinces to the capital caused partly by the attraction of the amenities of the Three Towns and partly by the demand for labour particularly in the building trade.'

The migrants from Northern and Western Sudan grew in number between 1946 and 1950. The inflow of migrants led to and was reflected in the extensive

building of 'Third Class' residential areas in the different parts of the Three
Towns, especially the *Deims* of Khartoum (Saad El Din Fawzi, 1954). The
growing number of urban migrants also led to a considerable employment
problem in Khartoum. For example in 1945: 'There was some unemployment in
Khartoum, at June 1945, some 750–1,000 workers were taken by the Forests
Department to relieve the situation and employed them at the Gadarif area. Thus
relieving the province of numbers of westerners' (*Annual Report, Khartoum
Province*, 1945).

Again according to the *Annual Report, Khartoum Province* (1950), the influx of
migrants, particularly Nuba (from the Nuba Mountains in Western Sudan) and
southerners, was increasing in the Three Towns. The rise of the population was
particularly noticeable in Khartoum where the numbers grew rapidly in the three
years preceding 1950.

Two important facts should be noted here. Firstly, since the earliest days of
colonial development, the largest section of the labour force of the Three Towns
consisted of migrants, largely men who first left their home areas in order to seek
wage employment. Many scholars, official statistics and reports have thus pointed
to rural–urban migration as the main factor underlying population growth in the
Three Towns (El-Sayed El-Bushra, 1971; Mohamed El-Awad Galal El Din,
1975).

The high rate of net migration to Greater Khartoum is a consequence of
increasing employment opportunities in tertiary, secondary and petty-commodity
production activities. The absence of cash–earning opportunities in rural areas,
coupled with the growing modern capitalist enterprises and service occupations,
has stimulated the flow of migrants. Each region of the Sudan sends at least some
representatives to the capital, though the absolute numbers from each region vary
considerably. The variations are strongly associated with regional disparities in
the levels of socio-economic development and in differences in opportunities for
earning cash.

Secondly, in the pre-war period, migration to the Three Towns was generally
characterized by its temporary nature. The migrants tended to oscillate between
urban wage-employment and their home areas, and many were engaged in
seasonal movements to agricultural areas, particularly the Gezira. However, in the
post-war period, the nature of urban migration to the Three Towns started to
change and most migrants have become increasingly dependent on wage-
employment. This proletarianization is reflected in the increasingly permanent
residence of migrant workers in town.

Thus, the pattern of migration now emerging is characterized by increasing
commitment to wage-employment and consequently a greater tendency among
migrants to bring members of their families to town. However, circular patterns of
migration still occur among some groups engaged in temporary contractual work
(e.g. in the building industry). It is, therefore, necessary to dwell on the nature of
industrial development that has been taking place since the colonial period, and on

the regional disparities in the levels of socio-economic development which have led to differential participation of migrant workers in the industrial urban economy of the Three Towns. The gradual and partial process of the proletarianization of migrant workers has to be viewed in relation to the uneven development of the urban economy itself. Declining income opportunities in the rural areas have increasingly made population movements in search of industrial employment inevitable. Simultaneously, however, the process of proletarianization has been constrained by the uneven penetration of capitalist relations in various rural economies, and the particular development of the modern capitalist sector. Thus it becomes imperative to consider patterns of industrial development in Sudan since colonial times.

Industrial development was held back for a long time by the unrestricted entry of manufactured goods from Britain and Western Europe. The inability of the existent handicraft industries to compete with imports limited the development of these industries and hindered the emergence of any new handicraft industry (Abdel Muhsin Mustafa, 1975: 14–15).

It was only in 1918–19 that the first modern factory – the Mukwar Cement Factory – in which machines and equipment were used, was established by the colonial authorities, but this was primarily for the construction of the Sennar Dam and the factory ceased production after the completion of the dam in 1925–6. This period also witnessed the establishment of some government units operating in the sphere of maintenance, and in producing spare parts for the trains and steamers of Sudan Railways.

During the Second World War there was an increase in industrial production, but various factors hindered importation. The colonial authorities then encouraged import-substitute commodities so that industries producing, for example, soap, textiles, oils, leather and sweets were established. These to some extent alleviated the shortages of the war period and served to keep down the prices of otherwise scarce commodities. For the purpose of organizing and regulating such industries, the War Supply Department was established. The Board of Economics and Commerce of this new department recommended setting up a committee to look into and advise on industries that could relieve the country from the need to import various products, in addition to finding what industries could be established through the use of locally-produced raw materials. Thus the Local Industries Investigation Committee came into being in 1942. It was, however, abolished in 1945, and most of the industries it proposed during the war period failed to establish themselves permanently when imports of British and other foods resumed in the post-war period. Again during the early 1950s a number of industries were established under the Prohibited and Restricted Goods Ordinance, 1939. These were mainly financed by private capital and included shoe manufacturing, meat, cement, cigarette and beverage factories.

This brief historical survey has aimed to show that the colonial administration did not systematically promote this sector of the economy. Even such modest industrial investment as was made during this period was mainly by private domestic and foreign investors. Industrial development during the colonial era has been summarized by Fatima Mahmoud (1978) as follows:

In the case of the Sudan, capitalists were encouraged to engage in activities that furthered the colonial government's designs. It was these designs that permitted and fostered the growth of merchant capital in foreign trade and implanted agricultural capitalists in the country. On the other hand, the development of handicrafts into full-fledged manufacturing industry was contrary to the colonial regime's desire to keep the Sudanese market open for their own manufactured goods. Consequently, an indigenous capitalist class remained non-existent throughout the colonial period.

After independence, primarily due to an absence of economic planning by the neo-colonial state, the industrial sector largely fell into the hands of private capitalists and was developing only through incentives without any central direction. The Approved Enterprises (Concessions) Act, 1956 did not consider establishing industrial priorities or rendering more facilities for the establishment of strategic industries or those dependent on local raw materials.

Thus, it is evident that although the public sector established a number of industries in different parts of the country, most of the industrial development in the Sudan has taken place in the private sector of the economy. According to the 1974 employment survey (I.L.O., 1975), the private manufacturing sector accounted for 91 per cent of all fixed assets, and 82 per cent of workers earning 76 per cent of all wages were employed in large-scale private industry.

The pattern of concentration of industrial plants is clearly reflected in the growth of Khartoum North as the major industrial town in the Sudan. Private industrialists have continued to concentrate their industrial investments in the capital city due to the availability of essential services and to the presence of a large flourishing urban market. The capital city provides the essential pre-requisites for private manufacturers and this only reinforces the existing pattern of concentration.

The rapid rate of industrial growth has resulted in an increasing demand for skilled and unskilled workers. It was this demand and the increase in income associated with it that attracted more migrants into the Three Towns. In 1968, Khartoum North, for instance, had the highest family income for wage earners among the eleven largest towns in the Sudan (Department of Statistics, 1970). The increasing number of migrants coming to the town 'has resulted in immense housing shortages and the emergence of shanty towns on the outskirts of the Three Towns' (Fatima Zahir El-Sadaty, 1972). By the late 1960s, the first industry-oriented 'cardboard settlement' was developed in Khartoum North by migrants from Kordofan and Darfur. In 1968, about 20,000 migrants representing about a quarter of Khartoum North's population were living in this settlement.

Thus, the demand for a labour force in the Three Towns initiated by the colonial authorities early in the century has been reinforced by the pattern of industrial concentration in the Khartoum urban area. However, despite the rapid growth of industry in the Three Towns, the number of new jobs created by the modern capitalist enterprises is insufficient to cater for the increased number of migrants who cannot be productively absorbed into the rural areas. The relatively high wage rates in the modern capitalist sector are up to two or three times the level of the average income of the small family farm. Young people naturally head towards places where they can expect higher incomes.

This situation has created an employment crisis in the Three Towns. In spite of the increasing flow of migrants, their participation in the labour force in regular employment is not rising commensurately. Similarly, the growing rate of industrial output is not matched by a corresponding increase in work opportunities, partly due to the increased dependence on capital-intensive technology. On the other hand, an increasing proportion of the urban labour force is relegated to casual and intermittent employment or to disguised or open unemployment and underemployment.

Thus, there are developing disparities between different categories of workers, these being reflected in the temporary character of much employment, in low wages, in the frequent absence of employment benefits, in underemployment, in the differential application of labour legislation, and in differences in the organization of workers.

Moreover, the inability of modern capitalist employment to absorb the increasing number of migrant job-seekers has in recent years enabled private employers (especially building contractors) to depress the wage levels even below the standard minimum wage, stipulated at L.S. 16.50 monthly in 1974 and L.S. 28.00 in 1978. The average wage of Nuer working in the building industry in Khartoum in 1976–77 was L.S. 0.70 a day. These facts indicate the limited application of protective labour legislation and the relatively free hand of market forces in determining employment conditions in these activities.

Essentially, two points have been emphasized in this section:

1. That rural–urban population movements in Sudan cannot be adequately understood without analysing the specific development of urbanization, of the urban economy and the pattern of industrial development. All these factors together have worked to create a class of urban wage labourers, specifically drawn from rural–urban migrants, particularly to the Three Towns and on which its urban economy has come to depend for its functioning.

2. That the participation of these migrant wage labourers in the urban economy is differential and essentially unequal, as witnessed from rates of underemployment and casual employment. This is only partially explained by the nature of the urban economy itself (especially industrial development). Further explanation has to be sought in other factors, which we turn to in the next section as we examine a specific type of rural–

urban population movement, namely circular labour migration of the Nuer to the Three Towns.

Circular rural–urban migration movements and regional disparities in Sudan

As we have stressed, there is insufficient employment offered by capitalist industry for the growing number of immigrants, most of whom do not have the qualifications and educational levels claimed to be necessary for work in a technically-advanced industry. Those who are considered deficient in these ways are mostly the recent comers and the migrants from the most depressed regions of the country, particularly the south, and they are thus relegated to casual or temporary employment.

In the early decades of British rule, the southern peoples were much less affected by the developing colonial economy than were many of the residents of Northern, Central and Western Sudan. But the developments in Northern and Central regions were nonetheless to be of crucial importance for the people of the south.

For geographical, administrative, historical and other reasons, it was relatively easy to stimulate the development of cotton growing on a capitalist basis, especially in the Gezira area. Cotton growing had existed in pre-colonial times. However, it should be stressed that cotton cultivation in pre- and post-colonial times was based on two different modes of production. The first was 'domestic', the second 'capitalist' but the first did not enable or facilitate the second (Barnett, 1977: 145). It is of interest to note that 'traditional' cotton cultivation was in fact banned by the colonial administration outside the Gezira area. The main areas of post-colonial cultivation were closer to the administrative and commercial capital of the country while the development of transport and communications in the region was given a high priority, as were the construction of rail links to the sea, and of port facilities, first at Suakin and subsequently at Port Sudan. This kind of development continued throughout the period of British rule and has in essence been maintained since independence. The net result is a marked disparity in the level of economic and social development achieved in different parts of the country.

For many reasons the development of the south was not as profitable or rewarding for the colonial power as was the north and to some extent the west. Not only was the southern region far from the sea but transport and communications to many parts of it were also particularly hard to establish because of swamps and forests. In addition, for primarily historical reasons, the cultural standards of the people in the south were different from those in the north and west. The latter had been exposed to a wide variety of commodities through extensive trade and exchange since the previous century. Thus in the colonialists' estimation, this was likely to lead southerners to the rapid establishment of a demand for manufactured goods. During half a century of colonial rule the British administration took advantage of previously existing differentials in the territory. Thus, the north experienced far more rapid rates of development than the south.

Great inequalities developed between northerners and southerners in occupational status and other achievements, and extreme differences developed between them in relation to social standing, political allegiance, access to power and influence. These were also developed and furthermore reproduced.

Nearly all jobs in the capitalist sector (both public and private), in road transport firms, in the Sudan Railways and in the few industrial establishments of the time were held by northerners. Being better educated and more literate, the population of the north became more mobile geographically and socially, achieving a position of over-riding economic advantage. We do not mean in this context that education is the main factor enhancing mobility but that it only reinforced this trend which, obviously, cannot be divorced from the objective conditions of the economic base, although both that material base and its superstructure share a dialectical relationship.

It is in the above types of historical process that the particular circular population movement practised by the Nuer, in addition to their specific pattern of participation in the urban economy, has to be sought. Thus, the involvement of Nuer in labour migration, as of many other peoples in the Sudan, was directly induced by colonialism. In pre-colonial times, the Nuer gained their livelihood from lands and tools belonging to them. In practising a subsistence economy, men would agree to be obliged to perform certain tasks together but there was no 'market' in which labour power was bought or sold. Men, their labour power, and the tasks they performed constituted a unity which could not be separated from the overall web of social relationships in which they were involved as members of a small-scale society. This whole situation changed with colonialism as various mechanisms (such as taxes and introduction of manufactured goods) were set in motion, in order to stimulate wage labour to meet cash needs. However, the inadequate opportunities offered by the Nuer domestic economy in the absence of any planned development led to their labour migration.

More specifically, in the case of the Nuer, we have to take cognizance of their relatively late entry into labour migration and how this has worked to curtail their access to better jobs. Furthermore, we have to add the factors of their illiteracy and their lack of particular occupational skills as one of the main reasons for their concentration in the manual building industry. This concentration in the building industry is an essential feature of their irregular participation in the labour force as day labourers and circulatory migrants.

Final comments

The main points we have emphasized in this paper are the following:

1. That traditional conceptions within various disciplines have led to inadequate understanding of population movements in Sudan, particu-

larly in the present century. Instead, we have proposed an approach which starts from the premise of looking at such processes historically, especially emphasizing that such movements are not voluntary or a matter of economic 'rationality', as proposed by conventional economics. They are, furthermore, more than spatial phenomena affecting the demographic make-up of areas where they occur. Rather, such movements are the consequence of colonial policies aimed at the creation of a class of wage labourers to accomplish the specific aims of the colonial state in Sudan, notably extraction of cheap raw materials and expansion of capitalist markets.

2. More specifically, particular types of population movement, notably from rural to urban areas, have led to the creation of urban wage labour classes. This particular phenomenon has been shaped by the very nature of urban and industrial development under colonialism, a development which has essentially been reproduced since independence.

3. The population movements of specific groups and their characteristic pattern of migration have to be linked to (1) and (2) above, and more so to the differential position they occupied during and subsequent to colonial rule. The circular migration of the Nuer and their unequal participation in the urban economy of the Three Towns is a case in point.

REFERENCES

Abdel Muhsin Mustafa (1975) The structural malformation of the Sudanese economy: a historical account of structural impact of colonial economic policies on the Sudanese economy, *Economic and Social Research Council Bulletin*, No. 24, Khartoum.

Abu Lughod, J. (1976) Development in North African urbanism, in B.J.L. Berry (ed.), *Urban Affairs Annual Reviews*, Beverly Hills, Sage.

Annual Report, Khartoum Province (1945).

Annual Report, Khartoum Province (1950).

Arrighi, G. and Saul, J. (1973) *Essays on the Political Economy of Africa*, New York, Monthly Review Press.

Barbour, K. (1961) *The Republic of the Sudan*, London, University of London Press.

Barnett, A. (1977) *The Gezira Scheme: An Illusion of Development*, London, Frank Cass.

Collins, C. (1976) Colonialism and class struggle in Sudan, *Middle East Research and Information Project*, No. 46.

Department of Statistics (1970) *Household Budget Survey 1967–68*. Khartoum.

Duffield, M. (forthcoming) West African settlements and development in the towns of Northern Sudan, in V.G. Pons (ed.), *Urbanization and Urban Life in Sudan*.

El-Sayed El-Bushra (1971) The evolution of the Three Towns, in S. Hale (ed.), *African Urban Notes*, pp. 8–23.

El-Sayed El-Bushra (1972a) The Development of Industry in Greater Khartoum, Sudan, *East African Geographical Review*, No. 10.

El-Sayed El-Bushra (1972b) *Urbanization in the Sudan*, Proceedings of the 17th Annual Conference of the Philosophical Society of the Sudan, Khartoum.

Fahima Zahir El-Sadaty (1972) Political Mobilization in a Western Sudanese Immigrant Group in Khartoum. D.Phil. thesis, University of Manchester.

Fatima Babiker Mahmoud (1978) Origin and Development of a Sudanese Private Capitalist Class. D.Phil. thesis, University of Hull.

Hale, Sondra (ed.) (1971) Sudan urban studies, *African Urban Notes*, 6, 2, 1–7.

International Labour Office (I.L.O.) (1975) *Growth, Employment and Equity: A Comprehensive Strategy for the Sudan*, Geneva.

Letter by Governor of Upper Nile Province to Civil Secretary (1927). Sudan Archives 212/11, Durham.

Magubane, Ben (1979) The city in Africa: some theoretical issues, in R.A. Obudho and Salah El-Shakhs (eds.), *Development of Urban Systems in Africa*, New York, Praeger.

M.E.F.I.T. (Consulting Engineers) (1974) *Regional Plan of Khartoum and Master Plan for the Three Towns*. Unpublished.

McLoughlin, P.M. (1970) Labour market conditions and wages in the Three Towns, *Sudan Notes and Records*, 51, 105–18.

Mohamed El-Awad Gala El Din (1975) International migration in the Sudan since the Second World War, D.Phil. thesis, University of London.

O'Fahey, R., and Spaulding, J. (1974) *Kingdoms of the Sudan*, London, Methuen.

Pons, V.G. (ed.) (forthcoming) *Urbanization and Urban Life in Sudan*, Khartoum, Khartoum University Press.

Saad El Din Fawzi (1954) Some aspects of urban housing in Northern Sudan, *Sudan Notes and Records*, 35, 91–109.

6 Africa's displaced population: dependency or self-sufficiency?

John R. Rogge

Over the past decade there has been an increasing volume of literature examining aspects of Africa's ever-growing refugee population (Gould, 1974; Rubin, 1974; Rogge, 1977; Adepoju, 1981). Also, after having largely ignored Africa's dilemma for so long, the international press has recently become aware of Africa's refugee problem, and particularly so with respect to the Somalian situation. What most of these writings have stressed is the almost total dependence that Africa's refugees have upon locally-derived solutions to their dilemma, since, in virtually all cases, African refugees do not normally resettle in third countries of permanent asylum. Since all asylum states in Africa are poor, the maintenance of large refugee communities, even with substantial international assistance, creates enormous economic and social burdens. This is especially so when refugees remain wholly dependent upon their hosts for their day-to-day needs. Clearly the quicker a refugee community can progress from its initial state of total dependency to one of self-support, and perhaps even complete self-sufficiency, the better it is for the host society. Moreover, in progressing along the road to self-sufficiency, refugees not only move into a position of providing for most of their daily needs themselves, but may also become integral components within a national economic system. This transition from being a total liability to becoming an asset to a state's productive system has been achieved, or is in the process of being achieved, in a number of Africa's asylum states. In contrast to some of the other papers in this volume, which examine the impact of development programmes upon population redistribution, this paper looks at the question of the extent to which involuntarily displaced people are contributing to, or have the potential of contributing to the development process of their adopted countries.

The nature and scale of the problem

Africa has had to deal with refugee populations since the 1950s, when the first major wave of displacees migrated from Algeria to neighbouring Morocco and Tunisia. Civil wars that followed Sudan's independence in 1956 and Zaire's independence in 1960 brought the refugee problem to central and eastern Africa, and, as anti-colonial movements gained momentum in Portuguese Africa, the number of displaced Africans passed the one million mark in the early 1970s. Since

68

then, even though some of the causative factors have diminished, and many refugees have returned to their countries of origin, the total numbers have continued to accelerate as new conflicts erupted in eastern Africa, the Horn of Africa, southern Africa and in Sahelian Africa. By the time of the O.A.U. conference on refugees in Arusha in 1979, it was estimated that the numbers of refugees had grown to between 3.5 and 4 million; and with the more recent intensification of the Eritrean conflict, with Somalia's futile attempt to annex the Ogaden, and with renewed disturbances in Uganda, the mid-1982 figure was undoubtedly around the 5 million mark.

A significant change has taken place in the type of refugee movements currently being experienced, which has a direct bearing on the probability for eventual repatriation of displacees. Much of the displacement during the 1960s and into the mid-1970s was a consequence of guerrilla warfare against colonial and white-supremacist forces. In virtually all of these cases, it was a foregone conclusion that the 'freedom fighters' would eventually succeed in their objectives, and thereafter civilian populations displaced by the respective conflicts would be able to return home. This did indeed happen in the case of Mozambique, Guinea-Bissau and Zimbabwe. It would also have happened in Angola, had independence not been immediately followed by civil war. And it may well happen soon in Namibia. However, for much of the rest of the continent where there has been involuntary displacement, other factors have caused the migrations, and resolutions to these conflicts appear to be much less straightforward. Indeed, much of the refugee movement since the Arusha conference in 1979, which has resulted in a dramatic increase of well over one million refugees in less than three years, has been associated with conflicts where there appears to be little or no chance of any resolution in the near future.

Consequently, much of Africa now finds itself in a paradoxical situation where, on the one hand, the individual refugees, as well as most of the governments of asylum states, still regard their exodus as but a temporary phenomenon. On the other hand, the realities of the various political conflicts, as evaluated by most objective analysts, suggest that the dilemmas are anything but ephemeral, and indeed, in many cases, the displacements are likely to be of very long-term, if not permanent duration. This means that there is an increasing need to re-evaluate the strategies that have traditionally been employed in many African asylum states. No longer should such strategies stress the temporary provision of relief and assistance in the expectation that refugees will soon return home; they should rather focus upon means of integrating refugees into the social and economic structures of the regions into which they have migrated as quickly and effectively as possible. Since asylum states seldom have the resources to achieve such integrative programmes themselves, it will also be necessary for the international community to adapt its strategies to these changing conditions. While refugee relief will continue to be the most immediately pressing type of assistance necessitated by new waves of refugee migrants, the many governmental and voluntary agencies must also move into the development field in order to facilitate the achievement of self-sufficiency for probable long-term or permanent refugees. Some agencies, including U.N.H.C.R. (United Nations High Commission for Refugees), are making this transition effectively. Others continue to adhere strictly to short-term relief strategies, although in many cases such positions are invariably predicated by limited availability of funding.

One of the characteristics that distinguish most African refugee movements from others around the world is that, at least until recently, they have been almost entirely rural-to-rural migrations. Moreover, they have invariably been short-distance movements, stopping just across the border inside the country of asylum. These refugees have been primarily peasant cultivators, seldom having much education or skills other than those associated with traditional methods of cultivation. Governments of asylum countries have been satisfied in keeping these refugees in or near their initial areas of in-migration, and most of the relief and development programmes have likewise focused in such areas. This situation has, however, begun to change. The number of refugees that are ending up in urban areas is certainly on the increase. Countries like Sudan or Somalia have found many of their cities swollen by in-migrating refugees. While many of them are clearly urban-to-urban migrants, and hence possess much higher levels of education and skills than the 'traditional' African rural-to-rural refugees, an ever-increasing proportion of the refugees that find their way into the cities is of rural origin, people who, in becoming displaced, have simultaneously become caught up in the urbanization process. Asylum states are clearly unhappy about this trend, since such urban refugees only exacerbate pressures on existing over-burdened urban infrastructures, and intensify already serious levels of urban unemployment.

Faced therefore with continuing growth in the number of long-term or permanent displacees, together with the increasing tendency for refugees to migrate to urban areas, asylum states must begin to modify their strategies in order to effectively cope with these trends. On the one hand, more commitment must be made to the creation of opportunities in rural areas for the rural refugees, that will permit them not only to achieve basic levels of self-support, but full self-sufficiency as well. In so doing, it becomes possible to temper some of the forces of urbanization that operate amongst many of the rural refugees. It also facilitates the incorporation of refugee communities into broader regional rural development programmes, so that the refugees' labour and their traditional rural skills can have national benefits as well as local benefits.

On the other hand, there must also be greater recognition of the fact that refugees of urban origins are best accommodated in urban environments. To date, no African country has effectively and successfully addressed itself to the problem of how best to integrate the potentially rich manpower resource into its urban areas. Clearly these changes in strategy in both rural and urban areas are tall orders for African asylum states, which invariably are unable to achieve successfully similar objectives for their indigenous people, let alone for alien populations. Nevertheless, given that considerable international assistance is often available for development-oriented programmes, and that such programmes for refugees often also have beneficial impacts for indigenous people, it is encouraging to note that some African asylum states have begun to tackle these issues in earnest. Among these are Botswana, Sudan and Tanzania.

Available options

The options that are available to asylum states which suddenly find themselves with large refugee populations are several. One is forcibly to repatriate the refugees to where they came from. The United Nations' convention on refugees, as well as that of the O.A.U., to which most African states are signatories, are both emphatically opposed to forcible repatriation or *non-refoulement*. It is encouraging to see that in spite of all the political turbulence prevailing in Africa there have been no serious cases to date of any African state not accepting a politically-displaced population. This is in contrast to several South-East Asian countries where seaborne refugees have frequently been towed back out to sea, and other refugees have been marched back across the border into the country they came from.

Voluntary repatriation is, in contrast, the most desirable option, and, as has already been stated, this has occurred in many cases. Algerians returned home from Morocco and Tunisia after 1962; Sudanese were repatriated to southern Sudan after the Addis Ababa Agreement in 1972; Guinea-Bissauans and Mozambiquans were able to go home once Portugal relinquished control in 1974 and 1975 respectively; and, most recently in 1981, the return of Zimbabweans was accomplished in record time. All told, close to a million of Africa's refugees have been fortunate enough to return to their countries of origin over the past 25 years. In spite of many of the difficulties returnees subsequently encountered when coming back to areas ravaged by war or years of neglect, these repatriations must clearly count among the success stories of Africa's refugee experience. Zimbabwe's recent experience illustrates this most vividly. Faced with the need to bring home over a quarter of a million refugees from neighbouring Zambia, Mozambique and Botswana, the newly-created Zimbabwean government, assisted by U.N.H.C.R., achieved a rapid and relatively trouble-free repatriation in a little over a year. Moreover, while the repatriation was under way from neighbouring countries, an even larger internal 'repatriation' of population that had been displaced to cities or to 'protected villages' during the civil war (approximately three-quarters of a million people) was also successfully executed. This total displaced population was rehoused, re-equipped with tools and seeds, and provided with food assistance until their first crop matured in 1981. Zimbabwe's experience is testimony to levels of success that can be achieved when repatriation is undertaken in an atmosphere of calm, order and freedom from corruption.

Where repatriation is not likely to become a viable option, alternative solutions are limited to essentially one of three possibilities. These are to retain refugees in camps; to resettle them in third and permanent countries of asylum; or to integrate them into the original asylum state, either in an organized way, or allowing such integration to proceed spontaneously. The first of these objectives is clearly the least desirable since camp populations remain dependent and largely non-productive. They create environments of discontent and despair, and in the long term usually become major political thorns. No nation better illustrates the dilemma created by such a solution to a refugee problem than the Palestinians (Barakat, 1973). Yet, in Africa, several regions are rapidly drifting into a permanent camp solution to their refugee problems. Such incidents are often less a result of deliberate government policies, than of misfortunes dictated by absence of alternative possibilities because of critically poor economies, or non-availability of adequate land resources suited for permanent settlement solutions. Certainly, there is little prospect for Algeria to develop the regions in which the Sahrawi refugee camps are located (Harrell-Bond, 1981), nor does Djibouti have many options for the support of its refugee camp populations at Ali Sabieh and Dikhil. And in Somalia's case, while some prospects for development exist in one of the five areas of refugee concentration – around Coriolei in the Shebele valley – in the other areas acute water shortages, together with poor soils, leave little scope for a progression out of totally dependent camp syndromes. Moreover, the permanent settlement of Somali refugees is incongruent with Somalia's political objectives for the Ogaden region whence the refugees came.

One of the major differences between the African refugee situation and that prevailing in South-East Asia is that, in the latter case, the majority of the refugees are resettled in countries of permanent asylum in the industrialized world. In contrast, very few of Africa's refugees ever leave the continent. Part of the reason for this has already been stated, namely that there is a tendency among most African refugees to view their exile as but a temporary phenomenon. However, the principal reason is more basic. African refugees, with their predominant rural, uneducated and unskilled character, are not regarded by principal immigrant-receiving nations as populations that could readily integrate and become economically self-sufficient. The fact that many of the South-East Asian refugees come from similar backgrounds and have equally limited skills or educational standing is frequently overlooked. For example, in the period from 1975 to 1979, the U.S.A. accepted 595,000 refugees; virtually none were from Africa. In the same period Canada accepted 74,000 refugees, also with virtually no African representation. Indeed, it was only after the passing of the U.S. Refugee Act in 1980, that Africa first received a quota for refugee resettlement, and Canada followed with similar legislation in the following year. In 1982, the U.S. quota for Africa was 3,000, and the Canadian quota was increased from 500 to 1,000. No other immigrant-receiving country in the industrialized world currently has an African refugee resettlement quota, although some European countries accept a few African refugees as immigrants under 'family reunion' provisions. Such data clearly show that very few African refugees find 'external' solutions to their dilemmas. Notwithstanding the small number that are being resettled, their departure does have a localized, albeit not a numerical impact. Since considerable screening of applicants for resettlement takes place, it follows that the most successful applicants are generally those with better education and urban backgrounds, who are most effectively able to impress their ability to integrate and assimilate into the U.S.A. or Canada upon harried immigration or consular officials. The successful candidates are also frequently individuals employed with aid agencies dispensing relief, or who have access to the informational services of such agencies. The consequence of this selection process is that, although few in number, the resettling refugees are drawn from a relatively small stratum of the refugee population. It is this fact that is causing concern among many development agencies engaged in refugee work, as well as among government officials in asylum countries, since all programmes aimed at generating self-sufficiency among refugees are critically in need of the very educational, technical and professional skills that are being drained off by the respective resettlement programmes. Little research has to date been addressed to this conflict of interest.

The third and most realistic option available to asylum states is that of local integration. This can be either spontaneously achieved, or can be a product of discreet government policy and programmes. Moreover, as stated in the earlier part of this paper, such strategies do not only bring about an independent and self-sufficient refugee community, but can simultaneously bring into fruition, for the benefit of all, the latent manpower resources contained in any given displaced population. Some of Africa's asylum states have succeeded admirably in developing policies aimed at meeting such objectives, and the remainder of this paper examines three case studies – the first being a small-scale programme, the second a moderate one, and the third a large-scale undertaking. In the case of Botswana, the scale of the development programme was modest, but it was significant because it was one of the first successful experiences. Moreover, Botswana was also the first to recognize that full self-sufficiency also implies the creation among refugees of a feeling of national responsibility, and that this was best achieved by giving refugees the option of becoming citizens of their adopted state. Tanzania has also attempted to integrate its refugees into respective regional development programmes, and, as with development programmes for its own rural population, has relied heavily upon the philosophy and principles of self-help. Like Botswana, it too has recently offered some of the refugees the option of becoming Tanzanian citizens. Finally, Sudan's experience is examined, because of the sheer size of its refugee population, and because it has such an extreme regional refugee concentration. The diverse approaches that the Sudan has adopted are further reasons for this examination.

Botswana

While Botswana's major dealings with refugees took place recently during the height of Zimbabwe's war of liberation, it also had earlier experiences with refugees originating from anti-colonial warfare in Angola. The movement of Angolan refugees into Botswana in 1967 was not large by contemporary African standards. During 1967–69, some 4,000 Angolans, primarily Hambukusha, fled into Botswana to escape the Portuguese programme of forcibly relocating rural people into 'protected villages' in areas affected by guerrilla war. For a small, recently independent, and relatively poor country of only 600,000 people, the sudden arrival of a refugee population of 4,000 presented a considerable challenge. Initially refugees settled among their kin on the Botswana side of the border on the western side of the Okavango Delta (Fig. 6.1). However, as their numbers increased to double the rural population of the region, it was recognized that a government-sponsored resettlement programme was needed. With the assistance of the U.N.H.C.R. and the World Food Programme (W.F.P.), as well as several voluntary agencies, development of a resettlement scheme some 90 km from the border commenced in 1969. The scheme, subsequently named Etsha, was located on some 260 sq km of land that had recently been cleared of tsetse fly. Not having been utilized before because of fly infestation, the fertility of the land was quickly recognized by the Hambukusha, and this was a sufficient incentive for them to cooperate in undertaking the 90 km move. Most of the refugees were resettled prior to the start of the 1969–70 agricultural season, and they were quick to clear lands for cultivation. Thirteen villages ranging in size from 170 to 470 people were established, and the settlers rapidly proved themselves to be energetic and enthusiastic cultivators. However, crop failure during the first season, resulting from severe drought, demonstrated that the settlement should attempt to diversify its economy if full self-sufficiency were to be achieved. Moreover, because the population was still being supported by relief agencies, and hence refugees were unable to acquire work permits, there was no opportunity for the refugees to sell their labour off-scheme to augment their economic base. Fisheries and handicraft schemes were introduced, and a highly successful cooperative was established. With these developments, as well as a successful harvest in the following year, the settlement rapidly progressed towards economic viability by 1971. Also, after the termination of W.F.P. aid, the refugees were granted permanent residents' permits, which permitted them to seek seasonal work away from the scheme.

The scheme acquired a school and health centre in 1971. The latter was especially welcome in view of two severe epidemics of measles and sleeping sickness that had claimed 39 and 35 lives respectively. By 1974 the scheme had become truly self-sufficient (Potten, 1976). It was at that point in time that the Botswana government offered the refugees the opportunity of taking up Botswanan citizenship. Although it was clear that the guerrilla war in Angola would soon be drawing to a close, since final preparations for the Portuguese

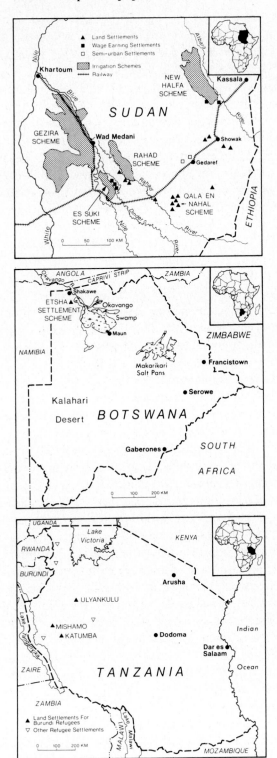

Fig. 6.1 Refugee settlements in eastern Sudan, Botswana and Tanzania

departure were well under way, few refugees opted to await repatriation. The general feeling was that they were better off than they had hitherto been in Angola, or were ever likely to be if they chose to repatriate. Hence, by mid-1975, 2,500 of the 4,000 refugees had opted for Botswanan citizenship.

Given that the total cost of the scheme was well under $100 per head, the creation of this viable agricultural community in the space of only five years must rank as one of Africa's most effective rural development undertakings. Moreover, the success is further evidenced by the fact that by 1975 the government inputs for infrastructural services at Etsha were no greater than those incurred elsewhere in northern Botswana. In achieving this successful resettlement, Botswana had simultaneously brought into production a tract of potentially fertile land that might otherwise have remained under-utilized, and indeed might well have been reinvaded by tsetse fly.

Tanzania

In Africa, Tanzania has one of the longest experiences with refugees. It has also been relatively successful in its programmes, aimed at making refugees self-sufficient as quickly as possible. Currently, it is in the process of granting citizenship to long-term Rwandan and Burundi refugees, the only African state other than Botswana to have adopted such a policy.

The first major wave of refugees to enter Tanzania came from Mozambique, fleeing from hostilities between the Portuguese army and anti-colonial guerrilla forces, as well as from the programme of forcibly resettling rural populations into 'protected villages' which the Portuguese authorities were implementing throughout guerrilla active areas in Africa (Jundanian, 1974). By the early 1970s, over 60,000 Mozambiquans had settled in five village groupings in southern Tanzania. Most were of the Makonde ethnic group, and hence were related to the indigenous Tanzanian Makonde in the area. Certainly, this ethnic affinity facilitated a rapid, and relatively harmonious integration, and it did not take the refugees long to achieve self-reliance in food production, based upon maize, rice, cassava and poultry. Even a few cash crops such as cashew-nuts, sesame and groundnuts were produced. Schools and health centres were established in the area with assistance of U.N.H.C.R., and these served not only the refugees, but also the local population. Given this relatively harmonious and viable social and economic environment, it is not surprising that, after Mozambique gained independence in 1975, many refugees chose to remain in Tanzania, or in some cases, came back to Tanzania after having repatriated to Mozambique only to find that their homelands had reverted to bush and that the local infrastructures had been totally destroyed by the ravages of war. Thirty-seven thousand Mozambiquans were repatriated in 1975, followed by 3,500 more in 1976. Thus a total of about 20,000 remained in Tanzania, where government authorities permitted their continued stay, although no longer as 'refugees' but as 'alien residents' (U.N.H.C.R., 1977:

27). The fact that as much as one-third of the refugee population decided not to repatriate is a testament to the success of Tanzania's refugee programme.

A similar level of success was achieved for Rwandan refugees who settled in north-eastern Tanzania in the late 1960s. Both the refugee populations that settled spontaneously and those that settled on government schemes rapidly achieved self-sufficiency. Indeed, it was from this Rwandan refugee community that most of the 36,000 refugees that embraced Tanzanian citizenship in 1980 were drawn.

Of all the Tanzanian programmes for refugees, the settlement schemes developed for Burundis stand out because of their size, as well as their impact upon the relatively unpopulated and unproductive regions of western Tanzania. Some 110,000 Burundi refugees entered Tanzania in mid-1972 following violent ethnic conflicts between the dominant Tutsi society and the traditionally subservient Hutu. It was the Hutu who fled to Tanzania (in contrast to the Tutsi who fled from Rwanda several years earlier, after similar clashes there between the same two tribal societies). By 1979, the Burundi refugee population had grown to 130,000.

Initially the refugees were able to settle spontaneously in Kigoma District (see Fig. 9.1), a region of Tanzania that is very thinly populated, but has considerable potential for agricultural development if some measure of tsetse-fly control is achieved, and provided effective dry-land farming techniques are introduced. However, as their numbers grew, it became clear that government-organized settlement schemes were needed. Thus the Ulyankulu and Katumba settlement schemes (Fig. 6.1) were conceived and developed under a tripartite agreement between the Government of Tanzania, the Tanzanian Christian Refugee Service (T.C.R.S.) and U.N.H.C.R. Katumba and Ulyankulu were very quickly to become the two largest refugee settlements ever to have been established in Africa. Indeed, when completed in the late 1970s they become the fourth and fifth largest population concentrations in Tanzania.

The Government of Tanzania set aside a land allocation of around 1,000 sq km at Katumba and 550 sq km at Ulyankulu for the development of these settlements. As already stated, the regions where the settlements were established were under-utilized, and there can be little doubt that, apart from wanting to reduce the burden of refugee support, the Tanzanian authorities simultaneously viewed the refugee communities as available manpower for the development of a hitherto unproductive region.

The settlement was executed using the same principle of self-help that was being applied throughout Tanzania in the government's reorganization of rural societies and economies under the 'ujamaa' villagization programme. Refugees were transported to the new village sites, and upon arrival were issued tools and seeds and assigned three-and-a-half-hectare plots of land. All land clearing, house construction and road building were carried out communally by the settlers. Even schools and clinics were built by the refugees with material supplied by scheme administrations. Indeed it has been suggested that the tolerant and understanding manner in which the administration promoted the development of self-reliance and cooperative action among the settlers contributed much to the scheme's successful establishment (Chambers, 1975: 19).

Cultivation began almost immediately at both settlements, based primarily on the traditional staples of maize, beans and cassava. In addition, cash crops such as groundnuts, tobacco, soya bean and sesame were introduced, and rice, which was completely alien to Burundis, was also promoted as a supplementary food crop as well as a cash crop. The Katumba settlement was especially successful, and had reached a level of self-support in cultivation by 1978, which permitted the settlement to be handed over to the Tanzanian local authorities at the end of that year. The settlement's population at that time was 69,000. At Ulyankulu, progress to self-sufficiency was retarded by some limitations in soil quality as well as by severe water shortages, primarily due to the fact that the settlement had greatly outgrown its initial planned size of 18,000. By early 1979, it had grown to 62,000. Because of these problems, a third settlement was started in 1979 at Mishamo, which, in addition to receiving some 23,000 refugees transferred from Ulyankulu, was also scheduled to receive an additional 20,000 Burundis who had remained spontaneously settled in Kigoma District. The transference of population from Ulyankulu made possible a reorganization of that settlement, which saw self-sufficiency in food production achieved in 1980, and resulted in its also being transferred to the local authorities' administration at the end of that year (U.N.H.C.R., 1980: 89). Mishamo has also developed along the same principles as its two predecessors, and it is currently scheduled to be handed over to local authorities in 1983 (U.N.H.C.R., 1982: 134).

Sudan

Like Tanzania, Sudan has also had a long history of refugee migrations. Refugees have fled into the Sudan from Zaire (mid-1960s); from Chad (mid-1970s and again in 1980–81); from Eritrea (since 1967) as well as from other regions of Ethiopia (since 1976); and most recently, from Uganda (since 1979) (Wright, 1980). In addition to all these in-migrations, Sudan has also witnessed an out-migration of Sudanese refugees to neighbouring countries during its civil war, as well as their subsequent repatriation, rehabilitation and resettlement in 1972–74. It is not surprising, therefore, that in the light of this diverse experience Sudan has developed a number of effective strategies for dealing with its refugees.

While Sudan's experience has been spread over two decades, the phenomenal surge in refugee numbers in the past five years, from a little over 100,000 to close to 550,000, has strained to breaking point the resources available for refugee support, as well as the traditional and generous Sudanese hospitality. Moreover, the problem has been intensified by the fact that the refugees have become heavily concentrated in only two regions of the country, one of which is characterized by a semi-arid environment and increasing competition for land between indigenous cultivation-based and pastoral-based societies, the other by extreme remoteness coupled with very poorly developed infrastructures. Of the more than half a million refugees in Sudan, about 350,000 are found in the Eastern Region (Kassala and Red Sea province) where the ratio of refugees to local population now stands at an incredible 1 : 4, and over 120,000 are in Eastern Equatorial Province, where the corresponding ratio is almost as high at 1 : 6. Clearly such concentrations of refugees place enormous strains on all types of services and resources, including the availability of essential foodstuffs.

In order to cope with the problems arising from these numbers, the Sudanese, in cooperation with U.N.H.C.R. and various voluntary agencies, have established a large number of settlement schemes in both eastern as well as southern Sudan. The policy is to resettle refugees on these schemes, and to discourage, as far as possible, spontaneous settlement of refugees in either rural or urban areas. This policy aims at creating self-sufficiency as quickly as possible, at standards of living comparable to those experienced by local populations. Some of the settlements that have thus been created are now very close to achieving these objectives.

However, Sudan's settlement policy must be distinguished from policies existing in most other African asylum states. This is because Sudan, in addition to the 'traditional' rural land settlements for refugees, has also created two other forms of refugee settlements – the wage-earning settlements and the semi-urban settlements. While the 'traditional' rural land settlements attempt to create self-reliant refugee communities based upon cultivation of their own land for subsistence and cash crops, the latter two are based on the premise that the refugees constitute a large but latent pool of human labour resources that can be integrated into the Sudanese economy, and in so doing become self-supporting from wages earned. Sudan is unique in Africa in this respect.

Clearly this policy makes sense. Sudan's ample land resources have great agricultural potential, but there are several constraints on the realization of this potential. One of these constraints is the shortage of agricultural manpower. This is especially the case in eastern Sudan where the development of large irrigation schemes, as well as the recent and rapid expansion of mechanized rainfed cultivation, has created a tremendous demand for seasonal labour. Traditionally, seasonal migration from other parts of the country, as well as from West Africa, was able to meet this demand. However, with increasing urbanization, with regional developments in other parts of the country, with restrictions on migrant labour from West Africa, as well as with the declining attractiveness of agricultural labour to many Sudanese, serious deficits in farm labour availability have been created. The objective of the wage-earning settlements is therefore to meet these deficits. Five rural settlements in two separate areas have been developed exclusively with this aim in mind. Many of the refugees on the other rural land settlements, however, also participate in the seasonal labour flows.

Sudan also has an inordinately high percentage of urban refugees, which is another characteristic that makes it unusual among African asylum states. This has prompted the creation of the third type of refugee settlement – the semi-urban settlement. As already stated, Sudan's policy is to discourage the spontaneous settlement of refugees. This is especially so with respect to urban areas, in spite of the fact that several of the major cities currently have refugee populations in excess of 30,000. The objective of the semi-urban settlements is to relocate spontaneously settled urban refugees to their own settlements located peripherally to cities. In this way they can be efficiently administered and serviced as a refugee community, while at the same time they are able to commute to urban areas to sell their labour. They are also strongly encouraged to sell their labour on nearby agricultural schemes.

By mid-1982, 15 cultivation-based rural settlement villages had been established in eastern Sudan, containing approximately 60,000 refugees. In southern Sudan, about 75,000 of the over 120,000 refugees had also been settled on rural land settlements. Levels of self-sufficiency achieved on these schemes are contingent upon a number of factors, not the least of which is the degree to which the settlers themselves wanted to cooperate. In southern Sudan, where the refugees' migration is less than three years old, rapid progress towards self-support was being made on most of the settlements, and by mid-1982 several were already on reduced W.F.P. rations as their farms became productive. In eastern Sudan, however, quite considerable ranges of success are being encountered. The oldest and largest of the land settlement schemes at Qala en Nahal illustrates many of the frustrations associated with land settlement programmes (Fig. 6.1) Started in 1969, the settlement was almost self-sufficient in 1974 when it was handed over to local authorities (Rogge, 1975). However a combination of neglect by the Sudanese local authorities thereafter, together with settler disillusionment, apathy and even outright resistance, rapidly saw the settlement stagnate, and many refugees left to seek their fortunes elsewhere, including in the cities. By 1979, U.N.H.C.R. funding was once more necessary in order to rehabilitate the scheme and settle some of the new Eritrean refugees (Spooner, 1981). Largely due to the establishment of an efficient agricultural extension and ploughing service by a voluntary agency, the scheme currently has over 30,000 settlers living in six villages and cultivating over 70,000 *feddans* (one *feddan* equals approximately 0.42 hectares). By mid-1982, it was approaching economic viability. Several other schemes, such as at Um Gargur and at Um Rakoba are also close to being viable. Others, on the other hand, are still too recent for their prospects to be accurately gauged, but indications are promising, especially for the three villages located adjacent to the Rahad irrigation scheme. On all these schemes, refugee families receive from 5 to 10 *feddans* of land, and it is considered that such holdings are sufficient not only for basic staple crops, but also for some cash cropping.

Progress on the wage-earning and semi-urban schemes has been less encouraging. The five exclusive wage-earning settlements (with a combined population of 18,000) are located either adjacent to the Es Suki irrigation scheme or near the Halfa irrigation scheme. In retrospect, the location of three villages at Es Suki was a poor choice for the refugee settlements, since Es Suki is one of the least successful of Sudan's modern irrigation schemes. Seasonal labour is primarily limited to cotton picking and weeding, neither activity being particularly attractive to refugees. Moreover, wages are extremely low, and there appears to be considerable discrepancy between what settlement authorities maintain refugees can earn, and what refugees are in fact earning. Throughout these settlements, refugees feel that they are being discriminated against *vis-á-vis* their kin on the rural land settlements by not having been given any lands to cultivate themselves. It is encouraging to note however, that the Sudanese authorities now recognize these problems and are beginning to modify the principles of this type of refugee settlement.

Similar difficulties are also manifesting themselves on the semi-urban settlements. One of the major problems with respect to the urban refugee appears to be the fear among many Sudanese that the refugees will take away employment from Sudanese nationals. There is some evidence to support this fear, especially in Port Sudan where there are about 45,000 refugees among a population of 350,000. Eritreans and Ethiopians are often prepared to work for less money, and to work for longer hours, and are frequently regarded by prospective employers as more diligent workers. Also, they are not unionized. However, given the very substantial drain of skilled and semi-skilled Sudanese labour to Saudi Arabia and the Gulf States, as well as the fact that many of the Eritrean refugees come from urban backgrounds where they have acquired high levels of skills, there would appear to be considerable scope for the greater integration of the refugee manpower resource into the urban economies.

Conclusions

This paper has examined some of the strategies that African asylum states have employed in dealing with their refugee populations. Given that very few African refugees are resettled in third countries of permanent asylum beyond Africa, and that the contemporary refugee populations are less likely to repatriate compared to refugees that fled anti-colonial wars in the 1960s and early 1970s, it is understandable that many governments have opted for programmes that generate a degree of self-support among refugees as quickly as possible. Not only do such programmes greatly reduce the economic burdens that refugees create, but often they can be beneficial to the host country in that refugee settlements in remote or under-utilized areas can be integrated into national development objectives. It is clear that most refugee communities contain latent manpower reservoirs which, if channelled into the right directions by government policies, can benefit both the state as well as the refugee. The three case studies from Botswana, Tanzania and Sudan that have been introduced here illustrate the various scales at which such strategies have been implemented, as well as the degrees of success that have been achieved. In Botswana's case, the Etsha scheme was successful because of its manageable size, because the refugees wanted to participate, and because effective and sympathetic administration was available to make the scheme work. In achieving its objective, the scheme also brought a large tract of hitherto unutilized land into the national economy. Likewise, Tanzania's experience at Ulyankulu, Katumba and Mishamo, while not without difficulties and frustrations, nevertheless has created among a very large refugee community a level of self-sufficiency comparable to that of indigenous Tanzanians in the region. Indeed, the settlement scheme has not only brought new lands into production, but has generated some of the most effective intensive farming enterprises in west–central Tanzania. Even in Sudan, where the successes of the settlement programme have been tempered with considerable periodic setbacks, the positive impact of the refugee manpower resource on the agricultural economy of eastern Sudan is very substantial. Without the refugees' seasonal labour inputs, many of the large-scale mechanized farms would not be able to produce at the levels they now do. And while the farmlands that the refugees have been allocated would undoubtedly be otherwise used by local farmers, the presence of the refugee settlements with their associated infrastructural facilities has clearly led to a general upgrading of rural facilities for all, since such facilities invariably become available to local as well as refugee populations. While rural land settlements, such as the ones described in this paper, clearly go a long way towards bringing refugees into the mainstream of national economies, their scope is clearly constrained by the ultimate number of refugees that have to be catered for, as well as the available land resource. Botswana and Tanzania both had adequate land resources to meet the immediate needs of refugees, but in eastern Sudan the sheer numbers of refugees that are now present make the provision of adequate settlement land an increasingly more problematic and politically contentious issue. It should be emphasized that, while rural land settlements are able to provide effective and lasting solutions to the problem of accommodating rural refugees, no similar set of solutions has yet been evolved to enable host countries to deal with the ever rising tide of urban refugees. This issue is now one of the major challenges confronting the continent's asylum states, as well as the international community in general.

REFERENCES

Adepoju, A. (1981) The dimensions of the refugee problem in Africa, *African Affairs*, 82, 21–35.
Barakat, H.I. (1973) The Palestinian refugees: an uprooted community seeking repatriation, *International Migration Review*, 7, 147–61.
Chambers, R. (1975) *Report on Rural Refugee Settlements in Tanzania*, U.N.H.C.R.
Gould, W.T.S. (1974) Refugees in Tropical Africa, *International Migration Review*, 8, 413–30.
Harrell-Bond, B. (1981) *The Struggle for the Western Sahara: The Sahrawi People*, American University Field Staff Reports: Africa, No. 37.
Jundanian, B. (1974) Resettlement programs: counter-insurgency in Mozambique, *Comparative Politics* (1974), 519–40.

Potten, D. (1976) Etsha: a successful resettlement scheme, *Botswana Notes and Records*, 8, 105–19.

Rogge, J.R. (1975) The Qala en Nahal refugee resettlement scheme, *Sudan Notes & Records*, 54, 130–46.

Rogge, J.R. (1977) A geography of refugees: some illustrations from Africa, *The Professional Geographer*, 29, 186–93.

Rubin, N. (1974) Africa and refugees, *African Affairs*, 73, 290–311.

Spooner, B.C. (1981) *The Qala en Nahal Resettlement Scheme*, Report to Euro-Action A.C.O.R.D., Khartoum.

U.N.H.C.R. (1977) *Report of the U.N.H.C.R. to the General Assembly*, New York.

U.N.H.C.R. (1980) *Report on U.N.H.C.R. Assistance Activities in 1979–80*, Geneva

U.N.H.C.R. (1982) *Report on U.N.H.C.R. Assistance Activities in 1981–82*, Geneva.

Wright, K. (1980) Sudan's refugees: 1967–80, *Disasters*, 4, 157–66.

7 Population redistribution and agricultural settlement schemes in Ethiopia, 1958–80

Adrian P. Wood

Agricultural settlement schemes are a major development measure through which the redistribution of a country's population may be achieved. In Ethiopia planned resettlement is of relatively recent origin, having occurred only since the 1950s. The schemes which have been developed over the last 25 years have been undertaken for a variety of reasons and have had differing degrees of success. Sometimes considerable redistribution of population has resulted, but this has often been of a local nature though not without important economic, social, and political implications.

This paper considers two groups of formal planned settlement schemes which have been carried out in Ethiopia since 1958: those which occurred before the Revolution in 1974, and those which have been begun since that date. The contexts in which these settlement measures have been developed are discussed and the specific origins of the various projects considered. Their impact upon population redistribution is then evaluated. The paper is based upon investigation carried out in Ethiopia in 1973–74 and 1980. The major sources of information were documents in government and independent agencies concerned with resettlement, and discussions with personnel in these organizations. Where possible this information has been checked through field visits and discussions with independent sources.

The population context for agricultural settlement schemes

Ethiopia is the sixth largest state in Africa covering 1.2 million sq km and has the third largest population, over 32 million in 1980 (I.B.R.D., 1980: 134; P.R.B., 1980). Dominating the country's relief are two major highland massifs, divided by the northern extension of the East African Rift Valley and surrounded by extensive lowlands below 1,500 m, which occupy almost 50 per cent of the national area. The population is concentrated in the highlands in which varied agricultural systems are practised (Westphal, 1975), while the lowlands support only 18 per cent of the people, the majority of whom are pastoralists.

Within the highlands there are considerable variations in population density, with the south-western extremities of both massifs relatively sparsely settled and the central areas more densely peopled. Population pressure is particularly severe

84

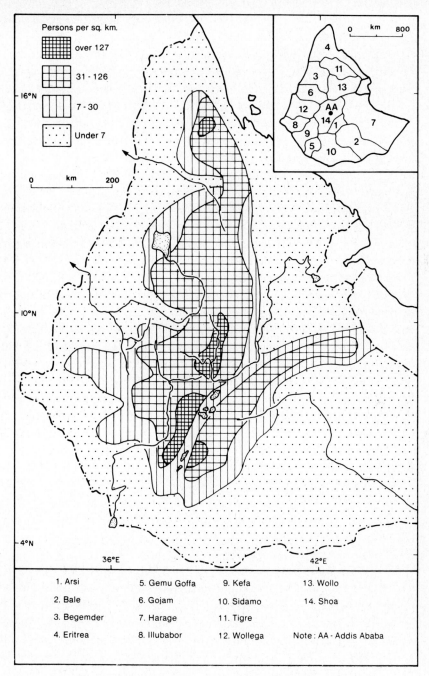

Fig. 7.1 Density of population in Ethiopia in 1970. (After Wolde Mariam, 1970.)

in the central part of the Northern Highlands where densities exceed 150 persons per sq km and the area of cultivated land falls below 0.2 hectares per person (Wolde Mariam, 1972: 173). This area includes the highland parts of Wollo and Tigre provinces, a region frequently affected by severe drought (Hussein, 1976). Other major population concentrations occur in the central part of the southern edge of the Northern Highlands and across the Rift Valley in the north-eastern part of Sidamo province in the Southern Highlands (Fig. 7.1). In contrast to these densely settled areas are several sparsely populated regions: a few forested parts of the highlands and extensive wooded and grassland areas at the edge of the highlands and in the lowlands. Agricultural settlement for rainfed cultivation is possible in many of these areas but is frequently constrained by malaria and trypanosomiasis, although other problems such as insecurity, isolation, and limited supplies of drinking water are also important deterrents.

Despite these difficulties and the strong ties which the highland population have with their home localities, there has been extensive spontaneous agricultural resettlement into these areas over the last 30 years. This has involved hundreds of thousands of households (Wood, 1982). While this resettlement has helped to slow the growth of population within the densely settled areas it has by no means solved the problems of population pressure upon arable resources in the highlands. In those areas, more frequent cultivation has caused serious damage to soil structure resulting in increased soil erosion and land degradation. Spontaneous resettlement itself has also caused ecological damage through exploitive land use practices and the cultivation of unsuitable slopes. With this continuing maldistribution of population relative to natural resources there is a major role for planned resettlement to play in helping to achieve the fullest ecologically-sound development of agriculture, the dominant sector in the Ethiopian economy (Bequele and Chole, 1969; Harberd, 1975).

Pre-Revolution settlement schemes

The economic and political influences

Under the Imperial Regime two major land tenure situations existed. In the northern half of the Northern Highlands tenures were based on kinship ties and village membership. To the south, land was owned by a small number of locally resident and absentee landlords and was farmed primarily by tenants. These parts of the country had been incorporated into the Ethiopian state in the late nineteenth century by a Shoan-led conquest, all land being alienated by the state (Marcus, 1975). Some of this land was distributed to soldiers in recognition of their service in the conquest and to local leaders prepared to support the new political situation, but much remained in the hands of the Emperor and was available for distribution or use by him and his government (Cohen and Weintraub, 1975: 43). This government land totalled over 50 million hectares. Most was lowland grazing used by pastoralists whose rights to land were not recognized by the Imperial Regime. However, 8.5 million hectares were suitable for cultivation (E.G., 1972a: 30), ranging from unsettled densely forested areas in the highlands to woodland savanna and grassland areas in the lowlands.

Despite this availability of unused government land suitable for arable farming, other considerations besides the clear need for planned agricultural resettlement had to be recognized in deciding the use of this land. In particular, there were strong political pressures upon the Emperor from the traditionally orientated elite who expected the continued use of government land for patronage purposes. These pressures were so great following the Emperor's return after the Italian occupation that this use of government land was institutionalized through a series of Land Grant Orders (E.G., 1972b: 15). Patronage thus continued as a major use of this land, some 2 million arable hectares being distributed permanently in this manner between 1942 and 1974 (Ibid: 16).

The agricultural development policy of the Imperial Regime also placed claims upon government land, further restricting the opportunities for planned resettlement. During the late 1950s and first half of the 1960s the country's balance of payments went into deficit and considerable quantities of foodstuffs were imported (Bequele and Chole, 1969). The need for increased home food production and for agricultural exports became clear. However, with the complex land tenure situations discouraging increased production by peasant farmers, and the political influence of the elite who strongly resisted any changes in the tenure systems, the government faced a major problem of how to achieve increased agricultural production. The solution chosen was to ignore almost completely the peasant sector and, by further land grants and subventions on farm mechanization, to encourage estate agriculture on the unsettled government lands, mainly in the lowlands (Bondestam, 1974; Stahl, 1974: 73–7). This policy also encouraged the development of mechanized commercial agriculture in some tenant-farming areas, and the resulting spontaneous resettlement of evicted tenants, numbering 6,000 a year by 1972, led to a further loss of land suitable for planned resettlement.

Settlement schemes and population redistribution

In view of the government's disinterest in peasant farming and its commitment of government land for political purposes and estate agriculture, it is perhaps surprising that any settlement schemes were carried out before the Revolution. However, more than 6,500 new farm units were created through 21 schemes before 1974 and some relocation of population was achieved. These schemes may be considered from the points of view of the quantity of assistance provided, the nature of the settlers involved, the reasons for resettlement, and their impact upon population redistribution.

Two types of settlement scheme, high and low cost (Fig. 7.2 and Table 7.1), can be identified in terms of the inputs provided. The high-cost schemes involved major land development costs through clearance and levelling and the construc-

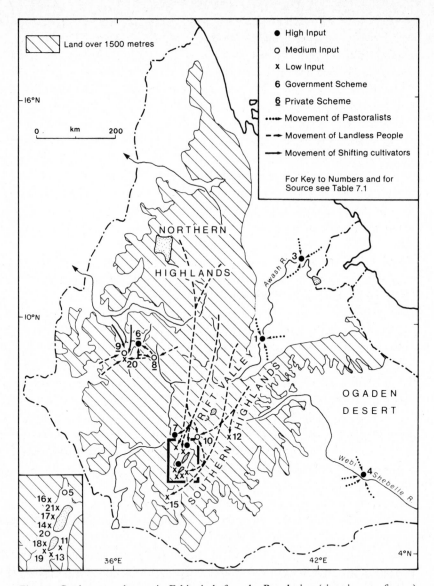

Fig. 7.2 Settlement schemes in Ethiopia before the Revolution (situation as of 1974)

tion of contour ridges or irrigation channels, but they were expected to produce considerable agricultural surpluses and aimed to give settlers relatively high incomes from which they could repay the development costs. In contrast, low-cost schemes involved little more assistance to the settlers than site identification and the provision, often very irregularly, of food during the first few months at the settlement site. In most cases these settlers were expected to achieve only an improved subsistence production. Between these two extremes were a few schemes which provided greater assistance than the low-cost type, but not the full-time technical advice and considerable expertise afforded in high-cost schemes (Simpson, 1975: 143).

Settlement schemes in this period involved two major and two minor groups of people. The first groups were nomadic pastoralists and peasant farmers; the latter ex-soldiers and shifting cultivators. The settlement of nomads, which involved some 900 settlers, 15 per cent of the settler households of this period, primarily sought to introduce them to settled agriculture through irrigation schemes located on their traditional dry-season grazing areas. At Gode, in the Ogaden Desert, the settlers took up cultivation wholeheartedly and accepted a sedentary life style. This success was partly due to the fact that they were not purely nomadic pastoralists but from one of the Somali clans which base their herding on the Webi Shebelle River along which they have always cultivated plots. In contrast, the schemes in the Awash Valley were less successful as the pastoralists visited their farms for only relatively short periods and developed little interest in agriculture. The scheme managers were in part to blame for this, as much of the cultivation and irrigation was carried out by the settlement authorities for the settlers (ibid: 88). The schemes which provided over 3,500 land-short peasant farmers with new farms were generally successful. In most cases strong motivation was exhibited by the settlers, the opportunity of access to land proving a sufficient inducement to these farmers who were previously short of land. This motivation was particularly important in helping the settlers to withstand considerable hardships which were often faced in the early years of resettlement due to poor site selection and limited assistance (Simpson, 1976: 23–4). The settlement of ex-soldiers and shifting cultivators proved somewhat less successful. The former were given plots on which to farm in lieu of pensions at three localities in the early 1960s (E.G., 1969: 44). However, despite their agricultural background, in most cases few of the soldiers found farming attractive and abandoned their plots, leaving only one viable site (MacArthur, 1971). Similar desertion affected the settlement of shifting cultivators in the Didessa Valley of Wollega province. Many of these settlers preferred to continue their old farming methods rather than accept the rigidities and extra labour requirements of permanent cultivation on a settlement scheme.

The reasons for these settlement schemes are numerous and different interpretations can be made of the reported justifications. However, two main groups of reasons may be identified: social or humanitarian, and self-interest on the part of the initiators. In the first case, many of the schemes sought to improve the welfare of land-short or disadvantaged people through the provision of land. In some schemes, such as the downslope movements in Wollega and Gemu Goffa, this assisted a spontaneous process, but in others, like those in Gemu Goffa for Menz settlers and at Koda Manuka and Wajifo involving settlers from outside the province, new directions of resettlement were established. In other cases the humanitarian motive stemmed from the way in which some groups failed to benefit from development schemes in their area. The Wollamo Agricultural Development Unit (W.A.D.U.) resettlements were established to provide

Table 7.1. *Pre-Revolution settlement schemes*

Map no.	Name	Location (province)	Sponsoring agency	Date of inception	Number of settler households 1974	Type of settler	Cause of resettlement	Origin of settlers	Nature of population redistribution
(a) High input – irrigated[i]									
1.	Amibara	Shoa	A.V.A.[ii]	1967	409	Nomadic pastoralists	Sedentarization	Surrounding area Awash Valley	Local[iii]
2.	Arba Minch	Gemu Goffa	M.N.C.D.	1962	44	Ex-soldiers	In lieu of pension	N. highlands Shoa, Wollo, etc.	Medium–Long distance H–L[iv]
3.	Dubti	Wollo	A.V.A.	1965	24	Nomadic pastoralists	Sedentarization	Surrounding area Awash Valley	Local
4.	Gode	Hararge	I.A.R.	1972	470	Nomadic pastoralists	Sedentarization	Surrounding area Ogaden Desert	Local
(b) High input – rainfed									
5.	Abele	Sidamo	W.A.D.U.	1958	984	Peasant farmers/ labourers	Land shortage/ landless	W.A.D.U.	Local downslope
6.	Angar Gutin	Wollega	A.S.D.	1971	200	Peasant farmers	Landless/ land shortage	Neighbouring highland Wollega	Local–medium distance H–L
7.	Bele	Sidamo	W.A.D.U.	1958	600	Peasant farmers/ labourers	Land shortage/ landless	W.A.D.U.	Local–medium 60 km distance. Downslope
(c) Medium input									
8.	Anno Gambella	Wollega	E.C.M.Y.	1971	55	Peasant farmers	Landless/ land shortage	Neighbouring highland Wollega	Local Medium distance within highlands
9.	Dimtu	Wollega	E.C.M.Y.	1971	200	Peasant and shifting cultivators	Landless and agriculture improvement	Neighbouring highland and lowland Wollega	Local Medium distance H–L
10.	Shemene Kedida	Sidamo	M.N.C.D.	1969	153	Peasants	Landless	Arsi, Shoa, Sidamo.	Medium distance H–L
(d) Low input									
11.	Alfacho	Gemu Goffa	M.N.C.D.	1965	8	Peasant farmers	Land shortage	Menz, Shoa	Long distance + 500 km H–L

No.	Name	Region	Agency	Year	Number	Settlers	Reason	Origin	Distance
14.	Chano	Gemu Goffa	M.N.C.D.	1970	300–547	Peasant farmers	Land shortage	Neighbouring Gemu Highlands	Local H–L
15.	Gato	Gemu Goffa	M.N.C.D.	1966	55–65	Peasant farmers	Land shortage	Menz, Shoa	Long distance +500 km H–L
16.	Koda-Manuka	Gemu Goffa	B.N.M.	1967	200–460	Peasants	Landless	Wollo and Begemder	Long distance +600 km H–L
17.	Lante	Gemu Goffa	M.N.C.D.	1968	570–600	Peasant farmers	Land shortage	Neighbouring Gemu Highlands	Local H–L
18.	Shelle	Gemu Goffa	M.N.C.D.	1965	700–800	Peasant farmers	Land shortage	Menz, Shoa	Long distance H–L
19.	Suga	Gemu Goffa	M.N.C.D.	1973	34	Peasant farmers	Land shortage	Menz, Shoa	Long distance H–L
20.	Tolle	Wollega	M.N.C.D.	1972	200	Shifting cultivators and peasant farmers	Agriculture Improvement of neglected community Landless	Neighbouring highland and lowland Wollega	Local, some downslope
21.	Wajifu	Gemu Goffa	M.N.C.D.	1966	400	Peasant farmers	Land shortage	Mehabrete, Shoa	Long distance downslope

Notes:
(i) *High input*: Characterised by resident agricultural extension staff; on-going assistance and services to settlers for forseeable future; production for market dominant.
Low input: Characterised by no resident staff; no on-going services provided to settlers after initial assistance with establishment; seeking to provide settlers with adequate subsistence.
Medium input: Characterised by resident staff – but not necessarily extension staff; limited emphasis on production for the market.

(ii)
A.S.D.   Association Solidarité et Développement (French mission)
A.V.A.   Awash Valley Authority (Government agency)
B.N.M.   Blue Nile Mission
C.A.D.U.   Chilalo Agricultural Development Unit (Government agency)
E.C.M.Y.   Evangelical Church Mekane Yesus (Ethiopian Protestant Church)
I.A.R.   Institute of Agricultural Research (Government agency)
M.N.C.D.   Ministry of National Community Development
W.A.D.U.   Wollamo Agricultural Development Unit (Government agency)

(iii) Local: Under 50 km
Medium: 50–150 km
Long: Over 150 km

(iv) H–L: Highlands to lowlands

Sources: E.G., 1969; MacArthur, 1971; Simpson, 1975 and 1976.

landless and land-short households with the same opportunities which peasant farmers with larger holdings were obtaining through the scheme (van Santen, 1980: 51). In the Awash Valley a similar principle was involved, the schemes being designed to provide opportunities for improved incomes among the nomadic population who had lost crucial dry-season grazing lands to the irrigated company estates as a result of the government's agricultural policy (Bondestam, 1974; Simpson, 1976: 27).

Settlement schemes were also carried out for less altruistic reasons on the part of the government. In the case of the Awash Valley, the government felt obliged to counter international criticism by making a token gesture towards the nomadic population whose livelihood the irrigated farms had undermined (Bondestam, 1974). Lessons were also sought from this experience on how to encourage the nomadic population to establish permanent bases which would facilitate both the provision of services to them and control over these frequently revolt-prone groups (Wood, 1983b). The resettlement of ex-soldiers also had political connotations, as did the establishment of Menz and other northern groups of people in the south, for the military dominance of Amhara over the southern peoples had been achieved in the late nineteenth century through the establishment in the south of northern communities loyal to the central government (Pankhurst, 1966: 135–48). The Chilalo Agricultural Development Unit (C.A.D.U.) and W.A.D.U. settlement schemes were also partly motivated by needs other than those of the settlers, the development projects needing land in the areas from which the settlers were removed; while the Schemena Kedida scheme, run by the Ministry of National Community Development (M.N.C.D.), was originally established to settle trainees from an agricultural project who could not find land or employment.

Under the Imperial Regime relatively little planned resettlement was carried out. Despite an expenditure in excess of U.S. $8 million, only some 6,500 new farm units were settled by 1974 (although the total number resettled before the Revolution was probably larger, but there were desertions). This represented the resettlement of between 0.1 and 0.2 per cent of the rural households at that time, a negligible amount especially when compared to the 5 to 10 per cent of the rural population which undertook resettlement spontaneously during the same period (Wood, 1982). Further, many of these settlement schemes produced little redistribution of the population, their aims often being to solve, with a minimum of relocation, problems other than the maldistribution of people relative to resources. Hence, only a little over 60 per cent of the 6,500 households settled moved more than 50 km and less than 50 per cent moved more than 150 km (Fig. 7.2). Nonetheless, some of the movements which took place in association with these schemes, particularly those from the highlands to the lowlands, and over long distances into other cultural areas, were important indicators of the feasibility of planned population redistribution in directions which had hitherto been regarded with some trepidation by settlers and agricultural planners alike.

The development of settlement policy

The schemes outlined above were carried out on an *ad hoc* basis, each one being planned as an independent entity to meet specific needs. No government policy existed concerning settlement schemes nor the redistribution of population. A *laissez-faire* attitude prevailed concerning spontaneous resettlement which it was felt provided a natural adjustment mechanism of population relative to resources and an important safety valve given the government's inability to introduce land tenure reforms and its consequent support of mechanized farming. Despite its stimulation of spontaneous resettlement through the neglect of peasant farming and the eviction of tenants to make way for mechanized farming, the Imperial Regime did not feel obliged to undertake any major resettlement measures. The schemes which it did carry out were mainly in association with other projects, population redistribution being a secondary goal to agricultural development (W.A.D.U., C.A.D.U. and Awash Valley Authority, or A.V.A.) or to the community development experience (M.N.C.D.). The only major resettlement schemes which were undertaken in their own right were those run by the voluntary agencies, mainly missions. Although these involved less than 1,000 settlers, they provided valuable information which supplemented the government's own experience when a resettlement policy was eventually formulated.

Towards the end of the Emperor's rule the importance of planned and spontaneous resettlement was finally recognized and some progress made towards the development of a policy concerning population redistribution (E.G., 1968: 375). This was undertaken primarily by the Ministry of Land Reform and Administration (M.L.R.A.) which was established in 1966 to control the distribution and utilization of government land, and to consider ways of reforming the use of this land and the land tenure situation in the country. This ministry had a land settlement department which, although never involved directly in resettlement, carried out and commissioned a number of studies.

The first of these was by World Bank consultants who suggested the use of the best remaining arable government land for the establishment of 10,000 family-run commercial farms of 12 and 140 hectares (E.G., 1969: 6 and Annex). Smaller farm units, with a social aim of accommodating landless farmers, were rejected as incapable of contributing to increased agricultural production, which the consultants, like the government, regarded as necessary and best achieved through medium and large-scale units. This suggestion was rejected by M.L.R.A., which was one of the most radical sections of the Imperial regime. The ministry felt that this use of the remaining arable government land to create better-off peasant farmers ignored social considerations and wasted one of the few remaining opportunities which the government had to avoid 'untoward social and political developments'. Consequently, alternative studies were commissioned. These suggested that government land should be used to facilitate a major redistribution of people from the overcrowded and eroded highlands to under-utilized areas, especially in the lowlands, and so achieve a better distribution of population relative to resources (E.G., 1971). This planned resettlement, it was thought, should channel the already considerable spontaneous movement and prevent ecological damage by providing these settlers with carefully-planned holdings, land-use advice and assistance in soil conservation (MacArthur, 1971). Besides this resettlement of 700,000 households to reduce population pressure in the most densely-settled parts of the highlands, it was suggested that resettlement opportunities would be needed for the annual increment on new households in areas where no land was available for them. This number would vary, depending upon other employment opportunities, population growth and the commercialization of peasant farming, but it was estimated that it could involve over 100,000 households a year (E.G., 1972c).

These ideas were accepted and incorporated, in 1972, into a policy document which outlined the Ministry's view that the redistribution of population through agricultural settlement schemes should be a major development measure for reducing poverty, increasing agricultural production, and protecting the country's natural resources. Although overtaken by political events, this documents marked an important step in the development of government thinking on the subject and was influential in post-revolution policy development.

Post-Revolution resettlement

The social, political and economic context

The Imperial Regime was overthrown primarily because it neglected the plight of the rural poor. The drought victims in Wollo who had been forced by famine to sell their land and the tenants and pastoralists evicted to make way for commercial agriculture were a major focus of public discontent at the time of the Revolution. As a result, the Provisional Military Administrative Council, which came to power at that time, has sought to pursue policies which it believes will produce greater equality of income throughout the nation, and, in particular, will rapidly raise the standard of living of the rural population. It hopes to achieve these goals through a fuller utilization of the country's natural resources, the provision to each rural household of sufficient land for its support, and the expansion of government services for the rural population (E.G., 1975a).

One programme in which these three methods are combined is agricultural resettlement. This policy received considerable attention particularly in the early days after the Revolution when a number of resettlement projects were being carried out in connection with drought relief (e.g. Wood, 1976). The importance of resettlement to the regime was confirmed when, in 1976, a little over a year after the Emperor was deposed, a Settlement Authority was established (E.G., 1976). This was charged with four main objectives:

1. the settlement of persons who have little or no land;
2. the utilization of lands that remain idle for various reasons;
3. the alleviation of the unemployment problems of the country; and
4. the conservation of forest, soil and water resources.

A fifth objective outlined in the introduction to the proclamation concerned the need to 'encourage nomads to develop their present holdings into modern pastoral and arable farming'.

These objectives, developed from the M.L.R.A's policy paper, went somewhat beyond those pre-Revolution ideas and beyond the primary aim of the Revolution to improve rural welfare by providing households with adequate land. They reflect a number of subsidiary aims which had become apparent in the first 16 months after the Revolution, and which in part explain the growth in resettlement since 1974. The second objective was motivated by the need for increased food production in the face of a growing food deficit, and has become an increasingly important goal because grain imports have risen to between 5 and 20 per cent of the country's needs. The third objective reflected the political as well as economic aspects of unemployment. The transition from a capitalist to a part-socialist economy involved a considerable increase in unemployment as some industries closed and commercial farms and coffee estates were handed over to the permanent workforce and the local population to run. The result was a potentially volatile situation, first in many of the rural towns which had been service and labour supply centres for the commercial farming areas and later in Addis Ababa. The fourth objective confirmed the government's recognition of the role resettlement can play in solving environmental problems, such as the destructive land use of spontaneous settlers, the severe erosion of the drought afflicted highlands and the clearance of forest, often on escarpments, by charcoal burners. The fifth aim continued government concern for the nomadic population. This was in part a desire to provide economic opportunities to formerly 'neglected' peoples and to support their rehabilitation after the economic disruption caused by the loss of animals in the drought. It also had political connotations, especially in the light of the 1975 Afar revolt and the unrest in the Ogaden. The new government, like its predecessor, is keen to achieve greater control over these intransigent peoples through sedentarization (Wood, in press).

At the same time a number of the reforms instituted since the Revolution have facilitated the work of the Settlement Authority. The most important is the nationalization of rural lands proclaimed in 1975 (E.G., 1975b), which abolished former land tenure systems, including private claims through the Land Grant Orders, and vested the ownership of all land in the hands of the state. Households were granted 'possessory', apparently usufructory, rights to holdings of up to 10 hectares, all surplus amounts being taken by the state for redistribution. Thus through this measure the government gained control over extensive private estates and abolished all competing claims to government land. Although the proclamation specifically recognized the rights of pastoralists to their customary grazing lands, these and other claims of communities can be overruled by the government's right to expropriate land for agricultural projects, including settlement schemes.

The proclamation which nationalized rural lands also established a new form of organization for rural communities – Peasant Associations. The rural population in each 800 hectare area is required to form an Association which is both a developmental organization and a legal body. Of particular importance for resettlement is the requirement of Peasant Associations to redistribute land among their members to increase equality of holding. In so doing it is envisaged that some households may remain with inadequate holdings and that this surplus population will need to be resettled. Further needs for resettlement will occur in connection with the enforcement by Peasant Associations of government land use directives when they are formulated. These, it is envisaged, will include the removal of land from cultivation in order to reduce erosion and so will involve the resettlement of people, some locally but others outside the areas.

The policy statement favouring planned agricultural resettlement has also been given strong political and financial support by the new regime. The government-controlled media frequently focus upon the successes in the resettlement programme, while this is a regular component in the speeches and tours of the country's political leaders. Financial support for resettlement has also been increased enormously, growing from less than U.S.$1 million a year before the Revolution to some U.S.$13 million in 1980 (E.G., 1979a).

Settlement schemes and population redistribution
Since the Revolution, and especially following the nationalization of rural lands and the establishment of the Settlement Authority, planned resettlement has proceeded at an increasing pace (see Tables 7.2 and 7.3 and Figs. 7.3 and 7.4). The annual number of households resettled has risen from about 700 before the Revolution to 14,000 in 1980, while expenditure on resettlement has risen from a negligible percentage of the National Budget prior to the Revolution to about 3 per cent in 1980 (Table 7.5) (E.G. 1979a and 1979b).

At the time of the Revolution a number of resettlement schemes were being implemented by the Relief and Rehabilitation Commission (R.R.C.), and other government and voluntary agencies, to assist people who had been made destitute by the drought (van Santen, 1980: 66). These schemes provided only limited assistance and the majority involved little relocation, the drought victims being re-established in their home areas. Most lasted only a year or eighteen months and assistance had been phased out by 1979, so they are not included in Table 7.2. However, relief schemes for pastoralists have proved longer-term undertakings. This is because they have generally experienced difficulties in trying to introduce destitute households to a sedentary agricultural existence, and because most of these schemes require continuing technical assistance, as they involve irrigation.

A second major development of settlement projects occurred in response to the land nationalization proclamation of 1975 and the rural unemployment which followed. When land was nationalized, most commercial farms were abandoned by their owners and managers and were taken over by local government officials. While the larger farms were turned into State Farms, the smaller ones generally were not and several were used for settlement schemes. This was done on local initiative by government officials from several ministries prior to the establishment of the Settlement Authority. The settlers at these sites usually included the former farm workers and neighbouring farmers, especially those who had lost land or had been displaced by the establishment of the commercial farm. At this time some unrest occurred in the rural service towns, especially in the coffee-producing areas, because of the reduced demand for labour on commercial farms owing to their redistribution to the local population and the banning of seasonal labour (Wood, 1983a). Because the land reform proclamation guaranteed land to landless rural households, there were demands among these unemployed agricultural workers to be given farms. As a result, a number of schemes were begun to establish these labourers as farmers.

While most of the resettlement begun in the period following the Revolution took place voluntarily, the settlement opportunities being provided in response to requests from the settlers, some resettlement at this time did involve coercion. In these cases the government decided to remove from the potentially volatile urban areas groups which they felt posed a threat to security. Those resettled in this manner included unemployed urban workers, or 'lumpen', thrown out of employment by the economic dislocation during the Revolution; some military personnel whose loyalty to the regime was questioned; and, in one area, charcoal burners whose profession was branded as counter-revolutionary. Settlers of this sort accounted for approximately 28 per cent of the total number during the period 1975–78 (Tables 7.4 and 7.5).

Following the establishment of the Settlement Authority in early 1976 all pre-existing schemes, including those run by private organizations, were handed over for the Authority to administer. The only exceptions were one or two famine relief schemes which the R.R.C. continued to operate, five settlement schemes for pastoralists which were placed under the Valley Agricultural Development Authority (V.A.D.A.) and some private schemes which were designated as self-supporting. Besides administering existing schemes and bringing them into a self-supporting state, the Settlement Authority has been required by the government to start a number of new schemes. The initiative for these has come partly from central government and partly from local government officials, the Authority being given little opportunity to initiate schemes itself. As a result, the Settlement Authority co-ordinates and services a widely scattered collection of schemes, of varying size and using different production methods, and with a variety of objectives.

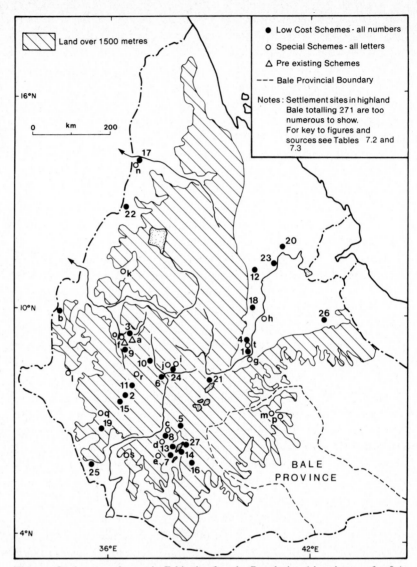

Fig. 7.3 Settlement schemes in Ethiopia after the Revolution (situation as of 1980)

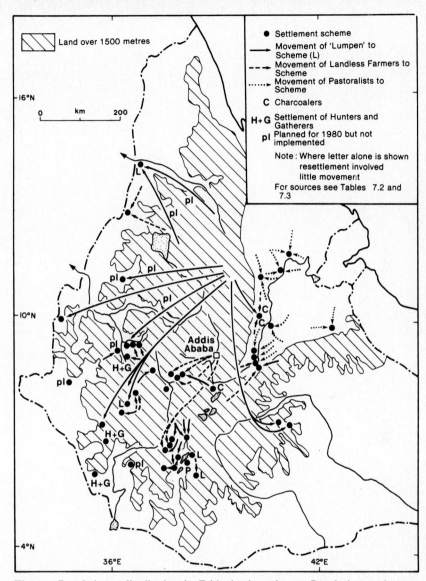

Fig. 7.4 Population redistribution in Ethiopia through post-Revolution settlement schemes (1974–80)

Table 7.2. *Post-Revolution settlement schemes, 1979*

Map no. or letter	Name	Location	Date of inception	Number of settler households (total number)	Type of settler	Cause of resettlement	Origin of settlers	Nature of population redistribution
(a) Special settlement schemes								
a.	Angar Gutin	Wollega	1977	504 (1,501)	Peasant farmers	Land shortage	Neighbouring highland Wollega	Local–medium distance H–L
b.	Asosa Hoha	Wollega	1978	114 (239)	Shifting cultivators	Agricultural Improvement	Surrounding area	Local
c.	Dana Gogora	Sidamo	1976	274 (1,246)	Peasant farmers	Land shortage	Surrounding area	Local–medium distance H–L (20–80 km)
d.	Dana Oreta	Gemu Goffa	1976	412 (1,029)	Peasant farmers	Land shortage	Surrounding area	Local–medium distance H–L
e.	Daramalo	Gemu Goffa	1977	600 (+1,200)	'Lumpen'	Urban unemployment/unrest	Arba Minch town, Gemu Goffa	Local
f.	Didessa Dimtu	Wollega	1978	493 (1,962)	Peasant farmers	Land shortage	Neighbouring highland Wollega	Local–medium distance H–L
g.	Golgotha	Arsi	1976	812 (2,522)	'Lumpen'	Urban unrest	Assela and Arba Guga towns, Arsi	Local–medium distance H–L for some
h.	Hali Debi	Hararge	1976	389 (1,730)	Nomadic pastoralists Drought victims	Sedentarization/ Drought relief	Surrounding area	Local
i.	Harole	Shoa	1978	2,981 (6,514)	'Lumpen': 80% Charcoal burners: 15% Peasant farmers: 5%	Urban and rural unemployment/unrest Shortage of land	Addis Ababa Zwai area, Shoa Neighbouring area	Medium distance and local
j.	Tadelle	Shoa	1977	2,322 (4,564)	'Lumpen': 95% Peasant farmers: 5%	Urban unemployment/unrest Land shortage	Addis Ababa Neighbouring area	Medium distance and local

(b) *Low cost schemes*

1.	Abadir and Addis Ketema	Shoa	1976	276 (1,804)	Sedentary pastoralists / 'Lumpen'	Rehabilitation of drought victims / Urban unemployment	Surrounding area / Metahara town, Shoa — Local / Local
2.	Andaracha	Kefa	1976	70 (152)	'Lumpen' / Unemployed coffee pickers	Unrest and urban unemployment	Andaracha town and environs — Local
3.	Angar Gutin	Wollega	Pre 1974	105 (529)	Peasant farmers—drought victims / Peasant farmers	Rehabilitation of drought victims / Land shortage	Wollo — Long distance / Neighbouring highland Wollega — Local and medium distance
4.	Awara Melka	Shoa	1976	324 (1,608)	Nomadic pastoralists—drought victims	Sedentarization, drought relief	Surrounding area — Local
5.	Blate	Sidamo	1976	199 (780)	Peasant farmers	Land shortage/landless	Highland Sidamo — Local–medium distance / H–L
6.	Botor Tole	Kefa	1978	143 (897)	Peasant farmers, some drought victims	Land shortage / Rehabilitation of drought victims	Kambata area / Shoa / Wollo — Medium and long distance / H–L
7.	Chano Dorga	Gemu Goffa	1977	440 (not known)	Peasant farmers	Land shortage	Gemu highlands / Gemu Goffa — Local–medium / H–L
8.	Dana Oreta	Gemu Goffa	1976	208 (709)	'Lumpen' Labourers / Peasant farmers	Urban unemployment / Land shortage / Rural unemployment	Addis Ababa / Neighbouring area — Local–medium distance
9.	Didessa Keresa	Wollega	1976	168 (873)	Peasant farmers / 'Lumpen' Hunters and gatherers	Land shortage / Unemployment / Agricultural improvement	Surrounding area — Local
10.	Didessa Kone	Wollega	1976	123 (527)	'Lumpen' / Unemployed coffee pickers	Rural and urban unemployment	Arjo town and environs / Kefa — Local

Table 7.2 (*cont.*)

Map no. or letter	Name	Location	Date of inception	Number of settler households (total number)	Type of settler	Cause of resettlement	Origin of settlers	Nature of population redistribution
11.	Didessa Limu	Kefa	1976	458 (910)	'Lumpen' Unemployed coffee pickers	Rural and urban unemployment	Agaro and Jimma towns, and environs Kefa	Local–medium distance
12.	Fecha	Wollo	1976	833 (1,548)	Pastoralists and cultivators Drought victims	Rehabilitation of drought victims	Wollo Highlands and neighbouring area	Local–medium; some H–L
13.	Gate, Shile, Mile, Ogao	Gemu Goffa	1976	156 (1,136)	'Lumpen' (includes unemployed fishermen)	Rural and urban unemployed	Arba Minch town Lake Chamo area Gemu Goffa	Local
14.	Gelana	Sidamo	1976	200 (not known)	Nomadic pastoralists– drought victims	Sedentarization Drought relief	Surrounding area	Local
15.	Gojeb	Kefa	1976	703 (1,719)	'Lumpen' Peasant farmers	Urban unemployment Land shortage	Jimma town Kefa Janjero area Kefa	Local–medium distance H–L
16.	Hagare Mariam	Sidamo	1976	200 (not known)	'Lumpen' Unemployed coffee pickers	Rural and urban unemployment	Hagare Mariam town, Sidamo	Local
17.	Humera	Begemder	1976	1,336 (2,856)	'Lumpen' Agricultural labourers from commercial farms	Rural unemployment	Humera area Begemder	Local
18.	Jewaha	Shoa	1976	711 (2,137)	Charcoal burners Peasant farmers– drought victims	Rural unemployment Rehabilitation of drought victims	Surrounding area Wollo	Local and long distance
19.	Kibish	Kega	1976	c. 200	Shifting cultivators Hunters and gatherers	Agricultural improvement	Surrounding area	Local

20.	Logia	Wollo	1976	160 (1,160)	Nomadic pastoralists— drought victims	Sedentarization Drought relief	Surrounding area	Local
21.	Meki	Shoa	1976	832 (2,842)	Charcoal burners	Rural unemployment Environmental conservation	Surrounding area	Local
22.	Metema	Begemder	1978	500 (500)	'Lumpen' Agricultural labourers and townsfolk	Rural and urban unemployment	Metema area and Gondar town Begemder	Local and long distance H–L
23.	Mile	Wollo	1976	252 (1,812)	Nomadic pastoralists— drought victims	Sedentarization Drought relief	Surrounding area	Local
24.	Tadelle	Shoa	1977	1,269 (5,198)	'Lumpen' Agricultural labourers and townsfolk Peasant farmers	Rural and urban unemployment Land shortage	Addis Ababa and surrounding area	Local and medium distance
25.	Tum	Kefa	1978	208 (1,216)	Shifting cultivators	Agricultural improvement Sedentarization	Surrounding area	Local
26.	Shinile	Hararge	1976	227 (1,558)	Nomadic pastoralists— drought victims	Sedentarization Drought relief	Surrounding area	Local
27.	Walleme	Sidamo	1976	204 (853)	'Lumpen' Unemployed coffee pickers	Rural and urban unemployment	Dila town Sidamo	Local

Note: See Figures 7.3 and 7.4. Some schemes are listed twice in the above table, because they have two sections, at which resettlement of different types, i.e. special and low cost, is being carried out.
Sources: Settlement Authority files.

Table 7.3. *Projected special settlement schemes, 1980*

Map no.	Name	Location	Projected number of settler households, 1980 (achieved)	Type of settler	Cause of resettlement	Origin of settlers	Nature of population redistribution
(a) Settlement Authority R.R.C.							
a.	Angar Gutin	Wollega	10,000 (not known)	'Lumpen'	Urban unemployment	All parts of country	Long distance
b.	Bambesi/Asosa	Wollega	4,500	Peasant farmers—drought victims	Rehabilitation of drought victims	Wollo	Long distance, c. 800 km. H–L.
k.	Beles	Gojam	2,000 (not known)	Peasant farmers—drought victims	Rehabilitation of drought victims	Wollo	Medium–long distance. H–L
l.	Gambella	Illubabor	2,000 (not known)	Hoe cultivators	Agricultural development of neglected peoples	Gambella area Illubabor	Local
m.	Harawa	Bale	3,000 (3,700)	Peasant farmers—drought victims	Rehabilitation of drought victims	Wollo	Long distance, c. 800 km.
n.	Humera	Begemder	8,000 (not known)	Peasant farmers—drought victims	Land shortage Rehabilitation of drought victims	Highland Begemder and Tigre	Long distance, c. 300 km. H–L
o.	Lower Didessa	Wollega	6,000 (not known)	Peasant farmers—drought victims	Rehabilitation of drought victims	Wollo	Long distance, c. 500 km. H–L
p.	Melka Oder	Bale	4,000 (not known)	Peasant farmers—drought victims	Rehabilitation of drought victims	Wollo	Long distance, c. 800 km.
q.	Sheko Bebeka	Kefa	2,000 (800)	Peasant farmers—drought victims	Rehabilitation of drought victims Labour for state farm	Wollo	Long distance, c. 600 km.
r.	Upper Didessa	Illubabor	2,500 (not known)	Peasant farmers—drought victims	Rehabilitation of drought victims	Wollo	Long distance, c. 600 km. H–L
s.	Woito	Gemu Goffa	500 (not known)	Shifting cultivators	Agricultural development of neglected peoples	Humer-Bako area Gemu Goffa	Local
(b) Valleys Development Authority							
t.	Amibara	Shoa	320 (not known)	Nomadic pastoralists	Sedentarization	Surrounding area	Local

Notes: See Figures 7.3 and 7.4. Some schemes are listed twice in the table because they have sections at which resettlement of different types, i.e. special and low-cost, is being carried out. In most cases where details are not known it appears that little or no progress was made, the resettled total for 1980 being only 14,000, of whom 12,820 are reported in known cases.

R.R.C.: Relief and Rehabilitation Commission.

Source: Settlement Authority files.

Table 7.4. Changes in the socio-economic background of settlers, 1974–80

Socio-economic background	1974–75 No.	%	1975–76 No.	%	1976–77 No.	%	1977–78 No.	%	1978–79 No.	%	1979–80 (proposed) No.	%	1979–80 (achieved) No.	%	Overall 1974–80[1] (achieved) No.	%
Farmers	260	22.6	2,953	56.3	2,621	56.0	2,236	44.4	No details available		28,000	68.6	12,500	97.5	20,570	71.1
'Lumpen'	901	77.6	1,003	19.1	1,048	22.4	2,247	44.6			10,000	24.5			5,199	18.0
Charcoal burners			239	4.6			342	6.8							581	2.0
Pastoralists			1,053	20.1	1,015	21.6	208	4.1			320	0.8	320	2.5	2,596	8.9
Neglected minorities											2,500	6.1				
Others	277	—	1,887	—	1,054	—	962	—							4,180	—
Total	1,438		7,135		5,738		5,995		12,953		40,820		12,820		33,126 (46,079)[2]	

Notes:
[1] Excludes 1978–79.
[2] Includes 1978–79.
The years designated here are by the Gregorian Calendar, but start in mid-September as according to the Ethiopian calendar. The Ethiopian year 1967 starts in September 1974.
Sources: E.G., 1978a: 5; E.G., 1980.

Table 7.5. *Volume and nature of planned resettlement, 1965–80*

| | Pre-Revolution | Post-Revolution | | | | |
	1965–73	1975–78	1979–80	1980[1]	1980[2]	1974–80[1]
Volume (annual no. of new settlers)	675	6,290	13,475	12,820–14,000[3]	44,820	8,928
Government expenditure (average annual expenditure, in U.S.$)	0.5 m	5.0 m	11.0 m	13.0 m	—	
Cultivated area (ha)	—	13,500 (1976–78)	—	—	—	
Production (quintals of grain)	—	68,000 (1976–78)				
Nature of settlers (percentage)						
Farmers	83.5	39.7		97.6	68.6	71.1
'Lumpen'	25.6				24.5	18.0
Charcoal burners		2.9				2.0
Pastoralists	14.9	11.2		2.5	0.8	8.9
Neglected minorities	1.6				6.1	
Others		20.6				
Distance of associated movement (percentage)						
Local (under 50 km)	38.8	48.9		2.5	6.3	30.4
Medium (50–150 km)	12.2	47.0		97.5	2.2	28.3
Long (over 150 km)	49.0	4.1		97.5	91.5	41.3

Notes:
[1] As achieved
[2] As planned
[3] Verbal report only
Sources: E.G., 1978a, 1979b; Simpson, 1975 and 1976; van Santen, 1980

Despite this diversity, the schemes can be divided into two groups: low-cost and special or high-cost (Fig. 7.3 and Table 7.2). Under the low-cost heading come most of the schemes inherited by the Authority from the pre-Revolution period, together with the bulk of the ones established in the early years of its existence. Although these vary considerably, they are characterized by:

1. limited government assistance to settlers, with few if any permanent staff;
2. extraction for cultivation; and
3. holdings of 2 hectares of cultivated land: 1 hectare for individual use and 1 hectare for communal use.

Settlers on these schemes are expected to have an agricultural background, and to need little incentive other than access to land to become successful farmers. They are also expected to be able to achieve reasonable agricultural surpluses without much advice or assistance, as the schemes are located in environmental zones similar to those from which the settlers come (E.G., 1978a).

In contrast, an alternative high-cost model for resettlement was developed in response to problems encountered in resettling unemployed persons with little or no agricultural background and in establishing settlement schemes in tsetse-infested areas where oxen need particular care. These schemes are characterized by:

1. a relatively high level of government assistance, including permanent technical staff;
2. payment of settlers for work in advance of harvest, in order to reduce the problems of the transition from urban employment to rural life;
3. mechanized means of production; and
4. 0.5 hectares holding for private use and 2.0 hectares of communal farm (ibid.: 2; E.G., 1978b).

During the period 1976 to 1980 the low-cost schemes have declined in importance, while the special settlement scheme model has been accepted for all future resettlement. This development is a result of changing emphases in resettlement needs which have been presented to the Authority by the government. In 1976 the Authority was asked to settle mainly farmers short of land and unemployed persons with an agricultural background. Most of this resettlement could be achieved through short-distance movement to sites within the highlands where agricultural practices required relatively little adjustment from those with which the settlers were familiar. However, as highland sites have become more difficult to find and settlement in tsetse-infested areas has become necessary, new farming methods for settlement schemes have been needed and greater assistance has had to be provided to the settlers. The introduction of payments to settlers prior to harvesting was also found necessary when in 1977 large numbers of unemployed urban workers, 'lumpen', were settled following the internal political conflicts which occurred in that year (Table 7.4), while the emphasis upon mechanization has increased as the government has sought to encourage communal farming and the production of food surpluses for sale to the state.

Another phase in the development of settlement schemes began in 1979, involving increasingly close co-operation between resettlement planning and relief and rehabilitation measures, and culminating at the end of that year in the incorporation of the Settlement Authority into the Relief and Rehabilitation Commission (E.G., 1979c). This change was stimulated primarily by the renewed drought in Wollo and Tigre provinces in 1977–78, which has confirmed amongst government leaders the view that the population in highland Tigre and Wollo exceeds the carrying capacity of that area. Hence a major relocation of people from that area is felt to be necessary, partly to reduce the population at risk from drought but also to allow the rehabilitation of these highlands to be achieved through land-use controls. This resettlement began in 1979 with the movement of 5,000 Wollo farmers to two sites – Asosa Hoha in the extreme west of Wollega and Melka Oder in highland Bale – and was planned to continue at the rate of 40,000 households a year; but in 1980 only 12,500 drought-affected households were moved. Nonetheless, this accounted for virtually all the resettlement carried out by the Authority in that year and confirms a major change of emphasis in the government's policy.

The other cause of this new phase of resettlement was the need to re-establish the farmers and pastoralists in Bale and Sidamo provinces who were left destitute by the scorched earth policy used by both protagonists in the Ogaden war. By 1980, although resettlement was still primarily at the relief camp stage in Sidamo province, in Bale 271 settlement sites had been established.

In both these resettlement projects the greater central government involvement and the tendency towards coercion noted in the mid 1970s has continued and developed. Famine victims identified for resettlement have their relief grain supplies withdrawn if they refuse to accept resettlement opportunities offered to them, while in Bale and Sidamo provinces the locations of the development villages are closely supervised by the government to ensure not only their suitability for development but also for defensive security. Government involvement in the internal organization of settlement schemes has also increased since the introduction of the special or high-cost model. In line with the development of government agricultural policy, settlement schemes are now organized as producer co-operatives, with settlers having private plots of only 0.1 hectare, and communal farming is increasingly subject to government production directives, almost like the State Farms (E.G., 1980).

Through these phases of resettlement policy a major change in the nature of the resulting population redistribution can be identified; a change from a dominance of local and medium distance movement not exceeding 150 km towards a dominance of long-distance resettlement (Table 7.5). In the early days after Revolution resettlement was used to solve, locally, a number of problems. Many schemes were implemented by local officials whose jurisdiction was limited, and so while political uncertainties constrained inter-regional cooperation long-distance population resettlement was negligible. However, as the coordination of regional administrations has improved and the government has had time to take stock of the population situation in the country, the need has been seen for long-distance resettlement in connection with the rehabilitation of the drought-affected areas of the Northern Highlands. Nonetheless, local resettlement remains important and although locally-initiated projects appear to have come to a halt, the Bale and Sidamo rehabilitation of war-displaced persons continues to be a major programme representing this sort of population redistribution.

Review and prospects

Prior to the Revolution, resettlement was of low priority to the government. No ministry or government agency was responsible for it and no national policy existed. A number of small schemes were undertaken, sometimes not specifically concerned with population redistribution, and the majority of resettlement was over distances of under 150 km. However in some cases people were resettled successfully over considerable physical, environmental and cultural distances, thus providing important indications of the feasibility of some forms of population redistribution previously felt to be impracticable.

Since the Revolution, resettlement has grown in importance, and is reflected in the establishment of the Settlement Authority, the 26-fold increase in government expenditure on resettlement and the 14-fold increase in the annual number of households settled between 1973 and 1980. The increased importance has been partly due to the drought in the Northern Highlands and the provision of land to landless households following the land reform proclamation. However, it is also a reflection of the interventionist approach of the new government, and of its policies of reducing inequality by achieving a fuller utilization of the nation's resources through a better distribution of population. Short-distance resettlement has been dominant since the Revolution primarily because of the local nature of many of the problems which this measure has been used to solve; it is occurring in Bale and Sidamo at present and will continue as government land-use directives are given to Peasant Associations. However, long-distance resettlement has grown in importance in recent years in connection with the rehabilitation of the drought-affected Northern Highlands. Population redistribution of this nature will continue for some years, and as the country's land resources are more thoroughly assessed further planned resettlement over considerable distances is likely to occur.

ACKNOWLEDGEMENTS

Financial support for this study was provided by the Social Science Research Council (U.K.) through a studentship held in the University of Liverpool from 1972 to 1975, and by the University of Zambia, which funded a period of study leave at the Institute of Development Studies, Addis Ababa University. The author thanks these organizations for their assistance. Many people in Ethiopia assisted this study by providing access to relevant material and discussions of this. In particular the author wishes to thank Ato Belai Abbai, Minister of Land Reform in 1973, and Mr G.C. Last of the Ministry of Education in Addis Ababa, without whose assistance this study would not have been possible.

REFERENCES

Bequele, A. and Chole, E. (1969) *A Profile of the Ethiopian Economy*, Nairobi, Oxford University Press.
Bondestam, L. (1974) People and capitalism in the north-east lowlands of Ethiopia, *Journal of Modern African Studies*, 12, 423–40.
Cohen, J.M. and Weintraub, D. (1975) *Land and Peasants in Imperial Ethiopia*, Assen, van Goroum.
E.G. (Ethiopian Government) (1968) *Third Five Year Development Plan*, Addis Ababa, Ministry of Planning and Development.

E.G. (1969) *A Policy-Oriented Study of Land Settlement*, V.E.M. Burke and F. Thornley, Addis Ababa, Ministry of Land Reform and Administration (M.L.R.A.).

E.G. (1971) *Environmental Problems, Policies and Actions in Ethiopia*, E. Jurket, Addis Ababa, Ministry of Planning and Development.

E.G. (1972a) *Draft Policy of the Imperial Ethiopian Government on Land Tenure*, Addis Ababa, M.L.R.A.

E.G. (1972b) *Settlement as a Government Land Use*, Addis Ababa, M.L.R.A.

E.G. (1972c) *Labour Absorption Prospects for Ethiopian Agriculture*, J.T. Goering, Addis Ababa, M.L.R.A.

E.G. (1975a) *Declaration of Economic Policy of Socialist Ethiopia*, Addis Ababa.

E.G. (1975b) *Proclamation to Provide for the Public Ownership of Rural Lands*, Proclamation 31 of 1975, Negarit Gazeta, Addis Ababa, Brehanena Selam Press.

E.G. (1976) *Proclamation to Provide for the Establishment of a Settlement Authority*, Proclamation 78 of 1976, Negarit Gazeta, Addis Ababa, Brehanena Selam Press.

E.G. (1978a) *Settlement Authority Annual Report 1970 E.C.*, Addis Ababa Settlement Authority.

E.G. (1978b) *Special Settlement Schemes: Organization and Management Manual*, Addis Ababa, Settlement Authority (mimeo).

E.G. (1979a) *Budget Summary, Financial Year 1972 E.C. (1979–80 G.C.)*, Addis Ababa, Relief Rehabilitation and Settlement Commission.

E.G. (1979b) *Budget proclamation for government services 1972 E.C. (1979–80 G.C.)*, Proclamation 172 of 1979, Negarit Gazeta, Addis Ababa, Brehanena Selam Press.

E.G. (1979c) *A Proclamation to Establish a Relief and Rehabilitation Commission*, Proclamation 173 of 1979, Negarit Gazeta, Addis Ababa, Brehanena Selam Press.

E.G. (1980) *Annex 2, Government Policies and Programmes, Lower Didessa Large-Scale Rainfed Settlement Project*, U.N.D.P./F.A.O. Assistance to Settlement Project, Addis Ababa, Settlement Authority.

Harberd, R.T. (1975) *The North East Escarpment and Sirinka Pilot Catchment Project*, Addis Ababa, Relief and Rehabilitation Commission.

Hussein, A.M. (ed.) (1976) *Rehab: Drought and Famine in Ethiopia*, London, International African Institute.

I.B.R.D. (International Bank for Reconstruction and Development) (1980) *1980 Development Review*, Washington D.C., World Bank.

MacArthur, J.D. (1971) *Some Aspects of Land Policies in Ethiopia*, Report to M.L.R.A.

Marcus, H. (1975) *The Life and Times of Menelik II*, Oxford, Clarendon Press.

Pankhurst, R. (1966) *State and Land in Ethiopian History*, Addis Ababa, Institute for Ethiopian Studies.

P.R.B. (Population Reference Bureau) (1980) *World Population Data Sheet*, Washington.

Simpson, G. (1975) *A Preliminary Survey of Settlement Projects in Ethiopia*, Research Report 21, Addis Ababa, Institute of Development Research.

Simpson, G. (1976) Socio-political aspects of settlement schemes in Ethiopia and their contribution to development, *Land Reform, Land Settlements and Co-operatives*, 2, 22–40.

Stahl, M. (1974) *Ethiopia: Political Contradictions in Agricultural Development*, Uppsala, Political Science Association.

van Santen, C.E. (1980) *Ethiopia. Rural Settlement Schemes*, U.N.D.P./F.A.O., Rome (Technical Report AG:DP/ETH/75/025).

Westphal, E. (1975) *Agricultural Systems in Ethiopia*. Wageningen.

Wolde Mariam, M. (1970) *An Atlas of Ethiopia*, Addis Ababa, Ministry of Education.

Wolde Mariam, M. (1972) *An Introductory Geography of Ethiopia*, Addis Ababa, Brehanena Selam Press.

Wood, A.P. (1976) *The Resettlement of Wollo Famine Victims in Illubabor, South-West Ethiopia*, Liverpool, Dept. of Geography, University of Liverpool, African Mobility Project, Working Paper 29.

Wood, A.P. (1982) Spontaneous agricultural resettlement in Ethiopia, chapter 22 in J.I. Clarke and L.A. Kosiński (eds.), *Redistribution of Population in Africa*, London, Heinemann.

Wood, A.P. (1983a) The decline of seasonal labour migration to the coffee forests of south-west Ethiopia, *Geography*, 68, 53–6.

Wood, A.P. (1983b) Rural development and national integration in Ethiopia, *African Affairs*, 82, 509–39.

8   Populating Uganda's dry lands

John B. Kabera

There are a number of forces which compel people to migrate to the drier areas of a country. Ideally, proper planning should precede settlement of such lands in order to avoid adverse consequences of environmental deterioration occurring as a result of land mismanagement. Uganda has a sizeable proportion of rather dry areas which have attracted settlements during the past few decades. This chapter reviews trends and impacts of contemporary migrations, and offers guidelines towards integrated planning for proper utilization of Uganda's dry lands.

Dry areas of Uganda

For a country whose mainstay is agriculture, rainfall is a dominant climatic factor contributing indirectly towards agricultural practices and, to some extent, the intensity of settlements. An understanding of the mean annual rainfall of Uganda is of some importance for assessing water resource potential and for agriculture in general.

The total amount of rainfall received in Uganda is the product of several factors. The effect of relief is exhibited by the orographic rains received in the hills and mountains of Kigezi and Ankole in the south-west of Uganda and on the Ruwenzori mountain in Toro, western Uganda. The influence of Mount Elgon in eastern Uganda is equally evident. Further, turbulence in the vicinity of isolated hills produces local increments of rain especially on their windward sides. This, however, does not seem to be the case with regard to the highlands of Karamoja in north-eastern Uganda. Likewise, proximity to Lake Victoria enhances annual totals around its shores, although this is not the case with the other lakes like Kyoga, Albert, Edward and George.

The areas receiving less than 1,000 mm (40 in) are considered dry in Uganda, even though this amount of annual rainfall would look equitable in drier countries. These areas may be arranged into four zones (Fig. 8.1). The first zone includes the depressed portions lying in the western rift valley and surrounding Lake Edward and George in south-west Uganda and Lake Albert further north. The rain-shadow effect could also offer part of the explanation as to why this zone is one of the driest parts of Uganda. These low-lying lands have high temperatures reaching 90–95 °F during the dry season and 80 °F during the wet season, thus leading to high evaporation rates. The zone also experiences long drought periods, especially in January and February as well as during June and July. The fact that air is descending from the hills to the west on to these low-lying areas means that the influence of the lakes themselves is very slight. The rain-shadow effect is so pronounced that virtually only the arrival of the equatorial trough during March and April and during October and November produces appreciable rain (Uganda Government, 1967: 16).

The second zone runs roughly from south-south-west to north-west-central Uganda being broken across by the Singo hills. This zone covers most of Ankole and western Masaka and south-central Mubende. It re-emerges after the Singo hills to cover the western fringes of Lake Kyoga and the surrounding region (Figs. 8.1 and 8.2). The reason for the dryness of this zone is not fully understood. It may be explained by the south-eastern trade winds moving over it, having deposited much of their moisture in Lake Victoria, producing a pronounced dry season in June–July. The other dry season is experienced between December and February when the zone is covered by the dry north-east monsoon, but this dry season is often broken, probably because of the air mass projectory during these months. The dry north-east monsoon becomes conditioned by the lakes and swamps of northern Uganda and may be expected to bring some occasional rain to this zone. Otherwise the two peaks of rain associated with the equatorial trough in April– May and September–November are evident.

The third zone comprises almost the whole of Karamoja in the north-east of Uganda and intensifies eastwards towards north-western Kenya (Figs. 8.1 and 8.2). Karamoja is the driest part of Uganda, with the lowest total rainfall and the longest dry season. It experiences pronounced drought spanning the months of November–March. The rainy season occurs from April to August with a marked minimum in June, and marked peaks in May and July. During the north-east monsoon, the area is swept by a dry wind which has traversed Somalia and passed the Ethiopian massif by the end of the year. On the other hand, the passage of the south-east monsoon by April–May crosses Lake Victoria and veers around Mount Elgon at the Uganda–Kenya border to bring moisture to this zone (Langlands, 1974: 308).

Coupled with the general aridity of these areas is the fact that unfavourable climatic fluctuations affect the dry lands. In Karamoja, for instance, there was an unprecedented cloudburst which resulted in a catastrophic flood in 1949, destroying experimental plots that had been established by government. In 1952 there was a long severe drought, in 1954 an unusual heavy storm and in 1955 no rain. Recently in 1979–81 there was a severe drought and cattle-raiding was at its height, so much so that international famine relief aid had to be sought to help the people of Karamoja.

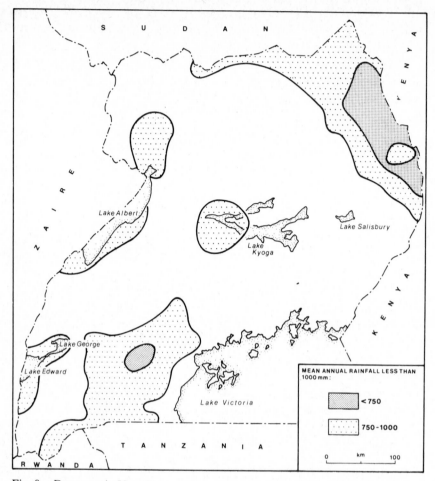

Fig. 8.1 Dry zones in Uganda

Factors affecting settlement of the dry lands in the past

In a country where peasant agriculture engages over 80 per cent of the population, soil productivity is an important factor in explaining population distribution. In most cases it helps to explain why agricultural communities tend to occupy the areas with better soils first, given, of course, other related factors. The productivity of a soil is the capacity of a soil to support a continuous crop growth, and hence is related to the chemical and physical nature of the soil, in addition to its moisture content. This concept differs a little from soil fertility, which concerns itself with plant nutrients in the soil. The productivity of soils in Uganda depends upon the material from which they are derived and the length of time they have taken to evolve under certain physical conditions. Their utility depends very much upon climatic conditions. Thus, unfortunately, some of the soils rich in basic minerals occur in areas which have either a low rainfall or a long dry season or both.

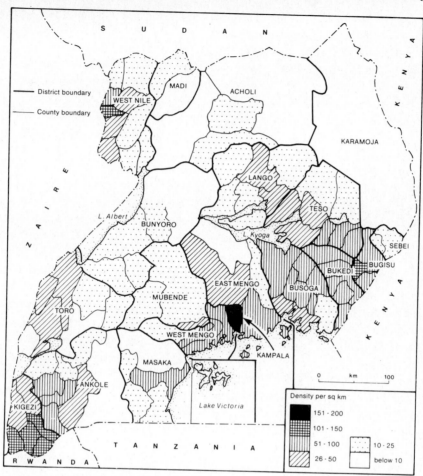

Fig. 8.2 Uganda's population density, 1948

Hence, the soils of western Uganda and Karamoja are categorized as of medium productivity but the areas are only slightly used, and are being populated as a last resort, because there have been better-watered areas to occupy. The soils of the dry zone of south-central Uganda are placed among those of fair productivity because they are ferralitic in nature, representing almost the final stage of weathering and with little mineral reserve left. They are leached to a considerable depth and have a fine granular structure and so are friable and porous. Coupled with the little rainfall received, such characteristics have ensured that these areas have been avoided and have only received sparse settlements in the past.

These dry areas are covered by a climax-vegetation cover of varieties of dry combretum, dry acacias and grass savannas, except in the drier eastern areas of Karamoja and along Lake Albert where bushlands and dry thickets abound. The drier the areas, the more scattered the vegetation cover. Added to this is the practice of starting grass fires every dry season, which results in poorer species being developed. These areas have in the past attracted traditional pastoral communities, and abound with wildlife, especially herbivores.

Until recently tsetse flies had been an important factor limiting population and settlement. They are the vectors of trypanosomiasis, which spread over most of tropical Africa reaching Uganda from northern Tanzania and from Zaire towards the end of the nineteenth century. Trypanosomiasis is a wide term which covers various diseases afflicting men and cattle. Two forms of the disease afflicting men have been identified: *Trypanosoma gambiense*, the milder form, and *Trypanosoma rhodesiense*, both of which are sometimes termed 'sleeping sickness'. Trypanosomiasis, or nagana, is normally used for the form afflicting cattle.

All tsetse belong to the genus *Glossina* (G) and of the 22 species which are known, 8 occur in Uganda (Uganda Government, 1967: 58). The more important species of tsetse which have caused concern in Uganda are three: *G. palpalis fuscipes*, classified thus to distinguish it from the *G. palpalis* of West Africa and Zaire, was widespread in the thickets and forests surrounding the shores and the islands of Lake Victoria as well as the lake shores of Kyoga, George, Edward and Albert. It has been of enormous significance as the vector of *Trypanosoma gambiense*, which decimated the human populations of these areas. The other two species are *G. morsitans* and *G. pallidipes*, which are effective vectors of trypanosomes pathogenic to cattle, *G. pallidipes* being also the transmitter of *Trypanosoma rhodesiense* to man. Both species thrive well in Ankole, around Kyoga and in most parts of north Uganda. The driest parts of Karamoja are relatively free from tsetse flies although *G. morsitans submorsitans*, a species of tsetse which abounds also in southern Sudan, is found in north Karamoja and the neighbouring Acholi and in West Nile.

Outbreaks of trypanosomiasis epidemics at the beginning of this century not only decimated people and cattle but also led to large areas being abandoned to tsetse flies. The savanna area, which covers the dry corridor from Ankole and Masaka to Mubende, and the environs of Lakes George and Edward and the western shorelines of Lake Kyoga, remain thinly populated, partly because of the effect of the sleeping sickness epidemics and the regulations which require the removal of people from the badly hit areas (Kuczynski, 1948: 290). Some of these areas have been turned into game reserves and the four national parks of Uganda, namely Rwenzori (Queen Elizabeth), north of Lakes Edward and George; Kabalega (Murchison Falls), north-east of Lake Albert; Kidepo in north Karamoja; and Lake Mburo in south-east Ankole, are all located in the dry areas under consideration.

Since the major fear of the infested areas was the presence of the fly, it meant that eradication of tsetse would encourage people seeking land for settlement to recolonize and settle in the areas freed from tsetse.

The establishment of the Department of Tsetse Control in 1947 was the beginning of a campaign to eradicate tsetse flies from infested areas in Uganda. By

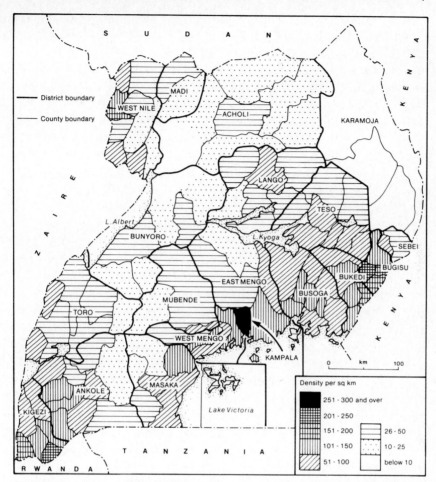

Fig. 8.3 Uganda's population density, 1969

1975, large areas had been cleared of tsetse flies in the Ankole–Masaka corridor, the area surrounding Lake Kyoga and large parts of northern Karamoja and neighbouring central Acholi.

Population increases in the dry lands of Uganda since 1900

By the beginning of this century the dry lands of Uganda carried densities in the region of 10 to 15 persons per sq km. Only a few parts of central Karamoja, eastern Lake Albert, the area north of Lake Edward and south-central Mubende exhibited higher densities, averaging 16 to 25 persons per sq km.

From the 1921 census records, the effects of sleeping sickness could be identified. The interior parts of the Ankole–Masaka corridor and the region from Lake Kyoga to Lake Albert had remained unpopulated. This situation persisted in the 1931 and 1948 censuses (Fig. 8.2). By 1952 the parts north-east of Lake Albert and the Edward–George areas were declared national parks.

By the 1959 census, the dry areas of Uganda never had densities above 25 persons per sq km. In the rift valley region of west Uganda and the Ankole–Masaka corridor, however, infiltration of people was beginning to be noticed. This in-movement increased during the intercensal period from 1958 to 1969. The western rift valley dry lands had attained densities of 26 to 50 persons per sq km. The Ankole–Masaka corridor had also reached densities of 10 to 25 persons per sq km (Fig. 8.3). In Karamoja the densities remained very sparse, averaging about 10 persons per sq km. The 1980 census has revealed that the dry lands have been receiving more in-migrants. The population increase in some parts of the Ankole–Masaka corridor and around Lake Kyoga during the 1969–80 intercensal period exceeded 50 per cent, and in a few cases 100 per cent. Under traditional agricultural practices, at low density levels, there was harmony between man and the land resources. But with increasing densities, either the agricultural practices have to change or the land must suffer.

A number of factors have combined to influence rapid population increase in these dry lands of Uganda. A strong influence on population redistribution to the dry areas and other areas affected by tsetse flies was the government policy to continue the war against tsetse flies, so that the flies are eventually eliminated from all areas with high agricultural and grazing potential. Between 1947 and 1973 some 40,000 sq km had been reclaimed although 48,000 sq km remained infested. Eradication of tsetse flies meant that the threat of the fly to man and his domestic animals was removed but, in the absence of total eradication, man had to come in to safeguard against tsetse re-invasion. It became necessary to resettle areas cleared of tsetse flies to form consolidation barriers. It was considered that a line of settlements could possibly form a permanent barrier to tsetse movement back into the reclaimed areas. This was a very attractive idea and fortunately there was a high density district, Kigezi in south-west Uganda, which was facing land shortage problems. By 1961 an estimated 80,000 persons from Kigezi had been resettled in various parts of western Uganda mainly in the consolidation areas (Kabera, 1982: Fig. 26.1).

Reclamation slowly outpaced resettlement. For instance in Bunyoro, west Uganda, it was difficult to get settlers, and the government had to offer room to settlers from the densely populated areas of western Kenya. Unfortunately, the Maragoli and Kitoshi who came had a cattle culture and brought cattle with them. This action helped to feed the tsetse with the blood meal requirement necessary for their multiplication and thereby formed a stepping-stone for tsetse to invade other cattle-grazing areas lying behind the consolidation line.

Having cleared large areas of tsetse flies, and without immediate repopulation, the government declared the freed areas as ranches, to be used by individuals, cooperatives and government. Ranching areas soon attracted a considerable number of people, who established ranches from the 1960s.

With the establishment of settlements, a number of infrastructures, dams and boreholes were constructed to provide water in these water-deficient areas. Roads were constructed to overcome the problem of remoteness and aided further movement of immigrants. Dispensaries and schools were erected to cater for the health and educational requirements of the people. These actions reassured the would-be immigrants. The result has been the rapid movement into formerly dry areas, especially those of central and western Uganda, within the last thirty years. Many people did not have to wait for the government to transfer them to the resettlement scheme areas. Large numbers have been moving on their own to find land to colonize in the dry western and central areas of Uganda; hence the recent increase in population density.

Current dry-land management

The potential land use of the dry lands is not easy to suggest. They remain areas for ranching, traditional pastoralism and wildlife reserves. Some cultivation of annuals is also possible, and crops like cotton, tobacco, ground-nuts and sorghum can grow well. With irrigation, crop growing can be increased greatly.

The problem, however, is that some of the dry areas of Uganda are being infiltrated by people who originate from better-watered areas. For instance, the out-migration district of Kigezi enjoys a cool climate where the annual rainfall is in excess of 1,000 mm per annum. The people from Kigezi are very hard-working. Back home in Kigezi, population pressure and land tenure have forced them to till the land intensively, but in the newly-settled dry areas they have resorted to tilling the land extensively. Their land management in Kigezi may well be fitted to areas where plenty of rain is received and soils are fertile, but such methods have been found destructive in dry areas. This is one group which has infiltrated into the dry areas of western Uganda and into Ankole, Toro, Bunyoro and Mubende.

Agriculture still depends on dry-farming methods over most of Uganda. People who have had a long history of dependency on adequate rain water supplies have now got to learn, by trial and error, how to live in harmony with the drier environment. This approach takes years and even decades to achieve the desired results, by which time the impact upon the environment may well have led to deterioration.

Moving through the areas occupied during 1977, it was observed that a lot of land had been opened up for cultivation, but that some fields had been abandoned and had been invaded by undesirable weeds, indicating that a degraded cover of vegetation had developed after the land had been opened up for cultivation.

What has been happening is a clear example of what land-hungry peasants can do when they get to an area where there is plenty of land to colonize. These lands had enjoyed a long period of rest. When passing through after the rains, the vegetation looks sufficiently enticing for one to recognize that cultivation is possible. It is interesting to note that pioneer resettlers were usually taken to inspect these lands after the first rains or during the rains (Ngorogoza, 1969: 96). Restricted by land shortage back home in Kigezi, these people tend to carve out very large pieces of land when they migrate, so that they will not have to face land-shortage problems in their lifetime. In order to ensure that they hold on to their lands, they must show evidence that they have actually cultivated the area at some time. This encourages them to open up large areas under extensive means of cultivation, leaving the plots after one or two crops have been grown. Emphasis is put on fast coverage of a man's land. The old well-developed methods of intensive cultivation are soon forgotten and are replaced by destructive methods employed under rotational bush fallow. These changes are not uncommon in Africa; they have been experienced among the Kofyar in Benin (Netting, 1965) and this could be the case with population movements from the Nuba mountains in Sudan.

In addition to the factors above, land tenure methods are not changed when these people move. In Kigezi, the system of land ownership and land tenure revolves around sub-division of a man's land between his sons, each son having the right to inherit a portion of land from his father's holding. In polygamous marriages, the sons inherit land from their own mother's portions. These practices of division of land are crucial in the present-day problems of land pressure, fragmentation of plots, landlessness and out-migration in Kigezi, and are being transferred to the new areas wholesale. So far there is little monitoring of what is going on in these newly developed areas. It would appear that when the peasants are not faced with critical food shortages, neither they nor any other person, body or department are concerned about the environment in which the peasants live.

Specific studies are to be organized to monitor the changes that have so far taken place, so as to guide future development of the dry areas, both those at present settled and those which pioneer settlers look poised to colonize.

The dry areas currently under game management are likely to persist under this land-use system. The present regulations governing these areas are clearly laid out, with the idea of conserving and protecting wildlife. They have been a major source of attraction to tourists, and by 1971 tourism ranked third to coffee and cotton in foreign-exchange earning.

The dry areas under cattle ranching are also specified. They have been laid out and most of them are now leased to individuals and cooperatives, and the government also has a few established ranches. Ranching for beef production is on the increase and new methods of livestock management are being encouraged. Dams have been constructed and valley tanks can be seen on many ranches. The idea is to start a revolution in livestock keeping.

The dry areas have, for a long time, been extensively used by the pastoral groups in Uganda; the Karamojong in north-east Uganda and the Bahima in Ankole in south-central Uganda, where traditional methods of husbandry still prevail, although attitudes to livestock ownership are being changed so that the traditional pastoral groups regard livestock as economic units. Whereas changes in attitudes are being realized among the Bahima, it may take much longer for the Karamojong to turn to modern ways of controlled grazing. Livestock-keeping will, therefore, continue to be an important economic activity in the dry areas of Uganda.

The need for integrated management of dry lands

Current utilization of dry lands through settlement, crop agriculture and animal husbandry requires a thorough study and appraisal. They are very delicate lands which require planned development.

It is essential that certain aspects which relate to settlement of the dry lands should be looked into. A thorough investigation into the water quality, quantity, availability, distribution and potential for channelling is essential. This requires feasibility studies by combined teams of physical scientists (e.g. hydrologists, engineers, meteorologists, geomorphologists, physical geographers, etc.) who will indicate the water potential of the dry lands and provide a framework for dry-land management.

Settlement of dry lands would appear to be a last resort in land colonization. Whereas the crop agriculturalists may be squeezed out of their better-watered areas because of high densities in subsistence economies, and find refuge in the dry areas because these seem to be empty, the pastoral communities slowly lose their pasture lands to crop agriculturalists, being relegated to the drier parts on the periphery of crop lands. Unplanned and uncontrolled settlement of dry areas by people from better-watered areas, in both groups, can result in dangerous degradation of the environment and lead to irreversible consequences and disharmony between man and his environment. It is for this reason that scientists in the field of human geography, sociology, agriculture, veterinary science etc. should form a team to study how best the dry lands ought to be settled and developed.

The knowledge supplied by the physical scientists, human scientists and development planners should be coordinated into a unified policy on dry-land utilization. Implementation of the policy formulated should be the concern of all relevant ministries, departments and organizations directly involved with dry-land management. There are, in many instances, cases where good plans are formulated but unfortunately left to one department to carry out. In Uganda, for instance, the Ministry of Local Administration is responsible for resettlement schemes; the final phase of implementation is left to that ministry, whereas prior planning involves many relevant ministries. The ideal situation should see the policy being carried out cooperatively by the relevant ministries that were involved in the planning stages. Given the lack of specialized manpower and other logistic problems, resettlers find themselves left virtually helpless in the new areas. The mere transfer of peasants from one area to another is not sufficient to make resettlers a happy and prosperous economic group. Practical guidelines ought to be laid out and implemented so that the new group moving into a new area, which may be climatically drier than the previous area, become better off than they had been, without endangering the environment. With these objectives in mind, the dry lands of our countries would become economic assets in reserve for current and future development.

REFERENCES

Kabera, J.B. (1982) Rural population redistribution in Uganda since 1900, in J.I. Clarke and L.A. Kosiński (eds.) *Redistribution of Population in Africa*, London, Heinemann, pp. 192–201.

Kangwagye, T.N. (1975) A report on current tsetse eradication schemes in Uganda, *East African Journal of Medical Research*, 2, 109.

Kuczynski, R.R. (1948) *Demographic Survey of the British Colonial Empire*, vol. 2, Oxford, Oxford University Press.

Langlands, B.W. (1974) *Uganda in Maps*, Part II, a preliminary non-edition, Makerere University, Department of Geography.

Netting, R.M. (1965) Household organisation and intensive agriculture: The Kofyar case, *Africa*, 35, 422–9.

Ngorogoza, P. (1969) *Kigezi and its People*, East African Literature Bureau, Kampala.

Uganda Government (1967) *Atlas of Uganda*, Department of Lands and Surveys, Entebbe, Government Printer.

9   Environmental and agricultural impacts of Tanzania's villagization programme

Michael McCall

A partial review is attempted of the development and under-development impacts of a massive population redistribution programme. Tanzania's villagization (*sogeza*) operations shifted over five million peasants from their former scattered homesteads into nucleated settlements of, in principle, 250–600 households each. The recent resettlement permanently altered the spatial, social and economic production relations of the peasantry as they were brought into approximately 8,000 *vijijini vya maendeleo* (development villages) and a new system of village government. In some quarters it has been praised as a model of socialist modernization, whereas in others it has been condemned as authoritarian state intervention in peasant relations of production.

After approximately one decade, villagization can be taken as established, but the relation between its original goals and the actual impacts requires critical examination. The focus in this paper is on the negative under-development impacts of the resettlement, both because these are already quite serious and could well be more so in the next decade, and because they are largely ignored in reviews of Tanzania's space economy and of the country's current economic crisis. Many problems can be ameliorated, though other negative impacts are unavoidable and justifiable. But certain basic changes must be implemented to reverse the environmental deterioration, the agricultural decline and a legacy of social discontent.

This is not a detailed study of particular aspects but a broad overview of problems and current solutions taken from contemporary studies. With 8,000 villages there are unavoidably some sweeping generalizations.

Ujamaa and villagization – origins and implementation

Resettlement schemes in Tanzania have a history going back at least to the population dispersals following the ferocious 'scorched earth' policies of German reprisals for Maji Maji in 1905. After the First World War and into the 1930s, the British relocated many thousands during the Swynnerton campaigns against tsetse encroachment which had partly resulted from the war. Peasants were brought into compact settlements, and then they gradually cleared bushland outwards by cultivating it (Kjekshus, 1977). In the 1950s, during the late colonial period of support for 'yeomen farmers', resettlement at low densities with larger farms was encouraged in the sparsely-populated frontier zones of Geita, Mbulu, Ismani and elsewhere. The most successful programme, the Sukumaland Development Scheme, assisted with the migration of 30,000 people in the peak five years, and the main destination zone, Geita District, doubled in population between 1948 and 1957.

The prelude to villagization, however, was the Village Settlement Schemes of the early 1960s, partly on former Groundnut Scheme land, and strongly supported by the World Bank. There were over 20 such villages set up as models, to be diffusion centres of modern farming. The total population was about 20,000 and most schemes had less than 200 settler households. They received considerable capital investment in machinery and services. At first settlers were paid an incentive agricultural wage and they worked under close supervision, but management was weak and the objectives ambiguous. Typically, accounting was deficient, equipment poorly maintained and productivity very low. The schemes were discontinued after five years, though they had absorbed three-quarters of the national agricultural budget; but from them was inherited the idea that nucleated settlements and broad extension services are the pre-requisite for rural development (Cliffe and Cunningham, 1973; McHenry, 1979).

Contemporaneously, spontaneous *ujamaa* villages were being formed by politicized cadres and poor peasants, motivated by Nyerere's ideology of self-reliance and equality based in an idealistic African tradition. *Ujamaa* in these villages was interpreted ideologically as a social mode of production founded on voluntary participation. At the same time communal agriculture was seen as a prerequisite for increasing productivity, and eventually leading also to communal small-scale industry. Around 50 small villages started spontaneously after independence (1961) and although 809 were recorded by 1969 they contained less than 5 per cent of the population. By this time, though some were motivated by socialist ideals, others were promoted by bigger farmers who hoped to benefit from government assistance to *ujamaa* villages. Many villages had only token communal enterprises.

One group of villages with a marked degree of communal activity and decision-making as well as self-reliance was in the isolated Ruvuma region. About 400 families from very poor scattered habitations voluntarily relocated into 17 new villages, developed communal farming systems and an interdependence in basic crafts, while investing savings in services and transport. In 1968, this Ruvuma Development Association was banned by the President, the official view being that the villages were not truly *ujamaa* but represented an elite (in the country as a whole) and were thus contrary to the 'frontal approach'. It is clear, though, that the Association posed an alternative decentralized development strategy to that of the party. At least one village, Matetereka, is still organized on communal labour and decision-making, and in other parts of Tanzania a handful of similar villages remains from the *ujamaa* experiment (McCall and Skutsch, 1983).

Table 9.1. *Rate of villagization*

	1969	1970	1971	1972	1973	1974	1975
Number of people living in villages (in thousands)	300	531	1,545	1,981	2,028	2,560	9,140
% of total rural population	2	4	12	15	16	19	80
Total number of villages	650	1,956	4,464	5,556	5,628	5,008	6,944

Source: Prime Minister's Office, *Maendeleo ya Vijiji vya Ujamaa.*

After 1968, despite the full support of the Arusha Declaration (1967), the number of new villages grew very slowly until the 'operations' of the early 1970s (Table 9.1). As the peasants were slow to respond voluntarily to the call for communalization, resettlement 'operations' villagized people, forcibly if necessary, in regions where there were extraneous justifications, as for example flood hazard in the Rufiji valley (1968), perpetual threat of famine in Dodoma (1971–72), Portuguese infiltration in Mtwara–Lindi (1973), and critical poverty in Kigoma (1972). But by 1973 the party leadership eventually grew impatient, and in August 1973 the President announced, and the party ratified, that it was compulsory for *all* rural people to live in villages by the end of 1976. Communal residence was declared as a first step towards real *ujamaa*; communal production was not imposed nor even particularly stressed. Thus the transformation to a social mode of production was reduced to a question of physical relocation, and the concept of *ujamaa* as a radical 'grassroots' movement was replaced by 'commandism' – enforced change directed and controlled from above (Boesen, 1979; McHenry, 1979; Hyden, 1980).

In the space of two years, probably over 5 million people were moved, although the exact numbers of people relocated are not known. The figures in Table 9.1 include several areas (e.g. Kilimanjaro, Rungwe district, West Lake) with already dense populations, though with each house set in its own one- to three-acre farm. In those regions, which also have political influence, boundaries were drawn round existing farm communities and they were declared villages. Elsewhere the rate of villagization accelerated as regional party officials competed to complete the exercise and gain kudos. Figure 9.1 brings out some of the regional variation.

The mechanisms of resettlement became increasingly energetic over the two years. Persuasion, building on the original *ujamaa* arguments for the advantages of communal life, was widespread though more in the national mass media than at local level. Inducements of status rewards and the material incentives of water, roads, clinics, schools and credit facilities were promised, often at unrealistically high levels. But the speed and scale of movement, and locally strong resistance, required also the use of coercion. The ultimate sanction was always force and the militia were quite widely used in violent operations, burning houses, food stores and crops, and there were some deaths. The operation arguably has left a legacy of

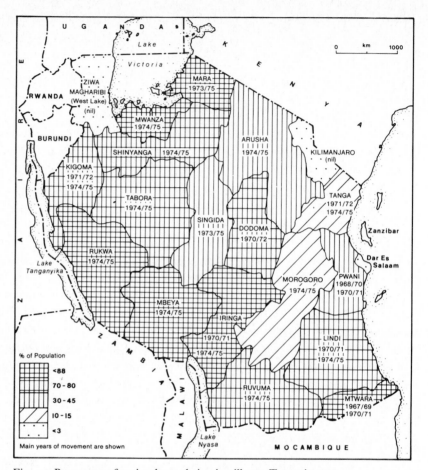

Fig. 9.1 Percentage of regional population in villages, Tanzania 1975

peasant alienation, mistrust and antagonism towards state rural development programmes, and of superiority and paternalism from the bureaucrats. Resistance came also from within the state. Local M.P.s (who are directly elected) objected to the coercion and sometimes administrative staff backed off, leaving the party officials to implement the moves (McHenry, 1979). During implementation there was very little emphasis on the productive potential of villagization. During the persuasion campaigns the peasants were promised rewards rather than joining discussion on their production responsibilities. Moreover the promised services have not subsequently been installed in all villages and so have lost much incentive value.

Some of the programme's implementors considered the peasants to be ignorant. Peasant involvement in the whole exercise, in the timing, site selection, layout of the new village and crop selection, was very limited. If peasants did not agree with the experts' findings they were overruled. Frequently their reservations about certain sites have been borne out by subsequent production declines or ecological deterioration. One outcome was the government directives and the presidential tours of 1976 which corrected some of the mistakes and re-resettled people (operation *Masahahisho*). By 1976 some people, in Mwanza for example, had been shifted three times to 'better' sites.

Remarkably little economic planning was done by the experts with regard to the new villages. The emphasis was on physical layout planning and house plot demarcation, often with little regard for environment. This resulted in inappropriate siting with regard to supplies of water and fuel, distances to fields and interaction between livestock and arable fields. It also meant slight consideration was given to potentials for village crafts, small industries or alternative energy sources. Too often blanket recommendations of village size were adhered to, without taking into account ecological and peasant economy variations. This is most serious in pastoral villages with cattle populations up to 20 times the human populations.

Ecological, social and agricultural impacts of resettlement into villages

Objectives of resettlement

The intended impacts of villagization were not spelt out very clearly by the government or party leaders. This absence of specified goals and objectives contributed to the implementation problems and to the resistance. However from the writings of Nyerere and from the 1973 declaration it can be assumed that the implicit goals included the following interrelated ideas:

(a) to achieve scale economies and save on overall transportation costs;
(b) to lay the foundations for a modernized rural economy, and to speed up the diffusion of information and modern farming techniques in particular;
(c) to facilitate national economic planning by transmitting objectives and targets to rural producers;
(d) to increase democratic decision-making by channelling peasants' needs and goals upwards;
(e) to lead towards equalization of rural income and wealth;
(f) to move towards communal ownership and communal relations of production;
(g) to provide health and welfare services to the rural population; and
(h) to improve security and national consciousness in the rural areas.

Village services

The most successful aspect of villagization is the provision of services to formerly isolated populations. At present there are no centralized data on the existence or levels of services; nevertheless some generalizations can be made:

(a) Service provision is generally much higher now than before villagization, especially for road access which had a high priority in village siting. There have also been large building programmes for schools, teachers' houses, clinics and party offices/community centres. Education is a high priority in Tanzanian rural development; the minimum population figure of 250 families per village was originally based on the threshhold of a single-stream primary school. On the other hand, the social infrastructure, including schools and markets, was sometimes destroyed during villagization. However, the distribution of services has not reached the levels promised and this has caused resentment in areas where they are seen to go to individually favoured villages. Over the decade, costs of provision have increased enormously and the state now relies on foreign aid for infrastructure and even operating costs, especially in rural water supply projects, where dams, equipment and running costs come from aid.

(b) The emphasis has been on service rather than productive infrastructure; thus dips, workshops, stores and irrigation schemes have received less investment. Studies (e.g. McHenry, 1979; Hyden, 1980) have pointed out that self-help labour participation is higher and more popular in non-farm service activities where benefits can be seen to be quickly applicable to all.

(c) There remain problems with the running of the village services. In the villages complaints are rife about clinics without drugs or bandages, water systems without spares or diesel, and so on. These are endemic with the accelerated action of the 'frontal approach' chosen by the party. But there are also many signs of poor organization, a tendency to respond to the latest 'campaign' and to neglect follow-ups, and, increasingly, corruption and *magendo* (non-legitimate and grey economic activities) among bureaucrats.

Environmental and agricultural drawbacks

The impacts of villagization discussed here are mainly in the deficit column. As far as environmental effects have been felt they have been mainly negative, and there is growing concern about the medium- as well as short-term agricultural costs.

(1) *Direct crop losses in early years.* In 1973–75, there were locally serious crop losses due to resettlement when, for instance, crops could not be harvested in time. Most moves however were in the slack season, and 1974–75 was in any case a drought year so that potential losses were reduced. In Mwanza, cotton suffered the following season from spiny bollworm because farmers had no time to uproot and burn cotton stalks.

Agricultural labour shortages continued for several years as labour was directed to house building and infrastructure self-help schemes as well as land clearing. For Kigoma Region, Loft (1981) has estimated this shortage as equivalent to 2 acres of crop farming over several seasons. Long-term losses have affected perennial tree crops: cashew-nut, coconut and sisal. The impact on cashew-nut production has been disastrous. The producer price incentive has been quite insufficient to compensate for the long walking distances to weed and harvest the trees. After weeding was enforced by edicts, peasants responded by burning the undergrowth, often destroying the trees or even villages in the process (Ellis, 1979).

(2) *Arable land shortage*. Villagization necessarily implies a reduction in acreage per household; problems arise because this is not balanced by intensification of production. Without intensification and with a significant reduction and usually elimination of fallowing, the consequence has been interrelated environmental deterioration – declining soil fertility and increased erosion. Marginal lands on steep slopes or poor soils within village boundaries are being cultivated increasingly. To compensate for lower fertility and yields, there has been a measurable switch from low-yielding, nutritious crops to high-yielding, low-value foods, particularly cassava, sweet potatoes and bananas.

A related question is, to what extent resettlement has redistributed village land more equably? In Mwanza immediately after the programme in 1975/76, there was some allocation in favour of the poorest peasants; those with no, or very little, land were given at least one acre per household (McCall, 1980). In a larger survey area, however, Collier (1981) found a marginally opposing trend. Most farm sizes were little changed, but new land distributed by village councils was positively correlated with existing farm size. It is possible that the initial equalization of *sogeza* is being slightly reversed.

(3) *Increased distances to fields*. For peasants this is the main drawback of villagization, to be balanced against gains in services and sociability. Most village case studies have shown that the average distance to plots has increased considerably (again owing to little intensification), with consequences for available field working time. For instance, assuming an eight-hour working day, walking time to a field 4 km distant (which is not at all unusual) will reduce the farming day by one-quarter. Over the whole season, the amount of walking required is inhibiting (Table 9.2), especially as a high proportion is by women producers also burdened by domestic activities. The impact is more than simply reduced field hours. The quality of agricultural work is bound to suffer because of extra weariness, especially as more midday field labour will be needed. Lighter loads of fertilizers and produce will have to be carried and therefore more trips made (peasants are anyway carrying loads of 25–40 kgs per trip). At a recommended input of over 7 tons per ha, it becomes virtually impossible to apply farmyard manure as recommended to save on imported fertilizers. It also becomes very difficult to protect the fields in the critical period before harvesting against birds, monkeys, hippos or thieves. Farmers often have to spend several weeks in temporary shelters in order to protect their vulnerable crops in distant fields, creating subsistence problems in the meantime. Yields are also reduced by the lower quality of farming input, especially poorer land preparation, less weeding and less careful harvesting. All these problems are exacerbated by the need to use more marginal land.

Table 9.2. *Walking requirements per ha per annum for different crops*

	Yield (kg/ha)	Man-days of labour (per ha) (including post-harvest operations)	Days in field	Total distance per season (km)
Maize (traditional)	850	111	107	1,070
Maize (improved)	2,200	141	136	1,550
Cotton (traditional)	350	169	141	1,410
Cotton (improved)	700	220	170	1,700
Rice	2,500	374	328	3,580

Note: Total distance is based on journeys to a field of 1 ha at a distance of 5 km plus headloading of a harvested crop with a 30 kg load.

(4) *Associated social and cultural impacts.* With longer journey times, women have less time for their normal household tasks, child care, and tending the sick. They can provide less cooked food for their children, and those who accompany them to the fields usually receive no midday meal. Additionally, there is the switch to low protein foods with reduction in groundnuts, though usually not beans. Consequently, child health may have deteriorated in some areas, due also to declining hygiene, where water is now less accessible or cholera more easily spread.

In Rufiji and Kilombero, for example, juvenile delinquency has appeared in the critical season when parents are guarding the rice paddies and the youths are less supervised. Village Councils have the right to allocate land on an usufructure basis, but land disputes in concentrated settlements have become more serious where different tribes or clans have been brought together and not yet adapted to cultural heterogeneity. Ordinary prejudices and suspicions are reinforced in land disputes, or simply by the social and economic disruption of resettlement. Customary laws and respect for natural rights of property and propriety are diminished. An outcome noted particularly in the early years was outbreaks of witchcraft and witch-hunting against real and imagined enemies, including state functionaries (Hyden, 1980; McCall, 1980). Witchcraft has been a normal response by the peasantry in periods of social upheaval since pre-colonial times.

(5) *Resource problems of water and firewood.* The firewood situation in Tanzania's villages is beginning to appear as the foremost environmental problem. Population concentration has obviously placed heavy pressure on surrounding *miombo* woodland and scrub. National data are not yet available, but scattered evidence shows that in the worst villages women are collecting fuel from up to 30 to 40 km away and they are carrying loads of over 30 kg. Very few villages have animal or mechanized transport for fuel gathering, though small towns truck in wood and charcoal. Within the villages firewood is sold by those with private woodlots. Around the villages can be seen deforestation and signs of consequent land degradation.

The government has instigated a massive Village Woodlot Campaign which has been successful in terms of initial mobilization for tree-planting. But past experience with similar campaigns has shown a heavy failure rate, due to not-watering, not-weeding or destruction by livestock or fire. Woodlots with their long-term individual costs and social benefits illustrate an extreme case of managing the commons and the problems of incentives and monitoring communal labour.

Water supply is locally a problem where villagization moved people away from streams or flood plains to interfluves or watersheds because they are the lines of roads. In other areas, there is heavy pressure on limited water sources since population growth and livestock requirements were often not considered in the resettlement. The government is making efforts to provide all villages with clean water by 1990, using active self-help, but also much foreign aid. Considerable investment is needed first to renovate previous schemes which are defective.

(6) *Livestock impacts*. The resource requirements of livestock were largely neglected during villagization and there was an implicit assumption of destocking. Without this destocking, the impacts have been formidable in the semi-arid central regions, including Shinyanga, Nzega, Singida, Dodoma, and parts of Iringa and Mbeya districts. Environmental pressures including overgrazing, damage to *mbugas* (a standard term used in East Africa to designate large, open, seasonally-flooded, alkaline, sandy clay grasslands, known as *dambos* or *vleis* in Southern Africa), water source pollution, gullying, and crop damage on the long treks to grazing land. The farming system is less integrated; for example, where pastoralists have moved cattle out of the villages there is less farmyard manure and fewer draught oxen are available. Where pastoralists and farmers (usually of different tribes) compete for limited land there have been violent clashes, as in the Usangu plains in Mbeya, and in Singida between Barbaig and Nyaturu. In some more settled areas, grazing land is beginning to be privately controlled, though not enclosed.

Despite these pressures, there is no evidence of destocking, rather the opposite. Large herds are kept partly for cultural reasons, but primarily for economic reasons, considering the returns to capital and labour on cattle compared with other rural investments. Like large families, a large herd is more productive and less vulnerable to risks of disease and predators. Small herds must be grazed close to home, whereas large herds associated with large families reduce overgrazing because young men can be spared for treks to distant pastures. Large herds are distributed in very complex kin and marriage relationships which eschew simple destocking or grazing regulations. Moreover, big owners who can afford to destock can most easily avoid it.

(7) *General land deterioration*. There are general environmental losses due to population concentration without adequate adaptation: soil compaction, erosion and gullying, damage to water sources, and loss of shade trees and communal space. Secondary bushland (thorny acacia spp) is spreading into previously cultivated areas and tsetse bush may expand, as earlier in the century (Vedasto, 1982).

What can be done towards solving problems of villagization?

Economic and land-use planners must attempt to overcome the worst of these population-resource pressures. In the present context this means identifying, evaluating and improving the status of the villages.

Identifying critical villages

Planning authorities have imperfect knowledge of the environmental conditions and farming systems of villages, and frequently underestimate the awareness shown at village level. The initial resource inventory can be based on a rapid, comprehensive, perhaps costly survey of all villages, or on estimates of carrying capacity at the level of agro-ecological zones. The former is more realistic because of the many different sources of pressure or viability problems, not all connected directly with villagization movements.

The spatial and resource problems should be distinguished from macro-considerations of political economy, although village in-depth surveys frequently show that the latter problems are more significant than the resource constraints:

(a) Low producer prices – the official marketing board prices range from 20 to 80 per cent of the usually illegal *magendo* prices.

(b) Transportation – rural accessibility is very limited and frequently restricted by seasonal conditions.

(c) Marketing and distribution parastatals – the parastatals have extremely high overheads and siphon off up to one-third of market value on administrative costs. Moreover they provide inefficient services to the farmers, through insufficient or late distribution of agricultural inputs and produce collection.

(d) Government campaigns and 'crisis planning' – there is a tendency for abrupt all-out campaigns which disrupt normal agricultural production and divert government staff effort from on-going programme support. Villagization was itself an extreme case of such a campaign.

(e) Leadership – common complaints concern alleged authoritarianism, disinterest, or corruption on the part of village officials and local bureaucrats.

(f) Shortages – in the current economic crisis, the villages are particularly hard hit by shortages of fuels, inputs, and all basic consumer goods.

The village-level resource planner can do little about these problems directly. Their implications should however be weighed against the usual village viability problems of resource pressure, sufficient resident labour; environmental hazards such as flooding; and specific socio-cultural problems such as in areas of conflict between pastoralists.

Evaluating village problems

Analysis of the relationship between population and resources has become developed in Tanzania through the Regional Integrated Development Plans

(RIDEPs). The methodologies now used are based originally on the Iringa RIDEP and adapted further in Tabora and Mbeya regions (Thomas *et al.*, 1975–76; Coleman *et al.*, 1978; Corker, 1982 and 1983; McCall, 1982). The basis is a rapid assessment of village (or zonal) area in terms of the land needed for subsistence production plus cash income, land needed for livestock grazing or stall-feeding, water and fuel supplies, and land for housing and infrastructure. Minimum food requirements and cash targets must be estimated. Then the carrying capacity is compared with suitable available land within reasonable walking distance to determine village viability. A sensitivity analysis of the key parameters should also be performed.

Some fundamental methodological problems occur in:

(a) the degree of change envisaged by the planners in the technology, land use and organization of production (the viability of a village is not a static measure but reflects the changing balance between village needs and resources);

(b) the extent to which planners perceive peasant behaviour as being rational though constrained, or as irrational, culture-bound and subject to limited goals;

(c) political goals, especially the selection of target incomes and the emphasis to place on communal farming;

(d) technical problems of estimating yields on peasant farms, livestock carrying capacity, fuelwood consumption, woodland regeneration rates and the vast sub-economy based on *pombe* (local beer) brewing and consumption; and

(e) conventional land evaluation methodologies of delimiting land systems and performing detailed soil analysis and agronomic trials not being rapid enough.

There is now a need to incorporate village viability assessment (VVA) into on-going settlement planning practice at regional level, and to cover four types of problem area:

(a) areas of high population density where carrying capacity is insufficient;

(b) areas of rapid in-migration from overcrowded zones;

(c) areas where overall carrying capacity is met but village shapes and boundaries mean insufficient land is within walking distance; and

(d) areas of land degradation.

Current strategy in Mbeya is to incorporate VVA into settlement planning procedures through proposed 'Land Use Planning Teams' in the coordinating Regional Planning Offices. The teams will provide a land use planning service to the functional ministries (of agriculture, livestock, water, natural resources and so on), rather than the responsibility being split between the ministries as at present. The main objectives of VVA in the proposed teams would be: initial checks on carrying capacities; identification of (potential) problem villages; estimation of the potentials of new settlement locations; initial identification and sensitivity analysis of possible solutions; and aid to village self-planning by providing technical resource information.

Planning and potential solutions

There is no single solution to villagization problems. They depend on the elements of viability and the specificity of village resources and potential.

(1) *Rural–rural migration.* A few areas experience permanent rural–rural migration, such as Usukuma, Unyamwezi and Unyakyusa. The determinants of rural–rural migration are not only land pressure but also culture and history; for example, the Wasukuma were traditionally involved in permanent migration of whole families to frontier zones where they reproduced their own farming system. Other tribes, such as the Wachagga, are more attached to their eco-cultural homeland. They move only to a few similar agricultural areas, and usually retain a home farm on Kilimanjaro. To encourage more permanent rural–rural movement as a solution, more is needed than short-term 'benefit packages' of seeds, tools and inputs. Long-term incentives are required, including better land than at home, permanent advantages in land tenure and first choice of new land, higher producer prices and solutions to marketing problems, and disincentives to staying in the same area.

(2) *Rural–urban migration.* This should not be encouraged as a solution. It is already high, though often temporary as young males may return to village agriculture after a period of formal or informal sector employment.

(3) *Temporary rural–rural migration.* This is more common where there is land pressure and cash incomes are limited by farm size than in areas of subsistence deficiency. The usual patterns are either three to six years' semi-permanent movement to areas with high cash-income potential – such as zones of tobacco, coffee, rice or finger millet production, extensive pastoral land, of gold-mining areas – or alternatively for longer periods but with seasonal returns for some work on the home farm. This is advantageous to the cyclical migrant but is problematic for both origin and destination areas. At the origin, it depletes the number of able-bodied males for individual *shamba* (small traditional farm or garden) work and for communal village activities. There may be heavy pressure on the family remaining at home, especially on females; hence the paradox that there is a labour shortage in the land shortage zones, which is currently resolved by reducing acreage further, or by hiring or reciprocal labour. At the destination, virtually no income is expended, except on *pombe* consumption. Since settlement is only temporary there is usually little effort in good farming and land conservation.

If the whole family moves, their land is often left idle in the midst of a land-hungry zone. Changes in customary land law are needed to enforce productive use of the land and changes in cultural attitudes in order to sanction this.

(4) *'Devillagization', or reduction in plot density.* The return of peasants to their former homes has been going on since 1974 but on a very small scale and illegally. It can now be considered as insignificant, but it might be a solution in some

migrant pastoral areas for the short term, until regional land pressures become too great.

A solution being promoted in several areas is to reduce intra-village densities and provide larger house plots. Specific plans depend on agro-ecological conditions, the main crops, subsistence and cash needs, the intensity of crop care and crop security. In Tabora Region, a U.K. Land Resources Development Centre team in the RIDEP has suggested an average plot size of 1 ha, half for the house and some subsistence, and half for individual woodlots. The argument is that a village size of 450 ha or so will leave all farmers within easy reach of village services whilst reducing the aggregate walking distance to fields. Farmers would have other fields for tobacco and maize just outside the central area, probably in block farms. (Water supply would not be adversely affected because it is mainly from shallow wells which should be dispersed.)

In some areas of Rukwa Region, densities have been reduced to a greater extent so that houses stand in 2–3 ha plots surrounded by all their crop fields. This implies fairly dispersed villages with longer distances to central facilities (Mlay, 1982). In Mbeya Region, on the other hand, decreased house plot sizes and higher densities have been proposed so as to reduce aggregate walking distances to external 2–3 ha fields (McCall, 1982).

(5) *Satellite villages*. The development of smaller satellite settlements to bring farmers nearer to their fields again was recommended by Dumont and Mottin (1979), and has been implemented in a few instances at least in Mwanza and Mbeya Regions (Vedasto, 1982; McCall, 1982). The concept has usually been strongly resisted. Jambiya (1982) has investigated Kanyelele village, Mwanza Region, where moves by individual farmers towards temporary satellites, although favoured by village leaders, were forbidden because higher-level authorities considered it to be 'anti-villagization'. No moves were permitted until the official land planning unit arrived for a post-villagization plot allocation. The unit agreed with the peasants and after one year, including quite thorough land evaluation and viability studies, demarcated layout and plots for two satellite villages of a couple hundred people apiece. The exercise was explicitly not equivalent to devillagization.

The satellite dwellers greatly reduced their farm-to-field journey times and their effective working time (Table 9.3), and after a season had increased their average worked holdings from 1.5 to 1.75 acres. Given the increase in working hours, satellites actually intensified agricultural production. The farmers now had access to higher quality land, and they raised the quality of their work through better husbandry. Significantly they were now able to carry fertilizers to the fields and to carry back more harvest. Crop losses were greatly reduced through night-time pest protection and secure adjacent storage. Central village dwellers also benefited from the reduced population pressure. Food crops increased only marginally because they are always the priority, but cotton production increased dramatically for the village as a whole. Other benefits felt in the satellites were more time for tending cattle, for planting trees and for social affairs and *pombe*

Table 9.3. *Effects of satellites on distance to fields: Kanyelele village, Mwanza*

	Igando satellite		Malilo satellite	
	Before move	After move	Before move	After move
Average distance one way to fields (km)	6.5	0.25	3.25	0.25
Average time one way to fields (hrs)	2.30	0.10	1.25	0.10
Effective increase in working time per day (hrs)		4.40		2.30

Source: Jambiya, 1982.

consumption. The women particularly responded favourably: closer to water and fuel supplies; far less walking to the fields carrying produce and children; the children having midday meals; more time for tending children and gardens, for washing, *pombe* brewing, attending clinic, food preparation and storage, and also for *ngomas* (dances).

The problem remaining is access to services – school, store, clinic, mill, Chama Cha Mapinduzi (C.C.M.) party office – which are found in the central village. Consumer items in the village shop are frequently sold out before satellite dwellers hear of their arrival. Children walk up to 13 km a day to school, or stay with relatives.

In similar parts of Tanzania there is much scope for satellites within registered villages wherever numbers are too high and fertile land is distant. Planning of such sites must be speeded up, as well as their legal recognition within the revised Ujamaa Village Act of 1982.

(6) *Redistribution of land*. Land is relatively evenly distributed within individual villages and there is no evidence that those with bigger plots live closer to village centres. Those with less land are usually the peasants who had to resettle in existing villages; for them, satellites are a feasible solution.

(7) *Reduction of land requirements (without intensification)*. There are other possibilities of increasing carrying capacity. Additional food sources might be found, such as better food processing, or exploitation of the considerable potential for fish farming. Off-farm income can reduce the need for cash crops and provide local employment. There are possibilities for small–scale village industries, such as food processing, crafts and implement manufacture, but investment costs are high and employment generation would be limited. For Kilimanjaro it has been suggested that densities could be raised in semi-urbanized 'retirement villages' where retired officials would need only a small plot.

Conclusions

The land resource pressures brought about by villagization should have been countered by developing communal systems of production and by agricultural intensification, but these have not materialized in practice, except locally.

Communal production

Communal farms are supposed to exist in all villages but many do so in name only. They are often individually worked, contiguous block farms rather than communal plots. Actual *ujamaa* farm areas are, relatively, very small. A sample of 32 Tabora villages showed *ujamaa* farms averaging only 13 ha, which was 25 per cent of the claimed size and only 10 per cent of the target area (Barrett, 1981). Communal work is not popular and has to be imposed by fines and other sanctions, though perusal of work records shows a very high rate of absenteeism. In a Tanga Region village, the turnout varied from 5 to 291 workers per day over the season (Rubin, 1982), which makes the planning of communal work very problematic.

Communal labour inputs are set unrealistically high; 4 hours twice a week in Tanga, and 12 hours a week per household in some Tabora villages (Rubin, 1982; Barrett, 1981). Labour payments, if any, are well below opportunity costs. Some villages have *mfumaki* plots where the crop income goes directly into the village treasury. The main constraint therefore is the lack of incentive for communal work, together with very deficient monitoring and recording of work performed and common allegations of embezzlement and cheating by leaders. Moreover *ujamaa* crops are sold solely to the parastatals at the low official prices. McHenry (1979) characterizes this as an extra taxation on an already unpopular exercise.

Finally, yields are extremely low. The Tabora data showed yields relative to those in private farming of 90 per cent for maize, 40 per cent for cotton, 22 per cent for sorghum, and 24 per cent for groundnuts despite higher levels of fertilizers. Moreover the labour inputs on average were about ten times as high per ha as on individual farms (Barrett, 1981). This misuse of labour time is probably the most deleterious and discouraging impact of communal farming.

Agricultural intensification

The intention of villagization was to bring about intensification, but the evidence shows that little has taken place. Areas which have intensified probably would have done so without the resettlement programme. Six interrelated reasons help to explain why intensification efforts have failed:

(a)   with excess land in most areas, farmers prefer to maximize returns to labour, and therefore devillagize;

(b)   price incentives for marketed crops are not sufficient to compensate for additional labour and inputs;

(c)   many areas of low fertility demand high capital inputs;

(d)   the distribution of limited fertilizers, chemicals and diesel is very unreliable;

(e)   modern varieties and monocropping are more risky because of greater vulnerability to environmental conditions; and

(f)   many farmers are not certain that villagization is here to stay.

In a detailed study, Loft (1981) has illustrated the failure of a large-scale World-Bank-assisted intensification programme in Kigoma Region. Peasants find that growing beans extensively for the private (*magendo*) market brings as much, or more, income than the planned returns from intensively cultivated cotton. Firstly, the price relations favour beans in terms of returns to labour. (Where minimum cotton acreages are enforced, peasants plant but do not cultivate.) Secondly, peasants avoid risk by not intensifying and becoming dependent on externally supplied inputs and on parastatal collections as well as on weather conditions or random calamities. Monocropping cotton is more risky than growing maize/beans/sorghum/groundnuts and other mixes where local seed varieties, staggered planting dates and wide spacing are used. Such traditional adaptations are inimical to modern input efficiency.

Population movements

At this juncture it is possible only to hazard what long-term effects villagization will have on the demographic surface of the country. At the national level, villagization brought about a vast, if uneven, removal of peasants into more concentrated settlements. The redistribution in principle has improved access, and facilitated service provision and the execution of development projects. Scale economies and communal efforts should have led to agricultural modernization. But the programme has itself brought about new constraints on agricultural production and therefore on the overall development trajectory, including foreign exchange earnings.

Under existing conditions of peasant production neither capital-based intensification nor labour communalization is immediately feasible. A significant solution for many areas, therefore, will be partial population shifts to satellite settlements within village boundaries. These should balance the advantages of proximity to productive land with access to the 'external economy', the contact points of which are located at the village centre. This will be supplemented by a small amount of unregulated returning to former homesteads. Thus the future population map of Tanzania may appear as diffuse blots rather than intense spots or the scattered dots of the pre-villagization era.

Concentration in villages is likely to mean less long-distance inter-regional migration such as the current movements of the Wasukuma and Masai. They will have fewer possibilities of finding new sites to settle for medium or long-term migrations, because of tighter restrictions towards living only in registered villages and the stricter limitations on movements between such villages. Traditional 'settler' farms of the Wanyakyusa from Rungwe in the Usangu Plains for instance have become more difficult to maintain (McCall, 1982). Villagization therefore can be expected to lead to a more static settlement pattern, with the exception of official new settlement programmes, which historically have not been very successful.

The stability of rural reorganization may be in contrast to increases in other population flows. The growing population of young men with scant prospects in peasant-based farming, and under the tight socio-political control of the village elders, will be unable to utilize the traditional escape mechanism of opening a farm on new land. Their solution will then be migration to frontier zones or to towns. Some village authorities are instigating new fiscal controls to limit the temporary (and permanent) movement of young men, for instance to plantations and to lumbering; the justification being the need for their labour power for village infrastructure as well as for family farms. Given the difficulties of opening frontier settlements, many more youths might opt for the less regulated peri-urban life if the relative quality of rural life deteriorates further.

Thus urban stability as well as rural productivity may be contingent upon ameliorating the environmental impacts of villagization.

In conclusion, villages are here to stay and there can be no solution which involves eliminating them. The impacts emphasized have been mainly the negative ones; there are of course positive effects on services, information and accessibility. A full evaluation would also have to address the methodological problem of comparing 'with and without' – what direction would rural development have taken in the past decade without villagization?

REFERENCES

Barrett, A.T. (1981) A note on communal agriculture in Tabora Region 1979–80, *Tabora Rural Integrated Development Project, Land Use Component*, unpublished report.

Belshaw, D.G.R. (1981) Village viability assessment procedures in Tanzania: decision-making with curtailed information requirements, *Public Administration and Development*, 1, 3–13.

Boesen, J. (1979) Tanzania: from *ujamaa* to villagization, in B. Mwansasu and C. Pratt (eds.), *Towards Socialism in Tanzania*, Toronto, University of Toronto, pp. 125–44.

Cliffe, L. and Cunningham, G. (1973) Ideology, organisation and the settlement experience in Tanzania, in L. Cliffe and J. Saul (eds.), *Socialism in Tanzania*, vol. 2, Dar es Salaam, Tanzania Publishing House.

Coleman, G., Pain, A. and Belshaw, D.G.R. (1978) Village viability assessment in the framework of regional planning in Tanzania, *University of East Anglia, Overseas Development Group*, UNDP/FAO Project URT/75/076.

Collier, P. (1981) *Ujamaa* and rural development: an assessment of Tanzania's experience, *Oxford University, Institute of Economics and Statistics*, unpublished paper.

Corker, I.R. (1982) *Human Carrying Capacity Assessment Model for Tabora Region*, Surbiton: Overseas Development Administration, Land Resources Development Centre, TRIDEP Project Record 65.

Corker, I.R. (1983) *Tabora Rural Integrated Development Project, Land Use Component Land Use Planning Handbook*, Surbiton: Overseas Development Administration, Land Resources Development Centre, TRIDEP Project Record 66.

Dumont, R. and Mottin, M-F. (1979) Self-reliant rural development in Tanzania 12 years after the Arusha Declaration on Socialist lines, Dar es Salaam, President's Office, draft report.

Ellis, F. (1979) A preliminary analysis of the decline in Tanzanian cashewnut production

1974–1979: causes, possible remedies and lessons for rural development policy, *University of Dar es Salaam, Economic Research Bureau*, paper.

Hyden, G. (1980) *Beyond Ujamaa in Tanzania: Underdevelopment and an Uncaptured Peasantry*, Nairobi, Heinemann.

Jambiya, G.K. (1982) The effects of establishing satellite settlements upon agricultural production: the case of Kanyelele village in Mwanza region, B.A. dissertation, University of Dar es Salaam, Department of Geography.

Kjekshus, H. (1977) *Ecology Control and Economic Development in East African History,* London, Heinemann.

Loft, M.V. (1981) A farming system's response to major state interventions in the seventies: a case study of the maize–beans villages of Kigoma Region, in P. Anandajayasekeram, B.J. Ndunguru and I.J. Lupanga (eds.), *The Proceedings of the Conference on Farming Systems and Farming Systems Research in Tanzania*. Morogoro, University of Dar es Salaam, Faculty of Agriculture, pp. 75–95.

McCall, M.K. (1980) The diffusion of regional underdevelopment: articulation of capital and peasantry in Sukumaland, Tanzania, Ph.D. thesis, Northwestern University, Illinois.

McCall, M.K. (1982) The population pressure on natural resources in Mbeya Region and potential solutions, *Mbeya, Regional Commissioner's Office, FAO Mbeya RIDEP Project*, GCP/URT/055 (DEN) (report).

McCall, M.K. and Skutsch, M.M. (1983) Which road for the peasantry? Strategies and contradictions in Tanzania's rural development, in D.A. Lea and D.P. Chaudri (eds.), *Rural Development and the State*, London, Methuen.

McHenry, D.E. Jr (1979) *Tanzania's Ujamaa Villages: The Implementation of a Rural Development Strategy*, University of California, Berkeley, Institute of International Studies, Research Series, 39.

Mlay, W.F. (1982) Personal communication, Dar es Salaam.

Rubin, D. (1982) *Bega kwa bega* and *msalagambo*: comparing constraints on peasant production, *University of Dar es Salaam, Department of Sociology*, paper.

Thomas, I.D., Coleman, G., Murray-Rust, H. *et al.* (1975–76) *Physical Planning and Resource Evaluation Follow-up Studies, Iringa Region, Preliminary Report (1975), Final Report Vol. 1 and Vol. 2 (1976)*. University of East Anglia, Overseas Development Group (for FAO).

Vedasto, F.R. (1982) The application of remote sensing and land evaluation as a basis for sustained land-use planning in the Kwimba District, (Tanzania), M.Sc. thesis, International Institute for Aerial Survey and Earth Sciences (I.T.C.), Enschede.

10 Development and population redistribution: measuring recent population redistribution in Tanzania

Ian Thomas

Types of development: the scale of their impact on population redistribution and sources of data

This paper will use the notion of development projects in two ways. The narrow, and more common, usage refers to readily identifiable schemes with a starting date, a specified location and extent, and – commonly – a pre-determined population size (or set of sizes), at least for the early years of the scheme (Lele, 1975: 8–11). In Tanzania, examples of the range of development projects of this sort include: estate production of tea, coffee, sisal and wattle; irrigation projects to extend rice farming on formerly uncultivated lands; the designation of forest reserves and game parks, such as that controlled by the Conservation Authority in Ngorongoro and in a host of less well-known but sometimes very extensive game reserves (the Selous and Ruaha Parks for instance); the planned expansion of existing towns, as in the case of Dodoma following its choice as the new capital; the construction of hydroelectric and water control schemes in the Pangani and Rufiji river basins; the mining of diamonds and gold, each with its peculiar organization and effects on population redistribution; and the building of cement, textile and other factories in towns or in the countryside. All of these were associated with the movement of people (Thomas, 1971; Egero, 1974). However, the numbers involved were relatively small – often only a few hundreds, occasionally up to tens of thousands, seldom more. In comparison to the total population – and especially that part of it still in the rural areas – these are relatively small numerical effects. They are usually measured as part of the project activity, and in national censuses they are often separately identified as institutional populations.

The second possible interpretation of a development project is broader but in most instances less tangible. This is what might be termed 'pervasive development' or 'enabling and attitudinal development'. It is widely replicated because easily replicable, and influences the majority of the population. Enabling development might be the construction of roads and the opening of bus services and transport enterprises, or it might be crop development and diffusion. Of course, it is as well to recognize that development is induced change and not necessarily wholly desirable change or desired change, especially in the short term. Enabling development of the sort noted might be part of the road to underdevelopment (Frank, 1969: 3–17). It could then be responsible for out-migration or natural decrease in relatively deprived areas. Attitudinal development, for instance, related to nutrition and hygiene or to accepted family size, is stimulated by advertising and by health and nutrition campaigns, as well as by other development programmes of a specific or a broadly educational nature. It too produces large-scale relative population redistribution by contributing to the emergence of regional and local differences in the chances of survival and the fertility of millions of inhabitants, and by influencing the decision to migrate among many. These effects of pervasive development, and the redistribution resulting largely from differential rates of natural increase and individual decisions to migrate, though often overlooked, are important because they affect such large numbers (see Table 10.1 and Fig. 10.1). The quantitative evidence for such large-scale redistribution comes from national censuses and surveys measuring population change and its components, natural increase and migration (Egero and Henin, 1973; Tanzania 1980, 1983).

Tanzania additionally, however, provides the somewhat unusual case of a development programme with a specified, and short, implementation timetable which nonetheless affected millions. This is the Tanzanian villagization programme of 1974 to 1976, and this paper concentrates on the limited problem of establishing some measures of redistribution – specifically, distances moved – for this sudden, massive and widespread but essentially short-distance relocation which, by its nature, has gone virtually unrecorded by the standard national statistical instruments.

Settlement reorganization 1973–76

The general nature of developments in the last ten years in Tanzania is well-known (Mwansasu and Pratt, 1979; Hyden, 1980) and will be described only briefly here. At the end of 1973 the political decision was taken to accelerate the purely physical dimension of the prevailing rural development strategy and to move scattered rural populations into nucleated settlements. Settlement sites were chosen within the next few months (by April 1974) and decisions taken as to which households would be relocated. The movements began in earnest in August and September 1974 and before the end of the year millions of people had new village homes. The relocation continued for the next few years, but judging from the results of the 1978 population census it seems to have been virtually complete by that time (Table 10.2). In 1976 the Prime Minister's Office, generally responsible for the villagization programme, issued statistics which suggested that some 13 million people had been villagized (Tanzania P.M.O., 1976). In all parts of the country, even before the villagization programme started, some people were already living in villages – local service centres and administrative headquarters – which became designated 'development villages'. In some parts of the country the traditional form of rural settlement was already the nucleated village (as in many

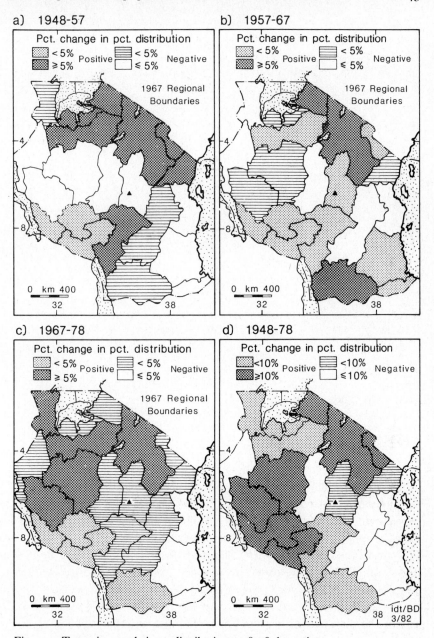

Fig. 10.1 Tanzania: population redistribution 1948–78, by region

parts of the coastal region of Tanzania). Elsewhere the rural inhabitants were living at such high densities that delimitating geographical areas and naming them as villages was equivalent to creating new nucleated settlements (as in Kilimanjaro Region and Bukoba and Kyela Districts). Thus, 13 million villagized did not mean 13 million relocated; perhaps eight to nine million were actually moved.

Table 10.1. *Tanzania: relative population distribution (1948–78) and natural increase (1967), by regions (mainland rural)*

Regions	Population no. 1948–78 (thousands)				Natural increase (thousands)	Regional population as % of total			
	1948	1957	1967	1978	1967	1948	1957	1967	1978
Arusha	325	408	611	929	33	4.4	4.7	5.2	5.7
Coast	386	408	512	517	18	5.2	4.7	4.4	3.2
Dodoma	466	514	709	972	25	6.3	5.9	6.0	6.0
Iringa	389	489	690	923	29	5.3	5.7	5.9	5.7
Kigoma	361	383	473	649	20	4.9	4.4	4.1	4.0
Kilimanjaro	354	474	653	902	37	4.8	5.5	5.6	5.6
Mara	283	380	544	723	24	3.8	4.4	4.7	4.5
Mbeya	569	686	969	1,386	21	7.7	7.9	8.3	8.6
Morogoro	478	548	685	939	19	6.5	6.3	5.9	5.8
Mtwara	680	747	1,041	1,300	13	9.2	8.6	8.9	8.0
Mwanza	655	804	1,056	1,443	26	8.8	9.3	9.0	8.9
Ruvuma	237	267	393	564	20	3.2	3.1	3.4	3.5
Shinyanga	560	660	900	1,324	30	7.6	7.6	7.7	8.2
Singida	355	373	458	614	18	4.8	4.3	3.9	3.8
Tabora	383	422	563	964	21	5.2	4.9	4.8	6.0
Tanga	472	579	771	1,039	29	6.4	6.7	6.6	6.4
West Lake	456	514	659	1,009	27	6.2	5.9	5.6	6.2
Mainland totals[a]	7,409	8,657	11,686	16,186	24	100	100	100	100

Notes:
[a] excludes Dar es Salaam Region and Zanzibar.
1978 data provisionally adjusted to 1967 administrative areas (and subject to amendment)
Sources: 1948–67: 1967 Census Report, Vol. 6, pp. 288–9.
1978: 1978 Population Census Report, p. 177.

There have been few systematic attempts to arrive at district estimates of the distances moved by the rural inhabitants in the course of the villagization programme. Maro and Mlay (1982) collected interview data from a selection of villagers in nine districts during the course of the University of Dar es Salaam's 'decentralization' research study. The proportion of respondents who had moved less than 5 km varied, among the districts, from 24.7 to 100.0 per cent. The proportion moving more than 16 km ranged from 0.0 to 32.8 per cent. No mean or total distances were given. Mascarenhas (1977), in a study of settlement distribution in Dodoma District, had estimated the distance between traditional settlements and *ujamaa* village sites, and from both of these to 1967 census enumeration area centroids, which he called 'hypothetical villages'. He provides a map showing the distances of the hypothetical villages from the nearest *ujamaa* village sites of 1974 but only tabulates the number of links within the categories: zero-move (35 per cent), within 5 km (48 per cent), and beyond 5 km (17 per cent). The remainder of this paper describes a method for estimating total distances moved by all the persons of every village and calculations of the village and district

Table 10.2. *Tanzania: percentage of rural households in villages, by region, 1978*

Regions	Number of rural households						
	In villages		Outside villages	Total households	% of Total		
	Registered	Non-registered			In villages	Not in villages	
Dodoma	175,458	3,985	6,986	186,429	96.3	3.7	
Arusha	120,002	21,377	15,621	157,000	90.1	9.9	
Kilimanjaro	139,940	10,093	2,893	152,926	98.1	1.9	
Tanga	157,832	5,801	18,268	181,901	90.0	10.0	
Morogoro	140,356	20,322	12,930	173,608	92.6	7.4	
Coast	96,437	9,308	5,707	111,452	94.9	5.1	
Dar es Salaam	15,184	2,888	314	18,386	98.3	1.7	
Lindi	105,847	0	538	106,385	99.5	0.5	
Mtwara	152,720	2,939	798	156,457	99.5	0.5	
Ruvuma	99,398	0	278	99,676	99.7	0.3	
Iringa	178,552	2,683	2,790	184,025	98.5	1.5	
Mbeya	181,049	10,824	4,850	196,723	97.5	2.5	
Singida	112,426	1,591	5,476	119,493	95.4	4.6	
Tabora	116,137	6,908	14,241	137,286	89.6	10.4	
Rukwa	72,876	12,128	1,499	86,503	98.3	1.7	
Kigoma	96,780	6,707	1,923	105,410	98.2	1.8	
Shinyanga	195,825	12,252	5,457	213,534	97.4	2.6	
West Lake	211,922	1,635	4,245	217,802	98.1	1.9	
Mwanza	197,545	6,105	3,160	206,810	98.5	1.5	
Mara	100,817	2,897	2,389	106,103	97.7	2.3	
Mainland total (rural only)	2,667,103	140,443	110,363	2,917,909	96.2	3.8	

Source: Tanzania, 1978 Census Report. DSM: Bureau of Statistics, 1980, Table 3.

mean distances moved per person. The method is applied to one district, namely Iringa District, which in 1967 had an enumerated rural population of 230,881 and in 1974 placed the rural inhabitants, then estimated at 238,818, into 159 villages.

Measuring short-distance redistribution

One reason for the absence of estimates of quantities for this large-scale redistribution is that the statistical (and cartographic) record from which one would calculate distance moved is fragmentary if not in many cases non-existent. This is because the movements were planned and implemented with great speed, because they were very many in number, and because although the decision to villagize was a central one, the decision-taking as to the choice of village locations was highly decentralized. Although there was a national census in 1978, again this has not provided data directly relevant to our question. The birthplace and residence data were collected only for a sample designed to produce regional and national estimates, the residence responses were pre-coded to record only inter-

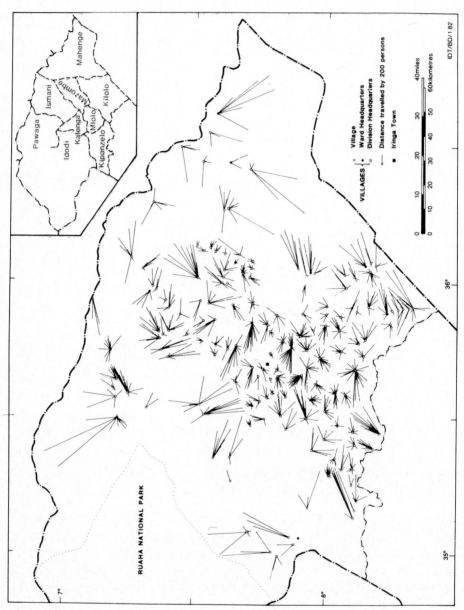

Fig. 10.2 Iringa District: villagization, 1974

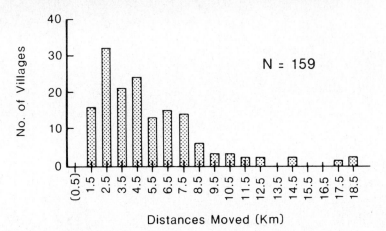

Fig. 10.3 Iringa District: village means. See Fig. 10.2: these are village mean distances moved per person.

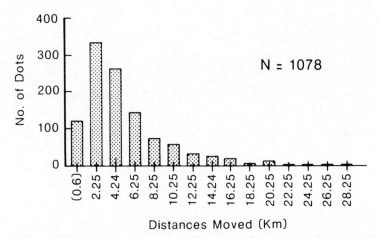

Fig. 10.4 Iringa District: 'dot' moves. See Fig. 10.2: distances are for moves of population aggregates, i.e. dots.

regional movements and those from rural to urban places and, finally, the published tabulations are aggregated by region.

Consequently it has been necessary to devise an indirect method to obtain estimates for each village and by aggregation for the minor administrative areas containing those villages. The method is demonstrated in Figure 10.2 which also shows the assumed pattern of movement and the distances involved. The derived measures of movement are given in Table 10.3 and the graphs (Figs. 10.3 and 10.4). As noted already, the 1974 villagization plan in Iringa District resulted in the creation of 159 villages. This study estimates the mean distance moved per person for Iringa District at 4.94 km. At first sight this may seem small, but it indicates that the aggregate movement for the villagization programme in this single district was of the order of 1.22 million km. The estimated average number of person-km of movement per village was 7,661.

Table 10.3. *Iringa district: population 1967 and 1974, and indicators of population movement resulting from the 1974 villagization programme, by divisions*

Divisions	Population no.		Movement indicators (estimates)		
	1967 census (a)	1974 estimate (b)	Dot moves (km)	Person-km of movement	Mean distance moved per person (km)
Ismani	34,044	27,869	781	152,110	5.46
Kiponzelo	27,150	25,206	666	144,715	5.74
Kalenga	22,571	27,643	469	124,660	4.51
Mlolo	38,191	37,104	734	146,420	3.95
Kilolo	46,372	52,413	1,188	250,275	4.78
Mahenge	9,107	10,227	384	91,330	8.93
Mazombe	32,121	50,198	688	192,800	3.84
Pawaga	14,035	8,492	278	48,180	5.67
Idodi	7,290	7,408	274	67,660	9.13
Totals	230,881	246,560	5,462	1,218,150	4.94

Notes: Col. 4, 'dot' moves, gives the length in km of the lines shown on Fig. 10.2, summed for all the villages of a division.
Col. 5 gives the product of the distance moved and the population value of the aggregate population dot for the village. All the dots for a single village have the same value, but the values are weighted for both the village and the Division to account for population change, 1967–74.
Col. 6 gives the total person-km of movement for the divisions and for the district divided by the 1974 population number for the administrative unit.
Sources: (a) Tanzania 1967 Census Report, vol. 1, p. 48.
(b) Iringa Regional Plan files, lists supplied by the District Planning Officers.

The graphs demonstrate that whereas the most frequent village mean distance moved per person was only 2–3 km (Fig. 10.3), there are many villages with a mean distance in the range from 3–8 km. (On both Figs. 10.3 and 10.4 the distances shown are the mid-points of distance bands.) Whereas the largest class of moves was for distances of 1.25 to 3.24 km (Fig. 10.4), a considerably larger number was for distances of 3.25 to 7.24 km and 20 per cent exceeded this latter distance. Figure 10.2 and Table 10.3 show that there are regional variations in the patterns of movement: settlement reorganization in the arid plains of the west (Pawaga and Idodi Divisions) and the mountainous areas of the east (Mahenge and parts of Kilolo Divisions) required proportionately more longer distance relocations than the central plateau (Mazombe and Mlolo). But because the population density is higher on the central plateau than in the peripheral areas, and because such a large proportion of the population everywhere was required to move to some extent, the total person-km of movement is high throughout the central area.

Method and assumptions used

The distance estimates were obtained by using the dot distribution map of the district compiled from the results of the 1967 population census; the village location map compiled in 1974–75 as part of a regional planning exercise; and the estimated village population size for April 1974 as used by District Planning Officers at the time of the villagization planning (FAO/ODG, 1976). The 1974 village locations were superimposed on the 1967 population distribution dot map. The 1967 dots (each representing 200 people) were then allocated to the new villages taking account of (a) the village population size, and (b) the proximity of the dots on the 1967 map. Where the 1974 population estimates for administrative divisions were significantly different from the 1967 census count for the same area (Table 10.3), the dots were weighted in value. (For example, if the population in 1974 was larger than that of 1967, each dot would represent proportionately more than 200 people, and vice versa. The assumption being made is that any population change affected all parts of an administrative division equally.)

The result is shown on Figure 10.2 where the number of lines, their orientation and their length represent respectively the volume of movement, the direction and the distance. Clearly, the 200-person aggregate involves a further assumption, namely that the persons aggregated in the dot representation are distributed about the dot's location (in relation to the location of the village to which all move) in such a way that their aggregate distance moved to the dot is zero. (This is the compensating sum of those moving from an original location closer to the village than the dot and those moving from a location more distant from the village than the dot. The geometry of this suggests that taking the distance from the dot to the village gives a conservative estimate of the distance moved.) A further assumption is attached to the representation of the village by a small circle. In fact it has been shown that village areas are quite extensive in many cases and within the village area there may be several settlement nuclei all registered as one 'village' despite there being as many as several kilometres between the various dwelling clusters of the same village (Fig. 10.5) (Thomas et al., 1976; Coleman et al., 1978). Two important conditions for the successful application of this method are a well-constructed dot distribution map, and a good village location map. There are reservations with respect to both of these in the present case study, in part because of the very rapidity of change which is being examined, but both are based upon extensive field investigation as well as reference to published maps of the Survey of Tanzania. The dot map was constructed with the aid of enumeration area mapping for the 1967 census, carried out for enumeration areas of 500 persons and recorded on 1 : 50,000 maps (Thomas, 1972). The villages' map was compiled by the author from published and unpublished maps held in the district and with the aid of District Planning staff and Divisional Officers (FAO/ODG, 1976). Village locations were all mapped with greater location detail in the 1978 census but summary district sheets from the 1978 census were not available to the author when this study was undertaken.

Conclusion

It was not the prime purpose of this paper to examine the implications of the distances moved nor to suggest a use for the measures devised; however, in keeping

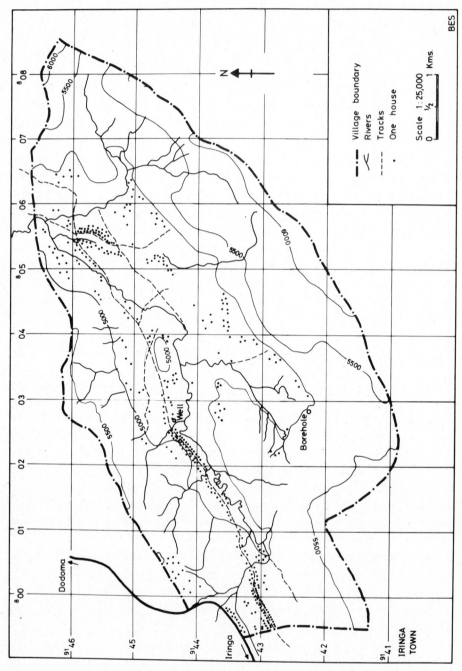

Fig. 10.5 Housing distribution of Kigonzile village

with the predominantly applied nature of much of the geographical – and other – research carried out in Tanzania, some tentative hypotheses are noted as illustrations of potential analyses of practical significance using these measures. They relate to the supposed benefits from villagization and some of the problems which village development faces. Is there a direct relationship between the mean village distance-moved and the savings achieved in providing any specified amenity (e.g. piped water)? Have longer distances moved or substantial moves across ecological boundaries increased the burden of agricultural adjustment (i.e. environmental 'risk') for villagers? And even more speculatively: with greater mean distances, have there been greater problems of social integration? With greater distance variation per village (range of dot-move distances), are there more likely to be resource distribution inequalities? And finally, with greater mean distances has there been a greater tendency to return from the village to the homestead area, and to return permanently? These all have considerable significance for an under-standing of the achievements and problems of the villagization programme. What is already indisputable is that, whereas mean distances moved per person were relatively small, the aggregate movement created by the villagization was immense. Further, there are differences in relocation distances between individ-uals, administrative areas, and ecological areas which may be a factor of considerable importance for the future development of the villages. The impact of the redistribution is sure to be felt for decades to come.

ACKNOWLEDGEMENTS

This is part of the paper delivered at the Khartoum conference. A revised version of the full paper presented at the 1982 meeting has been reproduced as Discussion Paper No. 118 of the School of Development Studies, University of East Anglia. Acknowledgement for assistance with costs of attending the conference are extended to the School and the Overseas Development Group of the University of East Anglia, and to the U.K. Overseas Development Administration and the University of Khartoum.

REFERENCES

Coleman, G., Pain, A. and Belshaw, D. (1978) *Village Viability Assessment in the Framework of Regional Planning in Tanzania*, Norwich Overseas Development Group (for United Nations Development Programme/Food and Agricultural Organization).
Egero, B. (1974) *Migration and Economic Development South of Lake Victoria*, Dar es Salaam Bureau of Resource Assessment and Land Use Planning, Research Paper No. 32.
Egero, B. and Henin, R.A. (eds.) (1973) *The Population of Tanzania: An Analysis of the 1967 Population Census*, Dar es Salaam, BRALUP/Bureau of Statistics, Census Volume 6.
F.A.O./O.D.G. (1976) *Iringa Region Tanzania – Integrated Rural Development Proposals for the Third Five Year Plan, 1976–81*, 2 vols. Norwich, Overseas Development Group (for U.N. Food and Agriculture Organization).

Frank, A.G. (1969) *Latin America: Underdevelopment of Revolution*, New York/London, Monthly Review Press.

Hyden, G. (1980) *Beyond Ujamaa in Tanzania: Underdevelopment and an Uncaptured Peasantry*, Nairobi, Heinemann.

Lele, Uma (1975) *The Design of Rural Development: Lessons from Africa*, Baltimore, The Johns Hopkins University Press (for World Bank).

Maro, P.S. and Mlay, W.F.I. (1982) Population redistribution in Tanzania, in J.I. Clarke and L.A. Kosiński (eds.), *Redistribution of Population in Africa*. London/Nairobi, Heinemann, pp. 176–81.

Mascarenhas, A.C. (1977) *Settlement and Population Redistribution in Dodoma*, Dar es Salaam, Research Paper No. 47, Bureau of Resource Assessment and Land Use Planning.

Mwansasu, B. and Pratt, C. (eds.) (1979) *Towards Socialism in Tanzania*. Dar es Salaam, Tanzania Publishing House.

Tanzania Prime Minister's Office (P.M.O.) (1976) *Vijiji Vilivyoshinda*, Dar es Salaam, Government Printer.

Tanzania (1980) *1978 Population Census, (Preliminary Report)*, Dar es Salaam, Ministry of Finance and Planning.

Tanzania (1983) *1978 Population Census, Volume 8: Population of Tanzania 1978*, Dar es Salaam, Bureau of Statistics.

Thomas, I.D. (1971) Population in the Southern Highlands of Tanzania, in S.H. Ominde (ed.), *Studies in East African Geography and Development*, London/Nairobi, Heinemann, pp. 239–58.

Thomas, I.D. (1972) Census mapping in Tanzania, in S.H. Ominde and C.N. Ejiogu (eds.), *Population Growth and Economic Development in Africa*, London/Nairobi, Heinemann.

Thomas, I.D., Coleman, G. and Murray-Rust H. (1976) *Physical Planning and Resource Evaluation Follow-up Studies, Iringa Region, Tanzania*. 2 vols, Norwich, Overseas Development Group (for U.N. Food and Agriculture Organization).

11 Communal villages and the distribution of the rural population in the People's Republic of Mozambique

Manuel G.M. De Araújo

Introduction

The People's Republic of Mozambique (P.R.M.) had adopted the socialist planning of its economy as the fundamental concern in its development. One of the essential bases for this planning is an exact knowledge of the nature of the population, not only its growth, but also the territorial distribution of population and the existing production relations.

For this purpose, a general population census of the whole country was carried out in August 1980. This showed a national population of 12,130,000 with an annual growth rate of 2.4 per cent for the period 1970–80. The mean demographic density is 14 per sq km, but the density is irregular, varying from 2 to over 30 per sq km. The birth and mortality rates are 45 and 19 per thousand respectively, with an average life expectancy of about 45 years old; more than 50 per cent of the population is less than 20 years old. Zambezia and Nampula, two of the ten provinces of the country, contain 40 per cent of the total population, with an average density of 23.6 and 28.6 respectively. In contrast, the largest province, Niassa, is the one with the smallest population, having an average demographic density of only 2 per sq km. The rural population makes up about 88 per cent of the total and is for the most part widely scattered.

The allocation of the rural population before national independence

Before independence in 1975, the territorial distribution of the Mozambiquan rural population was characterized by very irregular and scattered settlement, closely related to the form and distribution of land occupation and ownership. On the one hand, there were the foreign plantations, the colonial farmers and the large cattle breeders, who owned the most fertile and easily accessible land, having large areas of land taken over from their previous owners, Mozambiquan peasant farmers. On the other hand, one found the Mozambiquan peasant farmers being pushed on to the less fertile inaccessible land, where they occupied only small plots of unirrigated land for family agriculture, which was not very productive.

The areas of colonial agriculture forced the rural population to look for other areas to cultivate, but used a workforce recruited from among the same population, thus acting as areas which attracted population. Consequently, there was a higher population density in the plantations and areas of *colonato* (colonial farmer settlements) agriculture, but this did not reach a level of real concentrated settlement. The migrant population set up their family *machambas* (farms) and their dwellings around the plantations or *colonato*, but in such a way that while each dwelling and small family plot could be considered as a well-defined territorial unit, their distribution was scattered and irregular.

In 1970 the rural population accounted for about 95 per cent of the total population, with only about 5 per cent living in concentrated rural settlements. The major rural densities were in the Angonia and Chimoio plateaus and in the Limpopo, Zambezi and Incomati valleys, which were all areas of colonial agriculture. Taking as an example Gaza province, where the Limpopo agricultural *colonato* is, the data for 1970 show that from a total population of 756,315 inhabitants, only 20,890 were living in concentrated settlements. This 3 per cent of the population was in 8 population agglomerations, including the cities of Xai-Xai and Chokwé.

Throughout the national territory the centres of population concentration were provincial capitals, district capitals or small trading centres mainly inhabited by Portuguese, Indian and Pakistani settlers. These colonial settlements were surrounded by a belt of concentrated Mozambiquan population in residential quarters known as *caniço* (reed suburbs) which are characteristics of many African cities, and in Mozambique were essentially rural areas. In suburbs close to the commercial centres the population was very concentrated, but it became more dispersed the further one got away from the centre. The same happened with the plantations of the settlers, without giving rise to any real demographic concentration.

This scattered population was characterized by residential family groups made up of three or four houses surrounded by family *machambas*. Because of this population distribution, the majority of peasants did not have easy access to facilities such as communications, education and health, which were only in the few centres of population concentration. Moreover, the commercialization of the surplus production from the *machambas* was hindered by this isolation, and the small merchants took advantage of the situation to impose high prices in their shops and a system of unfair trade.

Bases for the transformation of the rural population

One of the first measures taken by the Frelimo party and the government of the People's Republic of Mozambique at Independence on 25 June 1975, was the nationalization of land, in order to do away with the disparities in the countryside, and to allow planning which followed the objectives of the country's economic development. As a result of this measure, the land now belongs to the working people; it cannot be taken over or sold. The land belongs to the man or woman who works it for as long as he or she works it. Pursuant to article 8 of the Constitution of the People's Republic of Mozambique, 'The land, the natural resources both on and under the soil, in the territorial waters of Mozambique, or within its jurisprudence, are deemed as the state's assets. The state is empowered to decide on the use of such resources and their respective destiny.' Thus, the basic conditions have been created which allow the state to plan the use of the land in accordance with the national goals for socio-economic development.

Article 11 of the Constitution of the People's Republic of Mozambique reads: 'The state encourages the peasants and private workers to gather and work in collective farms, whose development the state supports and directs.' Through the creation of state cattle-rearing and agricultural co-operative units, the bases have been created for direct rural socialization. For an efficient rural socialization it is necessary to change the territorial distribution of the rural population, and to create the conditions for the emergence of concentrated areas of population. The Communal Villages thus come to be not only a form of concentrating people but a way of organizing rural economic activity. The cooperative units of production, particularly in agriculture, are tightly linked to the Communal Villages to which they gave rise, or which created them.

The concentration of the rural population into villages of collective production began in the liberated zones during the armed struggle for National Liberation. In 1970 about two-thirds of Cabo Delgado province was already a liberated zone and all the population of this zone lived in Communal Villages; this population represented over 40 per cent of the total population of the province. The same thing happened, though on a smaller scale, in Niassa and Tete provinces. From this experience the eighth session of the Central Committee of Frelimo, held in February 1976, concluded that the Communal Villages 'should constitute the social framework of the future development of the Mozambiquan peasant'. The Communal Villages thus emerge as the means of attaining collective production and the balanced development of mechanization, agricultural specialization and the conservation of natural resources.

The formation of Communal Villages

During the armed struggle for national liberation we could not follow a planned system of land distribution. Thus, sometimes, the villages were built far from communications, fertile land or from other population centres.

Just after independence was gained, the Marrupa seminar was held in Niassa province, where a far-reaching political campaign was launched to organize the rural population into Communal Villages. Since then, new settlements of rural population have sprung up throughout the country, quicker than the growth in capacity for the planning and orientation needed for this new type of rural organization, both in population and economic terms. This situation leads to excessively large population concentrations without a previous or parallel socio-economic organization and sometimes without considering whether the geographical location was suitable, thus aggravating the existing situation, particularly with regard to water supply, soil maintenance and commercialization. For example, in the provinces of Cabo Delgado and Gaza villages have emerged with populations that can exceed 10,000, which spread in a line along the main roads. Here a serious imbalance develops between population and natural resources. This situation has led to the establishment of norms aimed at defining the optimum average demographic size of a village, which was calculated to be between four and five thousand when balanced against the available natural resources.

During this first phase, from independence up to 1978, there was no anterior planning of the geographical location and distribution of villages, which were instead sited according to the wishes of the local people, based on their empirical knowledge of soil fertility, and the existence of various natural resources. After 1979 a more planned process of territorial distribution was begun, and advice on population dimensions was given. At the same time the medium-scale extension of the habitational and agricultural space was begun in the villages in order to establish a balance between population and natural resources. However, this process is not yet complete, and it is still necessary to correct the remaining imbalances which emerged during the first period of Communal Village enlargement, and to plan scientifically all future development.

With regard to the process of formation of Communal Villages, various situations can be distinguished, which can be grouped into four categories.

Type 1: Communal Villages formed as a result of collective production
In this category are all the villages which were constructed in the liberated areas, and others which emerged after national independence as a consequence of peasants being organized into collective production in agricultural cooperatives. Most villages of this type can be found in Cabo Delgado, Niassa and Nampula provinces. In general, this type of Communal Village has better economic and social infrastructures than other types. A concrete example is Manjanga Communal Village in the province of Gaza with a population of about 5,000 inhabitants, which emerged as a result of the agricultural cooperative *Heróis Moçambicanos* which has a considerable commercialized production (over 50 per cent).

Type 2: Communal Villages formed as a result of natural disasters
After independence the peasants occupied the fertile lands of the river valleys, which had been abandoned by the colonial farmers. There, they established their *machambas* and houses maintaining their traditional ways of life with scattered and irregular settlement. From 1976 to 1978, as a result of heavy rains, particularly in the centre and south of the country, there were catastrophic floods which caused enormous material damage and loss of life. The Frelimo Party and the government

carried out a campaign to concentrate the affected population into Communal Villages in higher areas so as to be protected from future floods. This situation has led to the emergence of a large number of Communal Villages in the higher areas along the Limpopo, Incomati, Buzi, Pungue and Zambezi valleys. In this type of village, we first see population concentration, and only later on do we begin to see collective production. Due to this fact these villages are still connected to the old family productive areas which are sometimes located a long distance from the residential areas.

Type 3: Communal Villages resulting from former aldeamentos
The Portuguese colonization constructed various rural settlements (*aldeamentos*) which served, in some cases, as real concentration camps to control the Mozambiquan rural population, trying to keep them from the Frelimo action; in other cases, they were built up to accommodate specifically farmer settlers, and were named *colonatos*. As a result of the defeat of Portuguese colonialism, these *aldeamentos* were recovered, and many of them transformed into Communal Villages where Mozambiquan farmers or agrarian workers were installed to work on agro-industrial schemes or in the state agrarian units. That was what happened, for example, to the existing Communal villages of Chilembe, 1º de Maio, Malhazine and Lionde, all located in Gaza province. Similar cases can be seen in the provinces of Cabo Delgado, Niassa and Tete. A residential area has already been defined and built up for these villages, as well as an already initiated agrarian area; it was only necessary to adjust it to the new situation of collective production.

Type 4: Communal Villages of 'returned people'
With the coming of national independence, thousands of Mozambiquans living as refugees in neighbouring countries, particularly Tanzania and Zambia, returned to their country, settling in Communal Villages which they themselves con-structed, and in which they subsequently started collective production. These villages are found almost exclusively in the provinces of Cabo Delgado, Niassa and Tete.

Territorial distribution and evolution

The clearly-defined policy of land socialization and the role of the Communal Villages, their territorial expansion and impact on the geographical distribution of the rural population have been increasing at a satisfactory pace, although it is still necessary to correct some aspects which lead to imbalance. In the middle of 1978 their distribution was extremely uneven (Table 11.1).

By 1978 the province of Cabo Delgado already had the major part of its rural population organized in a concentrated settlement, which gives a clear idea of the impact of Communal Villages in the transformation of the territorial distri-bution of the rural population: before the beginning of the armed struggle on

Table 11.1. *Territorial distribution of Communal Villages in 1978*

Provinces	Number of Villages	% of total	Number of Inhabitants	% of the provincial population
Cabo Delgado	586	68.3	800,000	88.0
Niassa	40	4.6	72,000	16.0
Nampula	80	9.3	50,000	2.5
Tete	26	3.0	25,000	3.5
Zambezia	13	1.5	10,000	0.5
Sofala	13	1.5	10,000	1.0
Manica	9	1.0	4,500	0.9
Inhambane	5	0.5	2,500	0.3
Gaza	80	9.3	180,000	20.0
Maputo	5	0.5	40,000	4.0

Source: Comissão Nacional des Aldeias Comunais, 1978.
Comissão Nacional do Plano, 1980.

25 September 1964, only 2 per cent of the population in this province lived in concentrated settlements, including the urban population. This province is distinguished from the others because the process was started much earlier, during the armed struggle. In comparative terms this is followed by Gaza province, in the south of the country, which in 1978 had about 20 per cent of its rural population distributed in mass settlements; in 1970 only 3 per cent of the provincial population were living together, including the urban population. For the country as a whole, the group settlement of the rural population had already reached 10 per cent by 1978, whereas in 1970 the group settlement including the urban population had accounted for about 5 per cent.

We do not have enough data for the whole country to analyse completely the evolution between 1978 and 1980, but it is possible to follow the growth of the process through the example of Gaza province, where there has been a study of Communal Villages. In this province, from 1978 to March 1980 the number of Communal Villages increased from 80 to 104, and reached 131 by the middle of 1981 (Fig. 11.1). This means that during this period about 20 Communal Villages were constructed per year. The population living in the Communal Villages in March 1980 was 294,949, which corresponded to about 33 per cent of the total population of this province. Excluding the urban population, the percentage of the rural population living in Communal Villages reached 36 per cent. During this period (1978–80) there was movement of rural population towards the Communal Villages of about 57,500 people per year, which continued until 1981. During the first phase of the increase of Communal Villages in Gaza province, the movement of the rural population was from the Limpopo and Incomati valleys to the highlands, where the villages were constructed. Next, peasants from the surrounding dry ground joined them.

Another province where movement of rural population towards Communal Villages was significant in 1979 and 1980 was Nampula, in the north of the country. In this province the concentrated rural population doubled between 1978

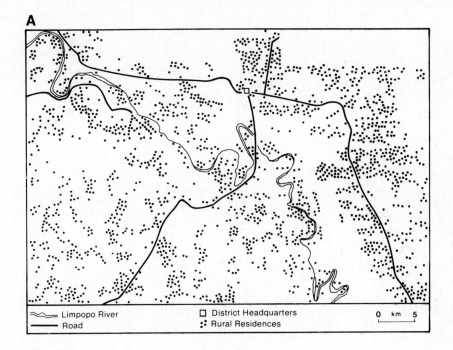

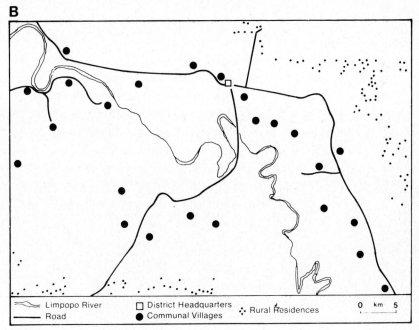

Fig. 11.1 Rural settlement in a section of the Limpopo valley, Gaza Province, Mozambique: A. Before 1975; B. In 1981

Table 11.2. *Population evolution in some Communal Villages of Gaza province during 1980–82*

Communal Village	Population		Growth
	1980	1982	
Julius Nyerere	9,741	20,015	10,274
3 de Fevereiro	5,311	12,976	7,665
Mao Tse Tung	3,558	6,293	2,735
Luis Carlos Prestes	5,743	8,337	2,594
Agostinho Neto	3,380	5,850	2,470
Marien N'Gouabi	10,300	19,050	8,750
A Vox da Frelimo	3,820	3,754	− 66
Fidel Castro	2,939	3,008	69
Coco-Missava	6,070	6,076	6
Guemelane	3,694	3,790	96
1º de Maio	10,550	14,000	3,450
Malhazine	3,899	4,356	457

Source: Comissão provincial das Aldeias Comunais (1980), *Mapa Estatistico do Distrito de Gaza*, Xai-Xai. Direcção Nacional de Habitacao (1982), *Levantamento das Aldeias Comunais*, Maputo.

and 1980, when it was approximately 10 per cent of the total population of the province.

The number of inhabitants varies from village to village. From the studies carried out, it appears that the normal number of inhabitants varies from 4,000 to 5,000. However, there are still villages with as many as 20,000 people, as in the case of the Communal Villages of Marien N'Gouabi and Julius Nyerere in Gaza province (Table 11.2). There are also others which still have not reached a population of 1,000.

The large size of some villages causes problems with regard to the distribution and rational utilization of land, the conservation of natural resources and the supply networks. Therefore, at the 1st National Meeting of Communal Villages, held in 1981, the ideal village was defined as one with four quarters, each of 250 families. The implementation of this measure has, however, faced some difficulties, because the movement of the scattered rural population towards the existing villages is not properly controlled. Thus, in many cases the Communal Villages still have very clearly accentuated demographic growth. A clear example can be seen at Machua Communal Village in Gaza province, which had 1,000 inhabitants in 1980 and about 10,000 in April 1982.

Just as the distribution among provinces presents quite a pronounced irregularity (Table 11.1), the intra-provincial distribution also presents the same irregularity from district to district, although there are no remarkable differences. Considering the situation of Gaza province, Table 11.3 does not mention Chicualacuala district because of the lack of recent data needed to be able to make a

Table 11.3. *Territorial distribution of Communal Villages in Gaza province, 1982*

District	Number of Command Villages	% of total	Population	% of total	Average of inhabitants/Village
Xai-Xai	24	18.9	82,692	24.3	3,445
Bilene	11	8.7	33,267	9.8	3,024
Chibuto	22	17.3	68,788	20.2	3,126
Manjacaze	14	11.0	26,393	7.8	1,885
Guijá	9	7.1	27,088	8.0	3,009
Massingir	25	19.7	23,967	7.0	958
Chokwé	22	17.3	77,671	22.9	3,530
Total	127	100.0	339,866	100.0	2,676

Source: Comissão Provincial das Aldeias Comunais (1982), *Relação das Aldeias Comunais existentes a nível da Província de Gaza com os respectivos números de habitantes,* Província de Gaza.

comparison, but this is the district where the movement of concentration away from rural population is in an embryonic stage. The districts situated along the valley of the Limpopo (Xai-Xai, Chibuto, Massingir and Chokwé) are the ones with a larger number of Communal Villages (Fig. 11.1), which also correspond to larger populations, except in the case of Massingir district which has the most villages but the least inhabitants.

Some actual problems and prospects of solution

There is an emergence of new rural settlements all over the territory of the People's Republic of Mozambique, where the population is essentially scattered. Besides the impact upon the territorial distribution of the rural population and the problems occurring there, it is also influencing many aspects of the socio-economic organization, causing new situations which are not always easy to resolve.

One of the problems which has arisen is related to the geographic location of the villages. During the first phase of development of the new type of settlement, the location was spontaneous, resulting from the peasants' empirical knowledge. The movement for the creation of Communal Villages could not be accompanied by scientific studies of physical and economic geography, as there were insufficient cadres available. That is why some villages are settled in unsuitable areas (on a slope, for example), without any articulation with road networks and with urban centres. Attempts were made to correct the situation during the second phase of this process through the relocation of some villages in the most critical situations and the creation of a trading and supplying system.

There was a pronounced imbalance between the quantity of population grouped together in villages and the available natural resources (land, water and forests), resulting in a shortage of arable land, water and firewood near some villages. Villages are frequently found where the average distance between residence and farm is more than 5 km and where the nearest source of water is more than 3 km away. Besides the relocation of some villages, other measures were taken to minimize these problems, by supplying pure water, creating satellite districts, giving greater incentive to agrarian cooperatives, reorganizing family properties and introducing activities other than agrarian production.

The People's Republic of Mozambique defined Communal Villages as the backbone of the development of productive forces in the countryside, based on socialist relations of production. Thus, considerable attention has been paid to the resolution of problems, and to providing long- and medium-term strategies for their development. The guidelines defined in the period 1978–80 and the guidance outlined during the 1st National Meeting of Communal Villages held in 1981 are bearing first results in the newer villages. Included in the guidance are the following:

> 'Communal Villages must be settled or re-settled on surfaces and require natural resources for the development of the production base. The spatial organization of the settlement of the people will therefore be a result of these factors.'
> 'A development programme for the Communal Villages will not be carried out without the existence of the possibility of investing immediately on limited principal factors. These investments imply, in general, studies, means and financing on the part of the state.'
> 'Production in the Communal Village must be developed on the grounds of a cooperative organization integrating the different types of economic unities of cooperatives.'

Communal Villages constitute an integral part of the socialization of the countryside, a strategy considered fundamental for victory over under-development in the People's Republic of Mozambique. The Prospective Indicative Plan for the decade 1981–90 refers to this task, mentioning that it will imply 'a movement of millions of peasants and rural workers'. The plan for the socialization of the countryside means 'to alter completely the class forces relations in the countryside, where the socialist sector will be dominant and determinant'. Therefore, the growth of a kind of concentrated settlement is not merely a movement of the population, but above all a territorial redistribution of the rural population regarding the creation of new relations of production in the countryside.

REFERENCES

Costiução da República Popular de Moçambique (1975), Maputo.
Comissão Nacional das Aldeias Comunais (1978) *O Processo de Desenvolvimento das Aldeias Comunais. Análise da Situação Propostas de Actuação*, Maputo (Mimeo).
Comissão Nacional do Plano (1980) *Informação Estatistica*, No. 1, Maputo.
Miro, C. and Potter, J.E. (eds.) (1980) *Population Policy: Research Priorities in the Developing World*, London, Frances Pinter.
Murel, V.N. (1970) Indicators characterizing systems of rural settlement, *Soviet Geography*, 11, 166–73.

12 A century of development measures and population redistribution along the Upper Zambezi

Adrian P. Wood

Over the last one hundred years a major change has occurred in the distribution of population on the Upper Zambezi flood plain and its margins (Fig. 12.1), involving a decline in the importance of flood-plain dwelling and a concentration of settlement along the margin of the plain. The process has been stimulated by economic, ecological, social and political factors and has proceeded in a series of surges in response to particular combinations of these influences. This paper focuses on the impact upon population redistribution of development measures introduced by the pre-colonial, colonial and independent administrations in that area.

The ecological basis of flood-plain settlement

The Upper Zambezi flood plain is a shallow depression some 30 km wide and almost 200 km long, cut into the gently undulating surface of the Kalahari (Barotse) sands which cover most of the Western Province of Zambia. The flood plain is bounded on the eastern side by a 50 m escarpment, but on the west the escarpment is more gentle and only 20 m high. The predominantly grassland flood plain stands out in contrast to the surrounding uplands which are forested. In the higher areas on the plain some trees are found, but these are now restricted to a few localities, although formerly they were more common.

The plain and its margins may be divided into a number of land facets (Peters, 1960: 30–1). The central part of the plain, known as *bulozi*, is the lowest-lying area. It is dominated by the present channel of the Zambezi river and by former channels now marked by numerous lagoons, *mulapo*. Although generally low-lying there are in *bulozi* small mounds which stand up to 6–7 m above the general level of the terrain. Some of these *mazulu* (sing. *lizulu*) are former levees, but the origin of others is unclear although some are reported to be former termite mounds (Gluckman, 1968: 6). The *bulozi* section of the plain varies in width from 4 to 15 km. In the area studied it was the most extensive land facet (Fig. 12.1). Bounding *bulozi* is the *saana*, a slightly higher area. As in *bulozi*, there are some *mazulu* within this zone. There is also, in many localities, a generally higher area of the *saana* with a number of *mazulu* parallel to the margin of the plain and close to the *saana's* boundary. Between the *saana* and the plain margin there is a lower, poorly-drained

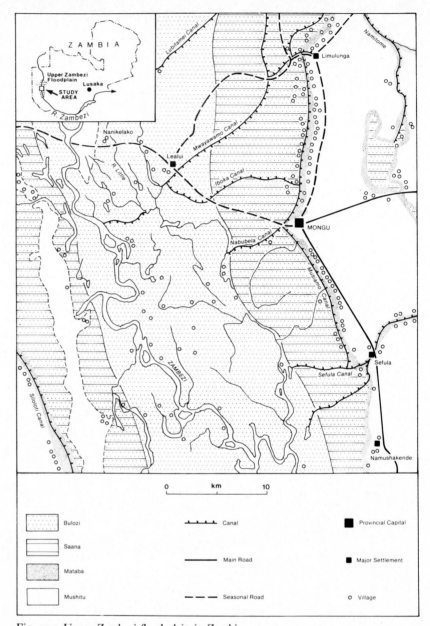

Fig. 12.1 Upper Zambezi flood plain in Zambia

area, although not as low as *bulozi*. This area, known as the *mataba*, is often called the seepage zone because its waterlogged condition is primarily a result of the continual seepage of water out of the Kalahari sands at the foot of the escarpment. Waterlogging is also caused by the annual flood and the limited number of gaps in the *saana* which allow water from this area to drain into the Zambezi. The *mataba* extends from the *saana* to the foot of the escarpment, an area known as the *mukulo* or edge of the plain. The scarp and the Kalahari sand 'uplands' are known as the *mushitu* or forest.

The ecology and economy of the area are dominated by the annual flood. Although the rainy season in this area usually extends from late October or early November to April, the flood does not start to rise until the end of December and reaches its peak in late March, or the first week of April (Gluckman, 1968: 4; Verboom and Brunt, 1970: 18). At that time the plain is almost completely covered with only a few mounds in *bulozi* and some of the higher areas in the *saana* above the flood. The flood recedes slowly. The plain is generally not dry enough to travel across on foot until late July, and parts may remain waterlogged or marshy until September or October.

Although a flood-plain area, the soils of the Upper Zambezi plain are not particularly rich or suitable for agriculture. The plain is dominated by the Kalahari sands, which form the plain *litongo* soils, and in only a few localities are clay or loam soils found. The major areas of good agricultural soils are the *mazulu* and the higher areas in the *saana* which have loamy soils; these are the most highly prized sites for cultivation, but they are strictly limited in number. The next most important sites for cultivation are depressions in the plain (*sitapa*, pl. *litapa*), which have particularly rich soils, renewed each year by silt deposited during the flood. Many of the *litapa* are found in old watercourses and their soils have a particularly high clay content. Another area where soils can be suitable for cultivation is in the *mataba* zone where a peat soil, *sishanjo* (pl. *lishanjo*), occurs, but it is naturally waterlogged and drainage must be practised to allow cultivation. At the forest edge of this soil there is a transition zone with moist *litongo* and dry *litongo* soils. The former includes some *sishanjo* humus and, with the water table low enough to prevent waterlogging but high enough to allow all-year-round cultivation, it is a particularly valuable soil. Unfortunately it occurs in a very narrow strip and the humus content rapidly declines away from the *sishanjo*. Above these *litongo* soils are the Kalahari sands, with little humus, on which cultivation is totally dependent upon rainfall. Gardens in this forested area are called *litema* (pl. *matema*) (Peters, 1960: 15–26).

Cultivation of these different soils involves careful adjustment of crop and farming practice to the impact of the flood and rainfall upon each type of garden. *Litapa* gardens are cultivated first after the decline of the flood; plant growth here relies on the moisture of the flood from mid-August, when sowing takes place, until late October, when the first rain occurs. Cultivation of these gardens involves considerable risks and despite the use of early-maturing flint varieties of maize, farmers lose their harvest from these gardens in many years (Peters, 1960: 22–4; MacLean, 1965: 6). This may be caused by a late fall of the preceding flood which delays cultivation or an early rise of the following flood, these depressions being the first parts of the plain to become flooded. Occasionally the late arrival of the rains after the water table has fallen below the rooting zone of these crops will also cause crop failure.

The *mazulu* (mound) gardens generally give a more reliable harvest, although early and particularly high floods can cause serious crop losses. These gardens are also used for the cultivation of maize, but in the past a variety of sorghum, *mumanan*, was grown which would ripen despite having its lower stem covered by the flood (Hermitte, 1973: 31). Since these gardens receive little benefit from flood silt they are usually manured prior to cultivation, especially in the *saana* area where the *mazulu* soils generally contain more sand. Planting has to await the onset of the rains, as the soil moisture is insufficient to carry seedlings through October, the hottest time of the year.

One other type of garden used in the plain is the *mukomena* (pl. *mikomena*), which is made on the plains' *litongo* soils by digging a trench around a small rectangular bed and piling the dug soil on top of the bed. A raised area is thus created with some extra concentration of humus from the grass surface layer of the trench. *Mikomena* gardens are therefore a little above the general surface of the plain and so allow crops, usually sweet potatoes and in recent years a newly-introduced type of cassava, *kapumba*, a few weeks longer growth prior to flooding (Peters, 1960: 17–20).

These three types of garden are found both in *bulozi* and in the *saana*, but the gardens at the edge of the plain are considerably different. In the peat *lishanjo* soils, gardens require the digging of a network of drainage channels. Provided these link up to a clear canal through to the main Zambezi channel, the water table in these areas can be lowered rapidly once the flood recedes. This is particularly important to provide a sufficiently long growing season prior to next waterlogging, which in the first instance is caused by the heavy rains rather than the rising flood. The *lishanjo* gardens can be used for a variety of crops. Traditionally they were used for the cultivation of maize and sweet potatoes, but now vegetables for sale in Mongu town are increasingly important, while a variety of cassava, *kapumba*, is also grown in these gardens. The moist *litongo* gardens can grow a wider range of crops than the dry *litongo* and *matema* gardens. Fruit trees, primarily the mango, now occupy a considerable proportion of this land, but maize, vegetables and cucurbits are also grown, and cassava in recent years. The dry *litongo* and the *matema* gardens were traditionally used for the cultivation of bulrush millet, one of the few crops to grow successfully in these heavily-leached sands with few nutrients. Today these gardens are increasingly dominated by cassava (Peters, 1960: 20–6; MacLean, 1965: iv–v).

Early population patterns and movements

The present inhabitants of the Upper Zambezi flood plain, the Lozi, are thought to have entered the area from the north during the seventeenth century. Although they were by that time grassland cultivators, their economy was dominated traditionally by hunting and gathering, fishing and herding, activities which provided the bulk of the food. The Lozi settled on the plain partly because of its defensive advantages and partly because of its good grazing and cultivation sites

(Hermitte, 1973: 19 and 22; van Horn, 1977: 144–5; Gluckman, 1968: 18–20). Their settlement was originally concentrated on *mazulu* in *bulozi* and the *saana*, but as the population grew, the higher areas in the *saana* close to the *mataba* were increasingly settled. With the annual flood, permanent settlement on the plain is not possible except on the few mounds which remain above the flood. Hence from the earliest days of their settlement in this area the majority of the Lozi have practised seasonal transhumance moving during the height of the flood either to higher *mazulu* in *bulozi* and the *saana* or to the uplands. The number of people involved in this movement has grown as the population has expanded and lower sites in the plain have been settled. Also, as the Lozi have acquired more cattle, the shortage of flood-season grazing in the plain has become more acute and an increasing number of people have been forced to move into the uplands for the duration of the flood.

Pre-colonial interest in the flood plain margins

Interest in the margins of the plain dates back to the eighteenth century when the Lozi, apparently for security reasons, defeated the Kwangwa in this area and forced these cultivators, whose drainage skills had allowed them to cultivate the *lishanjo* soils, to retreat to the valleys in the uplands. However, the Lozi themselves appear not to have taken any interest in these soils at that time, as in the 1830s they allowed an immigrant group from Angola, the Mbunda, to settle along the *mukulo*. Although these immigrants brought with them skills of forest cultivation, and suitable crops such as bulrush millet and a variety of cassava, *nalumino*, there is no evidence of any Lozi settlement or use of land on the forest side of the *mataba* prior to the 1860s (Hermitte, 1973: 40 and 53–4; Peters, 1960: 42; Gluckman, 1968: 37–8).

From the early 1840s until 1863 the Lozi were subjugated by the Kololo, a warrior people from the south. During this time some Lozi groups retreated to the north where, during 20 or more years in the forest, they learnt the skills of forest gardening. On their return some of the younger members of these groups had no knowledge of flood-plain cultivation and so settled at the *mukulo*, while others, now realizing the value of forest gardens, made claims for such land from the *Litunga* (the Lozi chief). The need to use forest land for grazing during the flood also increased at this time as the cattle population had grown considerably, the Kololo having brought considerable herds with them (Hermitte, 1973: 174; Mainga, 1973: chapter 4).

The first major shift of population from the flood plain towards the margin occurred during the reign of Lewanika, who was *Litunga* from 1878 to 1916. Prior to his reign the Lozi had suffered increasing food supply problems, caused in part by civil strife, but also by difficult flood conditions (Hermitte, 1973: 114 and 195). Population growth was also probably a contributory factor as lower *mazulu* and *litapa* gardens, both more prone to flooding, had been brought into cultivation to support them. At the same time population pressure had considerably reduced the *lechwe* herds which were hunted, and caused a scarcity of various foods obtained by gathering. Lewanika, realizing these pressures, encouraged a number of innovations in cultivation, which caused agriculture to grow in importance relative to other sources of subsistence (Meister, n.d.: 6). The most important innovation was the adoption by the Lozi of the Kwangwa's drainage technology to exploit the *lishanjo* soils. Their use was facilitated, and to a considerable extent dependent upon, the expansion of the canal network in the plain (Coillard, 1897: 515 and 559). In particular the construction of canals, such as the Sefula one which linked the *mataba* main drainage canal, the *Musiamo*, to the main Zambezi channel, was crucial in making it worthwhile for households or villages to dig trenches and subsidiary canals to drain areas of *sishanjo* soil.

The construction of canals was facilitated partly by the centralized nature of the Lozi state and in particular by the *makolo* institution of cooperative effort which, originally developed for use in warfare, was extended to civil works during Lewanika's reign. The construction of the major drainage canals was also facilitated by the slave population which the Lozi had acquired through raiding. By 1900, between one-third and one-half of the flood-plain population were slaves, who were used not only in public works but also by the households to whom they belonged, in order to intensify agricultural production in the face of the growing land shortage on the plain, which was in part caused by their numbers. As a result, despite the high labour input in digging the tributary drainage canals at one- or two-metre intervals, the *lishanjo* soils along the plain margin were rapidly brought into use (Hermitte, 1973: 37 and 214; Mainga, 1973: 168).

At the same time, the Lozi also began to grow cassava both as a subsidiary crop in existing flood-plain gardens and as a main crop in newly-established forest gardens. The ability of this crop to grow on poor sandy soils and to produce a reliable harvest which could be held in store in the ground for up to a year made this crop particularly attractive during the 1880s, when locust damage made it difficult to ensure adequate food supplies for the growing population from traditional crops (Hermitte, 1973: 196; Mainga, 1973: 154–6; Clarence-Smith, in press).

Colonial developments and agriculture

The British South Africa Company penetrated the north-western part of Zambia in the 1890s. It established its rule over Barotseland in 1890 through the Lochner Concession. The company, realizing quite soon after that there were few, if any, economically viable mineral resources in the area, sought to obtain from this territory labour for use in the mines in other areas under its control, especially Rhodesia (van Horn, 1977: 149). This was achieved primarily through an agreement with Lewanika whereby in return for freeing slaves – who would then be able to engage in labour migration – the company paid the *Litunga* and his councillors an annual sum (Hermitte, 1973: 230–1) from the proceeds of a tax, implemented as part of the agreement, to stimulate labour migration. The agreement, which was implemented in 1906, produced far-reaching changes in Lozi agriculture and society (Gluckman, 1943: 83).

The most immediate consequence of this agreement was the abandonment of the flood plain by the slaves, the Lozi only being prepared to grant land to freedom in the forest where the supply of land was plentiful (van Horn, 1977: 152). Decline in the labour supply to the Lozi households for agricultural work was aggravated by the growing involvement of the Lozi themselves in labour migration after 1906. Although many flood-plain households had considerable numbers of cattle which allowed the tax to be paid from cattle sales (N.A., K.D.E. 8/1/7, 8/1/4), men from poorer households and dependent males of wealthier households had to engage in labour migration. This was undertaken not only to earn sufficient to pay the tax but also to allow the purchase of imported commodities, which were increasingly demanded as the lower strata of Lozi society realized that their acquisition was not for the rich alone (Hermitte, 1973: 213).

The impact of this loss of labour upon agriculture varied, depending upon the labour needs of the different gardens and the combination of gardens worked by one household. Those households with widely scattered gardens requiring much time to be spent in travel and with extensive *lishanjo* gardens which needed considerable labour inputs were particularly severely hit by the freeing of the slaves and labour migration. In particular, the *lishanjo* gardens, with their need for annual repairs to the drainage trenches, begn to fall out of use. Now these were worked by the Lozi themselves rather than their slaves, the poor returns to labour which they provided were recognized, and some households decided to concentrate instead on the *matema* gardens where less labour was needed. Flood-plain agriculture was less severely affected because the work there was predominantly carried out by women. However, despite this and the introduction of the plough, some flood-plain gardens are reported to have fallen out of use because of labour shortage (ibid: 275–6 and 299). The gardens of the *indunas* (traditional area leaders) and of the *Litunga*, which had been worked by slaves, were particularly seriously affected.

The impact of labour migration upon agriculture increased after 1915 when bovine pleuropneumonia hit the Lozi herd, causing a two-thirds reduction in its number (N.A., K.D.E. 8/1/7). The colonial regulations concerning this disease prevented the sale of Barotse cattle outside the region from 1915 until 1940, thus eliminating an important source of cash for paying tax. Consequently, an increasing number of Lozi took part in labour migration, with up to 45 per cent of the adult males absent from their village at one time. Shortage of labour and to a lesser extent oxen caused a growing number of plain and *lishanjo* gardens to remain idle. Labour supply problems for the *matema* gardens were not so great, an influx of Mawiko forest cultivators from Angola providing a cheap source of labour during the 1920s and 1930s (Hermitte, 1973: 273 and 310; Peters, 1960: 42).

The freeing of slaves and the increased labour migration also affected flood conditions and hence, indirectly, agricultural production and settlement. The agreement abolishing slavery and instituting taxation also reduced the obligations of the population to the *Litunga*. Previously, people had been called upon frequently to provide *corvée* labour for public works, especially for canal construction and maintenance. From 1906 this was limited to 12 days per year, and in 1924, following the implementation of direct British rule that year, all labour obligations were abolished (Gluckman, 1943: 83). The result was a complete halt to canal construction and an almost complete end to maintenance. This resulted in poorer drainage of the flood plain, as the canals became blocked by weed growth and silt. The consequences were a slow but continual worsening of the annual flood. During the 1930s this does not seem to have caused a great deal of difficulty, probably because the lower *mazulu* and *litana* gardens had already been abandoned due to the reduced labour supply; but from the late 1930s floods are reported to have become progressively worse, leading to the abandonment of most *litapa* gardens, poorer yields on the *mazulu* and in *mikomena* gardens, and a general disenchantment with flood-plain agriculture by the Lozi. This resulted in increased labour migration during the 1940s which further reduced flood-plain agriculture, the population becoming increasingly dependent on remittances (MacLean, 1965: ii; Hermitte, 1973: 273; Gluckman, 1968: xi–xii). The *lishanjo* gardens were also particularly severely affected by the earlier rise of the flood and its slower decline. As the canals linking the north–south drainage canal through the *lishanjo* to the main Zambezi channel became blocked, the impact upon the water table of constructing subsidiary canals to drain a particular plot was greatly reduced. Hence these gardens almost all fell out of use, except near urban centres where vegetables were grown (Peters, 1960: 40–2).

A number of other influences during the colonial period encouraged flood-plain-based households to place increasing emphasis upon *matema* gardens and to relocate their main home from the *saana* or *bulozi* to the *mukulo*. In the early 1930s locust plagues affected many areas in the region. Fearing famine, the colonial administration, through the *Litunga* Yeta III, encouraged every household to grow cassava, especially the *nalumino* variety for which plentiful forest land was available. As this crop will not withstand waterlogged conditions, this was effectively a request for each household to have a *matema* garden. Further encouragement to settlement at the *mukulo* came in the late 1940s when a brick road was built there to replace the road along the *saana* ridge established by the missionaries and traders in the 1920s. Wells were also constructed along the *mukulo* and considerable and successful efforts were made by District Officers in the 1950s to encourage *saana* based villages to move to the dry *mukulo* rather than remain at locations which were seasonally waterlogged and regarded as unhealthy; the *Litunga* had set an example in the mid 1930s when he moved his flood-season capital from the *saana* ridge to the *mushitu* at Limulunga.

The introduction of the plough may also have had an impact upon flood-plain agriculture. It was a rather disappointing innovation, for although allowing more areas in the flood plain to be cultivated, these were inevitably areas more prone to flooding, at a time when the floods were becoming worse. Use of the plough may have caused a decline in the height of the *mazulu*, cultivation in this manner tending to spread the soil outward from these mounds and smooth their sides. Without slave labour to raise the mounds, and with increased flooding encouraging erosion many farmers report that their *mazulu* have become lower in recent decades.

Finally, some colonial development measures may be cited for their direct and indirect encouragement to movements from the flood plain. In 1947 the Barotseland Development Centre was established at Namushakende on the margin of the plain. The land used by this centre for its experiments was the *lishanjo* and the moist and dry *litongo* soils, confirming the government's lack of interest in the flood plain. Further, attempts to established 'improved' farmers in Barotseland concentrated on similar soils in the valleys in the uplands and on the plain margin (N.R.G., 1955: 5). Finally, although the colonial government did clear and reconstruct a number of canals between 1948 and 1960, these were mainly, like the Namitome canal, to drain the *lishanjo* soils of the valleys in the forest. Without improvement of the flood-plain canals, this more rapid flow of water from the upland areas led to earlier flooding at the edges of the main flood plain and increased losses in *litapa* and *lishanjo* gardens there.

Post-colonial settlement at the margin

Since independence in 1964, the rate of population movement to the margin has increased. Competition for land in this zone is intense and the plain margin from Limulunga to Namushakende is virtually one continual village. Over half the present villages along the *mukulo* moved from the flood plain within living memory, the majority of these coming from the *saana*. Although the bulk of people interviewed concerning the decision to move to the edge identified the worsening flood situation as the major stimulus, other social and economic factors have impinged on this decision.

Flood records of Mongu harbour for the 1970s show that there has been a general worsening of the flood conditions, the water is rising earlier, reaching greater heights and declining more slowly. The average height of the flood in the late 1970s was 30cm above that in the early 1970s. Although rainfall is one influence, this trend is probably the result of a reduction in the canal maintenance programme, the labour force having been reduced by over 50 per cent in 1970 so that today only 10 per cent of the total canal network is maintained. Given the integrated nature of this drainage system, especially the role of link canals to the main Zambezi, the limited and patchy maintenance which is carried out today is virtually useless for controlling the flood.

Worsening floods have affected the gardens of an increasing number of flood-plain households, causing higher crop losses and forcing such communities to rely increasingly on other gardens and sources of income. Some households, although still using their flood-plain gardens, no longer regard them as most important and concentrate attention increasingly on fishing, herding and the cultivation of more reliable *matema* gardens. Floods have also affected the cattle population. The longer absence which is required from the plain has caused increased cattle mortality during the flood season, as the loss of condition while on the upland grazing makes the animals more susceptible to disease (Abrahams, in press). Some households have lost so many cattle that they can find sufficient flood-plain grazing near the *mukulo* and no longer trek into *bulozi* during the non-flood season.

The flood conditions of recent decades have also meant that greater damage is suffered by property left in the plain. Huts need considerable repairs each year and frequent rebuilding, a particularly difficult and costly task now in the plain where wood is scarce. Increasingly, households wish to move all their possessions to the *mukulo* during the flood season, a lengthy and laborious operation given the more numerous possessions these days and the changing population structure of flood-plain villages.

Since independence, labour migration from Western Province (formerly Barotseland) has changed radically. Prior to 1965, most migrants were recruited by the Witwatersrand Native Labour Association (W.E.N.E.L.A.). They went to South Africa on two year contracts and had a portion of their earnings remitted to Mongu for use by their families and dependents. In 1965 W.E.N.E.L.A.'s operations were closed by the Zambian government and labour migration to Rhodesia and South Africa banned. Migrants from Western Province now have to compete in the Zambian labour market which has become increasingly competitive since 1970 as the growth of urban employment has slowed (Wood, 1982: 119). The competitive nature of the labour market together with changing values concerning urban residence, now colonial restrictions have been removed, have led to longer absence of labour migrants. Although it is now common for the nuclear family to leave with the migrant, the extended family of older and younger relatives remains. Remittances are fewer and smaller these days as urban–rural ties decline and responsibilities other than to parents are neglected. More young adult males are now absent from flood-plain villages, probably in response to the declining fortunes of agriculture and cattle rearing, and their growing aspirations, especially since independence. Hence many villages have no young adult males, their populations being predominantly female, with many children and a number of old people.

These changes in the structure of the flood-plain population have made life on the plain more difficult. Residence there requires mobility, primarily to practise the seasonal transhumance, but also for day-to-day activities. This involves considerable walking and the use of canoes which are the means by which *mazulu* are evacuated as the flood rises. Paddling a canoe is a skill usually reserved for men and so a considerable burden falls upon a few active adult males, particularly when numerous people and possessions, including furniture belonging to a whole village, must be taken to the *mukulo* during the flood. In some villages this problem, rather than flood damage to crops, has been crucial in stimulating permanent relocation to the plain margin.

Declining remittances from labour migrants combined with worsening floods have caused greater insecurity of income for flood-plain dwellers. Where no cattle are owned and fishing is not practised, there is little advantage remaining in the plain. What is needed by these people, many of whom are divorced or widowed women, is a secure income and the only garden to offer this is the *matema*. Relocation to *mukulo* to develop these gardens is also encouraged by the subsidiary sources of income possible there, especially near the urban centres. Considerable expansion of government employment since independence has brought more money into the economy of the urban settlements the *mukulo*. Much is used for local purchases, producing a multiplier effect in the urban-fringe economy. Thus sales of firewood, vegetables and local beers and spirits are important sources of income to many households along the *mukulo*.

Changing values in recent decades have also encouraged settlement at the *mukulo*. Labour migrants have for many decades returned to the flood plain and questioned the practice of transhumance and the effort involved in building a temporary flood-season dwelling. As household possessions have grown in number and become more bulky, transhumance has become more difficult. Hence returning migrants, and especially those retiring after many years in urban employment, increasingly regard it as wasteful to construct a home in the plain. They would rather work their flood-plain gardens, if it is worthwhile, using a temporary shelter there and have the security of a permanent home at the *mukulo* which will not require major repair every year and where they can safety store possessions accumulated when in town.

Attitudes to education have also changed since independence. In colonial days education was for a minority of children. It was often not begun until the age of 10 or over. The schools in Barotseland were mostly mission-run and these were adapted to the local pattern of transhumance, flood-plain schools having two sets of buildings, one in the plain and one at the *mukulo* or at the top of the scarp in the forest. Since independence all primary schools have been taken over by the government. Some years of schooling are now the right of every child and entry is at the age of 7. With worsening floods, maintenance costs of flood-plain schools have become exorbitant, and all but two of the six which formerly existed in the parts of the flood plain studied have been closed and are being replaced by ones at the *mukulo*. As schooling is regarded as very important by almost all parents, every effort is made to facilitate children's attendance. With the younger age of entry and the greater distances to schools in the plain, the only way in which some plain-dwelling families can ensure that their children receive education is by letting them stay at the flood-plain margin. In the past, family ties would have made it possible for a child to stay with relatives, and the establishment of a permanent home at the *mukulo* would not have been necessary. However, with the growing number of children in a household, now that infant mortality is lower, and the greater proportion of children attending school, relatives are averse or unable to offer such help, so flood-plain families must build their own dwellings at the *mukulo* to facilitate schooling.

Conclusion

The history of the Upper Zambezi flood plain and its margins during the last hundred years exemplifies the way in which development measures may directly and indirectly influence population distribution. The interest of the flood-plain-dwelling Lozi in gardens at the edge of the plain was first stimulated by government intervention when Lewanika sought to increase food production and reduce the risk of famine by encouraging the cultivation of cassava in forest gardens and the expansion of cultivation in the waterlogged *mataba* zone. The pre-colonial Lozi state's expansion of its slave population and use of military forms of organization for canal construction facilitated the drainage and cultivation of peat soil gardens in the *mataba* at the edge of the plain.

Agriculture and settlement in the flood plain was first undermined by the abolition of slavery and *corvée* labour by the colonial government and the consequent decline in canal maintenance and worsening of flood conditions. Freeing the slaves and the encouragement of labour migration through the introduction of taxation led to some labour problems in the flood plain which, combined with colonial encouragement of cassava cultivation to reduce locust damage, led to a further expansion of forest cultivation. The banning of labour migration to South Africa and the removal of colonial restrictions on the urban residence of labour migrants following independence has led to a change in the structure of flood-plain communities with a longer and perhaps permanent absence of economically-active males. This has caused a decline in remittances, which has forced female-dominated communities relying solely upon the uncertain flood-plain agriculture to abandon the plain in search of a more secure income from forest gardens to supplement their agricultural income through beer-brewing and other petty trades which can be carried out in the urban fringe economy along the edge of the plain. These changes in the structure of flood-plain communities have also led to problems in maintaining adequate mobility for flood plain residence especially during the flood season. The provision of services along the edge of the plain since late colonial times and the withdrawal of services from the plain since independence have given further cause for households to abandon the plain.

With the continuing provision of services along the edge of the plain and the worsening of flood conditions as the canal maintenance brigades remain understaffed, there is little prospect of a reversal of the abandonment of the flood plain. Increased accumulation of possessions will reinforce the desire for the end of transhumance and the establishment of permanent homes at the edge of the plain where flood damage does not occur. The gardens in the plain with the richest soils in this area will continue to fall out of use while the poor sandy forest gardens on which cassava is the main crop will grow in importance.

ACKNOWLEDGEMENTS

The research for this paper was carried out with financial support from the University of Zambia. The author is particularly grateful to Mr E. Beele, a University of Zambia student research assistant who accompanied him during the ten weeks of fieldwork. Mr M. Kamengo, the University's resident tutor in Mongu, kindly provided accommodation during part of the fieldwork and helped to make arrangements for visits to various parts of the study area.

REFERENCES

Abrahams, K.C. (in press) The cattle industry of Western Province, in A.P. Wood (ed.), *Western Province Handbook*. Handbook No. 5, Lusaka, Zambia.

Clarence-Smith, G. (in press) Climatic variations and natural disasters in Bulozi, 1847–1907, in A.P. Wood (ed.), *Western Province Handbook*, Handbook No. 5, Lusaka, Zambia.

Coillard, F. (1897) *On the Threshold of Central Africa*, London, Hodder and Stoughton.

Gluckman, M. (1943) *Essays on Lozi Land and Royal Property*, Rhodes–Livingstone Papers, No. 10. Livingstone, Rhodes–Livingstone Institute.

Gluckman, M. (1968) *Economy of the Central Barotse Plain*, Rhodes–Livingstone Papers, No. 7, Second Impression, Lusaka, Rhodes–Livingstone Institute.

Hermitte, E.L. (1973) *An Economic History of Barotseland*, Ph.D. thesis, North-Western University.

MacLean, H.A.M. (1965) *An Agricultural Stocktaking of Barotseland*, Lusaka, Government Printer.

Mainga, M. (1973) *Bulozi under the Luyana Kings*. London, Longmans, Green.

Meister, M. (n.d.) *Political Changes during the Colonial Era and its Consequences on the Social and Economic Structure of Barotseland*, mimeo.

N.A. (National Archives Files), K.D.E. 8/1/4. Report of the District Commissioner Barotse for the year ending March 1913.

N.A. (National Archives Files), K.D.E. 8/1/7. Report of the Resident Magistrate Barotse for the year ending March 1916.

N.R.G. (Northern Rhodesia Government) (1955) *Barotseland Protectorate – Schemes of Development, 1955–1960*, Lusaka, Government Printer.

Palmer, R.H. and Parsons, N. (eds.) (1977) *The Roots of Rural Poverty in Central and Southern Africa*, London, Heinemann.

Peters, D.U. (1960) *Land Usage in Barotseland*, Lusaka, Government Printer.

van Horn, L. (1977) The agricultural history of Barotseland, 1840–1964, in R.H. Palmer and N. Parsons (eds.), *The Roots of Rural Poverty*, pp. 144–69.

Verboom, W.C. and Brunt, M.A. (1970) *An Ecological Survey of Western Province, Zambia, with Special Reference to the Fodder Resources*, Land Resource Study No. 8. Tolworth, Land Resources Division, Directorate of Overseas Surveys.

Wood, A.P. (1982) Population trends in Zambia: a review of the 1980 census, in A.M. Findlay (ed.), *Recent National Population Change*, Durham, Institute of British Geographers, pp. 102–25.

13 Resettlement and under-development in the Black 'Homelands' of South Africa

C.M. Rogerson and
E.M. Letsoalo

Introduction

The study of settlement and resettlement schemes attracts researchers from a wide range of social science disciplines. Indeed, Chambers (1969: 12) once described the field as something of 'an academic no-man's-land'. Increasingly, however, human geographers are assuming an important role in the investigation of several programmes of population resettlement and their associated implications. Recent contributions by geographers include work on the resettlement of reservoir-evacuees in Thailand (Lightfoot 1978; 1979); the impact of Algeria's programme of *regroupement* (Sutton, 1977; Sutton and Lawless, 1978); spontaneous agricultural resettlement in Ethiopia (Wood, 1982); and the special problems of resettlement schemes for refugees in Africa (Rogge, 1981; 1982). Irrespective of the actual causes of resettlement, whether stemming from new dam/water schemes or military counter-insurgency operations, the process of relocation is one which inevitably results in considerable stress and trauma for the peoples involved. In particular, studies emphasize the adjustments that must be borne by resettled communities as a consequence of a disruption in social relations and possibly the loss of economic and social assets (Sutton, 1977).

During the past two decades major programmes of population removal and resettlement have occurred throughout the sub-continent of Southern Africa. The regional struggles for decolonization and African majority rule, the experience of post-independence civil strife and flight from apartheid contributed a flow of almost one million refugees (Hart and Rogerson, 1982). To this international migration flow must be added an even larger stream of 'internal' refugees in Southern Africa. Major internal population displacements in Zimbabwe, Mozambique and Namibia are engendered by military actions, clearing rural populations from strategic regions, and resettling them into 'strategic hamlets' (Weinrich, 1977; Isaacman, 1978). In South Africa the prime causes of population resettlement are linked to the implementation of apartheid policies. Here the term 'resettlement' is something of a misnomer, a misleadingly comforting rubric that masks 'the cruel business of arbitrarily uprooting helpless people and dumping them' (Nash, 1980: 4). Despite the occurrence of these types of population resettlement within Southern Africa, their nature and effects have received scant attention from geographers (Beavon and Rogerson, 1981). It is the intention in this paper to investigate the nature and implications of population removals into the Black Homelands or Bantustans of South Africa. More specifically, the paper describes the several categories of population removals which presently occur in South Africa, and examines the impact of resettlement upon two different village communities in the under-developed Lebowa Homeland.

Forced population removals in South Africa

Kane-Berman (1979) points out that behind the official pronouncements of 'separate development', 'separate freedoms' and 'multinational development' the real story of apartheid is that of the mass resettlement of South Africa's Black population. Official figures concerning the scale of African population relocation are notoriously inaccurate. The most recent estimates, however, suggest that at least 3 million and perhaps as many as 7 million Blacks have been affected by resettlement since 1948 (Maré, 1980, 1981; Marks, 1980; Murray, 1981; Surplus People Project, 1982; Platzky and Walker, 1983). This programme of mass displacement must not be construed as a random process, because resettlement takes on specific geographical forms. In particular, the policy is directed towards the removal of Blacks from parts of so-called 'White' South Africa and their resettlement into those other areas known variously as the Bantustans, Black Homelands or national states (Fig. 13.1). These latter regions, constituting 14 per cent of the land area of South Africa, are the cornerstones of the strategy of 'ethnic nationalism'. In terms of this strategy the Black population of South Africa is systematically 'deprived of basic political and economic rights' and 'restructured both in respect of its formal alienation and in respect of its physical relocation' (Murray, 1981: 133). As the focus of resettlement programmes, the Bantustans represent labour reservoirs from which employers in 'White' South Africa may draw cheap migrant labour. Also, increasingly these areas are assuming the role of hosting South Africa's 'surplus peoples', those identified as redundant in terms of the requirements of the White economy (Legassick and Wolpe, 1976; Surplus People Project, 1982). The groups in society most likely to be viewed in such a light are women, children, the elderly, sick and unemployed.

The programme of population resettlement has been interpreted as a key facet underpinning the maintenance of South Africa's 'labour-coercive' economy (Legassick, 1977), assuring the cheapness of Black labour through transferring some of the social welfare costs for the country's workforce onto the 'separate' economies of the Homelands (Rogerson and Pirie, 1979). For Maré (1981: 2) the policy of resettlement is also one of the 'disorganisation (fragmentation) of the dominated classes in South Africa'. In the view of South African government officials, the programme of resettlement is justified in the following statement made by Dr P. Koornhof, the Minister of Cooperation and Development:

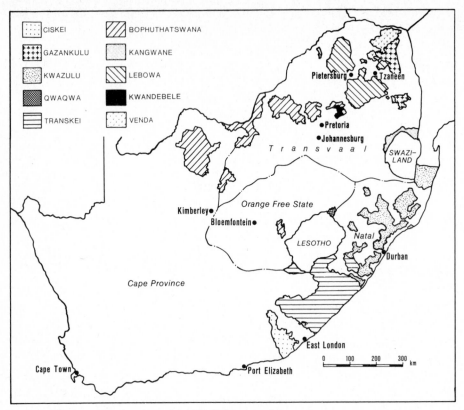

Fig. 13.1 The location of the Black 'Homelands'

The basic principle which must be applied throughout in the settlement of people is that we are dealing with the building of nations, with the improvement of people who are being settled to enable them, *inter alia*, to acquire a legal place of residence. The removal of people must therefore be development-oriented. (*Star*, 5/4/82)

Notwithstanding such assurances there are few supporters of the policy of resettlement outside the ranks of the ruling National Party in South Africa. The policy is bitterly opposed both by the mass of resettled peoples and by the Bantustan governments who perforce bear the burden of responsibility for caring for resettled populations (Dhlomo, 1981). Indeed, recent critical observers on resettlement describe the policy as 'diabolical' (Tutu, 1980), 'abhorrent' (Maré, 1981), a 'disaster' (Nash, 1980), a 'crime' (Bozzoli, 1983), a 'violation of human rights' (Rogers, 1980) and even as a policy of 'genocide-by-neglect' (Belcher, 1979). Against this background, attention turns to the specific causes of population removals into the Bantustans, using as a case study the Lebowa Homeland (Fig. 13.2).

The study region

In most respects Lebowa is typical of the ten ethnic Homelands which have been established under apartheid. This self-governing territory of South Africa is

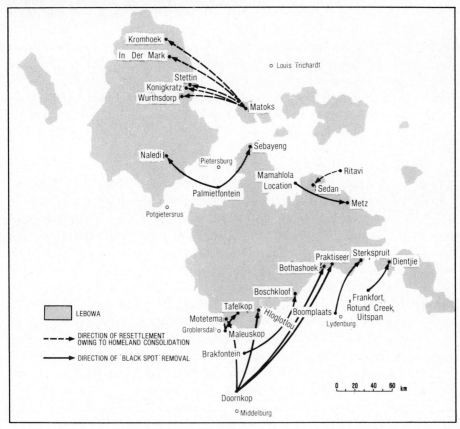

Fig. 13.2 Lebowa: resettlement associated with the clearance of 'Black Spots' and the programme of 'Homelands' consolidation

fragmented, impoverished and economically dependent upon migratory flows to the 'White' areas. The results of the 1980 census revealed that the Homeland has a *de facto* population of 1.65 million and a *de jure* population of 2.2 million, the difference being accounted for by migrants living or working in the White areas of South Africa.

The areas comprising Lebowa were largely established as African 'reserves' in terms of the 1913 and 1936 Land Acts, which laid the foundations for the (unequal) race-space division of South Africa. At this time, however, there was no division among the various reserves on the basis of ethnicity such that North Sotho, Tsonga, Venda and Ndebele peoples mixed together in the delimited reserves of the Northern Transvaal. With the introduction of apartheid policies, since 1948 ethnicity has become the primary factor in land allocation. In a modernized form of the 'divide and rule' philosophy, the Nationalist Government of South Africa proposed the establishment of a series of separate Homelands for the different 'ethnic' Black populations. Accordingly, in terms of the Promotion of Bantu Self-Government Act of 1959 the territory of Lebowa was constituted as the 'Homeland' for South Africa's North Sotho peoples. In 1962 a Lebowa

Territorial Authority was established and a decade later Lebowa was proclaimed a self-governing territory. In terms of apartheid ideology the Homeland is eventually to receive a form of so-called 'independence'. The current Lebowa leadership is, however, strongly opposed to the acceptance of this counterfeit form of 'independence'. Indeed, this opposition is well founded. With the 'achievement' of independence the people identified as ethnically associated with Lebowa, irrespective of where they are living, would be deprived of their South African citizenship and henceforth treated as 'foreigners' and 'guest-workers' in White South Africa.

The territory of Lebowa is fragmented, being composed of 12 seprate units of land. The non-contiguous nature of the Homeland is not peculiar to Lebowa, rather it is a distinguishing characteristic of nearly all the Bantustans. Attempts are under way to consolidate the territory and, in terms of the most recent set of proposals, Lebowa will be reduced ultimately to six parcels of land. Given the character of the Homeland it is difficult to speak of the Lebowa 'economy' *per se*. If such an economy can be recognized, then undoubtedly its most distinguishing trait is under-development. Like all Homelands, Lebowa is one of the most poverty-stricken and impoverished areas of South Africa. The region is manifestly unable to generate sufficient job opportunities with the result that unemployment is widespread. Indeed, two-thirds of the Homeland's estimated gross income derives from payments to migrant workers in 'White' South Africa. Agriculture is conducted overwhelmingly on a subsistence or, more correctly, on a sub-subsistence level. Commercial agriculture is undertaken only on a small-scale basis, primarily through projects operated by parastatal agencies of the Lebowa government. Industrialization is confined to a number of small bakeries, potteries and home-craft manufactures, which together employ only 2,000 persons. Of greater significance as an employer of labour within Lebowa is a series of chrome mines in the territory. But, despite some recent advances in increasing such employment opportunities (B.E.N.B.O., 1976), it is apparent that the Homeland remains unable to create enough job opportunities to match even the annual numbers of new entrants onto the labour market. Notwithstanding this situation, Lebowa – in common with all the Black Homelands – has been subject to mass population resettlement over the past three decades.

Population relocation

Following the pioneer studies of resettlement in South Africa by Desmond (1971), Baldwin (1974, 1975) and Maré (1980, 1981), six major forms of population removal into Lebowa may be distinguished. These categories of relocation relate to, *inter alia*, (a) the clearance of so-called 'Black Spots', (b) the programme of Homelands consolidation, (c) the abolition of labour-tenancies, (d) urban township relocations, (e) the operation of 'influx control' and associated legislation, and (f) the effects of agricultural 'betterment' policies. Each will be briefly examined.

The category of land known as 'Black Spots' constitutes the relics of the late nineteenth-century era of prosperous African peasant farming in South Africa (Bundy, 1979). These areas are lands of African freehold occupation which are located outside those areas of South Africa designated as Black race-space and hence fall within the boundaries of 'White' South Africa. The 'clearance' of these 'Black Spots' is one of the prime causes for mass population removals into the Bantustans. In the process of clearance, Blacks are despatched to their respective ethnic Homelands. Only large land-holders, those owning more than 17.3 ha of land, are entitled to compensatory land within the Homeland (Maré, 1980, 1981). Moreover, as Bundy (1979: 236) argues: 'The frequent assertions by official spokesmen that the new land provided was the equal of Black Spot land are not merely unconvincing but in the light of descriptions of Desmond and others are seen to be callous and threadbare deception.' Lebowa has been affected by the clearance of several 'Black Spot' lands throughout Northern and Eastern Transvaal since the period of the early 1950s. The major relocations associated with Black Spot removals are shown in Figure 13.2. In virtually all cases the uprooted populations are descendants of families that have owned and farmed the former 'Black Spot' land for at least a century.

A second genre of forced population removal, closely linked to 'Black Spot' relocations, is that which relates to the programme for consolidating the fragmented territories of the ten ethnic Homelands. In the area of the Northern Transvaal this process has necessitated an unravelling of the complex pattern of mixing of North Sotho, Venda, Tsonga and Ndebele peoples. With the formation of four ethnic states to 'cater' for these populations – Lebowa, Venda, Gazankulu and KwaNdebele – a considerable volume of resettlement was generated. Two types of relocations caused by Homelands consolidation affect Lebowa. First, areas declared as part of the territory of Lebowa may be excised and redesignated as forming part of 'White' South Africa. In this particular case, the peoples living on these excised pieces of territory are classified as constituting a 'Black Spot' and hence subject to mass removal back into Lebowa. Second, there occur situations where land is reallocated between the different Homelands. Again, the affected populations living under systems of either tribal or freehold land tenure become subject to removal. The most important mass removals into Lebowa as a consequence of consolidation arrangements are illustrated in Figure 13.2. The removal of at least 3,400 families from the Matoks area between 1976 and 1979 is typical of resettlement that results from the impending excision of land formerly declared as Lebowa territory. The movements from Ritavi to Sedan are illustrative of resettlement as a consequence of the ill-defined boundaries between Lebowa and the Gazankulu Homeland. It has been estimated that in total more than 130,000 'citizens' of Lebowa are affected by proposals for ethnic Homeland consolidation (*Rand Daily Mail*, 31/7/74). But these estimates exclude further removals that may occur from the still awaited proposals of another government commission examining consolidation issues.

A third category of 'discarded people' (Desmond, 1971) is those generated as a product of the abolition of the labour-tenant system and 'squatting' on White-owned farming land. The functioning of this system enabled families to subsist on their own plots of land on White farms while rendering a certain amount (usually six months) of labour to the farmer. This system of agriculture was widespread in the Northern Transvaal region and its progressive abolition has resulted, from 1964 onwards, in a steady flow of families being forced to return to Lebowa. The process of abolition is inseparable from the increasing spread of mechanization into White agriculture, reducing the need for the labour of the Black tenant. It is difficult to quantify accurately the extent to which Lebowa has been affected by resettlement of former labour-tenants. For South Africa as a whole, the crude figures for squatter and labour-tenant removals are estimated as 1.5 million people between 1960 and 1979 (Maré, 1981). That Lebowa has been affected greatly by this process is evident from the descriptions by Yawitch (1982) of the invasion of certain farm lands in the Homeland by resettled former labour-tenants. A further index of its significance is provided by the doubling of the population of one tribal authority between 1956 and 1980 as a consequence of the influx of former labour-tenants and squatters from the North-eastern Transvaal (Letsoalo, 1982).

The fourth type of relocation affecting Lebowa relates to the process of demolishing urban townships and squatter locations in 'White' South Africa and relocating their populations into new townships established within the Home-lands, where the inhabitants of these 'towns' become daily commuters, travelling to employment in the White areas. The extent of this form of relocation is indexed by the mushrooming of new Homelands settlements within the past two decades (Fig. 13.3). The process of urban township removal is being vigorously promoted throughout the Northern Transvaal with the object of creating towns which are 'white by night'. Illustratively, the town clerk of Pietersburg, the largest settlement in the Northern Transvaal, proudly claimed in 1980: 'We will have no urban blacks here next year' (*Star*, 7/3/80). In the pursuit of such goals, the old 'locations' at both Pietersburg and Potgietersrus were deproclaimed and their inhabitants moved to the more distant settlements of Seshego and Mahwelereng. Likewise the establishment of Lenyenye was linked to the resettlement of Blacks from White Tzaneen ostensibly 'because the White residents complained that the noise from the location disturbed the peace' (*Pace*, 1981). Perhaps the most disturbing example of this category of urban relocation affecting Lebowa is the coordinated removal of approximately 20,000 Blacks from the various townships at Ellisras, Vaalwater, Naboomspruit and Nylstroom. These peoples are being resettled together at the settlement of Steilloop. In this particular case, the resettled populations are inevitably forced into becoming weekly or monthly labour migrants rather than daily commuters.

The operation of the battery of legislation termed 'influx control', which regulates the place of residence and work of Black South Africans, is responsible for a further flow of people into the Homelands. The right of Blacks to a degree of

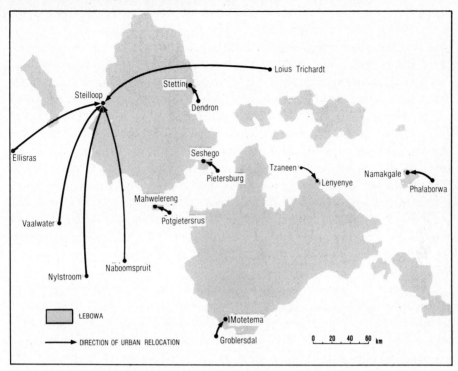

Fig. 13.3 Lebowa: resettlement associated with urban township relocations

permanency in the 'White' urban areas of South Africa is obtained only with great
difficulty through the provisions of the urban areas legislation. In terms of further
measures seeking to constrain the urbanward movement of Blacks, those persons
classified as 'unproductive' may be endorsed out of 'White' urban areas and
resettled into the Homelands. With the tightening of this legislation there has
occurred a growing stream of unproductive Blacks – the aged, women, young, the
infirm and disabled – who are forced to leave the urban areas. The 'rationale' for
such resettlement is stated in the notorious General Circular No. 25, of 1967,
issued by the Department of Bantu Administration and Development:

It is accepted Government policy that the Bantu are only temporarily resident in the
European areas of the Republic, for as long as they offer their labour there. As soon as they
become, for some reason or another, no longer fit for work or superfluous in the labour
market, they are expected to return to their country of origin or the territory of the national
unit where they fit in ethnically if they were not born and bred in the homeland (cited in
Maré, 1980: 75).

It is difficult to obtain accurate statistics of the numbers of such 'superfluous'
peoples resettled into Lebowa. Nevertheless, from the fragmentary data that have
emerged, it is apparent that this form of removal is common in Lebowa as with all
the Homelands (Smit and Booysen, 1977, 1981; Maré, 1980, 1981). In addition to

persons endorsed out of White urban centres as a consequence of influx control, the remoter areas of Lebowa have also been the foci for a steady stream of banished persons, most commonly long-standing opponents of the apartheid system (Letsoalo, 1982).

The final group of removals relates to the implementation of schemes for agricultural betterment in the Homelands, which involves the considerable spatial reorganization of dispersed rural communities and their resettlement in a series of planned agricultural villages (Letsoalo and Rogerson, 1982). Much population uprooting, albeit of a short-distance nature, is engendered as families accorded farming rights are concentrated in betterment villages, whilst those less fortunate are expelled into the bleak non-agricultural settlements known as 'closer-settlements' (Rogerson and Letsoalo, 1981). Despite mass resistance to the implementation of betterment schemes (Hirson, 1976–77; Yawitch, 1982), by 1980 almost three-quarters of Lebowa had been planned under betterment regulations producing a major stream of 'hidden' resettlement throughout the Homeland.

In summary, therefore, Lebowa continues to be one geographical focus of apartheid South Africa's extensive programme of population resettlement occurring over the past three decades. The mass removal of 'citizens' of Lebowa continues even in the face of opposition to removals as expressed by the Homeland government. The Chief Minister of Lebowa declared that he was 'opposed to our people being shunted around. We did not want to have a hand in this matter but these people are now in our Homeland. We have a moral obligation to care for them' (*Star*, 27/6/74). It is to an examination of the life-conditions of resettled peoples in Lebowa that attention is now turned.

The impact of resettlement

There exist, at present, few studies that capture the traumatic experience and stresses of population removals into the rural Homelands. The tragic experience of uprooting and 'dumping' into these impoverished areas cries out for research from a humanistic geographical perspective (cf. Ley and Samuels, 1978; Western, 1981). That said, the most important of the existing works are the descriptions by Desmond (1971) of the bleak living conditions endured by relocated populations throughout South Africa a decade ago and research by Clarke and Ngobese (1975) concerning the survival of 'women without men' in the resettlement areas of KwaZulu. The most important recent insight into the economic implications of resettlement throughout South Africa is that provided by the five volume study of the Surplus People Project (1982). The impact of resettlement in rural Lebowa is examined here through the results of an empirical investigation into the survival strategies of two resettled communities. In particular, the study seeks to highlight the modes of existence of relocated populations which have been subject to differing post-resettlement experiences. It is argued that resettlement in South

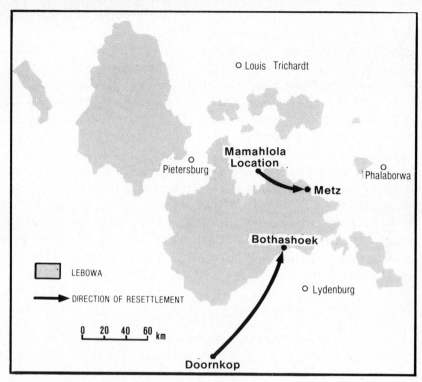

Fig. 13.4 Lebowa: the location of two case study villages

Africa is inseparable from processes of under-development and impoverishment for the African population.

The experience of resettled populations
The two selected case studies are of Metz, a rural betterment village and Bothashoek, an example of a closer-settlement (Fig. 13.4). Both villages may be considered as typical of these different forms of rural settlement which occur throughout all the Homelands. Rural villages are the products of the programme of agricultural betterment planning, the residents being in possession of the rights to conduct agriculture through ownership of a farming plot and/or cattle. By contrast, the closer-settlement is a non-agricultural community in which the inhabitants are almost invariably not permitted to farm, and there is a notable absence of any economic base. Colloquially they are known as *tickylaene*, a term which means, fittingly, a settlement where money is essential for survival.

The genesis of Bothashoek and Metz must be situated in the common process of clearing Black Spot areas of land in 'White' South Africa. The rural village of Metz was founded in 1957 after the removal of families from the Mamahlola location. In like fashion, Bothashoek was established for those Bapedi families uprooted from the Doornkop Black Spot in two separate removals beginning in 1970. Prior to their resettlement the Mamahlola people were a settled agrarian community engaged in the production of oranges, tomatoes, fruit and vegetables. The majority of the community were farmers either on a commercial or subsistence basis. Household incomes were supplemented by the practice of daily commuting to a variety of employment opportunities in the nearby urban centre of Tzaneen. There emerges a similar pattern of life prior to removal from the farm Doornkop, where fruit and vegetables were produced in addition to such staples as maize and sorghum. Outside agricultural pursuits, many members of the Doornkop settlement (particularly women) commuted daily to Middelburg for employment, especially in domestic service. Prior to resettlement, only a small fraction of the populations at Mamahlola and Doornkop were long-term labour migrants and absent working in the mines, on farms or in the factories of 'White' South Africa.

The process of excising the two Black Spots engendered considerable resistance amongst the affected populations. At Doornkop the *kgoshigadi* (chieftainess) was imprisoned for her refusal to hand over the effective title deeds to state officials. The chieftainess and her counsellor are reported as saying:

The government have offered us tents to live on strange land. We don't know what to expect. This is good land which we have tilled for years. We make our living from the land.

We have built our houses here, cared for the land, constructed our own churches and schools for the children. How can we leave the place where we have buried our fathers? (*Rand Daily Mail*, 24/4/64).

The struggle to remain at Doornkop repeated an earlier story of events at Mamahlola. Resistance on the Mamahlola farm was manifested in the tribe's refusal to move to Metz and in a demonstration by local women against the beginning of the mass deportation. At both Black Spots the local tribal leaders were unwilling to lead their peoples in a voluntary removal; as a consequence of their unwillingness, government deposed the existing chiefs and sought to install more pliant leaders. The final clearance of both Black Spots was achieved only after the issuance of eviction orders with resettlement occurring under police 'supervision' to the new locations. In both cases compensation was minimal with no monetary recompense offered for the Black Spot lands. Rather, the resettled peoples were 'given' the farms Metz and Bothashoek in exchange. That the resettled peoples did not perceive this exchange in terms of equivalence is apparent from their reactions to the new environments. It was reported after five months at Metz that the Mamahlola were so unhappy that they were preparing to disband entirely as a community (*Rand Daily Mail*, 5/8/58). And the new settlement of Bothashoek was described as a site 'not fit for human habitation' (*Rand Daily Mail*, 29/6/74).

The post-resettlement experience and modes of existence

The impact of resettlement was conditioned immediately by the different legal status of the two villages. The population removed to Metz was subject to the

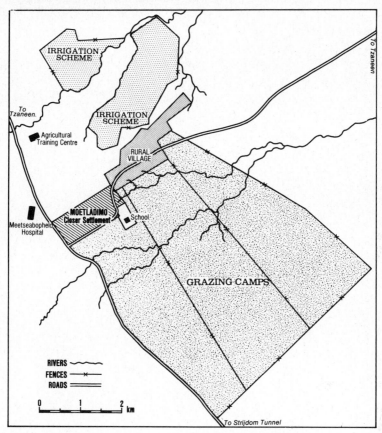

Fig. 13.5 Metz: the organization of a rural betterment village

regulations governing agricultural betterment, a programme seeking to improve the productivity of Black farming in South Africa (Yawitch, 1982). In terms of betterment planning the numbers of persons allowed to farm at Metz would be restricted to the numbers of available 'economic farming units', a sufficient area of land for a household to obtain a subsistence livelihood from agriculture. Only those persons permitted to farm, in terms of being allocated farming plots, were allowed to live in the Metz rural village (Fig. 13.5). The remainder, about half the families removed from Mamahlola, were resettled as a landless community at the adjacent non-agricultural settlement or closer-settlement of Moetladimo. It is the potential for obtaining a subsistence livelihood in agriculture through access to a farm plot and demarcated grazing lands that distinguishes life in a rural village from that in a closer-settlement. Bothashoek is the largest closer-settlement in Lebowa and is situated on land of agriculturally marginal potential (Rogerson and Letsoalo, 1981). Before the removal from Doornkop the resettled families were expected to dispose of all livestock (except poultry) in their possession as no grazing lands are planned for in closer-settlements. The original plans for

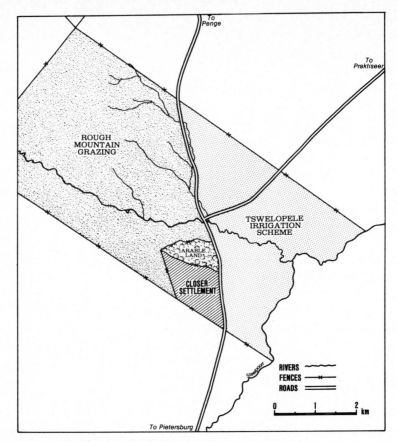

Fig. 13.6 Bothashoek: the organization of a closer settlement

Bothashoek provided only for a residential area. Nevertheless, a small area of arable land was subsequently demarcated (Fig. 13.6).

The difference between rural villages and closer-settlements has been progressively blurred. At Metz there emerged a group of landless persons residing in the rural village. Under the traditional system known as *go lotsha*, the village *kgoshi* has allocated dwelling plots to former labour tenants expelled from White farms in the Northern Transvaal. Although without formal farming rights, some of this latter group do undertake agriculture through a system of renting farm plots from those persons with farming rights. Together, the operation of the *go lotsha* system, the renting of farming plots and the provision of some arable land in the closer-settlement have combined to remove much of the legal distinction between life in rural betterment villages and in closer-settlements. In a survey of 112 households at Bothashoek, agriculture offered a subsistence base for only one household, notably that of a village headman. By contrast, the failure of agriculture to provide an economic base for the resettled population at Metz demands detailed comment. As a consequence of the unequal race-space division of land in South Africa, available farming land is limited in all Homelands, not least in Lebowa. At Metz there was insufficient arable land for full economic farming units to be allocated to households. Therefore, there began a process of land subdivision such that many families were allocated plots of land of only half or one-third economic unit size. Despite the planning of grazing camps, irrigated land and the availability of a government agricultural extension officer, a survey conducted of 51 Metz households showed that 90 per cent were wholly reliant upon purchased rather than home-produced foodstuffs. Thus, as a consequence of resettlement the populations of both the rural betterment village and the closer-settlement experienced a transformation from relatively stable agricultural communities to dependence upon the remittances of labour migrants or the returns from pensions and the rural informal sector.

At both Bothashoek and Metz it was apparent that resettlement was associated with increased levels of migration amongst the households. Indeed, the remittances of long-term labour migrants were the major household income source in both villages. In the absence of substantive local employment opportunities long-term migration is a necessity at both the closer-settlement and the rural village. The only regular wage-employment opportunities are as teachers, nurses or in government service. In addition, seasonal wage opportunities are available on nearby White-owned farms and on agricultural projects run by the Lebowa government, for example the Tswelopele cotton project which adjoins Bothashoek. That each settlement is located in the periphery of national economic space militates against future employment growth. The lack of substantive employment opportunities is particularly notable at the closer-settlement of Bothashoek because in the initial proposals for the establishment of such settlements it had been suggested that they be provided with an industrial base. Yet there is at present no industry at Bothashoek and no plans for encouraging future industrial growth through the programme of industrial decentralization. Indeed, the lack of correspondence between the planning of decentralized industrial growth points and the location of closer-settlements underscores the view that these settlements were founded primarily as locations for the migrant workforce and 'surplus' peoples of South Africa.

Beyond the remittances of migrant workers in 'White' South Africa and the limited opportunities for wage labour the only remaining household income sources derive from pension payments and the returns from 'informal sector' activities. The methods of payment of pensions for Blacks in South Africa reinforces the programme of coercing the old and disabled to relocate to the Homelands (Roux, 1981). The burden of pension payments falls upon the financially-strapped Homeland governments. Accordingly, many applications for pensions are turned down simply for lack of funds. The volume of pension payments at both Bothashoek and Metz is reduced further by bureaucratic difficulties experienced by Africans in securing such regular pensions. In the light of these difficulties many households seek monies through participation in one of a variety of informal sector activities, especially the brewing of traditional beer, petty commodity manufactures and the hawking of fruit and vegetables. The potential avenues for obtaining an informal income niche are, however, highly constrained, and the abject poverty of the two villages is mirrored in the limited opportunities for securing such an income. Indeed, resettlement at locations such as Metz or Bothashoek, far distant from the industrial and urban areas of South Africa, destroys the possibility of securing an income in such pursuits as gardening, washing or newspaper selling.

One crude index of standard of living in the two surveyed settlements is the computed monthly average income. The median income of households at Bothashoek and Metz during 1980 was R40 and R45 respectively which should be compared with the conservative estimate of the minimum necessary household budget for an average Black household, namely R170 per month (Potgieter and Levin, 1980). Only 10 per cent of the households in the two villages secure a monthly income in excess of that figure. The consequence of mass income poverty in these areas is reflected in the poor and monotonous diet of the populations, their crude conditions of housing, manifest undernourishment and poor health. It must be borne in mind that the people being resettled at Bothashoek and Metz are largely uneducated and illiterate, the products of South Africa's notorious 'Bantu education' system. Moreover, whatever degree of mastery resettled people have over their environment 'they have acquired as a result of experience and tradition' (Dhlomo, 1981: 8). For people to be uprooted, bundled on a truck and deposited in a new environment of which they have no experience precipitates extreme stress, which is reflected in a reduced ability of resettled peoples throughout South Africa to mobilize themselves to cope with their new (and often hostile) environment. In this fashion the major impact of resettlement for the communities at Bothashoek and Metz was to accentuate conditions of impoverishment and rural under-development.

Conclusion

In common with the resettlement experience of development projects in Africa, the programme of population removals in South Africa is one that generates considerable stress and trauma. 'Resettlement' in the South African context, however, is a misleading term concealing a cruel process of mass uprooting and continuing misery which afflicts the country's Black majority (Kane-Berman, 1979). The logic of apartheid allocates particular roles to the Homeland areas. On the one hand, these regions function as labour reservoirs on which employers in South Africa may draw for migrant workers. On the other hand, the Homelands are increasingly to function as disposal areas where the old, unemployed, sick and disabled may be sent when the White economy no longer has use for them. For the majority of the resettled peoples the experience is one which results in considerable economic and social disruption, reinforced by the characteristics of the environment into which resettlement occurs. Contrary to government rhetoric that the resettlement programme is 'development-oriented', resettled peoples are typically moved to locations where the opportunities for farming are either considerably reduced or non-existent and there exist few permanent wage-employment opportunities or avenues for casual or seasonal employment. As a consequence of the generally unfavourable nature of the places of resettlement, participation in the migratory labour system of South Africa becomes the major means for household survival. The programme of resettlement is thus associated with the transformation of formerly stable agrarian communities into broken communities chronically dependent upon migrant worker remittances, pension payments and the meagre returns from a rural informal sector. The findings of this study gainsay the view that the resettlement programme is linked to an ethos of improvement. Instead, it lends weight to the argument that the object of resettlement is to provide credibility to the notion of 'independent' Homelands, thereby entrenching ethnic partition within the Black population and serving also to 'legitimize' their exclusion from the major centres of political and economic power (Surplus People Project, 1982; Platzky and Walker, 1983). Under-development rather than development is therefore the major product of South Africa's programme for mass population resettlement.

ACKNOWLEDGEMENT

Mr P.J. Stickler is thanked for preparing the diagrams accompanying this paper.

REFERENCES

Baldwin, A. (1974) *Uprooting a Nation: the Study of 3 Million Evictions*, London, Africa Publications Trust.
Baldwin, A. (1975) Mass removals and separate development, *Journal of Southern African Studies*, 1, 215–27.
Beavon, K.S.O. and Rogerson, C.M. (1981) Trekking on: recent trends in the human geography of Southern Africa, *Progress in Human Geography*, 5, 159–89.
Belcher, T. (1979) Industrial decentralisation and the dynamics of forced labour in South Africa, *Journal of Modern African Studies*, 17, 677–86.
B.E.N.B.O. (Bureau for Economic Research re Bantu Development) (1976) *Lebowa Economic Review*, Pretoria, B.E.N.B.O.
Bozzoli, B. (1983) Marxism, feminism and South African studies, *Journal of Southern African Studies*, 9, 139–71.
Bundy, C. (1979) *The Rise and Fall of the South African Peasantry*, London, Heinemann.
Chambers, R. (1969) *Settlement Schemes in Tropical Africa*, New York, Praeger.
Clarke, L. and Ngobese, J. (1975) *Women without Men*, Durban, Institute for Black Research.
Desmond, C. (1971) *The Discarded People*, Harmondsworth, Penguin.
Dhlomo, O.D. (1981) Kwazulu and its stance and problems associated with resettlement

of persons in Natal. Paper delivered at the Annual Conference of the South African Institute of Race Relations, 1981.

Hart, T. and Rogerson, C.M. (1982) The geography of international refugee movements in Southern Africa, *South African Geographical Journal*, 64, 125–37.

Hirson, B. (1976–77) Rural revolts in South Africa: 1937–1951, in *The Societies of Southern Africa in the Nineteenth and Twentieth Centuries*, volume 8, London, University of London, Institute of Commonwealth Studies, pp. 115–32.

Isaacman, A. (1978) *A Luta Continua: Creating a New Society in Mozambique*, Binghamton, N.Y., Fernand Braudel Centre.

Kane-Berman, J. (1979) *South Africa: the Method in the Madness*, London, Pluto.

Legassick, M. (1977) Gold, agriculture and secondary industry in South Africa, 1885–1970: from periphery to sub-metropole as a forced labour system, in R. Palmer and N. Parsons (eds.), *The Roots of Rural Poverty in Central and Southern Africa*, Berkeley, University of California Press, pp. 175–200.

Legassick, M. and Wolpe, H. (1976) The Bantustans and capital accumulation in South Africa, *Review of African Political Economy*, 7, 87–107.

Letsoalo, E.M. (1982) Survival strategies in rural Lebowa: a study in the geography of poverty. M.A. dissertation, University of the Witwatersrand, Johannesburg.

Letsoalo, E.M. and Rogerson, C.M. (1982) Rural 'development' planning under apartheid: betterment planning in Lebowa, South Africa, *Geoforum*, 13, 301–14.

Ley, D. and Samuels, M. (eds.) (1978) *Humanistic Geography: Prospects and Problems*, London, Croom Helm.

Lightfoot, R.P. (1978) The costs of resettling reservoir evacuees in North-east Thailand, *Journal of Tropical Geography*, 47, 63–74.

Lightfoot, R.P. (1979) Planning reservoir-related resettlement programmes in North-east Thailand, *Journal of Tropical Geography*, 48, 47–57.

Maré, G. (1980) *African Population Relocation in South Africa*, Johannesburg, South African Institute of Race Relations.

Maré, G. (1981) *Processes, Policies and African Population Relocation*, Johannesburg, South African Institute of Race Relations, RR 46/81.

Marks, S. (1980) From *Difaqane* to discarded people: South Africa's internal refugees, *African Research and Documentation*, 22, 2–12.

Murray, C. (1981) 'Ethnic nationalism' and structured unemployment: refugees in the Orange Free State, *Disasters*, 5, 132–41.

Nash, M. (1980) *Black 'Uprooting' from White South Africa*, Johannesburg, South African Council of Churches.

Pace (Johannesburg).

Platzky, L. and Walker, C. (1983) Review of relocation, in South African Research Service (ed.) *South African Review I: Same Foundations, New Facades*, Johannesburg, Ravan, pp. 83–96.

Potgieter, J.F. and Levin, M. (1980) *The Household Subsistence Level in Urban Centres, October 1980 and Indexing of Salaries and Wages in the Republic of South Africa*, Port Elizabeth, Institute of Planning Research Fact Paper No. 39.

Rand Daily Mail (Johannesburg).

Rogers, B. (1980) Mass population removals in *apartheid* South Africa (1978–1980), *United Nations Centre Against Apartheid Notes and Documents*, 27/80.

Rogerson, C.M. and Letsoalo, E.M. (1981) Rural underdevelopment, poverty and apartheid: the closer-settlements of Lebowa, South Africa, *Tijdschrift voor Economische en Sociale Geografie*, 72, 347–61.

Rogerson, C.M. and Pirie, G.H. (1979) Apartheid, urbanization and regional planning in South Africa, in R. Obudho and S. El-Shakhs (eds.), *Development of Urban Systems in Africa*, New York, Praeger, pp. 323–44.

Rogge, J. (1981) Africa's resettlement strategies, *International Migration Review*, 15, 195–212.

Rogge, J. (1982) Refugee migration and resettlement, in J.I. Clarke and L.A. Kosiński (ed.), *Redistribution of Population in Africa*, London, Heinemann, pp. 39–43.

Roux, R. (1981) Striking for pensions, *South African Labour Bulletin*, 6 (8), 34–54.

Smit, P. and Booysen, J. (1977) *Urbanization in the Homelands – a new Dimension in the Urbanization Process of the Black Population of South Africa?* Pretoria, Institute of Plural Studies.

Smit, P. and Booysen, J. (1981) *Swart Versetedeliking: Patroon en Strategie*, Cape Town, Tafelberg.

Star (Johannesburg).

Surplus People Project (1982) *Forced Removals in South Africa*, 5 vols, Durban, University of Natal.

Sutton, K. (1977) Population resettlement – traumatic upheavals and the Algerian experience, *Journal of Modern African Studies*, 15, 279–300.

Sutton, K. and Lawless, R.I. (1978) Population regrouping in Algeria: traumatic change and the normal settlement pattern. *Transactions, Institute of British Geographers (New Series)*, 3, 331–50.

Tutu, D. (1980) Tearing people apart, *South African Outlook*, 110 (1312), 152–8.

Weinrich, A.K.H. (1977) Strategic resettlement in Rhodesia, *Journal of Southern African Studies*, 3, 207–29.

Western, J. (1981) *Outcast Cape Town*. Minneapolis, University of Minnesota Press.

Wood, A. (1982) Spontaneous agricultural resettlement in Ethiopia, 1950–74, in J.I. Clarke and L.A. Kosiński (eds.), *Redistribution of Population in Africa*, London, Heinemann, pp. 157–65.

Yawitch, J. (1982) *Betterment: the Myth of Homeland Agriculture*, Johannesburg, South African Institute of Race Relations.

14 Development programmes and population redistribution in Nigeria

Aderanti Adepoju

Introduction

Nigeria is a country of remarkable diversity in its economy, physical conditions, vegetation and ethnic groups. The four main physical regions consist of the sparsely populated dense belt of swamp and mangrove forest along the coast; the tropical rainforest area; the open woodland and grass savanna; and the southern Saharan region (F.M.E.D., 1975). The differences in physical conditions and soil fertility in the regions have, in combination, helped to produce complementary economies: cocoa, palm produce, and rubber in the rain forest fertile areas; groundnut and cotton in the sandy soils of the savanna north; and rich oil deposits in the east (U.N.F.P.A., 1980). These remarkable regional variations strongly influence both the pattern of development and population distribution (Adepoju, 1982).

The salient demographic features include the young population (48 per cent are under age 15), which results from the high rate of population growth; low literacy; and a low level of urbanization. In 1980, only about one-quarter of the population lived in urban areas of 20,000 or more inhabitants. However, major cities are growing rapidly, with annual growth rates of between 5 and 10 per cent, sustained by both high rates of natural increase (2.9 per cent per annum) and rapidly accelerating in-migration from villages and smaller towns.

The economic development strategy inadvertently shaped the pattern of population distribution. Beginning from the later part of the colonial rule, changes – administrative and political – were introduced which also had the indirect effect of diversifying migratory flows in the country. The development of provincial and divisional centres followed first the regionalization and later the granting of regional autonomy, providing employment opportunities for clerical and administrative cadres and expanded opportunities in trade and commerce. Artisans, labourers, clerks and traders were attracted to these centres, which were few in number, as was the choice of potential destinations for migrants.

The wage employment opportunities in these centres were considerably enhanced by the infrastructural investment in social amenities – roads, hospitals, piped water, electricity – which made the towns increasingly attractive to live in. Unlike the situation in Eastern and Southern Africa, with large and segregated

European settlements, there were no restrictive policies on movements of population; rather a policy mix of incentives and disincentives embracing the introduction of compulsory tax was introduced, to induce the required calibre and quantity of labour to service the rapidly growing, urban-centred administration, commerce and industry.

The improvements in transportation and communication networks have exerted a considerable impact on migration: these also facilitated the transmission of messages and impulses to different, widely located areas of the country. Improved transportation reduced the cultural gap and facilitated the integration of migrants to the host communities. It also had the added advantage of facilitating circulation or oscillatory migration. During the colonial era, a variety of migratory flows developed and some existing ones ceased or were modified as a result of political stability and the newly introduced economic structure geared towards the export of agricultural products to Europe.

In short, by the end of colonial rule in 1960, the development path had been clearly mapped out: this took the form of the agricultural, rural sector, and a rapidly growing small urban sector, marked by the concentration of development in a few cities. After independence, the policy of import substitution was vigorously pursued; the reliance on foreign sources of finance and manpower for the industrial sector, and the capital intensive nature of investment there, resulted in few employment opportunities for the rapidly growing labour force.

The spread of education, fostered by the rapidly growing population, created a pool of school leavers equipped with few or no practical skills for employment in the urban sector. The mismatch between the aspirations of the parents and the young school leavers and the type of employment available resulted in what initially became known as 'school leaver unemployment', which is particularly marked among school leavers of rural origin. Not all the migrants were educated and young: a significant proportion of city-ward migrants included adults, married and non-educated persons – traders, artisans, labourers – who invariably get absorbed into the informal sector and related activities.

Development plans and population distribution policies

In a restricted perspective, Nigeria has no explicitly formulated and well articulated population policy to influence directly the major demographic variables, especially migration (Adepoju, 1982). In a broad perspective, however, population policy embraces both explicit or population-influencing and implicit or population-responsive measures and programmes designed to contribute to the achievement of economic, social, demographic and other collective goals through their effects on demographic variables. In Nigeria, two areas of population concern and policy are explicitly stated: reduction of mortality (for non-demographic objectives) and the control of international migration, except for Economic Community of West African States (E.C.O.W.A.S.) nationals (for economic considerations of the absorptive capacity of the labour market (U.N.F.P.A., 1980: 58)). However, there are several aspects of implicit policies related to employment generation, skill development and rural development programmes; the relevant aspects will be discussed in relation to migration and population distribution policies and programmes.

During the operation of the First National Development Plan, 1962–68, government perception of the population issue was not clearly stated except in general terms relating the rate of population growth to that of economic growth. Likewise, the government position was not clearly stipulated as the post-independence planning efforts were geared towards achieving national unity and strengthening the infrastructural base of the economy.

Beginning with the Second National Development Plan, 1970–74, government concern over population issues became more articulated in the area of spatial distribution and movement of population (Adepoju, 1981: 143). Indeed, the plan stated that: 'For Nigeria, the distribution and movement of population to reflect relative economic opportunities is probably more important in the short-run than the aggregate size of the country's population' (F.M.E.D.R.A., 1970: 77). During the plan period, the government's population policy in the area of migration was aimed at encouraging skilled labour mobility and free inter-state population movement to exploit the 'resource base and development potentials' in various regions of the country. This, according to Acsadi (1971), is indeed, a 'partial' migration policy.

The Third National Development Plan, 1975–80, re-echoed the government position as briefly outlined in the 1970–74 plan by emphasizing that: 'The problem of the rapid rate of migration from rural to urban areas is recognized as an important aspect of population policy. Since rapid urbanization is accompanying social and economic development in Nigeria . . . the Government does not intend to discourage urbanization but rather to plan and control urban growth' (F.M.E.D., 1975: 77–8).

Several programmes were outlined in the plan; these included integrated rural development, community development activities, rural employment promotion projects and farm settlement schemes. The central aim was to improve rural incomes and living conditions and stem rural out-migration (Ayida and Chikelu, 1975). Besides, the plan stated further that, 'in order to reduce the problem of urbanization to manageable proportions, the Government will pursue a policy of integrated urban and rural development during the plan period' (F.M.E.D. 1975: 294).

More specifically, the regional development policy elaborated in the Third Plan aims at achieving a balanced development of urban and rural areas, balanced regional development, and creation of new urban management systems to overcome urban problems. At the rural end, the objectives include the diversification and intensification of rural production and the provision of basic social amenities, especially health centres, piped water, feeder roads and electricity. The plan emphasized that 'these measures should help to narrow the

disparities in living standards between the urban and rural population'
(F.M.E.D., 1975: 291–3).

Seven specific short-term objectives were set out, the aim being to achieve more
even distribution of income, reduction in the level of unemployment, diversification of the economy and balanced development. Apart from the objective of
achieving inter-state balanced development, 'another aspect of balanced development is the relative development of the rural and urban areas. In the past, the rural
areas have lagged behind the urban areas in development, resulting in increasing
disparity between standards of living in the rural and urban areas and in mass
migration of population from the former to the latter. The present plan aims at
checking this movement by especially promoting the development of rural areas.
Special efforts will be made to ensure that these rural development programmes
are effectively *implemented*' (F.M.E.D., 1975: 30).

In response to the 1978 Fourth Enquiry by the United Nations on the
perception of overall acceptability of the spatial distribution of the country's
population, the Nigerian government indicated that the current situation was
inappropriate. With regard to the desirable policy measures, the government
stressed the need to initiate policies to decelerate the basic trends in internal
migration. However, no modifications were anticipated in the formulation of
policies regarding the configuration of rural and urban settlements (U.N., 1981:
413).

At the time of writing, only the guidelines of the Fourth National Development
Plan have been published. One of the five objectives of the Fourth Plan is related to
the reduction of rural–urban migration (M.N.P., 1980: 22–3). The guidelines
include a series of strategies for stemming rural migration: agriculture, water,
rural economy, rural life styles, amenities (health and sanitation), new employment opportunities, etc. These are to be implemented mainly by local
governments, and aim at eliminating or drastically reducing the push factors of
migration from the source area. Information on how these would be implemented
is expected to be outlined in the plan document, when published.

Development programmes and population redistribution

The set of policies examined in this section has a close bearing on population
movement and distribution, although these were not the primary objectives. The
salient ones have been classified by Mabogunje (1981) as the new town
development policy; land colonization policy; resettlement schemes, administrative reforms; rural development programmes; and urban development schemes.

Rural development programmes usually aim at reducing the 'push' forces in the
rural areas by providing social amenities and enhancing employment opportunities there. The various activities of the executive agencies – health, education,
agriculture – are geared at promoting the living and working conditions of rural
areas and ultimately stemming the rural exodus.

Urban development programmes are accommodationist in nature. The regional capital cities, especially Lagos, Kano, Port Harcourt, Enugu and Ibadan, are obvious centres of attraction for most migrants since these are the major industrial, educational as well as commercial centres in the country. As a result, these offer readier opportunities for wage employment than medium-sized towns. The rapid growth of the urban industrial sector has been greatly fostered by the concentration of both government investment and the activities of private agencies – both local and international – whose investments are mainly urban-centred, and besides, are closely linked to the international economic system.

The development of the Lagos–Kano–Port Harcourt axes resulted from major concentrations of both public and private investment in these core areas. The influx of population there created, or more correctly exacerbated, the problems of congestion and crowding, unemployment and high house rents. All these placed severe strains on the limited urban social services. The problems of youth employment, delinquency, crime and congestion were politically and economically sensitive; as a result, a series of policies – low cost housing, expanded economic activities, massive investment in urban social services – were initiated in the urban areas in panic situations.

Thus, during the 1975–80 development plan period, the urban policy was systematically geared towards solving the problems created or exacerbated by rapid urban growth, inadequate infrastructure (roads, water, housing) and physical planning. Currently, house rents constitute about 40 per cent of the workers' monthly income. The policy is to reduce this to 20 per cent or less through direct government intervention in the provision of federal and state low income housing units (averaging 21,000 housing units per state) at subsidized rates in the towns. Associated with urban policy is the job creation which the massive investment in road and housing construction and industry is expected to generate. However, these have had the unintended effect of increasing the relative attractiveness of urban areas, thereby accelerating the inflow of migrants.

Only a few land colonization schemes have been successfully implemented. These include the agricultural towns of Mokwa and Shendam. While these have other non-demographic objectives, they nevertheless have some population redistributive impact, by attracting and more important, retaining, settlers there.

The new town development is by far the most recent and elaborate policy on which baseline data are sometimes available. The shifting of the federal capital from Lagos to Abuja and the creation of the agricultural company town of Bacita are viable examples; the Ajoda new town in Oyo State has not advanced beyond the preparatory phase.

Farm settlement schemes

Successive governments in the former regions of the country have since the late 1950s experimented with various programmes to create a more progressive rural economy and provide amenities and more remunerative occupations for village dwellers. These have a central theme: to increase the capacity of these villages to retain their adults and educated youths, thereby reducing the rate of out-migration from rural areas.

The West Regional Government, worried about the inability of the urban economy to absorb the first batch of the free primary school leavers, pioneered an ambitious and expensive farm settlement scheme in the rural areas. The scheme, launched in 1959–60, and later followed by somewhat similar schemes in the East, aimed to demonstrate the feasibility of scientific farming and to settle youths on such farms. Specifically, the aims were, among others, 'to test and later demonstrate modern commercial farming systems which are designed to attract young educated persons to take up farming as a profitable and worthwhile career; and create employment opportunities for some school leavers'. The programme encouraged the youths to stay on the land to reduce the drift to the towns, and sought 'to bring about a socio-economic revolution in the rural areas and reverse the trend of migration from rural areas by making life more congenial than it has been hitherto' (Alade, 1966).

Thirteen farm settlements were set up in Western Nigeria in 1960 and six in Eastern Nigeria in 1962. Between 1960 and 1965, 36 settlements were established in various villages and small towns, each designed to hold 100 to 150 families. Initially, young, unmarried boys with a minimum of completed primary school education were recruited. Progressively, married settlers were involved in the scheme. The cost per settler was very high and the objective to enlist youths in farming as a career was never realized. The drop-out rate was high; the demonstration effect of the 'modern' farms on surrounding farmers was minimal, and the expectations and aspirations of settlers that 'a comfortable living may be earned in the country' were never realized. Settlers had hoped, and the architects of the settlement programme gave the optimistic impression that, the scheme (now abandoned) would provide incomes and living conditions comparable to similar skill levels in urban employment. This never materialized. Likewise, the impact on migration was very minimal.

Promotion of small-scale industries

The Western State rural employment promotion project is one of the most elaborate and integrated schemes with the aim of reducing unemployment among school leavers who migrate to the cities in search of wage employment. The project includes vocational training for primary school leavers on infrastructural, agricultural and industrial programmes.

During the Third National Development Plan, 1975–80, various state governments formulated plans for small-scale industries, the objectives being to decentralize the nodes of development and achieve more balanced distribution. In the former Benue-Plateau State, a major objective of the government included 'the spatial distribution of industries, resources mobilization, diversification of the rural economy and the reduction of the rural–urban income inequality which spurs the rural–urban migration. The provision of the infrastructural facilities necessary to attract industries to the rural areas of the state will be complemented by a well-planned scheme of rural industrial credit' (F.M.E.D., 1975: 165). In Kwara State, industrial estates were planned in each of the 11 administrative divisions, apart from the industrial estates at Ilorin – the state capital – and Ajaokuta. The objective was to provide wage employment in several parts of the state and alternative destinations for migrants.

The former Mid-West government planned the establishment of 16 industrial estates in the divisional headquarters during the Third Development Plan period, 1975–80. The small-scale industries' credit scheme aimed at encouraging the establishment of small-scale industries in the rural areas 'as a means of increasing rural employment and income and of checking rural–urban migration' (F.M.E.D., 1975: 168). Provision was also made in the plan in the former North-Central State for the establishment of one industrial estate in each administrative headquarter to serve as the foundation of the future industrial growth of these areas to 'enhance the dispersal of small-scale industries to sub-urban areas'. The industrial location strategy was designed to check the widening industrial development gap between the Kaduna and Zaria zones and the remaining towns. Likewise, the small-scale enterprises' development scheme in the former Eastern State aimed at training small-scale entrepreneurs in 15 selected urban areas in the state. The scheme is expected to promote industrial dispersal, the aim being to 'mitigate the problems of rural–urban migration' (F.M.E.D., 1975: 173).

These various schemes, if effectively implemented, would have achieved the goal of promoting dispersed industrial development and possibly diversified the migration streams. But, given the wide gap between the formulation and implementation of government policies, as is characteristic of previous develop-ment plans, only a few of the projects outlined above were, in fact, implemented. Besides, very little information is available to facilitate a review of these projects, which are also too recent for their impact to be felt on population movement.

Administrative reforms

Two recent administrative reforms are relevant to the present discussion: local government reform and the creation of additional states in the country. In 1977, the existing administrative structure in the country was streamlined under a uniform system. About 300 local government councils were created and given considerable responsibility in areas that closely touch the people – sanitation, feeder roads, recreation, water supply, etc. By so doing, development was brought closer to the people (Olowu, 1980). One desirable impact of this is the development of local government headquarters as service points for their respective vicinities. It can be speculated that such centres also serve as 'receiving stations' for some migrants and ultimate destinations for others otherwise destined for the state capitals. This is most probably the case with clerks, artisans, traders and sundry workers.

Before 1963, there were three regional capitals – Ibadan, Kaduna and Enugu. These, along with Lagos, Port Harcourt and Kano, were the major administrative and industrial centres and served as major destinations for migrants. Benin joined the cadre in 1963, and by 1967 twelve state capitals had emerged, the major focus of massive investment in infrastructure and later light industries and commerce. The inter-state competition in development impetus promoted rapid growth of these state capitals, which also became growth centres. In this way, the creation of states indirectly promoted a decentralized urban development and diversified possible destinations for migrants. The 19-state structure introduced in 1976 further diversified the development of nodes, especially the new state capitals which enjoyed the patronage of the Federal Government in financial allocations to enable them effectively to take off. The result is that in the place of the former three nodes of development, a minimum of 20 developmental zones have emerged, coinciding with the state capitals.

The creation of states witnessed a massive influx of migrants – of the return migration stream – consisting of professionals, traders, artisans and kindred workers, to participate in the administrative and commercial activities of the new state capitals (Adepoju, 1981). So far, there is no study of the population-redistributive impact of the creation of additional states; it can be speculated, however, that a considerable amount of migration resulted from the creation of states and that the heavy urban population concentration in the old regional capitals has been greatly diffused since 1975. Apart from decelerating migration to the old centres of migration, the creation of states also fostered balanced development in the country.

Resettlement schemes

An equally significant measure – from the point of view of population-redistributive impact – relates to the resettlement schemes at Kainji and Bakolari dams, which involved the movement and resettlement of about 50,000 and 15,000 people respectively.

The Bakolari Dam and Irrigation Project, estimated at N110 million, is one of the largest agricultural projects in the country. It was designed to irrigate about 75,000 acres of land. The reservoir covered about 15,000–20,000 acres of land, and affected the homes and farm land of about 15,000 farmers who were resettled near the project site.

The construction of the Kainji dam involved the resettlement of people living in the area flooded by the dam. Initially, in 1963, when the resettlement started, four villages were involved; later 17 other villages had to be relocated. By 1965 when the resettlement was completed, an estimated 44,000 farmers from 239 villages and hamlets were resettled in 141 new villages (Mabogunje, 1973). Apart from these, some 12,400 workers were attracted to the dam site to work in various capacities. As Oyedipe (1977) puts it, 'equally significant was the influx of a large population of engineers, technicians, administrators, traders, unskilled labourers and other allied tradesmen into the area'. Like the Volta dam scheme in Ghana, this represents a concerted effort to redistribute population spontaneously.

Shifting the Federal Capital

The Federal Government invited the Economic Commission for Africa (E.C.A.) to conduct a series of surveys designed to provide 'basic demographic data for planning the new Federal Capital City'. Five surveys were conducted, including two demographic studies of households and the public service.

Among the 1,924,640 persons covered in the household survey, 55 per cent were classified as non-migrants. The migrants (45 per cent) were highly selective with respect to sex, the sex ratio of males to females being 125 : 100 (E.C.A., 1980a: 34). The heads of households were asked to indicate their plan to go to Abuja or stay in Lagos: their responses are *tentatively* indicative of planned movement to Abuja when this is inaugurated. Overall, 59 per cent were willing to move, 26 per cent were unwilling, while 15 per cent were undecided. These responses were significantly influenced by the origin of the respondents: less than 50 per cent of natives of Lagos State were willing to move, compared with 60 per cent of those of Oyo State and 96 per cent of those of Gongola State (E.C.A., 1980a: 184). In fact, except for the Yoruba-speaking states – Lagos, Ogun, Oyo and Kwara – more than 70 per cent of indigenes in other states planned to move to Abuja and a much smaller proportion among the others was undecided.

Factors such as the employment status of household heads, sex, house ownership and occupancy status influence the willingness or otherwise to move to Abuja. A higher proportion of employees than own-account workers, more males than females, fewer owner-occupiers than tenants were willing to move.

It was estimated that between 150,000 and 320,000 persons would probably be resident in Abuja in 1986. The initial master plan for Abuja assumes a target population of 1,642,000 for the year 2000 (Table 14.1), noting that the city 'will be permitted to grow to a maximum population of approximately 3 million, after which population growth will be accommodated in satellite towns' (E.C.A., 1980a: 214). What is perhaps intriguing is the projected annual growth of Abuja: 28 per cent in 1986–90, 14 per cent during 1990–95, and 10 per cent during 1995–2000, or an average of 17 per cent for the 1986–2000 period. Even under the low variant population projections, the rate of growth is estimated to be 12 per cent during 1986–2000. Further, it is projected that the number of households will increase sharply from 32,000 in 1986 to 205,000 by 1995, further rising to 335,000 by the year 2000. However, under the medium variant projection prepared by the E.C.A. (1980a: 217), the households in Abuja will vary between 257,000 and 522,000 in the year 2000, based on 32,000 and 65,000 households in 1986. Correspondingly, the total population is expected to vary widely between 1,261,000 and 2,559,000 in the year 2000 under the medium variant projections. The three different projections are based on 'the three likely initial population sizes at the inauguration of Abuja in 1986' (E.C.A., 1980a), derived from estimates made in the Master Plan (158,000), official estimate (200,000) and estimate by the E.C.A. (320,000).

The survey indicated that 78 per cent of all civil servants were willing to move from Lagos to Abuja. Very few (13 per cent) were unwilling to move and only 9 per cent had not made up their minds by the time of the survey. It is interesting to note that 60 per cent of the public servants' household population was not born in Lagos. Among the migrants, 36 per cent were of rural origin. There are differentials by sex: while 87 per cent of all male public servants were willing to move to Abuja, only 60 per cent of their female counterparts were willing to do so (E.C.A., 1980b).

Unlike most migratory moves, especially to new unexplored destinations, 93 per cent of the public servants who plan to move intend to move, with members of their households, to settle in Abuja. This is not surprising when it is realized that 47 per cent of migrants initially moved to Lagos to join their family/spouse employed in the public service. About another third (34 per cent) moved to Lagos to work or look for employment, while 19 per cent did so in order to attend school. It is to be expected that the different phases of the government move to Abuja will stimulate the movement of a large number of people from Lagos and other localities in the country. It is projected that 10,000 public servants will move there during 1982–83; 23,000 in 1984–85; 6,000 in 1985–87 and 31,000 after 1987. An estimated 281,000 public servants will be at Abuja by the year 2000: 17,000 by 1983; 68,000 by 1986; 83,000 by 1987; 172,000 by 1990 and 220,000 by 1995 (E.C.A. 1980a, b).

These various projections are based on estimates of the Lagos population alone. As a new federal capital, Abuja is expected to serve as the administrative and political nerve centre of the country; and, by so doing, to attract migrants from all parts of the country and beyond. The data base for estimating the magnitude of this flow is weak; nevertheless, the influx of migrants is expected to be rapid at first and may stabilize by the end of the century. It was indicated that the movement to Abuja would take off before 1 October 1982; in fact, it has taken off gradually: a few government ministries have moved their headquarters to Abuja, while others are expected to move during 1983–85.

Summary

The review of previous development plans in Nigeria shows that in spite of the concern by planners about the adverse effects of the rapidly increasing city-ward migration and the resulting distribution of population, few concrete policies have been introduced *and* implemented to achieve a rational pattern of population

Table 14.1. *Population projections for Abuja, 1986–2000*

Variant	Year				Implied annual growth rate (%),
	1986	1990	1995	2000	1986–2000
	(numbers in thousands)				
I Master plan	158	486	1,005	1,642	16.7
II High	158	486	978	1,872	17.6
	200	613	1,235	2,363	17.6
	320	981	1,975	3,781	17.6
III Medium	158	380	728	1,261	14.8
	200	482	923	1,599	14.8
	320	771	1,476	2,559	14.8
IV Low	158	324	534	838	11.9
	200	411	677	1,062	11.9
	320	657	1,084	1,700	11.9

Source: E.C.A., 1980: 218

distribution. The issue of population redistribution is addressed, in part, through regional planning policies. However, a few projects have been implemented which directly affect population redistribution, even though this was not the original intention. These include farm settlement schemes, rural industrialization and administrative reforms. Their impact on population redistribution has been minimal.

Two projects – resettlement schemes and shifting of the federal capital – exerted direct influence on population redistribution. The construction of the Kainji and Bakolari dams involved the relocation of 55,000 or so people; it is estimated that initially, in 1986, about 320,000 people will have moved to Abuja, the new capital whose population is projected at 3 million by the year 2000. The two examples are cases of organized movements of population consequent on the execution of development projects.

REFERENCES

Acsadi, G.T. (1971) Population policy and the Second Nigerian National Development Plan, Paper presented at seminar on population problems and policy in Nigeria, University of Ife.

Adepoju, A. (1981) *Migration and Development: The Case of Medium-Sized Towns in Nigeria*, Project report to be published by U.N.E.S.C.O. (Population Division).

Adepoju, A. (1982) Demographic aspects of internal migration policies in Nigeria, Paper prepared for the Working Group on Population and Development in Africa, C.O.D.E.S.R.I.A., Dakar.

Alade, C.A. (1966) *The Role of Farm Settlement Schemes in Western Nigeria Development Programme: Some Case Studies*, Institute of Administration, University of Ife.

Ayida, A.A. and Chikelu, G.P.O. (1975) Population aspects of development planning, in U.N., *The Population Debate: Dimensions and Perspectives*, vol. 1, New York.

Economic Commission for Africa (E.C.A.) (1980a) *Reports on Demographic Survey of Households, Housing and Living Conditions in Lagos*, Addis Ababa.

Economic Commission for Africa (E.C.A.) (1980b) *Reports on Demographic Survey of Federal Republic Servants in Lagos*, Addis Ababa.

Federal Ministry of Economic Development and Reconstruction (F.M.E.D.R.A.) (1970) *Second National Development Plan 1970–74*, Lagos.

Federal Ministry of Economic Development (F.M.E.D.) (1975) *Third National Development Plan 1975–80*, Lagos.

Mabogunje, A.L. (1973) *Kainji: A Nigerian Man-Made Lake, Kainji Lake Studies*, vol. 2, Ibadan, N.I.S.E.R.

Mabogunje, A.L. (1981) Effectiveness of population redistribution policies: the African experience, Solicited paper for session F.18 I.U.S.S.P., General Conference, Manila.

National Commission for Economic Planning Ministry of National Planning (M.N.P.) (1980) *Guidelines for the Fourth National Development Plan 1980–85*, Lagos.

Olowu, D. (1980) Local government and social services administration in Nigeria: the impact of urbanization, mimeo, Department of Public Administration, University of Ife.

Oyedipe, P.A. (1977) *Interrelated Changes in the Productive Activities and Demographic Characteristics of an African Population: A Study of the Impact of the Kainji Dam (Nigeria)*, Project Report to I.D.E.P., Dakar.

United Nations (1981) *Reports of Monitoring of Population Policies*, Document ESA/P/WP. 69, New York.

United Nations Fund for Population Activities (U.N.F.P.A.) (1980) *Nigeria Background Report: Needs Assessment for Population Assistance*, Office of the Coordinator, Lagos.

15 Population, disease and rural development programmes in the Upper East Region of Ghana

George Benneh

In the last decade, the question of rural development has come to the fore in the debate on the economic development of Third World countries. Not only have past development strategies been subject to enlightened criticism from policy makers, international financial organizations and social scientists, but new development strategies have been adopted with hardly any contributions to their formulation from their target populations. The lexicon of development has been enriched by the emergence of such new terms as 'integrated rural development', 'development from below' and 'basic needs approach'. But in all the twists and turns in the thread of the development debate, one thing on which there appears to be a convergence of views is the pivotal role of man in the development process. It is, therefore, surprising that the population factor has only recently been accorded the importance it deserves in the development strategies of developing countries.

There are several aspects of a country's population which have a direct bearing on its development. A United Nations (U.N., 1983) expert group on population resources, environment and development noted that 'an analysis of the population factors must take into account many other variables in addition to the number of persons, age, sex composition and geographical location. It must encompass socio-economic characteristics such as income distribution, level of education, health and family status.'

This chapter, however, focuses on only two of these variables: the health of the population with special reference to the incidence of onchocerciasis in the Upper East Region of Ghana and the geographical location of population in the region. The relationships between the two variables are examined and the problems of development arising from the incidence of onchocerciasis and the distribution of population are discussed. The second section of the chapter reviews two rural development programmes which have been designed and implemented to solve some of these problems.

A profile of the Upper East Region

The Upper East Region of Ghana borders on the Sahel zone. It shares common frontiers with the Republic of Burkina Faso (formerly Upper Volta) to the north and Togo to the east; its southern boundary with the Northern Region of Ghana is demarcated by the White Volta and Kulpawn rivers and the Gambaga scarp; and the Sissili river is its western boundary with the Upper West Region. The region comprises the three administrative districts of Bawku, Bolgatanga and Navrongo, and nine Local Council areas.

Annual rainfall in the region is about 40 inches (1,016 mm). The main meteorological station at Bawku records an annual average rainfall of 38.3 inches (925.5 mm), with an average of about 70 rain days; three-quarters of the rain falls between May and September. Thus, during six or seven months of the year, crops cannot be grown without irrigation. Drought occurs at irregular intervals, on an average once in five years.

The soils of the region are broadly classified into upland soils and valley soils. The upland soils are moderately well drained, and non-concretionary, or slightly concretionary when developed over sandstones and granite. Generally suitable for millet, sorghum maize and cowpeas under a system of hand cultivation or with bullock ploughing, upland soils have been subjected to intensive cultivation over the years. The valley soils, on the other hand, are quite deep, seasonally flooded and poorly drained. Mainly suited to rice cultivation, pasture and dry season vegetable gardening, they are difficult to cultivate by hand or by animal-drawn equipment (Adu, 1965).

The 1984 population census recorded a total population of 772,000 for the region compared with 543,000 in 1970, an intercensal increase of 43.1 per cent compared with a national increase of 42.6 per cent. Population density is highest in the upland areas, where it exceeds 160 per sq km, and lowest in the valley bottoms, where it is less than 40 per sq km. Most of the riverine areas are virtually empty (Fig. 15.5). A comparison of the population density maps over the years (Figs. 15.1, 15.3 and 15.4) underlines the overall trend in the concentration of population in the watershed areas and the near emptiness of the valley bottoms. The main empty areas comprise valleys of the Morago, Red and White Volta, Sissili and Tamne rivers. Outside these valleys, land is densely populated, with compound farming predominating. According to the 1970 population census data, the vast majority of the people lived in villages of less than 1,000 inhabitants. In the two Upper Regions as a whole, over 75 per cent of the population lived in settlements of less than 1,000 inhabitants, compared with the national average of 48 per cent.

The region is poorly served with all-weather roads, and during the wet season access to many places is difficult or impossible. A publication by the Rural Planning Department of the Ministry of Youth and Rural Development in 1970, which compared the Upper Region (of which the Upper East Region was then a part) with the rest of the country in relation to access to some basic needs, such as education, health facilities and potable water, observed that the Upper Region belonged to one of the least-developed regions of the country.

Incidence of onchocerciasis and the pattern of population distribution

Although the prevalence of onchocerciasis is not the only reason for the relative emptiness of the river valleys in the region, it is nonetheless an important factor.

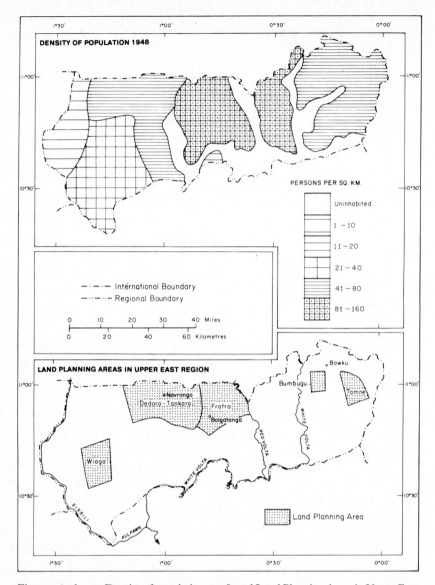

Figs 15.1 and 15.2 Density of population, 1948, and Land Planning Areas in Upper East Region, Ghana

Onchocerciasis is an infection by a parasitic filarial (threadlike) worm *Onchocerca volvulus*, transmitted in the region by the bite of an infected female blackfly of the species *Simulium damnosum*. The fly itself becomes infected by biting an infected human host. Both man and fly are therefore essential elements in the life cycle of the parasite.

The larvae of the insect vector *S. damnosum* can develop only in fast-flowing rivers. Onchocerciasis is therefore a disease of the areas flanking the rapids of

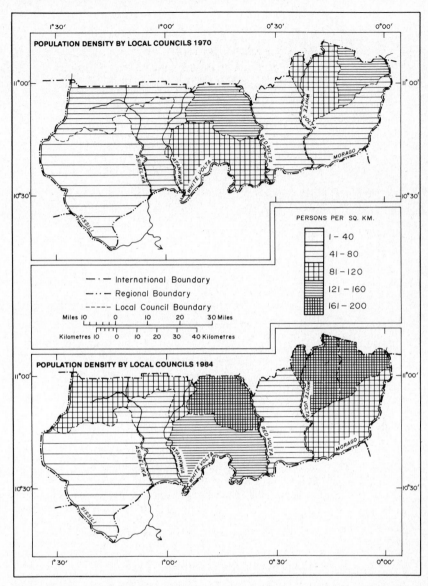

Figs 15.3 and 15.4 Population density by local councils, 1970 and 1984, Upper East Region, Ghana

rivers, hence its common name 'river blindness'. Apart from its role as a vector of disease the blackfly constitutes an intolerable nuisance. The average number of bites per day sometimes amount to several thousands, although only a small proportion of these result in infections. An infected person may ultimately go blind. Before the victim's sight is impaired, he would suffer from constant and excruciating itching caused by worms under his skin.

Onchocerciasis has a two-fold destructive economic effect: not only is there a

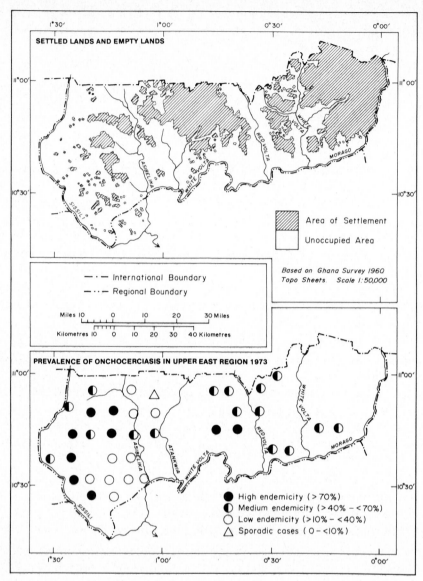

Figs 15.5 and 15.6 Settled lands and empty lands, and prevalence of onchocerciasis in Upper East Region, Ghana, 1973

reduction in the productive capacity of those afflicted by the disease, but the blind and the partially-blind become a charge on the society. The inhabitants of the onchocerciasis-ridden river valleys migrate to the upland areas which have, as a result, become overcrowded and overcropped. There are examples of desertion of former sites of villages or parts of villages at Tilli, Sekoti, Windenaba and Nangodi. These represent specific cases where the primary responsibility of onchocerciasis is not disputed. The disease has long been recognized by local communities, as evidenced by the terms in their local languages specifically describing the clinical symptoms of onchocerciasis. There are examples of traditional cures of the disease, albeit not effective, such as the chameleon fetish at Tilli.

Figure 15.6 shows the distribution of onchocerciasis by levels of endemnicity before the onchocerciasis programme was launched in 1974. Large hyper-endemic areas with prevalence rates of more than 70 per cent were found between the Red and White Volta rivers and along the Sissili river and its small tributaries.

As already pointed out, the presence of onchocerciasis and its vector may not always have been the sole factor leading to depopulation of the valleys. The present pattern of population distribution can be explained partly by the impact of the slave raiders who operated in northern Ghana during the nineteenth century (Lynn 1937; Dickson 1968). Other reasons have been put forward. According to one of the early writers on the subject 'Large areas of the country particularly on the . . . slopes toward some of the bigger rivers have been left entirely, and although tse-tse flies and slave raiders often receive the discredit, the stony condition and poor vegetation of the old farm lands round the compound ruins suggest that soil exhaustion was a factor not unconnected with their abandonment' (Lynn, 1942).

If soil exhaustion was a contributory factor in the depopulation of the valleys, then the problem was transferred to the upland areas where the high population densities had resulted in soil erosion and a decline in yields of crops by the late 1930s. Studies by agricultural officers in the region served to underline the seriousness of land degradation (Lynn, 1937).

Land planning, soil and water conservation programme

The land-planning policy originated from a genuine concern by the Colonial Administration about the deteriorating condition of soils in the upland areas in northern Ghana. In order to arrest the situation, the North Mamprusi Forestry Conference was convened at Navrongo in 1947. After proposals to establish Forest Reserves on the main watersheds in the region had been seen to involve the moving of too many people to be practicable, it was decided that the catchment areas and watersheds should be constituted into planning areas and that comprehensive measures should be taken to counteract soil erosion and to conserve water (Clancey and Ramsey, 1954). As a result of the recommendations of the conference, the Chief Commissioner of the Northern Territories (northern Ghana) set up a committee known as the Dedoro-Tankara Land Planning Committee in March 1948. This committee was to carry out a detailed survey of the Dedoro-Tankara land-planning area and to draw up a plan for soil and water conservation and general land use. If such a plan proved practicable, consideration would be given to setting up committees to do the same for other areas.

The survey was carried out by the Agriculture and Forestry officers jointly and a plan drawn up. When the practicability of such a plan had been established, the Dedoro-Tankara Land Planning Committee was redesignated as the North Mamprusi Land Planning Committee, in September 1949. Project committees were then set up under this for Dedoro-Tankara, Bumbugu, Tamne, Frafra and Wiaga (Fig. 15.2). Although there was local representation on these committees, the local population made hardly any contribution to the formulation of the land planning policy. It was mainly fashioned by colonial administrators and civil servants who, nonetheless, had detailed knowledge of the local conditions based on several years of field surveys.

The conservation measures taken in the land-planning areas consisted of establishing watershed protective forest reserves; contouring of arable land to control run-off from sloping land; construction of dams to regulate the movement of water and control gullies near the watershed; and demarcation and fencing of grazing areas. Productive measures included the planting of fuel-wood plantations; the introduction of improved farming methods and of fish farming; the building of clay-cored dams for supplying water for irrigation and stock; and the sinking of wells to provide water for human consumption. But to a large extent the success of the land-planning programme was to be judged by the improvement of farming methods based on the introduction of bullock ploughing, coupled with the use of farmyard manure and fertilizers on blocks of contiguous land of adequate size.

By the end of the financial year 1961/62, 135 dams had been constructed in the land-planning areas in the region; 1115.29 miles (1794.7 km) of narrow base contour bunds had been built; and 7,768 acres (3,144 ha) of land not suitable for arable purposes had been fenced and partially reseeded as grazing camps. Under completely or partially-controlled irrigation were 946 acres (420.9 ha) of bunded rice fields, and there were 335 acres (135.6 ha) of organized dry-season gardens. There was spectacular progress in the introduction of mixed farming: from one plough farmer in Bawku district in 1938 the number of bullock-plough farmers had increased to 2,645 by 1960. A publication of the Ministry of Agriculture (1962) commented on the success of the land-planning programme with particular reference to the Bumbugu Land-Planning Area as follows: 'The farming within the Land Planning Area has been established and the farmers are following a set rotational system using improved agricultural practices as taught by extension services of the Division; these have increased yields by over 100 per cent.' It concluded: 'The standard of living of the people has improved beyond all expectations.'

Nevertheless, the implementation of the programme encountered many difficulties, not the least of which was the lack of experienced professional specialists necessary to draw plans and train technicians for the follow-up work. In December 1959, the Government appointed a Working Party within the Ministry of Agriculture to carry out a thorough reappraisal of the Land-Planning Organization and its activities, with the objectives of achieving maximum long-range benefits from an expanded programme and preventing further deterioration of the land. Based on the recommendations of the Working Party Report, the Government of Ghana obtained approval in November 1961 for a United Nations Special Fund for the preparation of plans for the development of the land and water resources in the whole of Northern Ghana. F.A.O. was appointed as the Executing Agency for the project; field work was started in 1962 and was completed in November 1966.

Whilst the F.A.O. survey was under way, the Ghana Government launched a new agricultural policy in 1962 which shifted emphasis from smallholder agriculture to large-scale mechanized farming. The implementation of the new policy was entrusted to the following production fronts: the State Farms' Corporation, the agricultural wing of the Workers' Brigade, the United Ghana Farmers' Cooperatives' Council and the Young Farmers' League. Each of these production fronts established large-scale mechanized farms. The new socialized agricultural policy had the effect of dismantling the Land Planning Organization, whose personnel and machinery were withdrawn to the Vea Irrigation Dam near Bolgatanga, which was under construction. The United Ghana Farmers' Cooperatives' Council was made responsible for agricultural extension. Farmers in Manga Bawku, in the Bumbugu Land-Planning Area, complained to the author in 1969 that since 1962 the visits of extension officers had been most irregular (Benneh, 1972), which was confirmed by the poor condition of the contour bunds in the village at the time. Not only had parts been washed away due to poor maintenance, but some farmers had started growing crops on them, thus contributing to soil erosion.

The small dams or dug-outs which were constructed to conserve water for use in the dry season, and also for use by livestock and for crop irrigation, were not maintained. A survey in 1974 enumerated 68 dams, reservoirs or dug-outs of various sizes within the Bawku district, and most had either silted up from eroded top soils within their catchment areas or dried up because of high evaporation. Furthermore, as they became sources of water-borne diseases, their use became less attractive and the lack of treatment facilities and the incidence of river blindness forced many to move away from them. The survey concluded: 'In the present conditions of dug-outs, it is difficult to reckon their contribution to current water resources assessment of the area. They must first be rehabilitated, a task which must take into account the control of overland erosion and subsequent siltation of the reservoirs and the health hazards posed by man and animal utilising the same source of water' (C.S.I.R. and U.S.A.I.D., 1975).

If rural development should aim at building up the capability of the target population to solve their problems and improve their living conditions on a sustainable basis, then the record of achievement of the land planning programme has been disappointing. With the partial withdrawal of Government support after 1962, measures which had been introduced were allowed to lapse and facilities which had been provided were not maintained. This raises the fundamental question of the extent of the commitment of the local population to the programme and their understanding of the motives behind the measures which had been introduced.

Admittedly, there was local representation of the project committees for each of the land planning areas, but as Billes (1954) observed:

The local people have on the whole welcomed these operations and there has been no case of opposition. They appreciate very much the improvement of water supplies and the opportunity of earning wages, but do not always take advantage of all that is done for them, such as irrigation schemes, and they have little conception of the purpose of the operations. It is probably along broad lines of general community development that economic development will make the most progress.

The Onchocerciasis control programme (O.C.P.)

By the beginning of the 1970s, the strategy for solving the development problems in the region had changed. While the land planning programme had been focused on improving the watershed areas of the region, that of the Onchocerciasis Control Programme was centred on the relatively empty river valleys. This change in spatial orientation was partly due to a change in the perception, on the part of development agents, of the problems of the region and the technology necessary for solving them.

The change in orientation was aided by results of studies carried out since the 1940s on the spread of onchocerciasis in the region and the socio-economic impact of the disease. Systematic surveys such as Waddy's (1949) pioneering work drew the attention of policy makers to the severity of the incidence of onchocerciasis. Hunter's (1966) study of Nangodi posited a hypothesis of cyclical advance and collapse of settlements in riverine areas in the region. There were similar surveys in other West Africa countries in the Volta River basin.

Following these studies, it came to be accepted that the control of the *Similium* vector would provide the key to opening up the empty areas. Thus after preparatory meetings had been organized by the World Health Organization (W.H.O.) and U.S.A.I.D., seven countries (Benin, Burkina Faso formerly Upper Volta, Ghana, Ivory Coast, Mali, Niger and Togo) requested W.H.O. to combat onchocerciasis in the Volta river basin. A Preparation Assistance to Governments (P.A.G.) mission was set up by W.H.O. and F.A.O. in 1971–73, financed by the United Nations Development Programme (U.N.D.P.). Its task was to prepare a programme for the control of onchocerciasis over the entire Volta River basin, and to identify areas offering development possibilities in the light of their economic potential.

In its report, the P.A.G. mission recommended a plan of operation for a campaign to combat the disease under an O.C.P. to be executed by W.H.O. in association with F.A.O. and with the support of U.N.D.P. and the World Bank. The O.C.P. area in Ghana is the whole of northern Ghana, of which the Upper

East Region is a part. Funds for the programme, which began in 1974, were secured from various governments, including those of Britain, Canada, France, the Federal Republic of Germany, the Netherlands and the United States of America. Since the adult *Onchocerca volvulus* worm can live for as long as 15 years in an infected person, it was decided that the programme should last 20 years. The first phase (1974–79) cost $54 million, and the second phase (1980–85), which is being funded by the World Bank, the African Development Bank and 20 official aid agencies, will cost $110 million.

The control of the disease is on a regional basis with the headquarters at Ouagadougou, the capital of Burkina Faso. The O.C.P. has concentrated its efforts on the insecticidal attack on the larvae of the blackfly which are found on the swift-flowing sections of rivers. This strategy has been adopted because to attack the female blackfly with insecticides would mean spraying very large areas. Moreover, with a flight range of more than 150 km, the blackfly is not an easy target.

The choice of insecticide for the control programme has been crucial. D.D.T. was originally used, but because of its residual properties and its harmful effects on the environment its use was discontinued. Investigations led to the selection of temophos, Abate, which combined in a specific formulation the essential properties of high effectiveness against the blackfly larvae of all stages and low toxicity for the environment.

The massive spraying has resulted in a fairly spectacular control of the vector. According to the Director of the Onchocerciasis Control Programme, some 65 per cent of the original programme area is free of the infected blackfly. Fieldwork carried out by the author in the Nangodi, Zebilla and Tilli areas in the Upper East Region in 1978 revealed that the previously abandoned river valleys were being cultivated. Local inhabitants confirmed to the author that the nuisance caused by many bites from the blackfly had also been considerably reduced. But whereas a tolerable level of the incidence of the disease may have been reached in the area, the disease would not disappear for about 15 to 20 years, due to the longevity of the vector. Moreover, an onchocerciasis-free area could be reinvaded by the blackfly.

In view of this and the possible long-term effects of the massive insecticide spraying on the flora and fauna in the area (in spite of assurances of safety), a case was made for increase in funds for research into control measures other than spraying (Asibey, 1977). Furthermore, the scale and complexity of the control operation should be a case for concern in the long run. Neither Ghana nor any of the other six states connected with the programme has funds, materials, or human and technological resources to continue the fight after the end of the programme. The need to find cost-effective, intermediate and more appropriate techniques for controlling onchocerciasis cannot therefore be overemphasized.

Ultimately, the programme's success may largely depend on the development of a safe drug for effective mass treatment. Those developed so far, such as suramine and diethylcarbamazine, have been found to have damaging side-effects.

The O.C.P. has allocated $17.5 million for research and development over the next five years.

While the control of the disease is being done on regional basis and financed from a central fund, the economic development of the freed areas is a matter for each of the governments of the seven countries. The Ghana Government has established a National Onchocerciasis Committee with three sub-committees in the Upper East, Upper West and Northern Regions to implement this aspect of the programme. In addition there is a National Onchocerciasis Secretariat located in Accra.

Although the development of the freed areas is the responsibility of the individual governments, some guidelines provided by the P.A.G. mission became the F.A.O./I.B.R.D. (1975) methodology for planning the development of the O.C.P. zones in each country, in three stages:

(a)   the gathering of basic information by making an inventory of existing studies and undertaking new ones, with particular emphasis on basic data generation by remote sensing;

(b)   the utilization of this information for preparing development plans; and

(c)   the implementation of specific development projects.

These guidelines have been designed to encourage rational use of the freed lands and to avoid the ecological abuse that could follow unplanned or unguided occupation of these lands.

The national Onchocerciasis Control Committee of Ghana has achieved some measure of success in using the above methodology. A data bank has been built about the onchocerciasis-free areas (National Onchocerciasis Secretariat, 1984), including the report on the landsat-related study for regional planning of onchocerciasis-free areas, prepared by the Tippetts-Abbetts MacCarthy Straton Company. Moreover, six development areas in the O.C.P. region of Ghana have been selected for planned development, one of which is the Fumbisi/Yagaba/Soo area, located mostly in the Northern Region but with a spillover into the Upper East Region. South of Navrongo, near the confluence of the Sissili and Kulpawn rivers with the White Volta, this is the first planned resettlement programme to be implemented, and it is to be financed by the Ghana Government and U.N.D.P. each contributing about the equivalent of U.S.$394,500 and U.S.$815,200 respectively.

Since the inception of the O.C.P., the Fumbisi area in the Upper East Region has witnessed large-scale rice farming with motorized modern machinery. The soil in the area is a very fine silt-loam and can be very productive under irrigation if special cultivation measures are employed. It is estimated that as much as 100,000 ha can be cultivated under irrigation, but only a small fraction of this areas is actually being cultivated, mainly by farmers who have come from outside the area practising a form of mechanized shifting cultivation of upland rice. The influx of 'stranger' rice farmers has been resented by the local population, and has also created problems of land tenure which was the subject of a Ghana Government Committee of Inquiry. It is to be hoped that, with the implementation of the planned resettlement scheme in the area, the living conditions of the people will be changed for the better. The target population of the programme is composed almost entirely of the most poor, least-favoured groups: precisely the groups which are presently the concern of international funding agencies and the governments of most developing countries. Thus, in terms of helping the poorest of the poor and meeting basic needs, it is hard to conceive of a better-targeted programme.

While the control of the blackfly has made an impact on the health of the targeted population, the economic development of the onchocerciasis-free areas has yet to take off. Indeed, given the parlous economic situation of the country, it may well be argued whether or not they deserve priority attention with respect to investment as against other areas which may yield higher and quicker economic returns. It is also important to bear in mind the fact that the eradication of onchocerciasis is only the first step, albeit an important one, towards the development of the empty valley lands of the region. Solutions will have to be found to such other limiting factors as inadequate infrastructure, unreliable rainfall and other health problems, for example, human and animal trypanosomiasis and malnutrition.

The justification for giving some priority to the development of the onchocerciasis-free areas rests not only on the physical potentialities of the area but more importantly on the need to improve the quality of life of a people who for decades have been left helplessly on their own to cope ineffectually with the scourge of river blindness. But if their hope for a better future is to materialize, then the kind of development which is pursued should be centred on them. The only way to bring this about is for the poor people to be involved in the identification of their needs and in the formulation and implementation of development programmes to achieve these needs. This would have the added advantage of building up the capability of the poor people for achieving sustainable development when outside help is withdrawn.

REFERENCES

Adu, S.V. (1965) *Soils of Navrongo-Bawku area, Upper Region, Ghana*, S.L.U.S. Memoir No. 5.

Asibey, E.O.A. (1977) Blackfly dilemma, *Environmental Conservation*, 4, 291–5.

Benneh, G. (1972) The response of farmers in Northern Ghana to the introduction of mixed farming: a case study, *Geografiska Annaler*, 54, Ser. B, No. 2, 95–103.

Billes, D.J. (1954) The planning of land use and soil and water conservation in the Northern Territories, *Proceedings of the 2nd Inter-African Soils Conference*, Leopold-ville, 1148.

Clancey, J.L. and Ramsey, J.M. (1954) Land use soil and water conservation in the Northern Territories of the Gold Coast, *Africa Soils*, 3, 338–53.

C.S.I.R. and U.S.A.I.D. (1975) *North East Ghana Savannah Research Project*, Final Report, vol. 1, mimeo.

Dickson, K.B. (1968) Background to the problem of economic development in Northern Ghana, *Annals of the Association of American Geographers*, 58, 685–98.

F.A.O./I.B.R.D. (1975) *Economic Development of Areas Freed from Onchocerciasis in Dahomey, Ghana, Mali, Togo and Upper Volta*, Rome.

Hunter, J.M. (1966) River blindness in Nangodi Northern Ghana: an hypothesis of cyclical advance and retreat, *Geographical Review*, 56, 398–416.

Lynn, C.W. (1937) Agriculture in North Mamprusi, Gold Coast, *Department of Agriculture Bulletin*, No. 34.

Lynn, C.W. (1942) Agriculture in North Mamprusi: A review of a decade's progress, *Farm and Forest*, 3, 81.

Ministry of Agriculture (1962) *Miscellaneous Information 1961–62*, Accra.

National Onchocerciasis Secretariat (1984) *Socio-Economic Development in the areas freed from Onchocerciasis in Ghana*, cyclostyled report, Accra.

Rural Planning Department (1970) *A Regional Summary of Socio-Economic Survey*, Accra.

U.N. Economic and Social Council (1983) *Recommendations of the Expert Group on Population, Resources, Environment, and Development*, E/Conf.76/PC/8.

Waddy, B.B. (1949) *Onchocerciasis and Blindness in the Northern Territories of the Gold Coast*, cyclostyled report, Ministry of Health, Accra.

16 Demographic intermediation between development and population redistribution in Sudan

Abdul-Aziz M. Farah

Introduction

During recent decades, several less-developed countries have experienced relatively rapid economic growth rates. However the benefits of overall economic growth have been unjustifiably distributed in favour of a few localities, with large population sectors of each country remaining peripheral to such benefits. The process of development that generates the structural changes associated with socially- and morally-orientated productive and distributional systems is still in the infant stage.

A distinctive feature of an undeveloped country is the existence of a large subsistence sector embracing the majority of the population, characterized by low productivity, low income, lack of access to innovation and widespread disguised unemployment. This sector contrasts with the other sector, which combines small growth poles that are either urban or crop-producing centres. In such a dualistic setting, the heart of the development problem lies in the gradual shifting of human resources from the subsistence sector to the other sector (Fei and Ranis, 1963), resulting in the uneven distribution of population in a country. But as regards scale and tempo of population mobility, the share of urban centres in many developing countries is significantly larger than the share of crop-producing centres. The environmental contrast in these countries is particularly striking between urban and rural sectors, which activates the preponderance of urban-ward migration.

However, the unevenness of population distribution, or changes in the shape of its distribution over time, is not only a product of spatial mobility of people, but also of relative differences in rates of natural increase among regions in a country. For instance, higher rates of natural increase specific to areas within a country may cause imbalances in population distribution even in the absence of the internal migration. The differences in rates of natural increase are caused by differential levels of birth and death rates which are determined by region-specific underlying socio-economic, demographic, medical and ecological conditions. Therefore, the basic element in the formulation of a study of this kind should rest on specifying theoretical relations between such underlying factors and population dynamics that have latent impacts upon the pattern of population distribution. Hence our immediate objective is to develop a theoretical framework that incorporates various hypotheses with regard to the expected effects of development-related variables upon the dynamic determinants of population distribution. The second objective is to test for the various hypothesized relations outlined in the proposed framework, using data from the 1973 census of Sudan.

Theoretical formulation

Our attempt to formulate a theoretical framework that explains causes of population redistribution is based upon the following two premises. First, population distribution at a given time and in a given country is a function of fertility, mortality, and net migration observed within its various areas. The spatial differences in the interplay and balances of these forces uniquely define the overall picture of the population distribution. In other words, the relative differences in population growth rates among the areas of a country determine its geographical distribution, and stand as strong predictive variables in its future redistribution. Area-specific population growth is defined in the traditional manner of births minus deaths and net migration:

$$d(P)(i) = B(i) - D(i) \pm NM(i),$$

where $d(P)$ = change of population, B = births, D = deaths,
NM = net migration, and i = area in a country.

Second, changes in these variables are primarily caused by changes in socio-economic factors prevailing in each area. This premise stems from increasing recognition and realization of the role of social, economic and cultural factors in shaping levels and patterns of demographic variables. Unlike most neo-classical growth theories which have treated population growth as an exogenous variable, recent development theories have incorporated population growth as an endogenous variable, affecting and being affected by economic growth (Solow, 1956; Nelson, 1956; Lewis, 1954; Leibenstein, 1957; U.N., 1973). Although recent economists and demographers have emphasized the importance of development-related variables in determining the demographic variables, there are wide differences in views concerning the nature and timing of their impacts.

(i) *Fertility*: Under Malthusian influence, some economists contended that fertility is a direct positive response to rising income. They suggested that rapid increase in the birth rate in response to rising incomes would cause the income *per capita* to fall back to its original subsistence level (Smith, 1951). However, empirical consideration of demographic transition in historical perspective and in contemporary developing societies indicates the implausibility and inapplicability of their proposition in all settings and circumstances. Generally, they overlooked circumstantial and external influences upon the nature of the relations between fertility and development-related variables. According to the threshold hypothesis (Easterlin, 1975), fertility is a positive function of income up to a certain high level of income, after which fertility decreases with an increasing income. Such a decline occurs at higher levels of income because changes in the economic and social structure influence the values and goals of the population and raise the cost of rearing children (Friedlander, 1965). These changes are usually associated with some modernization and urbanization factors which impinge on motivation, attitudes towards and knowledge of methods of fertility control by individual couples.

According to Easterlin, societies, in terms of fertility transition, evolve through two major stages. The first is the traditional stage where the potential supply of children for married couples is less than their actual fertility. The deficit situation occurs as a result of factors like poverty, prevalence of diseases, particularly venereal diseases and malnutrition, all of which lead to fecundity impairment. In similar conditions, any economic improvement reflected, say, in rising income is likely to generate a rising trend in fertility. The second is the modern stage where the actual fertility deflects to take a downward trend below the potential supply of children. The deflection point in fertility transition is an outcome of an interplay of socio-economic, health and modernization factors. In this stage the relation between the development-related variables, for example, income, and fertility is negative.

Symbolically, the general relation between fertility and economic development reflected by levels of some indicators can be interpreted by the following expression:

$$\mathrm{d}(B)(i) = f(Y/P)(i),$$

where $\mathrm{d}(B)$ = changes in fertility, Y/P = level of income *per capita*, i = area in a country. In the early stages of economic development, the growth of income, working by itself or being a proxy for other development-related variables, stimulates an increase in fertility by reducing biological and non-biological constraints in the natural fertility regime. According to the threshold hypothesis, fertility responds negatively to increasing income during modern stages. The mechanisms through which income generates its negative effects on fertility are of a different nature from those in the traditional stage.

Empirically these two types of relations have been observed by some economists and demographers using time-series and cross-sectional data. Because of the unavailability of the first type of data, this analysis will be based on cross-sectional data.

(ii) *Mortality*: The second important demographic intermediating factor in the process of development and population redistribution is regional variation in mortality levels. There is ample evidence that within countries, as well as between countries, survival rates and socio-economic conditions are positively related (Adelman, 1963). It has been argued that the poor have a consistently higher probability of early death than the rich, even if both groups have equal access to publicly-owned health services (Antonovsky, 1967; Carvalho and Wood, 1978). In the absence of equal distribution of income, the rich have more access to specialized, hospital-based medicine (within a country or abroad), better food and a healthy life because they can afford to pay.

Among various development indices, *per capita* income is universally used as an indicator of an area's economic well-being in terms of food, housing, infrastructure and social services. The lower the level of development reflected in *per capita* income, the more constraints an area has on items of food, shelter, public utilities (sanitation, transportation, etc.) and social services. Therefore, an area-specific mortality level (gauged in terms of overall measure of mortality or probability of dying by a certain age) is an inverse function of its *per capita* income:

$$d(D)(i) = f(Y/P)(i).$$

However, the function may not be sufficient in interpreting regional mortality differentials.

The following limitations may be of interest in the formulation of regional analysis of mortality. First, an aggregate level of mortality is affected by the nature of income distribution observed in a given region. If regional levels of *per capita* income are the same, mortality is likely to be higher in areas where income distribution is more uneven. Second, the income variable may not be a good proxy for some socio-economic variables, and therefore may not reflect their effects on mortality. In a given society, individuals vary in their inability to improve health for themselves and their relatives. An improvement of health is not only a function of the economic means available, but also a function of individuals' level of knowledge regarding ways to combat diseases (Preston and Gardner, 1976). One of the fundamental ways of increasing such knowledge is education. An inverse relation between education and mortality has been observed empirically by many researchers (Farah, 1981; Cochrane, 1980; Caldwell, 1979), even if other socio-economic variables, including income, have been taken into account. Therefore, the use of *per capita* income alone is not sufficient in the analysis of regional mortality differentials. Of course, this limitation can be effectively controlled by using a multivariate analysis, preferably on micro- and community-level variables. Third, beside the income level variable, and sometimes independent of it, there comes the role of status of medical technology in a society. In many less-developed countries, the recent sharp decline in mortality has been mainly attributed to large-scale government expenditure on imported medical facilities. In most of these countries, it has been argued that mortality rates have been declining rapidly since the Second World War, while the rate of increase of *per capita* in food production has been slowing down (U.N., 1975: 449). The unprecedented rate of population growth in these countries (mainly due to a decline in mortality) associated with the diminishing rate of food *per capita* persuaded some analysts to conclude that the introduction of public health programmes (immunization, malaria control, sanitation and the like) was the major cause of the observed mortality decline. The case for this kind of argument is supported by research from both less- and more-developed countries (Stolnitz, 1955; Arriaga and Davis, 1969). Preston (1975), examining and comparing life expectancies of various countries in the 1930s and 1960s, arrived at a greater shift in the income–life-expectancy curve attributed to imported medical technology, 'exogenous factors', as compared to the movement along the curve attributed to the rise in *per capita* income. Using a decomposition procedure, the author found that decreases in mortality over a period of about 30 years for most countries with low *per capita* incomes in the 1930s was much greater than would be expected on the basis of the increase which occurred in *per capita* incomes. Hence, the author concluded that the general improvements of mortality over the period considered were primarily due to public health and sanitation measures.

From the above discussion we can propose that regional mortality variations are attributable both to differential levels of income *per capita* and to medical technology in those areas. Therefore, our previous expression is extended to incorporate the exogenously determined factor:

$$d(D)(i) = (Y/P, MT)(i),$$

where MT is the state of medical technology in area (i).

If we assume momentarily that net migration in area (i) is zero, the growth rate of population is unequally defined by the birth and death rates; and, hence, is a function of level of *per capita* income and medical technology of area (i). Symbolically:

$$d(P)(i) = (Y/P, MT)(i).$$

As indicated before, this relation is positive in the early stage of development, owing to the effects of *per capita* income on fertility and mortality. The level and variation in population growth rates in area (i) are determined by various forms of behaviour of the two rates during the development period.

(iii) *Net migration*: The third component of population growth is the volume of net migration. The pattern of population distribution is partly, and sometimes primarily, marked by the pattern of geographical mobility of population in a country. In the case of developing nations the most dominant type of migration is the shift of people from rural to urban centres. Another type of migration is the movement of people from the less productive and subsistence economy to the more productive and modern sector, encompassing both industrial and agricultural areas.

Concerning theoretical formulation of internal migration, most scholars in the field recognize the imperfect state of theoretical and empirical knowledge of the migration phenomenon. There is no doubt the deficiencies in such knowledge have hampered the study of underlying causes of migration; many attempted theories tend to be 'time-bound', 'culture-bound' and 'descriptive-bound' (U.N., 1973: 209). To some extent this situation may be attributed to the greater complexity of migration and limitations in migration data as compared with the other two components. Some of the causes of its complexity stem from the fact that migration involves a move from one place to another and, thereby, necessitates understanding the conditions of those places.

Due to the above-mentioned difficulties, most migration studies tend to be descriptive and to be partial in describing the volumes and characteristics of migrants. Among others, two distinct generalized approaches have gained importance in the field of migration research. The first is the 'push–pull' hypothesis, which considers relative differences of characteristics of place of origin and destination. The second approach has sought to formulate empirical generalizations describing patterns of migration, sometimes in the form of mathematical models. On the basis of the first approach a simple system is offered that considers net migration in a place as a function of the differentials of *per capita* incomes between the place and other places in the country:

$$\mathrm{d}(MN)(i) = f[(Y/P)(i) - (Y/P)(n-i)]$$

However, the above formulation is not sufficient to explain the characteristics of migrants and the other determinants of migration for which relative differences in area-specific *per capita* incomes do not stand as proxies. Nevertheless, the model is an easy procedure for discerning empirically some of the effects of the development-related variables assumed to have impacts on migration streams.

So far we have considered the theoretical framework that specifies the channels through which development-related factors affect population redistribution in low income countries. The basic feature of this framework is that basic demographic variables (fertility, mortality, migration) are located in the intermediate stage between development actions on the pattern of spatial distribution of population. In essence, the key to the proposed framework is the change in the level of development. Its latent dynamic features activate a set of conditions that generate influences on those intermediate variables which, in turn, contribute to change in geographical distribution of population.

Although the proposed theoretical scheme is likely to be a good starting-point in the study of this topic, some limitations are inherent in the system. First, there are many physical geographical factors which influence population distribution independently from factors of development, such as the nature and degree of fertility of the soil and climatic conditions, and regional variations in these factors have influenced the habitability of many areas in Sudan. However, they may be less effective through socio-economic processes. Second, the influence of social policy and social organization has been overlooked in the formulation of the framework. Within limits, people may deliberately choose not to respond to pressure to move to areas with evolving economies. The reluctance of many nomadic groups to respond positively to the government's policy for their settlement is a good example of that. Internal mobility may also be affected by governments' efforts to control population distribution within countries. The third limitation is that the mutual relations between the intermediate variables have not been considered by the framework. There is a possibility that inter-regional migration may contribute to changes in the pattern of internal distribution of fertility and mortality, or changes in mortality are likely to be associated with changes in fertility.

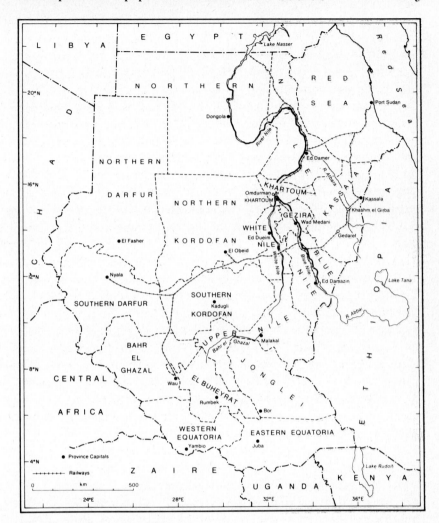

Fig. 16.1 A location map of Sudan

As it is, the framework is a reasonable tool for analysing the intricate relations between development and population redistribution. Our strategy to operationalize the theoretical relations discerned by the framework will also be limited to the extent allowed by the nature of data available in Sudan.

Geographical distribution of population and development activities

Sudan presents a good opportunity for studying the correlates of population distribution and factors governing its redistribution. It is one of the 25 least-developed countries by U.N. designation. The largest African country in area, Sudan, is also a land of rich ecological contrasts, stretching from desert areas in the north through Savanna areas to dense equatorial jungle in the south. It also comprises wide variations of geological, climatic and cultural features which have a significant bearing on its regional development and on its demographic conditions. About one-third of the land is desert or semi-desert, mainly occupied by the nomadic population.

The most prominent feature of Sudan is an extensive plain that covers almost the whole area, except for some highlands in the east, west and south. Being fortunate in having the Nile and its tributaries and adequate rainfall in the south, the country has great potential for agricultural development. At present, the agricultural sector, which is the dominant sector in the Sudanese economy, contributes about 40 per cent of its gross domestic product. It also accounts for nearly 75 per cent of the total employment. On the other hand, the sector of manufacturing industry accounts for 4 per cent, as against 12 per cent for the service sector.

The development of agriculture and its related socio-economic activities in Sudan has been marked by a dualistic structure between high-income, irrigated and mechanized rainfed agriculture on the one hand, and low-income, traditional agriculture and livestock-raising on the other hand (I.L.O., 1976). The dualistic structure of development activities is also regional. The highest concentration of these activities is biased toward the old provinces of Blue Nile, Khartoum and Kassala, leaving other provinces, especially the southern ones, lagging far behind. This dualism has contributed to a pronouncedly unequal development between regions. Most of the irrigated and mechanized rainfed agriculture is located in central and eastern parts of the country. These two regions have most of the transport, power, schools and health centres, and also have the greatest concentration of industrial activities. The activities in manufacturing industries indicated by either money invested, or number of workers employed, or total values of production, are heavily skewed towards the three old provinces (Table 16.1): in 1971 they shared 88 per cent of the manufacturing industries in the country, employed over 90 per cent of the total workers in the manufacturing sector, and contained over 85 per cent of capital investment in these industries. Khartoum province alone, by embracing the Greater Khartoum metropolitan complex (the Three Towns), has the largest concentration of educational, professional, commercial and administrative activities. It is also the area that enjoys a preponderance of raw materials, energy, transportation, labour and market accessibility (Nimeiri, 1976). Considering the geographically-unbalanced growth of the banking network in Sudan, El-Shibly (1982) demonstrated that the banking facilities are largely concentrated in the three provinces (Khartoum, Kassala and Blue Nile), with the largest proportion in Khartoum. Out of 176 branches operating various banking facilities in 1980, 59 were located in Khartoum, followed by Blue Nile (32) and Kassala (17). The existence of such prerequisite factors for the growth of manufacturing industries accompanied by a growing population and market potentials has led to increasing industrial activity

Table 16.1. *Percentage distribution of manufacturing industries by provinces, 1970–71*

Provinces	Number of establishments	Total production	Value added	Number of workers	Salaries	Capital invested
Khartoum	73.2	66.1	61.5	64.6	67.2	47.2
Blue Nile	8.6	16.3	19.1	19.9	14.3	24.3
Kordofan	7.7	1.7	2.0	2.3	1.6	2.6
Darfur	1.4	0.2	0.1	0.2	0.1	0.2
Northern	2.4	2.6	3.1	2.7	2.9	4.4
Kassala & Red Sea	6.2	12.7	13.7	9.7	13.0	20.4
Bahr el Ghazal	0.5	0.4	0.5	0.6	0.9	0.9
Upper Nile	—	—	—	—	—	—
Equatoria	—	—	—	—	—	—
Total	100.0	100.0	100.0	100.0	100.0	100.0

Source: Sudan Government, Department of Statistics, 1976

within the triangular complex of Khartoum, Blue Nile, and Kassala provinces, with the centre of gravity of their distribution falling within Khartoum.

Many researchers into geographical patterns of agricultural activities (Farah, 1981) have demonstrated that Blue Nile (old definition) and Kassala have gained the largest shares in overall capital investment and labour input in the country's modern agricultural operation. According to them the agricultural subsistence sector dominates Kordofan, Darfur, Red Sea and the Southern region and shrinks significantly in Kassala and Blue Nile.

These unbalanced development features have greatly influenced geographical population distribution and population densities (Fig. 16.2). Aridity in the north and swamps in the south retarded the development in those areas and inhibited dense settlement. The highest concentration, as shown in this map, is observed in the triangular complex of Khartoum, Blue Nile and Kassala and along the Nile and its tributaries. This wide regional variability of population densities has been primarily caused by the regional variability of population growth rates.

Before the first census of 1955–56, virtually no data were available concerning Sudan's population size, growth rate or any other demographic characteristics. Information on the components of growth were obtained, though with questionable reliability, for the first time from that census, when the population reached about 10.3 million.

The 1973 census was the first complete enumeration of the country. The census covered the basic structural and dynamic aspects of population as well as economic and housing characteristics on a *de facto* basis. The population was enumerated at 14.9 million, indicating an intercensal growth rate of 2.2 per cent, though the urban growth rate was 7.4 per cent and the rural rate 1.5 per cent.

The provinces of Khartoum, Blue Nile, and Kassala reveal the highest growth rates and population densities (Table 16.2). As will be seen later, these provinces

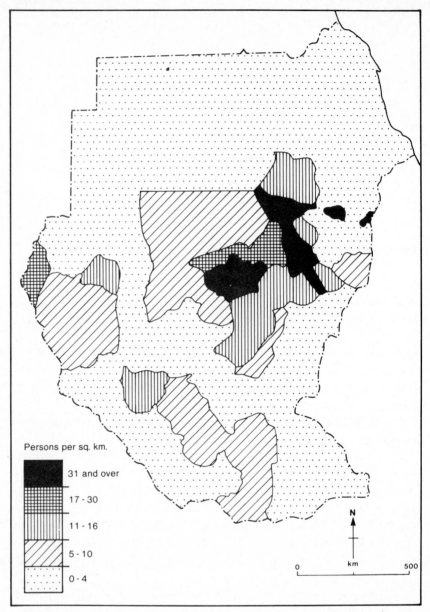

Fig. 16.2 Population density by councils, Sudan 1973. *Source:* Census Office, Department of Statistics

also have the highest fertility in the country, and relatively low mortality. The other northern provinces have shown slight increases in population growth rates and densities. Our regional analysis of fertility and mortality will show that these provinces exhibit intermediate levels of fertility and mortality in Sudan. In the

Table 16.2. *Size, population density, growth rate and nomadic population by province, 1955–56 and 1973*

Province	1955–56 total (thousands)	Density per sq km	Nomads (thousands)	1973 total* (thousands)	Density per sq km	Nomads (thousands)	Intercensal growth rate
Khartoum	505	24.0	53	1,146	52.2	55	4.7
Blue Nile	2,070	14.6	124	3,740	25.4	248	3.2
Kordofan	1,762	2.8	394	2,202	4.4	406	1.3
Darfur	1,329	2.7	266	2,140	4.2	405	2.7
Northern	873	1.8	67	958	1.9	93	0.5
Kassala & Red Sea	941	4.6	502	1,547	5.5	415	2.8
Bahr el Ghazal	991	4.6		1,397	6.2		2.0
Upper Nile	889	3.8		836	3.2		−0.4
Equatoria	903	4.6		792	3.6		−0.7
Total	10,263	4.1	1,406	14,758	5.6	1,622	2.2

Note: *Not adjusted for the under-enumeration.
Source: Department of Statistics, Khartoum, 1976 (preliminary tabulations by the census office).

south, two provinces (Upper Nile and Equatoria) have shown a decline in their population densities and exhibited negative intercensal growth rates owing to the highest mortality and lowest fertility in the country.

Regional variability of population growth rates is not only attributed to regional differences of fertility and mortality rates, but also to internal mobility of people, mainly towards urban centres. Sudan has a predominantly rural population, of whom about 11 per cent are nomadic. Urbanization in the country has reached only a modest level, and much of the urban population is concentrated in a few large towns, while some of the smaller towns exhibit only limited urban features. Vast stretches of the country are as yet remote from any major urban areas. In 1955–56, less than 5 per cent of the total population lived in centres of 20,000 or more, and more than half were concentrated in the Greater Khartoum complex. In 1973, about 14 per cent of the population lived in centres of 20,000 or more, and approximately 30 per cent of them were enumerated in the Greater Khartoum area. Forming the capital city complex, Greater Khartoum by and large benefits most from development performances in the country. It constitutes the primate city with a noticeable increase in the degree of primacy over time. Kawabe and Farah (1973) have demonstrated that the degree of primacy, in the way they defined it, increased from 130 in 1955–56 to 203 per cent in 1973. According to that study, in 1966 the largest eight towns (those above 30,000), all in the Northern region, had over 70 per cent of the public hospitals, commercial and insurance banks, professional technical groups, educational institutions and administrative and political personnel. The majority of the largest centres were located in Khartoum, Blue Nile and Kassala provinces, and their intercensal growth rates were the highest (5–8 per cent per annum), partly because of net migration.

Table 16.3. *Some socio-economic and health indicators by province, 1977*

Province	Per capita income (LS)	% urban (10,000+)	% female literate above 10 years	% never attended school among 7 to 9-year-olds	Population per doctor	Total fertility rate	$q(2)$
Khartoum	377	68.2	44.9	40.3	3,200	6.8	0.121
Blue Nile	288	10.6	24.3	56.1	28,500	8.1	0.147
Kordofan	229	9.5	7.4	68.9	45,300	6.2	0.176
Darfur	251	11.2	10.8	70.5	43,900	6.6	0.148
Northern	258	12.3	31.1	40.0	20,300	7.5	0.143
Kassala	293	18.0	25.6	53.5	18,800	8.9	0.136
Red Sea	238	33.4	25.3	54.0	16,800	6.4	0.159
Bahr El Ghazal	134	7.8	1.7	93.7	74,600	6.0	0.253
Upper Nile	147	4.6	4.7	83.4	63,500	6.2	0.241
Equatoria	157	9.5	11.7	72.5	62,200	6.0	0.234

Source:(a) *Per capita* income drawn from Farah (1981).
(b) Population per doctor computed using official figures (Ministry of Health) and population figures (census).
(c) Other variables are obtained from the census results.

Relations between development indicators and demographic variables

Without indulging in philosophical debates about the concept of development, we will spell out, as far as the data permit, some of its indicators that have relevance to the proposed scheme of analysis. Table 16.3 indicates that Khartoum, Blue Nile and Kassala, in contrast to the southern provinces, occupy the top portion of the income ladder with most education, urbanization and health measures. The other northern provinces occupy the intermediate stage.

(i) *Mortality*: For simplicity we will use the level of child mortality as an index of the overall level of mortality observed in a province. The preferred index of this mortality is $q(2)$, the probability that a newborn will die before reaching the age of 2. It is based upon 1973 data of reported deaths among children born to women aged 20–24, taking account of the observed age pattern of fertility. It is clear from Table 16.3, that there are enormous regional differences in child mortality in Sudan. As a group, the three southern provinces – Upper Nile, Bahr El Ghazal, and Equatoria – had roughly 66 per cent higher child mortality than the northern provinces, the national level being 0.170, with a range extending from 0.121 to 0.253, and Khartoum province having the lowest level.

The sharp regional differences in $q(2)$ are highly correlated with other socio-economic and health indicators. For the ten provinces, the correlation coefficient between $q(2)$ and *per capita* income is -0.97; with adult female literacy rates -0.80; with population per doctor $+0.90$. It is clear that the most disadvantaged areas from the point of view of development also have the highest mortality. But ten observations are certainly too few to permit such analysis. Farah and Preston (1982), using a sample of household-level census returns, found that the regional dummy variables in their regression model proved to have very large effects upon mortality variation. Being located in one of the three southern provinces raises

Table 16.4. *Net intercensal inter-provincial migration by sex, from birth-place data of 1955–56 and 1973*

Province	Numbers (in thousands)	
	Males	Females
Khartoum	160	85
Blue Nile	235	151
Kordofan	172	126
Darfur	177	86
Northern	117	72
Kassala and Red Sea	57	40
Bahr El Ghazal	15	5
Upper Nile	22	18
Equatoria	7	3

Source: Population Census Office (1980)

mortality rates relative to Khartoum province by 48–71 per cent, controlling for socio-economic characteristics introduced in the model. Location in one of the other northern provinces also raises mortality relative to Khartoum, but by a smaller amount. One logical reason for the observed regional variability of mortality is the variability of disease endemicity, particularly malaria, and of levels of development, including the existence of a health system.

(ii) *Fertility*: The preferred index for fertility of a region is total fertility. Provincial total fertility levels were estimated through the familiar P/F method, which compares reported current fertility to cumulative lifetime fertility and corrects for discrepancies between them. As shown in Table 16.3, the national total fertility rate is 7.1, with an inter-provincial range of 6.0 to 8.9. The correlation coefficient between *per capita* income and total fertility rate is $+0.67$; hence fertility is positively related to provincial income, evidently reflecting a very high incidence of fecundity impairment in the poorest southern areas. For example the Infertility Survey among the Murle tribe in Southern Sudan uncovered a 10 per cent incidence of primary sterility and 41 per cent of secondary sterility. Gonorrhea, malaria, malnutrition and lack of medical care were cited as the major contributory factors.

(iii) *Migration*: Table 16.4, showing the net intercensal migration based on place of birth data of the 1955/56 and 1973 censuses, revealed that Blue Nile, Khartoum and Kassala provinces gained substantial numbers of migrants during the period. The other northern provinces generally witnessed negative net migration, while among the southern provinces, Bahr El Ghazal lost population, but Equatoria and Upper Nile gained slightly. The general pattern of migration is also consistent with the regional level socio-economic indicators in Table 16.3.

Concluding remarks

Our analysis shows clearly that the population distribution among the geographical regions is primarily shaped by the differential development actions during the last two decades. The regional variability of population growth and density largely reflects regional development. One of the most interesting features of inter-regional variation in the two vital rates (mortality and fertility) is their negative correction coefficient of −0.65. Areas of higher mortality have, in general, lower fertility, as clearly shown by plotted points in the scattergram of Figure 16.3, where there is no linear relationship, and the general direction, excluding Khartoum, is negative. The negative trend of vital rates is presumably caused by the socio-economic and environmental factors that have opposite effects upon fertility and mortality. Mortality shows the expected negative relation with a province's economic circumstances; for instance, the mortality/female education relationship was proved to be very strong and negative in direction (Fig. 16.4). On the other hand, fertility and socio-economic conditions are positively correlated; for example, there is a strong and positive relation between *per capita* income and fertility, at least in nine provinces (Fig. 16.5).

In conclusion, provinces can be classified into three groups, according to stages of factors of population growth. The first group is composed of the three Southern provinces, characterized by the highest mortality and lowest fertility, by a marginal volume of net migration and by the lowest overall population growth rate during the last two decades. These are the poorest provinces in terms of *per capita* income, education and health measures. Communications are poor and much of the south is cut off from the stream of progress in the rest of the country. The

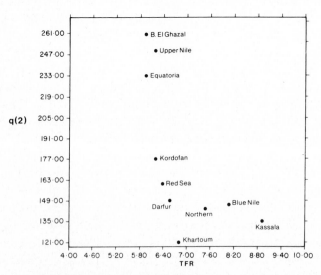

Fig. 16.3 Relation between total fertility rate and child mortality in Sudan. Correlation of q(2) with TFR = −0.650; significance = (0.021)

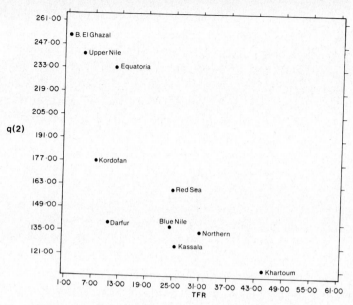

Fig. 16.4 Relation between percentage female literacy and child mortality in Sudan. Correlation of q(2) with PFL = −0.804; significance = (0.003)

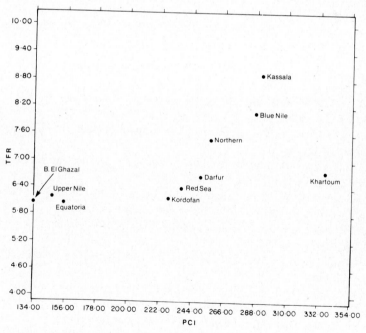

Fig. 16.5 Relation between *per capita* income and total fertility rate in Sudan. Correlation of TFR with PCI = 0.670; significance = (0.017)

outbreak of civil war in this region during the 1950s and 1960s intensified socio-economic and health problems. Presumably, these factors played effective roles in reducing fertility, increasing general mortality and prohibiting immigration.

The second group comprises Darfur, Kordofan, Northern and Red Sea, which generally reflect an intermediate stage in the demographic evolution in the country. Evidently fertility is positively correlated and mortality is inversely related to the level of *per capita* income, resulting in an inverse relationship between the two vital rates. Therefore it can be postulated that natural growth will probably increase. However, they are also areas of out-migration. Their future population growth and density will depend on the extent to which the out-migration affects their natural growth rates.

The third group is composed of Khartoum, Blue Nile and Kassala provinces. They have the highest fertility, lowest mortality and highest volume of in-migration. Therefore, they witnessed the highest population growth rate and population density during the period. They encompass the largest urban centres with the highest degree of modernization and family planning activities, so we may postulate that future fertility and mortality will decline in varying degrees. Their future population growth will depend on the pace of decline of each vital rate and the trend of migration.

In the end, the regional patterns of population growth and redistribution are likely to be uneven in the foreseeable future, unless a genuine policy of regionalizing development programmes is effectively implemented.

REFERENCES

Adelman, I. (1963) An economic analysis of population growth, *American Economic Review*, 53, 314–39.

Antonovsky, A. (1967) Social class, life expectancy and overall mortality, *The Milbank Memorial Fund Quarterly*, 45.

Arriaga, E.E. and Davis, K. (1969) The pattern of mortality change in Latin America, *Demography*, 6, 223–42.

Caldwell, J.C. (1979) Education as a factor in mortality decline. An examination of Nigerian data, *Population Studies*, 33, 395–413.

Carvalho, J.A. and Wood, C. (1978) Mortality, income distribution and rural–urban residence in Brazil, *Population and Development Review*, 4, 405–16.

Cochrane, S.H. (1980) *The Effects of Education on Health*, Staff Working Paper, no. 405, Washington, D.C., World Bank.

Easterlin, R.A. (1975) An economic framework for fertility analysis, *Studies in Family Planning*, 6, 54–63.

El-Shibly, M. (1982) Eliminating dependence on foreign aid: marriage or reality? Paper presented in seminar series held at the Development Studies and Research Center, Faculty of Economic and Social Studies, University of Khartoum.

Farah, Abdul-Aziz (1981) Child mortality and its correlates in Sudan, Ph.D. thesis, University of Pennsylvania.

Farah, Abdul-Aziz and Preston, S.H. (1982) Child mortality differentials in Sudan, *Population and Development Review*, 8, 365–83.

Fei, J.C.H. and Ranis, G. (1963) Innovation, capital accumulation and economic development, *American Economic Review*, 53, 283–313.

Friedlander, S.L. (1965) *Labour Migration and Economic Growth*, The Massachusetts Institute of Technology.

International Labour Office (1976) *Growth, Employment and Equity: A Comprehensive Strategy for the Sudan*. Geneva, Imprimeries Populaires.

Lewis, A. (1954) Economic development with unlimited supplies of labour, *The Manchester School of Economics and Social Studies*, 22, 139–91.

Leibenstein, H. (1957) *Economic Backwardness and Economic Growth*, New York, Wiley.

Kawabe, H. and Farah, A.M. (1973) An ecological study of Greater Khartoum, in *Urbanization and Migration in Some Arab and African Countries*, Research Monograph Series No. 4, Cairo Demographic Centre.

Nelson, R.R. (1956) A theory of the low-level equilibrium trap, *American Economic Review*, 46, 894–908.

Nimeiri, S.M. (1976) Industry in the Sudan, in Ali Mohamed El-Hassan (ed.), *An Introduction to the Sudan Economy*, Khartoum, Khartoum University Press.

Preston, S.H. (1975) The changing relation between mortality and level of economic development, *Population Studies*, 29, 233–50.

Preston, S.H. and Gardener, R. (1976) Factors influencing mortality levels in Asia: international comparisons and Japanese case study. Paper presented at the Seventh Summer Seminar in Population, East–West Population Institute, Honolulu, Hawaii.

Smith, K. (1951) *The Malthusian Controversy*. London, Routledge and Kegan Paul.

Solow, R.M. (1956) A contribution to the theory of economic growth, *Quarterly Journal of Economics*, 70, 65–94.

Stolnitz, G.J. (1955) A century of international mortality trends, *Population Studies*, 9, 24–55.

United Nations (1975) *The Population Debate: Dimensions and Perspectives*, Vol. 1, New York.

United Nations (1973) *Determinants and Consequences of Population Trends*, vol. 1, New York.

17 A typology of mobility transition in developing societies, with application to North and Central Sudan

Mohamed el-Hadi Abusin

An attempt is made here to present a general model of mobility transition in developing societies that are undergoing a steady although imbalanced process of transformation. These societies are characterized by a sharp dualism in economy. They have a broad base of a traditional sector (pastoral nomadism and peasant economy) and a small highly localized modern sector in agriculture and industry.

Mobility transition is viewed here as transition of individuals and groups of people on the socio-economic ladder either spatially, temporally or both. In developing societies such a process ranges from transition within pastoral and peasant societies and between them, and from these sectors of the economy into the most modern sectors in agriculture and industry. Consequently we encounter two types of transition: a conservative one represented by transition within nomadism and the peasant economy, and an innovative one represented by mobility from this traditional sector into the modern sector.

Alternatively, mobility transition may be viewed as a process of transition from the local system represented by both nomadism and the peasant economy, into the regional system. Both constitute the complex national mobility transition (Symanski, Manners and Bromley, 1975).

The mobility transition so defined will be tested in North and Central Sudan as a step towards ascertaining its validity for similar areas.

Presentation of the general mobility transition model

Mobility transition in its three interrelated forms and types of local, regional and national systems is a function of a number of integrated variables with special characteristics in developing societies which distinguish them from developed societies. These variables in their interaction constitute a form of feedback system in which they interact by a two-way process of feedback compared with the simple unidirectional system. Essential for the understanding of the mobility transition and constituting the components of the society, these variables are listed below:

1. The economic base, mode of living and regional complementarity (Ullman, 1956)
2. The physical environment and distribution of resources

236

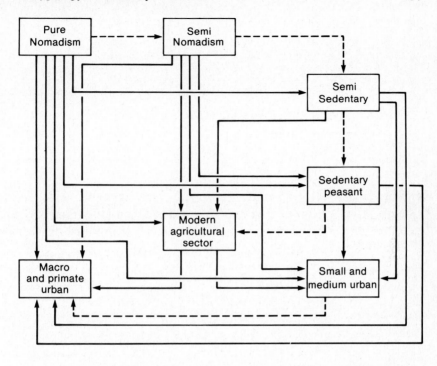

————— Normal and sequential transition   ————— Non - sequential transition

Fig. 17.1 A simple model of stages of the general mobility transition in a developing society

3. The cultural configuration and cultural space (Ginsburg, 1961)
4. Degree of economic rationalization of behaviour
5. Demographic index (Berry, 1964)
6. Technological index (Berry, 1964)
7. Modernization process and resultant value system, perception and preference of individuals and groups
8. Development continuum (Hodder, 1968)
9. Accessibility and communications media
10. National planning models of regional development and their role in the process of achievement orientation of individuals and groups

Each of these variables constitutes a sub-system of the society, and their interaction generates a mobility transition unique to such societies. The resultant model of transition is tentatively summarized in Figure 17.1.

The complexity of these variables and the interaction between them has made the modelling of transition in developing societies a difficult task. Therefore any attempt here is aimed at presenting the broad framework of a model that is intended to stimulate research in this area and to introduce a systems-analysis approach into the study of such societies.

Table 17.1. *Variables that initiate mobility transition in developing societies*

Variables	Characteristics in each of the sectors of the society		
	Pastoral nomadism	Peasant economy	Modern sector in agriculture and industry
1. Economic base and mode of life	Subsistence	Subsistence/exchange	Exchange and market-orientated
2. Distribution of resources	Uneven in space and time	Uneven in space and time	Fairly even
3. Cultural configuration	Uniform	Uniform	Medium to highly complex
4. Degree of rational economic behaviour	Fairly rational	Fairly rational	Satisfactory
5. Demographic index	1st–2nd stage of demographic transition	1st–2nd stage of demographic transition	2nd–3rd stage of demographic transition
6. Technological index	Low	Low/medium	Medium/increasing
7. Value system	Traditional	Traditional/ semi-modern	Modern and western
8. Development continuum	Imbalanced economic system	Imbalanced economic system	Satisfactorily balanced economic system
9. Accessibility	Low	Low and increasing	Medium and increasing
10. National planning models	Imposed and structurally different, resulting in minimum achievement orientation	Imposed resulting in minimum achievement orientation	Self-generated, resulting in satisfactory achievement orientation

Note: This table is based on personal evaluation of the variables, and attempts to simplify a complex situation in order to have a broad idea of the expected transition.

To begin with, a tentative evaluation of these variables is attempted in Table 17.1, according to the three major sectors comprising a typical developing society. These sectors or modes of life are pastoral nomadism, the peasant economy, and the modern economy in agriculture and industry. The modern economy is concentrated in government-controlled tenancy, or in agro-industry enterprises, or in urban-orientated industries and services. The modern sector in both forms is mostly polarized and centralized, producing growth poles that are developing at a faster rate than the broad traditional base of the economy. It is this contrast that has generated a high rate of sector-bypassing transition. It has deflected the normal transition from nomadism into a peasant economy towards the modern sector of agriculture and industry, the initial base of transition outlined in Figure 17.1.

The general model in its initial form, summarized in Figure 17.1, assumes that transition starts from nomadism, moves into peasant economy, and then into the modern sector under a normal and simple social configuration, balanced economic development, relatively uniform population and resource distribution, etc. (Table 17.1). Under such conditions, transition is expected to be self-generated, sequential and attaining a satisfactory level of socio-economic harmony and balance, normally characterizing societies with the minimum of government intervention. In the majority of developing societies, governments with limited resources have failed to attain a sufficiently-balanced regional development to produce a normal and balanced transition process.

Government intervention, in adopting national plans and provision of services which favour areas of relatively high potential, has created growth poles that have disturbed what we refer to here as a normal sequential process of transition, producing a complex and unpredictable one. The role of governments may be indirect, in placing basic services in rural areas (water supply, educational and health facilities, etc.) in specific centres, which have acted as central villages, generating mobility within each sector of the society. The role of governments may also be direct, as for example recruiting nomads and peasants in specially-structured settlement projects; transferring people after real or expected disasters; or resettling over 50,000 Nubians in the Khashm el-Girba project in Eastern Sudan after the construction of the High Dam. Government is contributing to the disparity at the regional level by further investment in agro-industry in modern-agriculture areas, resulting in an increasing gap between such areas and the broad traditional base of the economy, as well as the major urban centres. It is this growing regional or sectoral disparity which has generated excessive inter-modal and inter-regional processes of transition (represented by the longer arrows in Figure 17.1, compared with the short arrows referring to the normal sequential transition within each sector or between closely-related sectors shown in the model).

Although this model is discussed in relation to societies with an initial nomadic sector, it can be applied to any society with a basic subsistence sector, a partially-commercial sector in agriculture, and a modern sector in agriculture and industry which is mostly primate-city- and urban-orientated.

Types of mobility transition

As stated earlier, the complex model of transition characterizing developing societies can be divided into three major interrelated types, summarized in Table 17.2:

1. Transition within pastoral nomadism as a local sub-system which is linked in a different process with the peasant economy sub-system. The latter process, whether regional, temporal, or both, is termed here as inter-modal transition, while the former is termed as intra-modal transition.

2. Transition within the peasant economy, as an intra-modal process which

Table 17.2. *Components and types of sequential and normal mobility transition processes*

Types of transition	Transition processes
1. Local sub-system (intra-modal, spatial, temporal or both)	
(i) Within pastoral nomadism	Pure nomadism → semi-nomadism → semi-sedentary
(ii) Within the peasant economy	Daily movement to supply labour deficiency within the village → seasonal movement, but within the peasant economy
2. Regional sub-system (inter-modal, spatial, temporal or both)	
(i) Between the local sub-systems	From all stages of pastoral nomadism → peasant economy or the reverse
(ii) Between local sub-systems and the modern sector of the economy	From pastoral sub-system into the peasant economy sub-system into the modern sector in agriculture, agro-industry and micro- and macro-urban
(iii) Transition within the modern sub-sectors	Labour circulation within the modern sub-sectors
3. National system	Local → regional, i.e. from pastoral nomadism → peasant economy → modern sub-sector in agriculture → agro-industry → urban

Note: It is the deviation from this pattern, associated with disparity in regional and sectoral development, which has complicated mobility transition in developing societies. Therefore it should be the target of any sound development plan to attain the smooth and sequential transition outlined in this table.

   is linked with the modern sector through a process of inter-modal transition, whether inter-regional, temporal or both.

3. The transition process from nomadism as a local sub-system into a peasant-economy local sub-system, and from both into the modern sector of agriculture or into urban-based industries.

In order to understand the model suggested earlier it is appropriate to consider briefly these types or components, with a few comments about the resultant national transition.

Local sub-system of mobility transition
(i) *Transition within pastoral nomadism.* Pastoral nomadism can be classified as an intra-modal sub-system of the socio-economic structure of the society in which migratory processes are mainly within the pastoral ecosystem, especially when it is subjected to the minimum external forces of change (Fig. 17.2). Such migratory processes represent an original, conservative (Petersen, 1965), pre-agricultural type of mobility. In many developing societies it is still important in terms of size of population involved, area annually or seasonally covered and ecological impact (El-Hassan, 1982). Pastoral nomadism in all stages is a form of human adaptation to ecological and environmental conditions, through a complex but self-organized process of seasonal, reciprocal and extensive pattern of mobility. Moreover, it is

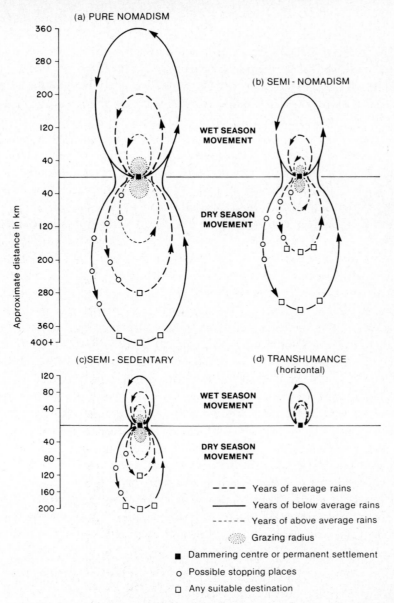

Fig. 17.2 The components of local nomadic mobility transition. Modified from Johnson (1969).

undergoing a continuous process of change (Prothero, 1964) which may be self-generated, induced or imposed (Abusin, 1983).

Pastoral nomadism in all stages is connected to the resource base and its carrying capacity, as well as the size and nature of development projects in the traditional grazing and range lands. Such projects range from provision of permanent water supply sources stimulating transition into sedentary life, to large-scale agricultural projects superimposed on the nomadic ecosystem, generating a complete inter-modal transition among the nomads. At the same time, the mechanism of internal transition within the nomadic community and its transition into the modern sector in agriculture is a function of such variables as the range carrying capacity, overstocking rate, size and composition of herds, socio-economic network and returns from development projects established in the nomadic areas (Abusin, 1981).

Pastoral nomadism in many of the tropical developing societies extends from marginal semi-arid areas into semi-humid areas, therefore we may expect a wide range of transition process. In marginal semi-arid areas transition is slow, unpredictable and more connected with purely environmental and ecological variables; semi-humid areas are more attractive to development projects and provide a better chance of contact with settled communities and exchange economy.

The transition processes by which pastoral nomadism is linked with sedentary life as a more advanced stage in the socio-economic evolution of societies are attributed to two main factors. First, there are purely ecological conditions connected with the continuous degradation in the range carrying capacity through frequent drought, overstocking and shrinkage in natural grazing land as a result of the horizontal expansion of modern agriculture. Secondly, there are the factors external to the nomadic ecosystem, including the increasing contact of nomads with sedentary economies in traditional or modern form, the provision of basic services in the nomadic areas and even more recently, the recruitment of nomads as tenants in modern agricultural projects that are structurally contrasted with the nomadic mode of life. Both factors may interact in some nomadic societies in semi-arid areas producing a rapid rate of transition of nomadism into sedentary life, reducing the purely nomadic section of the population, and in a way smoothing out the socio-economic disparities in such societies.

The processes of transition of pastoral nomadism within its different stages, whether gradual, sequential, sudden or structural, and its linkage with other sub-systems of the economy at the regional level has the following main features:

(a)   that it tends to be reversible in the three first stages (pure nomadism, semi-nomadism and semi-sedentary), generally self-generated, initiated by ecological factors and therefore involuntary;

(b)   that nomadism in all stages is normally linked with other sub-systems of mobility, through the sedentary peasant stage of the economy. The passage from nomadism straight into other sectors of the economy is increasing, especially when 'push forces' at the local level and 'pull forces' at the regional level are strong enough to transfer nomads into sedentary life, hence reducing the cultural configuration in developing societies. At the same time when 'the transition gradient' is sharp, i.e. from pure nomadism into urban (Fig. 17.1), the socio-economic consequences are generally very serious.

(ii) *Transition within the sedentary peasant economy.* The sedentary peasant economy represents the largest sector of the economy in developing societies in terms of population involved and contribution to domestic production. It acquires its significance in representing the intermediate phase in linking nomadism with other sub-sectors of the economy under normal conditions.

Mobility transition in the initial stage of peasant economy is restricted in terms of people involved, duration of change of residence and space covered (Table 17.2). It takes the form of daily or periodic movement of surplus agricultural labour within the same peasant economy, and hence is termed, like nomadism, conservative mobility transition, in which the individual or the group is migrating to maintain the same way of life (Petersen, 1965).

Transition within the peasant economy has increased in frequency and volume in many of the developing societies as a result of an increase in population pressure, the over-use of land and a drop in returns from cultivation, associated also with ecological factors and excessive migration, especially of young people, into other sectors of the economy and urban centres. Farms close to villages fail to absorb the surplus labour force above the marginal productivity level. Such surplus is normally absorbed by distant extensive farms owned by wealthy farmers or village merchants. This movement is gradually spreading beyond the 'boundary of the peasant economy' into the modern sectors of the economy, in the form of seasonal and reciprocal migration at the beginning, into labour circulation within the modern sectors of the economy, and gradually changing into permanent transition. Mitchell (1969: 179) has summarized its regional process and pressures in origin and destination that maintain its seasonality. Seasonality will end when the pressure is released in origin or destination. With more development in industry in destination areas, permanent stay is steadily in favour of those areas in which chances of permanent jobs are rapidly increasing in agro-industries and urban centres.

Regional and inter-modal mobility transition
This refers to the pattern of mobility mechanism by which local sub-systems are interrelated and become functionally integrated in the national system through a series of interrelated regional sub-systems of linkage. The regional sub-system of transition is in the form of a chain of local micro-regional sub-systems of mobility, through an interchanging mechanism of seasonal or permanent mobility into enterprises of large regional and national influence. Although regional transition is merging into the national system so that it cannot easily be distinguished, in its initial form it is simple and sequential.

In its present form it is (i) rural–rural mobility from nomadism into peasant economy or from both into areas of more advanced agricultural economy, and (ii) rural–urban mobility mainly from the traditional sector of the economy, directly or passing through a long process of circulation within the modern sector in agriculture.

Four factors are important in explaining regional or inter-modal transition in most developing societies. First, the increasing frequency of voluntary or compulsory sedentarization among nomads gives the peasant economy a large surplus of population discharged from nomadism which feeds the regional process of transition. Second is the dependence of the modern sector on hired labour and its role in increasing the demand for labour. Third is the absorption of a large part of the land people in the traditional sector formerly cultivated or used as pasture; this has limited the potentialities of the economic base, hence generating more frequent inter-regional mobility. Fourthly, the modern sector has provided an alternative source of supplementary income for quite a long time for seasonal movers from the traditional sector. Therefore, it has generated a reciprocal mobility, maintaining a safe level of manpower 'spill-over' limit necessary for a productive traditional sector and a smooth gradual transition in the society (Oesterdiekhoff and Wohlmuth, 1980). Seasonal mobility is gradually turned into a circulatory pattern within the modern sub-sectors with an increasing tendency towards permanent stay. This has produced a new type of transition which is not necessarily spatial and termed here 'within the modern sector transition'. It is a form of 'job transition', from agricultural worker into industrial worker, whether in agro-industries or urban centres, without even changing the place of residence.

National mobility transition
National mobility transition refers to the whole process of linkage between all sectors of the economy within a specific nation or political unit. In a situation of uniform economic base, a cultural configuration and minimum government intervention, it tends to be smooth, sequential and to have minimum adverse socio-economic consequences. In many developing societies the physical and the cultural landscape is by no means uniform and the role of government is leading to even more diversity, whether regional or sectoral, resulting in a non-sequential pattern of transition (Fig. 17.1).

National mobility transition is a function of the following main factors:

(a)   the nature and size of the traditional sector and the degree of diversity;
(b)   the nature and size of the modern sector and the resultant difference from the traditional sector – the sharper the differences the greater the frequency and volume of transition;
(c)   the priorities and strategies of national planning policies – empirical evidence suggests that priority in development in most developing societies is given to high-potential areas, at the expense of depressed areas;
(d)   the urban growth rate and distribution which is more in favour of more developing areas – the majority of developing societies are characterized by strongly primate cities. Mostly the national capitals act as termini of national mobility transition, resulting in urban congestion, uni-modal distribution of population, uneven allocation of manpower and social friction. National mobility in its present form is uni-directional, from the

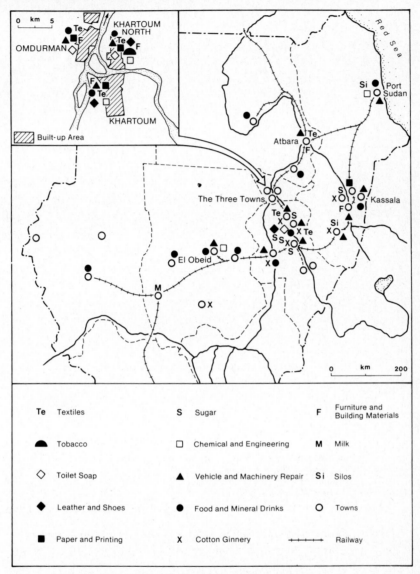

Fig. 17.3 Distribution of industries in North and Central Sudan

large population base into the small terminal centres, with a nominal counter-stream.

The case of North and Central Sudan

North and Central Sudan represent a wide spectrum of physical landscapes, ranging from pure desert in the northern part to a semi-humid zone with about 800 mm of annual rainfall in its southern part. The result is a diverse distribution of natural resources. The Nile and its tributaries, as the most important physical feature in the region, have an important role in this diversity, which is clearly

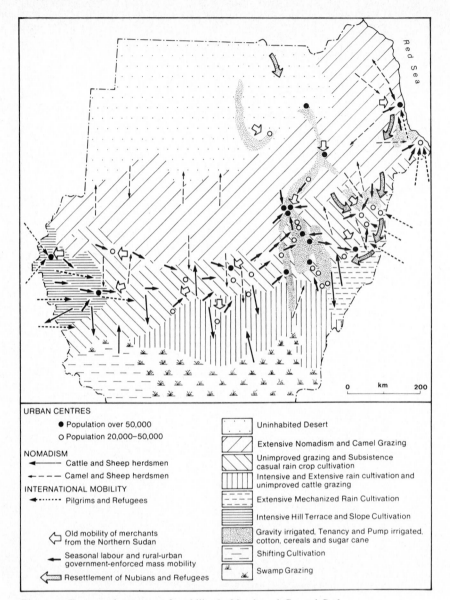

Fig. 17.4 Types and patterns of mobility in North and Central Sudan

reflected in population distribution, human activities and attraction of development projects (Figs. 17.3 and 17.4).

Cultural configuration is also sharp, because the region represents a crossroad between the Western and Islamic cultures, and the associated human migration into Africa along the Nile and across the Red Sea as well as the *hajj* from West Africa.

Economic dualism is also sharp and regional disparity is even further increasing as a result of concentration of development projects in agriculture and industries

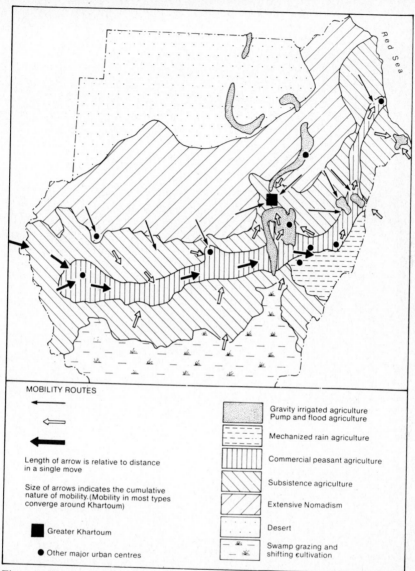

Fig. 17.5 Intensity of mobility in North and Central Sudan

within the Middle Nile area with more concentration of industries in Greater Khartoum (Fig. 17.3).

With such characteristics, North and Central Sudan constitute a typical developing society, in which mobility transition had started as sequential, but has been disturbed by environmental changes and uneven regional and sectoral development.

In order to test the validity of the general model discussed earlier, it is appropriate to examine very briefly mobility processes in the North and Central Sudan in the 1970s, a typology of which is outlined in Table 17.3, and illustrated in Figures 17.4 and 17.5.

Table 17.3. *A general typology of mobility in North and Central Sudan*

A

Type of mobility	Pattern and direction	Motivation	Barriers to mobility	Mobile unit
Nomadic pastoralism	Repetitive, cyclic and seasonal North-to-south	Conservative, maintaining the same standard of living Utilization of pastures properly	Available pasture at origin, loss of livestock or ownership of cultivable land	All the family when in pure form, and part of it when in the stage of semi-nomadism
Seasonal labour circulation	Repetitive, cyclic and seasonal Mostly west-east	Innovating, aiming at improving standard of living – income supplementation motive	Family size, annual crop yields, transport cost and income from other sources	The productive member of the family or group of own tribe
Rural–urban	Step-like under normal conditions and long distance when 'push' factors are strong	Innovating, aiming at structural change of economic pursuit and residence	Family size, transport cost, lack of education, risk of unemployment and failure to fit into urban life	Single males, mostly in a group of own tribe
Government-controlled mass mobility	Single move to a pre-determined destination	To solve a problem in which the mover is not involved	The government is responsible for removing any barriers	The whole family

B

Type of mobility	Category in regard to the choice of move and destination	Migratory force	Mobility defining boundaries	Response to the intervening opportunities
Nomadic pastoralism	Voluntary and free	Ecological 'push' and ecological 'pull'	Intra-regional or intra-community under normal conditions	High, being governed by the availability of water and pastures
Seasonal labour circulation	Voluntary and impelled, due to the government labour supply annual campaigns	Ecological 'push' and ecological 'pull', stimuli of change feedback and inducement by the government	Inter-regional and inter-community to similarly rural areas but offers better income and service	High when the economic motive in pure form is ruling or a previous contract does not exist
Rural–urban	Voluntary and free	Ecological 'push' and ecological 'pull', stimuli of change and feedback and inducement by the government 'Relative and friend'	Inter- or intra-region. In both cases of an inter-community type	Highest among the five types, still follow more favourite routes and destinations
Government controlled mass mobility	Enforced by a pre-determined decision in which the mover is not involved	The government	Inter-regional and inter-community	Does not exist

Type of mobility	Selectivity differential		Duration of stay in destination	Effect on (1) origin and destination; (2) on the mover
	Sex and age	Education and skill		
C				
Nomadic pastoralism	No specific selectivity when in pure form. Young males with or without families when in the stage of semi-nomadism or horizontal transhumance	No specific selectivity	Few days to few weeks during the wet season and 3–9 months during the dry season	Reservation of pasture for later use, overgrazing and overstocking in destination Cultural change only after contact
Seasonal labour circulation	High selectivity of young males over long distance	When in pure form, no selectivity; relatively high when taken as a stage before movement to the town	6–9 months	Solving seasonal unemployment; solving seasonal labour shortage Material success, social and cultural contact
Rural–urban	Highest selectivity among young males over long distance or where 'push' forces are strong	Highest among the five types	Lifetime	Loss of the most productive element of the population and family disintegration solving a permanent labour problem Socio-economic transition
Government controlled mass mobility	No selectivity because it involves a non-potential mover	No selectivity	Lifetime	Evacuation of the origin and population of destination Material improvement but minimum change in social integration

The mobility transition outlined is by no means simple, but is increasingly complex and undergoing a rapid rate of change in pattern direction and frequency. The normal sequential process has been disturbed in many parts of the study area by the following main factors:

(a) the degradation of the environment in the marginal semi-arid parts of the region as a result of drought, desertification and over-use of resources;

(b) the high degree of regional concentration of the modern sector and of diversity of the traditional sector (Fig. 17.3); and

(c) the role of the government in recruiting labour for the modern sector from the traditional sector by adopting an organized annual campaign. This campaign, which had originally started to provide cotton pickers for the Gezira scheme, has been extended to provide workers to meet manpower demand in other irrigated schemes and agro-industry. Consequently, and as a result of the purely ecological push, the modern sector pull and the government efforts in securing labour for the modern sector, the linkage between the traditional and modern sectors has produced a complex and non-sequential transition process. The role of the government in disturbing the normal transition is more evident in recruiting nomads as tenants in irrigated projects, transferring people into a new way of life (e.g. the resettlement of the Nubians in Khashm el-Girba and the Eritrean refugees in Eastern Sudan).

Consequently, the mobility transition has the following broad characteristics:

(a) a rapid transition of nomadism into sedentary life in irrigated projects without first passing through the peasant economy stage;

(b) excessive mobility from the peasant economy into the localized modern sector of the economy;

(c) a high rate of labour circulation within the modern sector and 'job transition' before permanent stay; and

(d) the urban primacy of Khartoum has produced a uni-directional mobility transition, mobility into Khartoum and smaller regional capitals being from all sub-sectors of the economy.

The most important results of such a transition can be summarized as follows:

(a) the increase in population concentration in the Middle Nile zone – the Blue Nile province (now the Middle Region) in 1973 had 26 per cent of the total population in the country compared with 20 per cent in 1955 and Khartoum province had 8 per cent in 1973 compared with 5 per cent in 1955;

(b) the rapid increase of urban centres, especially medium-sized towns, beyond their job- and services-absorbing capacity, hence feeding the current of mobility (Table 17.4); and

(c) the disturbance of the spatial and temporal transition necessary for

Table 17.4. *Percentage growth rate of seven medium-sized towns in North and Central Sudan, 1955–73*

Towns	Population (in thousands)			Aggregate percentage growth rate			Average annual growth rate due to migration
	1955/56	1964/65	1973	1955/56–1964/65	1964/65–1973	1955–1973	
Nyala	14	27	60	93	122	329	19
Gedaref	18	46	66	156	43	267	16
Kosti	26	38	81	46	113	212	13
Geneina	12	21	35	75	67	192	11
Shendi	11	16	24	45	50	118	7
El Dueim	13	16	26	23	63	100	6
En Nahud	17	20	26	18	30	53	3
Totals and averages	111	184	318	65	70	182	11

Notes: Towns are ranked according to the average annual growth rate due to migration.
The towns are selected on the following bases:
(a) they are distributed in the central belt from west to east where mobility is concentrated;
(b) they show a reasonable indication of the volume of rural–urban migration into medium-sized towns as a step to larger towns and to Khartoum as the primate centre of mobility transition;
(c) the approximate average annual increase due to migration between 1955 and 1973, shown in the last column.
The average national increase of population per annum is about 2.5 per cent.
Source: Dept. of Statistics – Sudan, The Second Population Census, 1973

gradual evolution of the society, contributing to an uneven allocation of human resources. The manpower discharged from the traditional sector into the modern sector, whose labour absorption capacity is limited, has resulted in an increasing rate of redundancy in a large segment of the population. The result is an improper transference of human resources, attained in the past by proper linkage of the traditional and modern sectors by seasonal migration, through which a smooth transition could be attained.

Conclusion

The initial sequential transition characterizing purely traditional societies has been disturbed as a result of the superimposition of a highly-localized modern sector whose manpower capacity is incompatible with the surplus in population discharged from the traditional sector, especially when the ecological push is increasing. This has been the norm in the majority of developing societies, especially those with a sharp diversity in resource and population distribution and a wide cultural configuration. Under such conditions the 'transition gradient' is equally sharp, linkage between economic sectors is improper and resultant socio-economic consequences are serious.

Current transition in its spatial and temporal forms is an integral component of development and associated changes in technology, flow of information, and in the demographic index, as well as of ecological changes at the local or the regional levels which frame the national transition process.

Mobility transition in its normal path is sequential and gradual, from the local sub-systems within the traditional sector into the sub-systems of the modern sector. It is now getting more complex, because of the increasing gap between the traditional and the modern sectors of the economy, as a result of further concentration of development in the modern sector induced or directed by national planning policies.

The current transition process is not only economically wasteful; it also has far reaching socio-economic and demographic consequences. Therefore a careful framing of correction policy and the means of its application at the national level is essential, looking into transition as an integrated system rather than as separate isolated components (nomadism, seasonal migration, etc.). It is necessary to revise carefully national planning models, in objective, structure, design and management, as well as in regional and sectoral orientation of development, in order to provide a proper linkage between the different sub-sectors of the economy as a pre-condition of a smooth and healthy transition process. Such measures prove to be more pressing when environmental and cultural diversity is sharp. The expected results of such measures are: minimum cultural friction, reduced overcrowding and proper allocation of human resources, along with the balanced development and urbanization which are normally associated with a gradual transition process.

REFERENCES

Abusin, M.E. (1975) A survey and analysis of internal population mobility in North and Central Sudan, Ph.D. thesis, University of London.
Abusin, M.E. (1980) Nyala: a study in rapid urban growth, in V. Pons (ed.), *Urbanization and Urban Life in the Sudan*, Development Studies and Research Centre, University of Khartoum and Department of Sociology and Social Anthropology, University of Hull, pp. 352–80.
Abusin, M.E. (1981) A change in strategy of animal herding among the nomads of the Butana – Eastern Sudan, in G.J. Heinz (ed.), *Problems of Agricultural Development in the Sudan*, vol. 4, D3400 Gottingen, Federal Republic of Germany, pp. 87–104.
Abusin, M.E. (1983) *Livestock Economy and Attitude of Tenants: A Comparative Study of Rahad and Khashm el-Girba projects*, Rahad Corporation and Ford Foundation.
Agrar- und Hydrotechnik GmbH – Essen (1980) *New Halfa Irrigation Rehabilitation Project*, Report prepared for the World Bank.
Berry, B.J.L. (1964) Approach to regional analysis: a synthesis, *Annals of Association of American Geographers*, 54, 2–11.
Department of Statistics, Sudan (1977) *Second Population Census, 1973*, Khartoum.
El-Hassan, A.M. (1982) *The Environmental Consequences of Open Grazing in the Central Butana – Sudan*, Institute of Environmental Studies, University of Khartoum, Environmental Monograph Series, No. 1.

Ginsburg, N. (ed.) (1961) *Atlas of Economic Development*, Chicago University Press.

Hodder, B.W. (1968) *Economic Development in the Tropics*. London, Methuen.

International Labour Office (1976) *Growth, Employment and Equity in the Sudan: A Comprehensive Strategy for the Sudan*, Geneva, Imprimeries Populaires.

Johnson, D.L. (1969) *The Nature of Nomadism*, Research Paper 118, Department of Geography, University of Chicago.

Mitchell, J.C. (1969) Structural plurality, urbanization and labour circulation in Southern Rhodesia, in J.A. Jackson (ed.), *Migration*, Cambridge University Press, pp. 156–80.

Oesterdiekhoff, P. and Wohlmuth, K. (1980) *The Bread Basket is Empty, The Option of Sudanese Development Policy*, Bremen, F.D.R.

Petersen, W. (1965) *Population*, New York, Macmillan.

Prothero, R.M. (1964) Continuity and change in African mobility, in R.W. Steel and R.M. Prothero (eds.), *Geographers and the Tropics: Liverpool Essays*, London, Longman, pp. 189–213.

Symanski, R., Manners, I.R. and Bromley, R.J. (1975) The mobile-sedentary continuum, *Annals of Association of American Geographers*, 65, 461–71.

Ullman, E.L. (1956) The role of transportation and bases for interaction, in W.L. Thomas (ed.), *Man's Role in Changing the Face of the Earth*, Chicago University Press, pp. 826–77.

Zelinsky, W. (1971) The hypothesis of mobility transition, *Geographical Review*, 61, 219–49.

18   Rural population and water supplies in the Sudan

Yagoub Abdalla Mohamed and
Mohamed el-Hadi Abusin

Introduction

It is universally accepted that an adequate supply of water for drinking, personal hygiene, and other domestic purposes and adequate means of waste disposal are essential to public health and well-being. In arid areas the presence of water has long been regarded as the most valued asset of a country, a wealth, a way to progress and economic development. Unfortunately, vast numbers of people in developing countries, most of them living in rural areas, do not have access to safe sources of water. Thus, there is naturally a world-wide concern about water supplies, highlighted by the International Drinking Water Supply and Sanitation decade.

In the Sudan, in areas away from the Nile, water supply for domestic purposes is a chronic problem. People have long tried to solve it with their local primitive means. They have dug shallow wells and pools but they faced many difficulties when they were confronted with rock layers or hard non-cracking clays.

Water-shortage problems started to be critical in the 1940s when population density around the permanent water sources increased, leading to concentrations of both humans and animals, to conflicts between individuals and tribal groups, and to environmental deterioration and cover removal.

The Sudanese government recognized the problem of rural water supplies very early, and embarked on ambitious programmes to solve it. The problem of improving rural water supplies in the Sudan differs from one area to another. In drier areas improved supplies may mean simply increasing the water quantity; in less arid areas, it is more a question of quality. The minimum daily water requirement for a healthy and normal life is estimated at 18 litres (4 gallons) by W.H.O.; but the average *per capita* water consumption in the Sudan is about 7 litres (1.5 gallons) per day. This disparity between the amount of water required for healthy living and the actual consumption is the central problem of rural water supplies in the Sudan.

Rural water-development programmes in the Sudan may be divided into four phases, according to the objectives behind the programme.

1. Conservation phase, 1942–56

Water provision during this period was aimed at environmental conservation and protection. The policy was to provide new water sources to achieve population redistribution and migration to the newly opened areas, reducing grazing pressure and overcultivation in already degraded areas. To achieve this policy a Soil Conservation Section was established in the Department of Agriculture, which started a programme of *hafir* (excavated reservoir) construction and small dams in areas of rain cultivation to provide workers with water supplies and also to open new areas for settlement and grazing and relieve the overgrazed areas.

2. Land use phase, 1956–66

With independence, the rural population still suffered from a lack of drinking water. At this stage more ambitious programmes were implemented to solve the problem and to combine water provision with some form of land use planning. Thus water provision was used to help in proper land use and to reduce environmental degradation around existing water sources, but still the scale of the programme and the financial resources available were not sufficient to achieve the declared objectives, so a more ambitious programme started in 1967.

3. Anti-thirst campaign, 1967–69

The concern for pasture deterioration, soil and forest destruction was over-shadowed by a thirst cry, resulting in an anti-thirst campaign, launched by the government, for national and international support to achieve this human goal. The output of this campaign was some 4,200 water points provided in most of the thirst-stricken areas in Western Sudan, making water available to a large portion of the rural population. In executing this campaign, water points were opened, completely ignoring environmental potentialities of the area, leading to more destruction and deterioration. Land-use planning was abandoned and political pressure prevailed.

4. Rural development and water supplies, 1969–80

The anti-thirst campaign did not totally eradicate the problems of thirst in all areas, but the policy changed towards using water as a catalyst to stimulate development activities. A Ministry for Rural Development was established incorporating the Rural Water Development Corporation (R.W.D.C.), the only agency for rural water provision. During this phase more emphasis was given to development potentialities of the areas selected for water provision and the role of popular participation. Thus for the first time the local community began to be concerned with the problems of water provision and started through self-help to contribute effectively to solving it.

This brief summary shows that the government programmes for water provision are based on a number of assumptions:

1. provision of adequate water in a deficient area will stimulate development, so water is regarded as a catalyst for stimulating development activities;

2. water provision will open up new areas for grazing and agricultural activities, which will help in proper land utilization and reduce environmental degradation observed around water sources;

3. water provision may help in population redistribution, by influencing the establishment of new settlements, and may control their size by controlling the capacity of the water source.

To achieve these objectives thousands of water sources were provided, their distribution, capacity and permanency depending very much upon the physical environment of the country (Table 18.1). The geological structure influences the distribution of the water-yards; 49 per cent of the country's area is underlain by basement complex with very low underground water capability, 28 per cent by Nubian sandstone with high water capability, 19 per cent by Umm Ruwaba series and Gezira formation with high water capability and 4 per cent by other formations, generally with low water capability.

As a result of these physical factors, the types of water supplies found in rural Sudan are:

1. surface water sources – natural (including natural depressions, streams and wadis which are seasonal, and the Nile and its tributaries) or constructed;

2. sub-surface water sources – hand-dug wells;

3. underground water sources tapped by boreholes and water-yards;

4. filters – canal water treated through slow sand filtration; and

5. tube wells with hand pumps (Fig. 18.1).

This paper attempts to assess the impact of rural water provision on population distribution with the aim of delimiting areas of adequate, deficit or surplus water supplies so as to direct future planning and action to these areas. It also attempts to analyse the impact of the declared policies of water provision on rural population distribution, and to get an idea of the degree and magnitude of the problem of water shortages and problems hindering the achievement of the goals and objectives of the government. To achieve these aims, the general policies are discussed and the relationship of population distribution and water supply sources are assessed with particular reference to the supply/demand situation.

The data for this paper were collected as part of a larger survey project carried in 1980 on 'Social and Managerial Aspects of Rural Water Supplies in the Sudan' sponsored by the International Development and Resources Centre, Canada (I.D.R.C.). In that survey, four communities were assessed with respect to their

Table 18.1. *Existing water sources by region, 1980 (rural areas)*

Region	Water-yards	*Hafirs*	Dams	Hand pumps	Improved hand-dug wells
Darfur	395	107	25	—	243
Kordofan	628	337	10	330	444
Khartoum	220	8	—	—	52
Central	1,300	183	1	—	106
Eastern	180	130	13	—	327
Northern	114	—	—	100	49
Southern	500	78	—	—	—

Source: National Administration for Water, 1981.

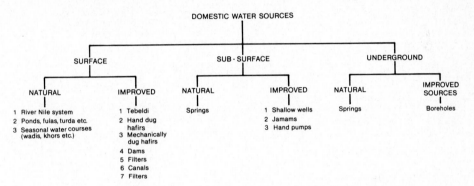

Fig. 18.1 Types of domestic water supply sources, Sudan. A water source is termed as 'improved' when constructed, modified, deepened or widened by human or mechanical effort. Improvement may or may not produce a healthy hygienic water. *Fula* is a natural depression where rain-water collects. *Hafir* is an excavated reservoir, man-made. *Turda* is a natural depression larger than *Fula*. *Tebeldi* is an African baobab; the trunk is hollowed to store water. *Jamam* is a small hole dug in a wadi bed where the water table is shallow.

water supply situation and their future aspirations. Also we benefited from the records of the National Administration for Water.

Present situation

At present, the efforts of the different departments responsible for water supplies have made it possible to extend the service to over 40 per cent of the rural population, but still there are regional variations with regard to water adequacy and sufficiency. Large areas where water shortage is very acute include most of Western Sudan and large areas of the central clay plains (Fig. 18.2).

Water provision through boreholes is controlled by the geological structure and policy considerations. The Land Use Department, which was responsible for water provision and for maintaining the healthy condition of the land, tried to follow some form of spatial planning with respect to borehole and *hafir* locations.

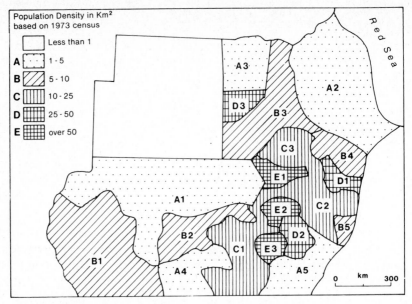

Fig. 18.2 Population density and domestic water supply and adequacy.

A Areas of acute water shortage:
A1 Supplied by boreholes and wells
A2 Wadis and wells
A3 Water shortage away from the Nile
A4 *Hafirs* and wadis
A5 Wells and wadis
B Areas moderately supplied:
B1 Mainly wells and boreholes
B2 Boreholes and *hafirs*
B3 Nile and wells
B4 Mainly wells
B5 Mainly wells
C Areas in central clay plains, moderately supplied:
C1 Mainly *hafirs*, dams and wells
C2 Mainly *hafirs* and wells
C3 Nile and wells
D Areas adequately supplied:
D1 Gash delta boreholes and wells
D2 Blue Nile and *hafirs*
D3 Nile and wells
E Areas adequately supplied with improved sources:
E1 Khartoum Province – Nile, wells, boreholes
E2 Gezira – Nile, filters, wells, boreholes and canals
E3 Kosti Area – White Nile, wells, *hafirs* and boreholes

Water provision was used as a catalyst to achieve proper land use and soil conservation. Criteria were set for the location of boreholes and other water sources which included population density, the animal population, the potentiality of the area for development and nearness to the site to water sources. Based on these guidelines, survey teams inspected the proposed sites and recommended water points at distances according to carrying capacity of the areas. However, after 1967, the Land Use Department was incorporated into a bigger department named Rural Water Development Corporation (R.W.D.C.) with the main objective of executing an anti-thirst campaign. As a result of the ambitious policies pursued by this new department as well as political pressure, there was no strict application of the criteria and the attempt in spatial planning was abandoned. In many instances water-yards are found close to each other, leading to over-grazing, over-cultivation and general degradation of the environment around water-yards. This is because water points attract more people and encourage seasonal migration, exerting pressure on local water supplies and natural resources. It is clear that lack of spatial planning has contributed effectively to the desertification process in the Sudan.

Despite these efforts in water provision, the quantity of water annually available for rural populations (humans and animals) from the present sources amounts to 189.76 million cubic metres (145.5 from water-yards, 37.5 from *hafirs* and dams and 6.76 from improved hand-dug wells and hand pumps), while the present demand in rural areas is for about 340 million cubic metres, of which about 160 million cubic metres are for humans and 180 million cubic metres for animals.

The expected water demand by 1990, according to the National Administration for Water, is about 490 million cubic metres, of which 220 are for human use (assuming a growth rate of about 3 per cent) and 270 for animals (assuming a 50 per cent increase in demand). The above calculations do not take into account the water supplies provided by hand-dug traditional wells. These traditional wells are dug annually in wadi or dry stream beds especially in areas underlain by basement complex structures. Due to their wide distribution, it is very difficult to estimate their contribution, so these estimates considered only the amounts provided by improved sources.

Distribution pattern of water supply

The distribution pattern points to areas of adequate water supply, deficit or surplus. It is not only shaped by financial and technical limitations, but also by variations in landforms, geology, drainage and soil types. As a result, areas dominated by boreholes and water-yards are separated by wide stretches with only hand-dug wells or no water. There are few areas having all types of source. The hand-dug wells and *rahads* (elongated natural depressions where rain water collects) are the most widespread sources in the country, with a wide impact on population distribution because they are easy to construct and to manage. The traditional hand-dug well in the pre-borehole period had been the main cause of wide dispersal of rural population, limiting its localization to small villages matching the well's capacity and permanency; now it is losing its importance in shaping the distribution of population because of the change in aspirations and availability of better improved sources. The growth of central villages, rural markets and service centres is now closely associated with the distribution of improved water sources, especially in areas away from the Nile.

As mentioned already, domestic water supply sources in the Sudan are either natural or man-made. The natural sources are concentrated in areas of heavy rainfall south of latitude 14° on clay soils. In spite of their important role in providing more water than improved sources for both human and animal populations during the wet season, their high seasonability restricts their use, as well as records of their distribution and capacity (Fig. 18.2).

Man-made sources are either improved or unimproved. Water-yards have a wide distribution in the country, while filters are confined to irrigated areas as a device to purify canal water, acting as a substitute to water-yards in areas of poor or saline underground water (e.g. Managil).

Borehole development started as an alternative to the traditional inadequate sources as early as 1919, but its remarkable increase was in the period 1961–78. Over 80 per cent of all boreholes were drilled in the years 1961–81, and about two-thirds were constructed during the anti-thirst campaign of 1967–69.

The unimproved sources include traditional hand-dug wells which form the domestic water supply base in most of the rural areas of the country. Unlike improved sources, whose distribution is controlled by the geological structure, they have a wider distribution in the country, being within the expertise and financial ability of the local communities. Unfortunately, information regarding their number and distribution does not exist.

Hafirs and dams tend to have a different or even contrasting pattern of distribution from boreholes, and are mainly found in areas underlain by non-water bearing rocks.

The water supply situation has resulted in the present patchy and clustered distribution of rural population. It also reflects the phases of water provision policies in rural areas since the 1940s as well as subsequent political and economic development. An early phase emerged from the soil conservation attempts in the 1940s when soil conservation and proper land use were the main criteria for siting water points, the aim being to achieve a balance between resources used and conservation. The result was a careful distribution of water sources but far below the requirements and needs of the rural population. Such policies continued up to late 1960s. The second phase started after independence in the form of the anti-thirst campaign. During this period water sources were constructed without any environmental consideration. The target was to provide domestic water for the rural population, especially in areas of scarcity. The result was completely unbalanced distribution with a remarkable concentration in areas that had been able to exert political pressure. This extensive development is reflected in the budget of the Rural Water Development Corporation which shows that two-thirds went for water development. Despite these efforts, the disparity is still remarkable. It became clear that the government could not provide water to every

Table 18.2. *Domestic water supply by region – North and Central Sudan*

Region	Rural population estimates, 1981 (in millions)	Area in sq km	Density (persons per sq km)	Number of boreholes and their equivalent	Number of persons per borehole or equivalent	Number of sq km per borehole or its equivalent
Kordofan	2.67	380,549	7.0	1,919	1,392	198
Darfur	2.64	496,373	5.3	1,900	1,389	261
Central	4.63	142,139	32.6	2,188	2,116	65
Eastern	1.54	263,361	5.9	1,334	1,154	198
Khartoum	0.4	20,971	19.1	510	784	41
Northern	1.2	477,078	2.52	347	3,458	135

Notes:

1. Borehole (water-yard equivalent is estimated to be about 10 shallow wells yielding 5 cubic m/day and a *hafir* of average size with capacity of 15,000 cubic metres).

2. Figures for Central Region, Northern Region and Khartoum must be considered in the light of the fact that such regions have alternative sources in the Nile system, where the problem of water availability is replaced by one of quality.

settlement, and opted for self-help effort, thus adding a new dimension to the disparity of water distribution. Communities with better financial resources benefited from this policy.

Improved sources have a high tendency towards clustering, separated by areas of unimproved and deficient sources. The maximum concentration of boreholes or equivalent is found in Khartoum Province and in the Central Region, where there is a borehole within every 41 and 65 sq km respectively. The number of persons per borehole or its equivalent is generally high in most of Northern Sudan (Table 18.2) and these areas have few alternative sources of water supply.

Domestic water source and population distribution

The Sudan's rural population is sparsely distributed with an average density of 12 per sq km. The 1973 census gave a rural population of 10.7 millions, projected to 13.1 millions in 1981 and expected to be over 14.8 millions in the year 2000.

The majority (57 per cent) are confined to the Nile system, according to 1981 estimates, and the rest (43 per cent) are widely scattered all over the country.

Away from the Nile, population distribution is controlled by (a) available water supply, and (b) land available for agriculture and pasture, which in most cases do not coincide with areas of water supply. The degree of such relationship varies from one area to another, but tends to be greater in the central belt of the Sudan. There is an observable association of heavy population concentration in areas with natural resources. Apart from their uneven distribution, water sources in all forms do not provide the amount of water required annually for human and animal population in rural areas (Table 18.3).

Under the open free land use system, water is the key factor to the exploitation

Table 18.3. *Minimum annual water requirements of rural human and animal population, 1980*

Type	Water/one unit		Total population in millions	Total water required (in million cubic metres)
	Per day (in gallons)	Per year (in cubic metres)		
Humans	4	7.2	8.0	57.6
Camels	2	3.6	2.0	7.2
Cattle	6	10.8	10.0	108.0
Sheep and goats	2	3.6	10.0	36.0
Horses	5	9.0	1.0	9.0
Donkeys	4	7.2	3.0	21.0
Average and total	3.8	6.9	—	238.0

Source: Rural Water Corporation, Khartoum, 1981

of resources, the quantity available influencing the size of population. If water is unlimited, control on the size of population is exercised by the size of the available land. Usable land is a function of distance from a water point, and hence the time spent in fetching water or travelling to and from farms daily becomes crucial to population size.

This statement is supported by results of a study carried in East Kordofan (Yagoub and Abusin, 1982) where the population of some villages might rise by 40 per cent after water provision, most in-migration taking place from neighbouring villages during the first five years after water was provided. Meanwhile land is fixed. More land could be worked only at the expense of walking greater distances. The alternative which is practised now is to over-work the land within easy reach, and this leads to deterioration. This vicious circle could be broken by providing water at the sources of migration.

Water provision through boreholes has added a new dimension to the water supply situation. It provides a permanent water supply, which reduces time and effort and which is perceived by the local inhabitants as of good quality and healthy. This perception shaped the type of water distribution, based on the aspirations of villagers. For example, in areas along the Nile more and more villages are provided with house connections. In the Gezira, about 60 per cent of the homes have yard taps, and those with no private connections take water from their neighbours. About 4 per cent use raw water from nearby canals or rivers, 6 per cent get their water from open hand-dug wells and the remaining 30 per cent use water-yards and filters.

Water provision also has an impact on the nomads. The objective was to use water as a mechanism in inducing their settlement. Studies carried out in southwest Kordofan showed the response of some nomads. Before the provision of water, Adapetu (1971) found that in some villages about 52 per cent of his respondents led one form of nomadic life or another; after water provision, only 19 per cent reported that they still moved personally with animals. The overall percentage reduction varied directly with the length of time a village had been provided with water. The rate of settlement tends to be fairly rapid initially, but tapers off with time.

Water provision also has an impact on settlement distribution and size. Closer examination of the pattern of settlements reveals the uneven distribution of water supplies. Thus those fortunate areas that have perennial water sources become centres of large concentrations of both humans and animals, attracting services and emerging as nodes of development. It is found that the number of services declines from the oldest to the newest water point, services and age of water points being strongly correlated. These services and facilities have a major role in attracting people to settle round or near water supply centres, especially in nomadic and traditional communities. In most irrigated areas and along the Nile the situation is rather different. Villages are planned with an almost fixed size, and a water supply is provided with all the necessary services. Therefore distribution of water sources and population tends to be uniform and regular in pattern, thus contrasting sharply with the clustered, patchy and irregular pattern of distribution characterizing nomadic and traditional communities.

Conclusion

From the above discussion, the following features emerge:

(a) The overall distribution pattern of water points is patchy, clustered, irregular and closely associated with the variations in the physical landscape, geological structure, soil types and drainage.

(b) Physical variations do not have the only impact on the distribution of water sources, but the policy of water provision is also influential.

(c) Boreholes have the greatest role in shaping population distribution, but the fact that they are unevenly distributed and do not provide what is required by the people leads to instability in population distribution, especially among the nomads and semi-nomads during the critical dry months.

(d) Due to financial and technical limitations, the annual increase in water supply is far less than the annual requirement of the rural population. Moreover, there is a general deterioration in water sources as a result of managerial problems, lack of spare parts and fuel shortages. It is estimated, for example, that *hafirs* lost half of their designed capacity due to sedimentation.

(e) Water provision programmes have led to human and animal concentrations with serious effects on cover removal and general environmental deterioration. In this connection, we need to ask ourselves, is the cure for water shortage in such semi-arid areas more water, or how to deal with water?

(f)   In view of the current problems the country faces with regard to the desire to provide safe and adequate water supplies, and at the same time to achieve a rational use of resources, a new orientation is required as to the role of water in these semi-arid areas. In this respect the main question to be asked is: what type of management is required to achieve the aims and objectives of water provision?

ACKNOWLEDGEMENT

Acknowledgement is made to the International Development and Resources Centre (I.D.R.C.) for their financial assistance.

REFERENCES

Adapetu, A.A. (1971) The impact of improved rural water supplies on the Hamar and Humur tribes of S.W. Kordofan, Unpublished Ph.D. thesis, University of Ibadan.
Department of Statistics (1981) *Preliminary Population Projections, the Sudan 1975–2000*, Khartoum.
National Administration for Water (1981), Unpublished report, Khartoum.
Yagoub Abdalla and Mohamed el-Hadi Abusin (1982) *Social and Managerial Aspects of Rural Water Supplies in the Sudan*, unpublished report.

19 The impact of the Kenana project on population redistribution

Babiker Abdalla Abdel Rahman and
Amna Beshir Homoudi

Development is a necessary element of normal population adjustment and equilibrium. Within the Sudan, like most other countries, some areas have expanding employment opportunities while others are stagnant or declining. In general, development programmes, especially in less developed countries, are a predominant force in dictating the redistribution of human resources in response to changing opportunities among regions. The Sudan, now experiencing technological change in the form of capital investment in new industrial plants, large-scale irrigation schemes and other facilities responsible for the production of goods or services, all of which provide new employment opportunities, is subject to large-scale redistribution of its population.

Here we attempt to examine the relationship of demographic factors to agricultural production and development through a case study of the Kenana Sugar Scheme. Two aspects of the relationship will be considered: first, an analysis of the trend and magnitude of population changes that were a result of the scheme; secondly, the impact of the scheme on the demographic, social and economic conditions of the population.

As in many developing countries of Africa, so in the Sudan a study of this kind is hampered by the absence of reliable published demographic and socio-economic data. It has, therefore, been necessary to undertake a sample survey to collect data concerning the social and economic conditions of the population, their origins and their perception of the scheme. The sample was stratified into four classes according to type of economic activity: agricultural workers, factory employees, Camp Five residents (mostly the sector engaged in non-basic activities) and the original population of Kenana who live on the boundary of the scheme. Invaluable information has also been obtained from interviews with key officials in the factory.

The sample size (120 households) although arbitrary, was considered to be sufficient for the purpose of the paper. The head of the household formed the primary unit and the enquiry was directed at him. Thirty households were then randomly selected for interviewing from each of the four classes.

The Kenana Sugar Project is located south of Rabak on the White Nile, approximately 240 km south-west of Khartoum (Fig. 19.1). The total estate area is 150,000 feddans (one feddan = 1.038 acres = 0.425 hectares). At full

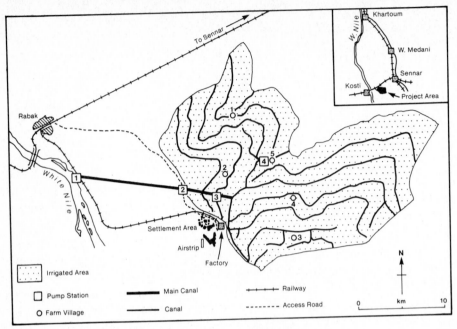

Fig. 19.1 The Kenana Sugar Project: general layout

development, 81,000 feddans will be supplied with irrigation water for growing sugar cane. At full capacity, as during the season 1982–83, the factory is expected to produce 330,000 tons of white refined sugar annually so as to meet local demand and to fulfil an export target of 150,000 tons. The plantation is divided into five 16,000 feddan areas, each subdivided into 4,000 feddan farms, which are further divided into 1,000 feddan sections, each run by a section manager. Each of the five areas is supposed to be a self-contained community, having its own social services, for example, schools, clinics, social centres and a market. The possibility of the estate becoming wholly self-supporting is also being considered. A horticulture scheme for the production of vegetables is already established. There are also plans for beef and dairy cattle farms, as well as for sheep, chickens and an orchard.

Water is drawn from the White Nile and carried to the cane area via a main supply canal, 29 km long. There are four pump stations along this canal with a combined lift of 40 m. The capacity of the irrigation system is 42 cubic metres per second, which is over half-a-million gallons per minute. After the water has been lifted at the main pump station it is distributed entirely by gravity through a series of primary canals following the contours of the land.

The normal planting rate is approximately 42 ha per day using a combination of hand and mechanical planters. Seventy-five per cent of harvesting is done by mechanical harvesters. The balance of 25 per cent is cut by hand. Cane is transported by truck-trailers to the factory, which is designed to crush 17,000 tonnes of cane daily and operates in the dry season, between November and June.

It is important to note that the project does not involve any tenancies, but wage labour only. This explains the fact that most of the original inhabitants refrained from working in the scheme. They are basically self-employed, traditional farmers or nomads who look down on any form of wage labour.

Changes in population size

Before the establishment of the scheme, the Kenana area was inhabited by a large number of semi-nomadic tribes who practised rain-fed agriculture, mainly for subsistence. Settlements were composed of straw huts which were usually abandoned during the dry season as some villagers went in search of grazing grounds and watering points, while others moved into the nearby White Nile pump schemes to sell their labour during the picking of cotton. Within the Kenana Scheme there were 27 villages with a total population of only 3,700 persons.

Of the total inhabitants, 344 villagers needed to be moved when work on the site started in January 1976 with the construction of the 24km-long main canal. Those who were moved were compensated with cash. They were paid 12 Sudanese pounds for a hut and 70 piasters for each feddan of agricultural land, and were rehabilitated in one conglomeration outside the Kenana Scheme.

The total population living in and around the site is now estimated at approximately 75,000. This is, of course, a substantial increase in absolute and relative terms, since the area in 1975 had no permanent population, only nomadic farmers during the rainy seasons. During the seven years from 1975 to 1982 the population increased more than 20 times. Only about 13 per cent (10,000) of the total population are employed by the factory either in cane production, sugar production or in finance and administration. Approximately 20 per cent are engaged in secondary employment to provide services for the workforce. The remainder are villagers who live in the proximity of the scheme and are in no way wage earners. This means that the number of the original population (3,700) increased nearly 12 times to reach 43,500.

The major component in the remarkable increase in the size of population is undoubtably migration. The results of the sample survey revealed that almost 65 per cent of the total population migrated to Kenana after the establishment of the scheme. However, a distinct variation is evident in the proportion of migrants in each of the four classes. The highest proportion of migrants is noticed among the agricultural workers (97 per cent) followed by factory workers (70 per cent). The exceptionally high percentage of migrants engaged in production is mainly due to the fact that agricultural operations are hard and involve great effort, which the original population were not used to. In fact, the survey revealed that the indigenous population look down on work in cane fields and consider it an unworthy menial job. Those involved in agriculture come mainly from Darfur, almost 1,500 km away. They leave their areas of origin as a result of the push factors of unemployment and underemployment, rather than the attraction of Kenana as a pull factor.

Regarding workers in the factory, the factors which attract them are many.

Perhaps the most important is the expected availability of jobs for those unemployed, higher income for those already employed and the general belief that the standard of living can be improved. It is also important to mention that some were pulled to Kenana, especially from the nearby sugar estates of Assalyia and Sennar, because Kenana offers free housing, and free water and electricity supplies, as well as free medical and educational services.

However, the most important factor relating to the increase of population in the area is the drift from nearby villages. The population of this sector increased from 3,000 in 1976 to approximately 43,500 in 1982. It is important to note that the survey revealed that a negligible percentage of these villagers are employed in the factory. This is mainly because the factory demands skilled labour, while the majority of the villagers are young, not properly trained for any specific skilled occupation and are often illiterate, or at best primary-school leavers.

The stream of movement to Kenana is very strong. As the survey showed, people are suffering from the relative decline in rain-fed agriculture rewards relative to the increasing cost of living. So people move to Kenana in the hope of finding a job in the factory or a part-time job to supplement their income. Some people are attracted to the scheme in the hope of being allotted a plot of land, as they know that the authorities intend to plan the villages around the scheme. Planning involves the provision of basic services such as piped treated water, electricity, education and health facilities. Moreover, villagers move near to the factory area to make use of the surplus water for watering their livestock. This practice means a basic change in their mode of living as seasonal semi-nomads. The villagers believe that this is the biggest benefit to be derived from Kenana. The all-year-round availability of water saves them the trouble of travelling long distances, increases the number and improves the quality of their livestock. Being near Kenana also creates the opportunity of supplementing their income by selling milk, charcoal and wood.

Short-distance migrants as well as the relocated population occupy an area on the southern boundary of the scheme in scattered unplanned villages. People from the same tribe tend to conglomerate in the same area. Those working on the scheme live in new villages designed for them by the project.

Demographic structure and socio-economic conditions

The survey revealed that the sex structure of the population is typical of migrant groups, with a ratio of 162 males to every 100 females, the excess of males reflecting their greater independence and the type of jobs available in the scheme, which are overwhelmingly male-orientated. Women represent 13 per cent of the workforce in Camp Five, where they are engaged in selling food or tea, and only 3 per cent of the total economically-active population. They all come from Kosti or Rabak towns, and are either old, self-dependent or young women who support their families.

Table 19.1. *Percentage educational attainment by sector*

	Illiterate	*Khalwa*	Primary	Lower Secondary	Higher Secondary	N
Original population	63	28	6	3	0	30
Agricultural labourers	21	33	21	25	0	30
Camp Five residents	33	27	20	20	0	30
Factory labourers	19	15	21	8	27	30
Total population	37	26	18	12	7	120

Note: N = Number of respondents

In addition to sex imbalance, the population of Kenana is predominantly composed of young adults. The survey revealed that 71 per cent were below 35 years of age, and of those three-quarters were between 20 and 25. This finding is not unusual as the majority of the population are migrants and migration is most frequent among these groups. People are more mobile in their late teens and early twenties, as this is the period when schooling is terminated and entrance into the labour force and the formation of new family units begins. Family ties are less inhibiting, for in the Sudan usually after the age of 18 a male is considered mature and is given the freedom to choose.

The sample survey suggested that 37 per cent of all residents are illiterate (Table 19.1) and 26 per cent have attended only *Khalwa* schooling, which is basically an informal type of education directed towards the teaching of the Koran. The highest percentage of illiterates is observed among the original population. Eighteen per cent of all residents have had primary education and a further 19 per cent have attended lower and higher secondary schools.

The level of education is higher among factory workers. It has been noticed that even higher secondary school leavers are engaged in skilled or semi-skilled work on the scheme. This implies that factory working conditions are attractive even to the young and educated. This is undoubtedly a healthy trend. If such development projects continue to attract this sector of the population, movement to the urban centres may be reduced.

The main goal of development is to improve the standard of living of the population, as people are contributors and ultimate beneficiaries of development. Benefits of development are measured by certain indicators, such as the rate of growth *per capita*, the size of income, the proportion of population benefiting from development and, even more important, the creation of social and economic forces that lead to desirable change in the social structure and in the people's values and attitudes.

The survey results provide information about the earnings of the respondents before the scheme and their present earnings. Table 19.2 shows that 64 per cent of the respondents improved their income after the establishment of Kenana.

Table 19.2. *Percentage comparative level of income by sector*

	Increase in income	Decrease in income
Original population	40	60
Agricultural labourers	75	25
Camp Five residents	87	13
Factory labourers	57	43
Total population	64	36

However, there is a distinct variation in income improvement according to sector. Camp Five residents have benefited most, as the majority in this area engaged in non-basic activities, such as trading, carpentry and tailoring. At the other end of the scale, 60 per cent of the original population claim that their income is now lower than before the establishment of the factory. This result may be doubted, as most of the villagers are very bitter towards the scheme. It stands to reason that their income must have increased, for two reasons:

1. The influx of the villagers to the scheme is strong and gaining momentum; the new settlers must have gained information about better living conditions in the area or otherwise they would not have been attracted.
2. Because of their location in the vicinity of the site, the villagers enjoy several advantages that must have contributed to an improvement in their economic conditions. The factory influences the rural area economically: it acts as a market centre for their local products and needs, and it provides employment opportunities.

Regarding the relation between population and development in the context of social change, the respondents were asked to mention the benefits the project had brought to the area and to what extent they made use of them. They felt that water supply, education, health services, electricity, transport and trade are the most important. However, the results also revealed that there is a distinct variation in the degree of use of the social services between groups (Table 19.3). For example, of the original population 43 per cent claim that they never used any of the social services; of those remaining, only 29 per cent made use of health services supplied by the project. Conversely, of the agricultural and factory workers only 4 and 13 per cent respectively made no use of the social services. This variation is expected, in view of the project regulations limiting use of services to its employees only.

The nil percentage of those who benefited from education services among the agricultural and factory labourers is explained by the fact that the vast majority of the respondents are either single or unaccompanied by their families, while the meagre use of social facilities by the original population is explained by the

Table 19.3. *Percentage use of services by sector*

	Education	Water supply	Health services	Electricity	Transport	Trade	None
Original population	40	54	29	—	17	3	43
Agricultural labourers	—	96	66	—	50	25	4
Camp Five residents	4	85	92	85	85	10	8
Factory labourers	—	69	20	—	20	47	13

bitterness of the original population and their feeling that they have been cheated by the Kenana Sugar Scheme authorities.

Summary and conclusions

This study has examined some of the links between the social and economic development on the one hand and population on the other. Results of the study show that development projects act as nodes which attract a certain sector of the population, namely young and adult males. However, irrespective of the economic success of the Kenana project, the majority of the people in the rural areas have been left as poor as they were. In fact, the project has not only failed to solve the problem of widespread poverty among the rural residents, but it has also helped to aggravate the inequalities in living standards, since it has failed to bring about desirable changes in the quality of life. It is important that efforts towards economic development should be balanced by efforts towards positive social progress.

20 Migrant labour in the New Halfa Scheme

Mohammed Osman El Sammani

Introduction

The New Halfa Scheme is the outcome of the resettlement of the Nubian Halfawyeen population (from Wadi Halfa), whose land was drowned by the High Dam, along with the partial settlement of the local nomadic groups (e.g. Shukriya, Lahawiyeen, Khawalda), the indigenous owners of the land, in return for their accommodation of the Halfawyeen coming from the north. The scheme was developed in five phases (Alam, 1971: 45) that involved land reclamation with the essential canalization network and development of settlements, spanning the period 1962–69. The first of these phases was devoted to the resettlement of the uprooted Nubian Halfawyeen communities (from Wadi Halfa), while the later ones were directed to beneficaries from the local nomadic groups.

The scheme was founded on the waters of the Khashm el-Girba dam on the River Atbara. Initially it was designed to conserve about 1.3 milliard cubic metres of water, but because of siltation it presently provides about 0.8 milliards. The area targeted for development is 500,000 feddans (one feddan = 1.038 acres), yet about 300,000 feddans are cropped annually. The drop in acreage is mainly due to shortage of irrigation water, inefficiency of the irrigation system, and lack of other basic agricultural inputs; which in totality induced the government to launch the present rehabilitation programme, financed by the World Bank.

The land is divided into tenancies of 15 feddans size, of which 5 are under cotton, 5 under groundnuts, and 5 under wheat in the Halfawyeen-settled part of the scheme, and under dura in the part settled by the nomads. Cotton is the government crop, in the sense that it is produced and marketed as a state monopoly crop; while groundnuts, wheat and dura are the tenants' crop, in the sense that the proceeds from them go wholly to the tenant, after the deduction of those costs of inputs provided by the management.

Besides crop production, tenants at New Halfa keep livestock of various types and numbers. The tradition of livestock raising is well-established among the former nomads as compared to the Halfawyeen; however, many of the latter have effectively adopted this type of economy, especially cattle raising. Recent surveys (Agrar-Und Hydrotechnik GmbH, 1980: Phase II, vol. 1.1, Annex 4) on the income of the tenant have revealed that in some cases returns from livestock are

Table 20.1. *Family labour contribution to different agricultural operations for the production of three crops in the Halfawyeen and nomad areas of the New Halfa Scheme, 1980*

Operations	Halfawyeen area						Nomad area					
	Wheat		Groundnuts		Cotton		Wheat		Groundnuts		Cotton	
	No.	%	No.	%	No.	%	No.	%	No.	%	No.	%
Land preparation	94	21.8	51	7.5	87	6.6	51	12.1	94	5.5	119	3.3
Sowing	4	0.9	34	5.0	114	8.6	52	12.3	193	11.3	172	4.7
Irrigation	107	24.8	36	5.3	106	8.0	20	4.7	40	2.3	53	1.4
Weeding	48	11.1	176	26.0	651	49.2	90	21.3	834	48.8	2,296	62.6
Fertilizers (applying)	80	18.6					61	14.4				
Thinning			25	3.7	83	6.3						
Harvesting	3	0.7	137	20.2			59	14.0	33	1.9	184	5.0
Threshing			94	13.9					230	13.5		
Picking	27	6.3			150	11.3			150	8.8		
Packing			85	12.6			45	10.6	98	5.7	332	9.1
Baling					132	10.0					246	6.7
Transportation	68	15.8	39	5.8			45	10.6	38	2.2		
Pulling of roots							45	10.6			264	7.2
Total	431	100.0	677	100.0	1,323	100.0	423	100.0	1,710	100.0	3,666	100.0

Source: Agrar-Und Hydrotechnik GmbH (1980), Phase II, vol. 1, Annexes 4, 33, 43

higher than those from the three crops (cotton, groundnuts and wheat), especially in those parts of the scheme settled by tenants of nomadic origin. Apart from the fact that it is a source of income, livestock in the New Halfa area plays the important role of financing agricultural operations from the sales of animals when need arises; plus the traditional prestigious role it gives to its owner, especially among the former nomads.

The migrant labour situation

Crop production in New Halfa is managed by the tenant, mostly in a supervisory capacity, contributing little work with his hands as compared to migrant labourers. Results from survey findings in 1978 and 1980 by a West German consultancy firm, including the author, support this argument (Agrar-Und Hydrotechnik, GmbH, 1980, Phase II, vol. 1: 30–41). Counting families who contributed their labour more than once to the production of the three crops shows that out of 61 cases interviewed in the Halfawyeen area, 9 families reported contributing their labour to production of wheat, 10 to groundnuts and 25 to cotton; out of 184 cases interviewed in the nomads' area, 16 families reported contributing their labour to production of wheat, 33 to groundnuts, and 62 to cotton.

To make up for the limited labour contribution by the family, the tenant resorts to hired labour. It is apparent from Table 20.1 that the contribution of hired

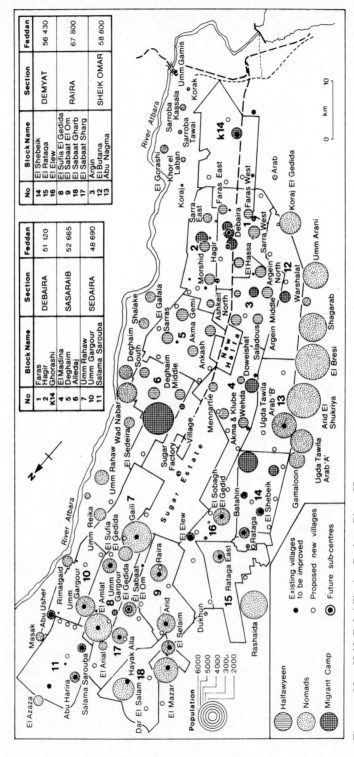

No	Block Name	Section	Feddan
1	Faras	DEBAIRA	51 120
2	Hagir		
K'14	Ghorashi		
4	El Madina	SASARAIB	52 665
5	Deghaim		
6	Alledaji		
7	Umm Rahaw	SEDAIRA	48 690
10	Umm Gargour		
11	Salama Sarouba		

No	Block Name	Section	Feddan
14	El Shebeik	DEMYAT	56 430
15	El Rataqa		
16	El Elew		
8	El Sufia El Gedida	RAIRA	67 800
9	El Sabaat El Om		
18	El Sabaat Gharb		
17	El Sabaat Sharg		
3	Argin	SHEIK OMAR	58 800
12	El Butana		
13	Abu Nagma		

Fig. 20.1 New Halfa Rehabilitation Project, Phase II.
Source: Agrar- und Hydrotechnik GMBH

labour to agricultural production is substantial, using the New Halfa Area as a readily available labour market. This is further reflected in the population composition and distribution in the scheme area. The total population in the scheme, including the Sugar Estate, was 266,310 persons in 1980, of whom 51,106 were Halfawyeen, 139,689 nomads, 40,515 migrant labourers and 35,000 inhabitants of New Halfa Town (Fig. 20.1).

The previous discussion is intended to serve as a background to a presentation on the socio-economic forces conditioning the distribution of migrant labour population in New Halfa Scheme. Two sets of forces are distinguished as having an impact on (i) sending migrant labour populations into the New Halfa Scheme, and (ii) directing this population to certain parts of the scheme. In what follows the former will be referred to as the external forces, and the latter as internal forces.

External forces affecting labour migration

The areas of origin from which migrant labour comes are indicative of the trend of the flow of labour to the scheme. It comes from Western Sudan in particular, but also from Eastern Sudan and to a very limited degree Southern Sudan:

	Tribe	Area
i	Fur	
ii	Zaghawa	
iii	Bargo	Darfur (Western Sudan)
iv	Masalit	
v	Bergid	
vi	Nuba	Kordofan (Western Sudan)
vii	Gawaama	
viii	Beni Amir	
ix	Hadendowa	Kassala and Red Sea (Eastern Sudan)
x	Amrar	
xi	Dinka	Lakes and Jonglei (Southern Sudan)

The data from 100 samples surveyed at random in five labour camps substantiates the above picture, as their percentage distribution by area of origin reveals: Darfur 50 per cent; Kordofan 30 per cent; Khartoum 11 per cent; Kassala and Red Sea 8 per cent; and Gezira 1 per cent.

Migrants saying they came from Khartoum are of diverse origin, dominated by elements from Western Sudan; however, they have not entered the scheme directly from their area of origin, but have stayed in Khartoum temporarily before coming. Most migrants seemed to have looked for employment opportunities in other areas before coming to the scheme, since 52 per cent of those questioned reported that they had not moved to the scheme directly from their area of origin (Agrar-Und Hydrotechnik GmbH, 1980: Annex 4, 19).

The following factors seem to be the main influences upon labour movement to the New Halfa Scheme:

(1) *The development gap.* For a variety of reasons, the country's development has not been balanced, registering economic and social gaps between the areas of irrigated schemes and the rest of the country under traditional modes of production. All the 11 tribal groups listed previously as constituting the migrant labour elements at New Halfa come from areas with poor economic bases and low standards of living.

(2) *Slow rates of development.* Owing to limited resource potentials, lack of infrastructure, slow progress of local economies, bad planning and a multitude of other factors, the share of these traditional areas supplying migrant labour in regional and national economic development has continued to be negligible.

(3) *Population/resource ratio.* The economic and social progress of those traditional areas has been delayed by increase in population, due to improved health care and control of epidemics, while little has been done in the area of productivity. The result has been in many areas less production from the same lands, evident in declining soil fertility and yields, the pushing of the northern grazing belt southwards, and the prevalence of environmental degradation.

(4) *The historical factor.* Migration for employment in irrigated agriculture, particularly from Darfur and Kordofan, started as early as the mid-1930s; and from Kassala and Red Sea into the Gash Delta Scheme during the 1940s. Since then the trend has been maintained. With time, the populations of these traditional lands have become convinced that their local economies are not capable of securing them a sustained living. Migrations for employment have therefore become part of the culture of these populations.

(5) *Social and economic motivation.* Migrants move from areas of origin to those offering employment prospects to take advantage of the economic and social opportunities offered by the latter areas. In this way migration is a means of upgrading social status, especially if the migrant is highly motivated. Sources of aspiration in these traditional communities are to return home with new goods, ideas and styles of life, and to gain enlightenment through new impacts and the influence of education.

(6) *Psychological factors.* Since the mid-1970s more people are migrating from the rural areas, in pursuit of jobs, to the developed parts of the country and to countries outside Sudan. The fever of migration has become a hysterical situation; migration is preferably to the oil-rich countries, but if that is impossible, then to those places within the country that offer employment opportunities. Among the latter the irrigated schemes, including New Halfa, are important centres of attraction.

(7) *Catastrophes.* Sometimes those traditional areas supplying labour are hit by catastrophes, causing the dispersion of large populations into other parts of the country that provide temporary or permanent refuge. The many famines hitting the Red Sea Hills area from time to time send populations into the Gash Delta and the New Halfa Scheme. The 17 years of unrest in Southern Sudan resulted in

migrations to the Gezira and New Halfa Schemes and the Sugar Estates. The Sahelian drought of 1976 pushed many of the Zaghawa to head for New Halfa, where they presently constitute large communities. One in every five years in the semi-arid and savanna low-rainfall zones registers rainfall failure, which means unreliable pastures and a bad harvest. Similarly, during one in every five years the plains of the Jonglei area experience flood hazards that lead to the loss of the dura crop, the main staple food of the population. Inevitably, a bad harvest results in more migrants from these traditional areas.

(8) *Locational factors.* Locational factors are important in three ways in the case of New Halfa. The first of these is the location of the New Halfa Scheme within a convenient range of the zone of irrigated schemes in the country, especially in relation to Rahad and Gezira, whereby labour can assess employment opportunities in the three and choose the most economically rewarding location. The proximity of the three schemes to each other facilitates labour mobility, particularly with the development of the national road network. Secondly, the special location of the New Halfa Sugar Estate within the New Halfa Scheme area, with its different scheduling of labour requirements, enables the same labour supply to be available for agricultural operations within the New Halfa Scheme at other times of the year. Finally, the proximity of New Halfa to the nomads of Eastern Sudan, and the acquaintance of the latter with the scheme area, give New Halfa the advantage over other irrigated schemes of attracting a substantial labour supply from these areas.

(9) *Fodder requirements.* The livestock economies of the Sudan depend very much on natural grazing. Even in the irrigated schemes natural grasses on the edges of canals and in fallow areas are the main source of fodder supply for the tenants' livestock, supplemented with straw, the residue from the cotton bushes and, recently, purchased dura, cotton seeds and oil-seed cake. From the beginning of March to some time in July, depending on the onset of the rains, there is a critical shortage of pastures so that the nomads of Kassala and the Red Sea Hills go to the New Halfa Scheme to seek employment as cotton pickers and to establish grazing rights for their animals over the tenancies they pick. The cotton residues in the tenancies support their herds and flocks for a period of at least one month, and admit them to the grasses on the edges of the canals, to the stored straw and to the abundant supply of cotton seeds which they can purchase from local merchants.

(10) *Complementarity.* It is apparent from the above disposition, that there are many interrelationships connecting the areas of labour supply to those of labour demand. In summary, there is an evident complementarity between the two economies of the traditional areas and the irrigated ones.

Internal forces affecting labour migration

The majority of the migrant labour settlements are to be found in the southern two-thirds of the scheme (Fig. 20.1), where the Halfawyeen settlements are concentrated and the New Halfa Sugar Estate exists, while very few of these settlements are to be seen in the northern parts of the scheme, where tenants of nomadic origin are preponderant. Obviously this pattern of distribution of settlements corresponds to labour employment opportunities in the scheme.

The factors governing the distribution of labour inside the scheme are various:

(1) *Share-cropping in groundnut production.* It has become an established practice in the New Halfa Scheme, especially in the Halfawyeen settled area, that the groundnuts crop is produced through share-cropping between the tenant and the migrant labourer. This might take one of two forms: (i) renting the land to the migrant labourer in return for part of the produce, or (ii) providing the land and the inputs, while the migrant contributes his labour, with the crop shared between the two according to certain agreed ratios. The first is preferred by those share-croppers from among the migrants who managed to accumulate adequate savings to enable them to rent the land and support themselves throughout the production season. The second arrangement is the one preferred by the majority of migrant labourers, because it relieves them of the burden of outlays, these being shouldered by the Halfawyeen tenant. Since the latter is more affluent than the nomad tenant, his part of the scheme attracts more migrant labour settlements.

(2) *Share-cropping on the amlak land. Amlak* land is the freehold land owned by the Halfawyeen close to their settlements, and in addition to the tenancies, as individual property, in compensation for the agricultural land they once owned at old Halfa. Individual ownership varies from one family to another, depending on the size of previous property. However, all the *amlak* land of one village exists in a consolidated form receiving irrigation throughout the year. Usually, this land is cultivated with vegetable crops which are another form of production managed through share-cropping, on similar arrangements like groundnuts. Research findings on migrant labourers' incomes reveal that their returns from the *amlak* share-cropping activity are among the most rewarding of their economic pursuits. The fact that the nomad-settled area has no *amlak* land explains the tendency for migrant labour to concentrate in the Halfawyeen-settled area.

(3) *Attraction by the financially-able tenant.* Successful tenants at New Halfa are the ones who are able to pay for agricultural operations from their own resources and at the right time. These have proved to be the ones who receive additional incomes from outside agriculture. Migrant labour is attracted by the financially-able tenant, who pays him his fees immediately after finishing his work. He is reluctant to work for the poor tenant, who has as his only source of finance the cotton advances credited to him by the management. Since the majority of the Halfawyeen tenants have sources of income other than agriculture, they are in a position to attract more migrant labour than the nomad tenants.

(4) *Joint livestock-raising ventures.* Livestock compounds (mainly for cattle) are found near a number of the Halfawyeen settlements. The herds in these camps belong to both Halfawyeen settlers and livestock raisers from Eastern Sudan. Keeping cattle in large numbers is one of the practices adopted by some of the Halfawyeen families after entering the New Halfa area. Livestock are tended by

the tribal elements from Eastern Sudan as part of their herds, and they market the milk surpluses in excess of the needs of the owner at New Halfa town. In return for these services, the Halfawi livestock owner secures an adequate amount of grazing from his fellow villagers to allow collaborators from Eastern Sudan to utilize the grazing lands surrounding the village.

(5) *Attraction by earlier in-migrants of same stock.* In-migrants change jobs. There are some who manage to obtain permanent jobs and settle in the New Halfa Scheme area. Remarkable among these are the guards at the irrigation regulators, and the other categories of workers employed by the management of the scheme. The majority of these workers are from Western Sudan with a few from Southern Sudan. Initially they entered the scheme as unskilled labour employed in the construction phase. When the scheme was completed, some of them were absorbed permanently in labouring jobs, and their presence attracted others of the same tribal origin so that many of the migrant labour settlements at New Halfa are found near the main canal regulators, where the houses of the guards are built, or near the section and block headquarters, where the workers employed by the management have their homes.

(6) *Special employment opportunities.* Both the agricultural management of the scheme represented by the section and the block headquarters, and the irrigation services represented by a hierarchy of officers, carry out many jobs for which they recruit labour regularly or when need arises. For example, all clearance work outside tenancies, besides those agricultural operations which the tenant fails to carry out in time are done by the agricultural management through labour recruited for this purpose. Again, the clearance and maintenance of canals is regularly done by labour paid by the Irrigation Department.

(7) *Attraction by tribal affiliation.* This is more pronounced in areas inhabited by tenants of nomadic origin especially by fellow-tribesmen, who being motivated by the cotton residues as fodders for their animals head to certain parts of the scheme, where they are admitted as cotton-pickers by tenants who come from the same tribe. The two have continued relations outside the cotton-picking operation, maintained through their mutual interests in livestock raising in rain-fed agricultural production away from the scheme, and in cultural relationships.

Compared to this situation the nomads have limited relations with the Halfawyeen due to cultural differences and to some degree to the physical separation of the two communities, since the former occupy the northern and fringe areas of the scheme, while the latter are to be found in its middle southern parts. They perceive the Halfawyeen as the well-to-do population of the scheme, who have benefited more than they have from the resettlement programme. They point to their settlements as having good housing and adequate social services, and generally view them as an affluent society compared to themselves, judged from the agricultural machinery co-operative societies established in nearly all the Halfawyeen villages.

(8) *Social and cultural distance.* Though the majority of the migrant labour

settlements are found in the Halfawyeen part of the scheme, these settlements are located away from the Halfawyeen villages, with the exception of the livestock-raising compounds. There are social and cultural gulfs separating the two populations. Though the Halfawyeen need the labour of the migrant population, they look down upon them. They discredit their communities as sources of many social evils – drunkenness, crime, gambling and prostitution – with whom their young should not mix. These migrant communities wanted a secure water supply and so established their settlements freely near canals, in shanty housing away from the planned Halfawyeen villages.

Conclusion

The migrant labour situation in irrigated agriculture as illustrated by the case of New Halfa is a dynamic one, where in time both the external and internal forces are open to changes leading to new situations. To what degree we can project these situations with precision is not easy to predict. However, there are indications that labour will continue to flow from the traditional and less developed areas of production of Western and Eastern Sudan into the central parts of the country including the irrigated schemes. Even with more attention devoted to these lands, their carrying capacities are limited, and therefore can absorb only part of the future increases in population. The interplay of other forces such as education, rising life expectations, economic and social equity, and increased accessibility will maintain the flow of migrant labour from these areas.

Presently the benefits accruing to the migrants from their coming to the irrigated areas are many. Compared to their areas of origin, they have more secure living conditions, abundant water supply (though it may be unhygienic), plenty of food, better job opportunities, higher incomes, and access to social services (though they were not initially planned for them).

On their labour depends agricultural production in the irrigated schemes, but they are socially looked upon as outsiders by the tenant communities who have title to the land.

It may be concluded that the flow of migrant labour to the irrigated scheme is partly a result of the existence of a development gap between two areas in the country, which might be held as a necessity of the time. Whether migration will continue at the same rate or not will very much depend on future changes in the structure of employment in the sending and receiving areas.

REFERENCES

Agrar- und Hydrotechnik GmbH – Essen (1980) *New Halfa Rehabilitation Project*, Phase II, vol. 1. Support Measures Phase I, Annexes 1–8.
Alam, H.A. (1971) Khashm el-Girba Development Project, paper for the Cairo workshop on Land Reclamation and Resettlement in the Arab World, The American University at Cairo.

Fahim, H.M. (1971) The Study of the New Nubian Community in Upper Egypt, Abstract, paper for the Cairo Workshop on Land Reclamation and Resettlement in the Arab World, The American University at Cairo.

Khogali, M.M. (1982) Western Sudanese migrants to Khashm el-Girba agricultural region: a case study, in J.I. Clarke and L.A. Kosiński (eds.), *Redistribution of Population in Africa*, London, Heinemann, pp. 166–75.

Sorbo, G.M. (1977) *Nomads on the Scheme: A Study of Irrigation Agriculture and Pastoralism in Eastern Sudan*, unpublished.

Waterbury, J. (1972) *The Cairo Workshop on Land Reclamation and Resettlement in the Arab World*, Northeast Africa Series, vol. 17, no. 1.

21 The Gash Delta: labour organization in pastoral economy versus labour requirements in agricultural production

Hassan Mohamed Salih

Introduction

Traditionally, the Hadendowa pursue activities of a mixed economy, which comprises herding of cattle, camels, sheep and goats with rain cultivation of dura (*Sorghum vulgare*). In 1923 flush irrigation was established in the Gash Delta, where cotton was introduced for commercial production. More recently, castor has replaced cotton as the main cash crop in the scheme. That shift started in the late 1950s when the yield of cotton began to decline owing to factors such as pests and heavy growth of weeds, increasing the cost of production and decreasing the tenant's income, which was further affected by the international fall in cotton prices. Moreover, soil and agricultural research in the Sudan have proved that the Gash Delta is a suitable place for the production of castor (Abdel Rahman, 1970). Eventually, the area under castor cultivation increased gradually at the expense of cotton until the latter was abandoned completely in 1970–71 season.

Although the largest part of the Delta is allocated to the Hadendowa tenants, few of them have changed their pastoral mode of life and settled in the agricultural villages of the scheme. Today, their main interest is to look after their herds and to raise food crops. In the combination of these two activities pastoralism has continued to be the dominant mode of livelihood while commercial agriculture is pursued as a secondary activity. Since the inception of the Gash Delta Scheme in 1923, the Hadendowa have continued to create intricate administrative, political and economic problems for successive administrations whether at regional or national level.

It is true that their tribal structure with its territorial system, their unstable environment and the prevailing administrative and economic circumstances in the scheme are important background factors which militate against the development of commercial agriculture. The established argument in anthropological literature has maintained for some time that the policies for settlement of pastoralists are always obstructed by cultural values associated with animals. The Hadendowa are no exception, as animals to them have significant social aspects around which kinship ties and political interests are moulded. Though recognizing the importance of these factors, here it is emphasized that the factors which hinder full participation in commercial agriculture can be understood and illuminated by

282

focusing on the differences between the patterns of labour allocation in the pastoral economy and those in agricultural production.

The purpose of this paper is therefore to show that incompatibility is not between pastoralism and agriculture *per se* but between labour requirements for herding on the one hand and those for cotton and castor production on the other. Animal husbandry and cultivation of food crops have always been complementary to each other in the pastoral economy. Historically, the Hadendowa were exploiting the Gash Delta resources successfully, though by a rudimentary irrigation system, to produce considerable quantities of dura for local consumption as well as for export. The delta was one of the main grain supplying areas in the Sudan, with an exported surplus to Arabian markets across the Red Sea (Burckhardt, 1819: 400). Therefore, as pastoralism and modern cash cropping are two different economic systems with different labour requirements, it is necessary for the Hadendowa to adopt a different pattern of labour organization if they are to adopt cash cropping or to combine both animal husbandry and modern agricultural production.

Labour organization in the pastoral economy

The main sphere of production in this situation is herding. Obviously, productive activities require rights in animals, natural resources and human labour. Access to labour resources is established through the principles of kinship. The elementary family is the smallest kinship unit of economic integration within which individual rights and duties with regard to animal husbandry are allocated, so it constitutes a basic unit of production to fulfil the requirements of daily consumption, marriage transactions and other kinship obligations. The achievement of these objectives needs an adequate number of animals as well as the cooperative work of several males to carry out herding duties and of females for domestic tasks. The elementary family will be a viable household when it satisfies such demands from its own animal and labour resources without receiving substantial help from outside.

Household composition

The typical residence of the Hadendowa elementary family is a single tent. The tent starts with a nuclear family, since it is pitched for the bride on the first day of her marriage. Eventually, this develops into a complete elementary family with the birth of children. Normally the children move out, on their marriage, to establish their own tents and subsequently the parents live alone. Therefore the social composition of the tent varies through time, depending on the procreation or non-procreation of the spouses, on the number and sex of children and on the marriage of these children. Membership of the tent is restricted to marital and parental links and does not extend beyond the limits of the elementary family.

Table 21.1. *Household composition in the Gash Delta*

Type of household composition	Occurrence in the camp	%
1. Newly married couple without children	7	10
2. Elementary family (parents with children)	44	62
3. Old couple without children	4	6
4. Divorced woman without children	3	4
5. Divorced woman with children	1	1
6. Widow without children	6	8
7. Widow with children	2	3
8. Widower with children	2	3
9. Unmarried children of dead parents	2	3
Total	71	100

This ideal natural development cycle may be modified by circumstances of divorce and death in the household. Although these social and natural factors can reduce the membership of a tent to one sex only, no tent will continue to exist without a female member. Typically, every tent represents only one married women, or a women who has been married, whether she is divorced, widowed or in certain circumstances even dead.

Table 21.1 shows the main features of household composition among the Hadendowa, though it is based on information obtained from three camps near the Gash Delta. The majority of the households are based on married couples, with or without children. This pattern is represented by 55 cases or about 77 per cent, mainly comprising 44 elementary families, approximately 62 per cent.

The tent always remains the property of the wife, even if she is divorced or becomes a widow. In both situations she will continue to live in her tent, either with unmarried children or alone when all the children are married. If a man survives the death of his wife and still has unmarried daughters, they remain together in the tent. If a deceased woman leaves no daughters or all her daughters have already married, then in both cases, as well as on the marriage of the last daughter in the tent, the tent is finally pulled down. So the physical existence of the household will come to an end with the final dismantling of the tent.

Herding requirements

The coordination of tasks and allocation of duties in the household depend on the division of labour according to sex and age. First, there is the division of labour between men and women, the former on the pastures, the latter inside the tents. The tent is the sphere of female activities, and no male over the age of seven, except the husband, sleeps in a tent or carries out any activity inside it. The most important domestic functions are the preparation of food and the care of children. Young daughters assist their mothers in the running of the domestic work by collecting brushwood for the cooking-fire and by bringing water from the wells on donkeys or by attending to small children. If a household does not have younger daughters, then the water and brushwood are fetched by young boys, as a girl approaching (or at) puberty is never allowed to mix with males. Generally, young children of both sexes look after goats and small calves which graze close to the camp. But in most cases, this job is left to boys only, so that they can be trained in herding techniques and be prepared as potential herders.

Apart from that, women spend the rest of their time in making clarified butter, braiding straw mats, weaving woollen rugs or making leather containers and decorative articles for the tent. Such items are prepared either for personal use, or taken to the local markets by old widows and sometimes by men. Many families supplement their livelihood by selling straw mats, baskets and woollen rugs in the local markets. Another important female job is the setting up of a new tent or striking and repitching it. Because women are responsible for pulling down and rebuilding tents, the movement of any camp cannot be undertaken without their consent.

Generally, women are not allowed by custom to work on the herd or to undertake any activity related to animals. Particularly, milking is an exclusively male job, and women will never do it, as it is prohibited to them, and it is considered extremely shameful.

While women are confined to domestic work inside their tents, the men are responsible for the management and the maintenance of animals. Although herding is the main feature of the Hadendowa economic life in their harsh and variable environment, they are not a highly nomadic society in the full sense of the word. They are not engaged in long seasonal migration like the Beggara and the Kababish in Western Sudan or the Rufaa Al-Hoi of the Blue Nile. The scattered, limited water supplies and poor pastures throughout their country, and importantly their traditional tribal system which confines each tribal section to defined territorial boundaries, seem to preclude long seasonal migration on a large scale. Thus, ecological conditions do not permit large concentration of animals in one grazing area, except in the Gash Delta. Instead, the Hadendowa tend to move and graze their animals in small family groups, of not more than three or four tents, within the orbit of their traditional watering centres. However, concentration of tents may occur, especially on the outskirts of the Gash Delta, depending on the availability of water and grass.

The average individual ownership of animals among the Hadendowa is remarkably low in comparison with the major pastoral tribes in the Sudan, partly because they live in one of the poorest marginal environments. Frequently, they face successive years of drought, to the extent that a large section of their population fails to find milk or dura for daily consumption. But in spite of the fact that animal husbandry among the Hadendowa does not involve long-distance movement, and the size of the family herd is small, still herding remains an arduous task with relatively heavy labour demands.

Scarcity of grazing and water resources creates acute continuous conflicts and friction over pastures and watering centres, frequently leading to homicides, injuries and animal thefts. Therefore security for both human beings and animals requires more vigilant labour. Normally it takes two men to attend a herd of 30 to 35 cattle on pastures, and another two men for watering. Similarly a flock of 50 to 60 sheep needs at least two men for shepherding and one more man for watering. Such high labour demands are also necessary because the Hadendowa herd their animals during the night and this requires more labour to keep constant watch on the animals, otherwise they will easily go astray and eventually be attacked or driven off by thieves. Friction on pastures is intense during May and June (Table 21.2), the peak months of the dry season, when grazing and water resources are extremely scarce and so a large number of herds concentrate around wells. However, Table 21.2 includes only those cases which are reported to the police; many incidents are not reported.

The herding duties require the division and coordination of tasks among the male members of the household. Attending animals on pastures and watering them is always the responsibility of unmarried adult men. These divide themselves into two working-groups, one to go out with the herd overnight, and the other to water it next morning. Also it is the duty of the latter to repair wells and build large troughs from which animals drink. Usually the animals come to the wells at about mid-morning. They are watered and remain to graze and rest around the wells, while the herders sleep under shady trees or temporary shelters. At sunset, the herds are driven to the camp, for the cows to be milked near the tents where the calves are kept. After that, the members of the household will take their evening meal, each sex separately. As soon as they finish their meal, the group responsible for herding takes the animals to the pastures, while the others go to their sleeping place on the edge of the camp. All young unmarried men of the camp sleep around the tents to guard against trespassers. Then early in the morning they go to the wells to start a new working day.

The older men spend the day around the camp, discussing herding arrangements and settlement of disputes or receiving guests, with whom they usually discuss tribal affairs. They may also visit the wells to supervise the work of young men and inspect the condition of the herds, and they go frequently to the local markets, either to sell an animal and local products (charcoal, mats and ropes) or to bring the household needs, such as coffee, sugar, grain and occasionally clothes. Importantly, rain cultivation is the duty of old men, mainly on small plots during years of good average rainfall. Traditional cultivation of food crops does not consume a long time or involve much work. It needs one man to make rows of holes on the ground, using the sowing-stick *saluka*, and another man to drop seeds in these holes and cover them with soil shifted by his feet. The crop will grow with the early showers in July, and a man must visit his cultivation plot frequently to be sure that it has not been damaged by animals, locusts or birds. Apart from that, it requires no specific labour input until the harvest time in September.

There are some seasonal and regional variations in this arrangement of herding.

Table 21.2. *Cases of animal thefts, injuries and homicides among the Hadendowa in the Gash Delta, 1969–70*

Month	Animal thefts	Minor injuries	Serious injuries	Attempted murders	Homicides
June 1969	145	114	34	2	8
July	27	32	3	1	—
August	36	42	6	1	—
September	69	43	6	1	—
October	104	47	17	2	5
November	48	54	8	1	4
December	67	63	12	1	4
January 1970	58	63	19	—	4
February	50	53	26	—	4
March	91	45	30	1	5
April	58	65	31	2	5
May	116	115	30	2	7

Source: Aroma and Wagar Police Stations' Reports

The Hadendowa in the Gash region breed mainly cattle, sheep and goats, but they have in addition a few camels, which are kept by those Hadendowa who live further to the north on the Red Sea Hills, where climatic conditions are not favourable for cattle. Rearing of camels is not common in the Gash Delta, especially as the Hadendowa here are transhumant and they are not in need of camels for carrying household equipment on long seasonal movements. In addition, camels graze on different pastures away from cattle and sheep, and this entails extra labour and different herding techniques. So most families find it difficult to provide labour for both camels and cattle or sheep unless they are rich enough to hire herders. Accordingly, large herds of camels in the Gash Delta are owned mainly by a few wealthy people and tribal leaders who have resources to provide the necessary labour requirements. Ultimately, such ownership confers prestige among the Hadendowa.

Usually, with the early flood of the Gash River at the end of June or the beginning of July, the tents are moved to the open plains west or east of the Delta. But during years of low flood most of the people may remain on the Delta, pitching their tents on higher sites beyond reach of the flood. By this time of the year, young herders start their rainy season movements, taking the animals to graze on the annual grasses and herbs outside the Delta. The frequency of herd movements in this season depends on the rainfall situation. Generally, pastures and water supplies are not sufficient for the animals to remain in one place more than three to five days. So, they move frequently and for short distances. Normally, old men, women and children do not follow the herds, but stay behind camping near the Delta with milch cows and some goats. Thus during the rainy season, from July to September, young men remain with the herds away from the tents on distant pastures. At this time of the year, animals may drink from rain-pools, and thus the herders are released from the laborious task of drawing water every morning.

Moreover, even for those who continue to use wells, working demands for watering animals are not heavy during the rainy season and winter, because cattle and sheep are watered every other day, in contrast to summer when these animals need to be watered daily, and sometimes twice a day. So watering of herds during the summer requires more work, especially towards the end of the season when the water level in the wells becomes noticeably low.

When the rain pastures are over-grazed and the pools dry up, by the end of October, the cattle and sheep are rushed back at great speed towards the Gash Delta in order to be near the watering-centres. However, on reaching the fringes of the Delta, the animals are not allowed to proceed further into the agricultural area, so as to avoid damage to the crops. They continue grazing on the outskirts of the Delta until the end of the harvest in February. During this period the animals come close to the fields, creating a constant threat to the cultivation and causing many disputes between the herders and the tenants. The administration of the Gash Delta Scheme has tried to protect the crops and reduce the scale of such disputes by providing a number of defined tracts on which animals can pass between the pastures and well-centres. In addition, the administration maintains some of these well-centres in the Delta. Each well-centre is partially surrounded by banks to retain water during the flood and allow it to filter deep down into the ground. This is because underground supplies are limited all over the region, due to the existence of a bedrock of basement complex. So, the herders depend mainly on surface wells fed by infiltration from the Gash flood. These well-centres are confined to certain sites of good percolation, like sandy belts and the bed of the main Gash River. Otherwise the largest part of the Delta is unfavourable for adequate water supplies. Besides watering the well-fields, the administration of the scheme provides a number of *hafirs* to reserve more water from the flood for the dry seasons. Such water supplies maintain large numbers of people and animals during both winter and summer.

While cattle and sheep spend the winter grazing near the Gash Delta, the camels, though limited in numbers, are taken either to the western plains of Sinaib towards River Atbara, or to the eastern plains near the Eritrean borders. They do not need frequent watering during this season and they can travel easily for long distances from remote pastures to the watering-centres. More important, the traditional grazing system is trying to reduce the pressure on the limited pastures near the wells and save them for cattle and sheep as both of these require frequent watering.

After the harvest, cattle and sheep are allowed to move into the Gash Delta. Also by the end of March, the tents are moved back into the Delta. At the same time the camels return from their winter pastures to rejoin the rest of the herds on the Delta. All the animals spend the summer in the Gash Delta where cattle and sheep graze on varieties of grass and herbs. The pastures here remain palatable for a long time, even when the surrounding areas have dried up. Moreover, the ample trees and bushes provide favourable browsing for camels and goats.

Normally during the summer there are crowds of animals in the Gash Delta. The scantiness of rainfall in the region, averaging less than 15 mm in northern and eastern semi-deserts, has more often forced large numbers of herds to move towards the Gash by the beginning of every summer. The natural qualities of the Delta soils allow them to absorb a considerable proportion of water and retain moisture for a long period after the flood, but the concentration of animals on the Delta during the summer makes competition for pastures and water very acute, and therefore herds need intensive care. Equally, this creates more constraints on the family labour.

Herding partnership

So far, the pattern of labour deployment in the pastoral economy has been outlined, and the necessary herding requirements for the elementary family to maintain itself as a unit of production. Herding is a difficult job which demands skills and physical ability to protect oneself and animals in a hostile environment. So it is usually carried on by males who are above the age of 15. In a sample of 71 households, only three households fulfil herding requirements independently; the majority do not have an appropriate demographic structure, in terms of age and sex, for providing labour for herding duties. Therefore, it is necessary for each household to join a wider grouping in order to overcome this problem of labour shortage. When looking at the general patterns which govern and regulate the formation of such groups, we find that cooperation in herding activities follows the dynamic of patrilineal segmentation. Therefore, the herding-group is a cooperative unit of production, which usually consists of households either belonging to a father and his married sons, or brothers and their married sons.

   Table 21.3 shows that 13 out of 19 herding groups in the sample consist of more than one household. The prevailing ties which link the co-herders in these groups are those of patrilineal and patrilateral kinship. Usually, the division of animals among brothers after their father's death does not lead to the breakdown of the herding-group. Although the father's herd is divided into individual shares and each son obtains control of his own share, brothers continue their cooperation as before by keeping their animals together in one herding-group. The adult male members in such a group provide a collective labour force for herding and watering their animals together. So this cooperation does not always imply that co-herders have collective rights in the joint herds, but in some cases the members of a herding group constitute an anticipatory inheriting-group. This occurs particularly when married brothers continue working on their fathers' herd as prospective partners after his death.

   Though membership in a herding-group seems to be based on patrilineality or patrilaterality, there are other variables which can influence the composition of such groups: the availability of labour resources in each household and the size and composition of its herd. There are three households in the sample which fulfil

Table 21.3. *The composition of herding groups, Hadendowa*

Number of households	Number of unmarried adults	Cattle	Sheep	Camels	Goats
2	5	25	65	2	—
3	7	37	70	—	20
3	4	25	60	—	—
6	6	40	70	1	15
4	5	20	40	—	10
6	8	59	65	3	30
3	4	35	60	—	—
5	8	42	55	15	20
6	4	34	20	—	10
3	5	27	55	4	—
4	4	19	45	—	30
2	2	7	—	—	—
5	7	60	45	—	—
1	2	3	—	1	100
1	3	27	—	—	—
1	6	40	—	—	—
1	2	60	100	30	—
1	3	100	200	70	—
1	—	40	60	—	—

herding requirements independently. One of them consists of a father with his two unmarried grown-up sons, owning a herd of 100 goats, three cows and one camel. The second is a household which includes a father and his three unmarried sons owning 27 cows only. The third household consists of a father and his six unmarried adult sons, maintaining a herd of 40 cows which are looked after by the four oldest sons, while one is a migrant labourer and another younger son attends secondary school.

It is clear from these examples that labour sufficiency does not depend only on the number of adult males in the household, but also on the variety of livestock kept. Two of these three households keep one variety of animals, cattle. At the same time, the first household manages to cope with labour needs for three varieties because herding goats does not entail heavy labour demand, the herd of cattle is very small and the one camel is always kept near the camping area. Accordingly, it will be difficult for the three households to diversify their livestock without running into labour shortages.

Moreover, herding partnership depends also on reciprocal advantages among partners. So it is preferable among brothers who have nearly equal numbers of animals. It is not advantageous for a man owning a few animals and having a number of adult sons to cooperate with another brother who keeps a large herd with one or two adult sons only. Each household is trying to make the benefits deriving from joint herding equal to its labour input.

Thus, generally, co-herding among brothers is characterized by equal benefits as there is no great wealth differentiation among them, since they get nearly equal shares from one patrimonial herd. Normally, brothers form a herding-group, unless one of them is exceptionally industrious, or increases his animal wealth by utilizing other resources, such as tribal and administrative jobs, or by being a successful cultivator in the Gash Delta Scheme. Further, a man can have more animals than his brothers if he has been favoured by his father, or if he marries a woman who gets a large number of animals from her father. Such circumstances help a man to accumulate more animals and build a big herd. Such herd-owners always keep their animals separately because they can supplement their labour force by hiring herders.

In the sample (Table 21.3) there are three households hiring herders, though all of them have more than one brother in the camp. One of them has only two sons, but he affords to manage herds of 60 cows and 30 camels and a flock of more than 100 sheep. The two adult sons in the household herd about ten cows which are always kept near the camp for milk, while the rest of the animals graze on distant pastures and are looked after by hired herders. The second household belongs to a tribal leader, who is also a successful cultivator in the Gash Delta Scheme. He owns about 100 cows, 70 camels and 200 sheep. Some of these animals are cared for by his three adult sons, while he hires six men to provide the herding requirements for the rest of his animals. It is necessary to mention here that the animals of tribal leaders are more secure than those of the ordinary tribesmen. This is because thieves either respect these leaders, or are afraid of their influence and authority in the local courts. The third case is a household of a government employee who has no adult sons, but he hired four herders to work on his herd of 40 cattle and a flock of nearly 60 sheep.

These three households show that rich people can easily manage to keep large herds of more than two varieties of animals because they can afford to hire the necessary labour. Each of the three types of livestock, cattle, camels and sheep, requires different herding techniques on separate pastures at different seasons of the year. Camels are tree browsers, so they graze on thorn bushes in the hill country. On the other hand, cattle and sheep need to be kept on relatively green pastures and are watered more frequently than camels. The ability of rich men to hire labour enables them to provide a labour force for the various herding duties required by different types of livestock. But, shortage of labour in the majority of households exerts constraints on the available labour force. As these households do not have the ability to hire labour, they depend mainly on the system of herding partnership. Also labour requirements limit the size and diversification of the herd.

Pastoralism and labour requirements in agricultural production

Commercial agriculture has been established in the Gash Delta depending on flush irrigation from the seasonal flood of the Gash River. The administrative set-up of the scheme has undergone several changes from the Kassala Cotton

Company in 1923, to the Gash Board in 1928, and finally the Gash Delta Agricultural Corporation in 1967 which continues to the present day. In spite of these changes in the administration, the agricultural system continues to operate on the same principles laid down in 1923. Today, the Corporation is responsible for clearance of the land, canalization, technical supervision and other administrative duties. It is also responsible for provision of seeds, castor hulling and marketing. After covering the cost of irrigation and agricultural supervision, the revenue is divided according to the following percentages: tenants' joint account: 57, corporation: 25, central government: 11, social services: 3, tenants reserve fund: 3, and Aroma Rural Council: 1.

On the other hand, the tenants are responsible for the clearing and maintenance of feeder channels, the erection and repairing of interplot banks, the sowing and picking of the crop, together with other agricultural operations like weeding, resowing, thinning and the transport of castor to the hulling stations.

In the pastoral economy, cultivation of food crops does not make heavy demands on the labour force because it can be carried out by one old male member of the household. Once the seeds are sown during the rainy season the crop does not need continuous work, until the harvest time. If the harvest does not meet the food requirements of the household, some lambs or a calf will be sold to make money to buy the supplementary grain from the local market. Now under the new circumstances of agricultural production in the Gash Delta, cultivation is the dominant occupation and the agricultural operations determine the allocation and use of labour. Also, the new system implies a different kind of production which is no longer organized and controlled by the household, but by the administration of the scheme, and it extends beyond the limits of kinship, since it necessarily involves wider sectors in the network of the market economy. Further, castor cultivation is more demanding in labour and needs continuous work throughout the agricultural season, which extends from September to April.

Generally, castor takes about six months to be ready for harvest. When the operations of irrigation are completed by the middle of September, the castor seeds must be sown within seven days, or as soon as the land gets sufficiently dry for walking on. Sowing is carried out manually, using the *saluka*. Instructions are given by the agricultural inspectors concerning spacing between holes and rows and the number of seeds in each hole. Usually it takes a man about three days to sow one feddan of castor. In addition to heavy demands on labour during the peak seasons of sowing and picking, the tenants in the scheme are faced with the problem of the vigorous growth of weeds which germinate during the flood and curtail the yield of the crop. It is an arduous task for the tenants to carry out weeding by hand which costs time and labour, especially when it has to be done three or four times every agricultural season.

Table 21.4 shows the average number of working days for one feddan during various stages from sowing to picking. The tenant has to start the first weeding ten days after sowing and before the grass develops and covers the crop in the seedling

Table 21.4. *Average tenant labour required per feddan*

Agricultural operations	Labour required in man-days
Sowing	2.4
First weeding	5.6
Second weeding	3.4
Re-sowing	1.3
Third weeding	2.2
Fourth weeding	2.5
Thinning	1.3
Picking	13.7
Building of shelters	1.7
Transport of drinking water to the workers	17.2
Packing and transport	4.6
Total days of work	55.9

Source: Ahmed, T.H., Economic aspects of production in the Gash Scheme, Eastern Sudan, in *Agricultural Development in the Sudan*, Philosophical Society of the Sudan. Thirteenth Annual Conference, Khartoum, 1966.

stage. This is the most difficult part of the agricultural operations and must be completed within one week to allow the crop to grow. The most threatening species of weed is *haya* (*Phynchosia memonia*), a creeper which climbs over castor plants. Then the second weeding begins by late September, to be followed by the third weeding which continues until the middle of October. During the same time thinning and resowing are going on, adding more pressure on the labour resources of the tenant. Finally comes the fourth weeding, at about the end of October or early November. The laborious task of picking, done by hand, starts in January and continues until early April, the peak period being from the middle of March to early April.

Several attempts have been made to mechanize cultivation, weeding and harvesting of castor in order to increase production and to reduce the heavy labour demands, but since the seeds are sown immediately after the flood subsides, the land is not sufficiently dry to implement mechanized sowing or weeding effectively. At the same time mechanized picking requires mechanized sowing for the plants to grow in straight rows with specified distances between them. The complexity of such problems has obstructed the mechanization of agriculture in the Gash Delta. Ironically, the same soil qualities which always support the plans for continuing castor cultivation are also the main obstacles for mechanization. Until now no effective method has been devised for the control of weeds in the Gash Delta, but the use of various weed killers has been tried.

It is clear from the foregoing discussion that the traditional grazing system of the Hadendowa is incompatible with the demands of agricultural labour. Firstly, the time of sowing in September is in conflict with labour requirements for herding, as at this time most of the adult men have to be moving with the herds away from the Gash Delta. Secondly, the harvest period from January to April coincides with the annual rush of the animals towards the Delta. So there is a need for more herders to hold them back from causing serious damage to the crop. Therefore, most of the pastoral families cannot carry out herding and agricultural duties simultaneously. This is understandable if we bear in mind that it is always difficult for the household to fulfil all herding requirements independently.

As shown earlier, among 71 households there are only 3 households with sufficient labour supply to meet the herding demands from among their members. The remaining 68 households are facing labour shortage, three of them hiring herders, and the rest entering into herding-partnerships. The permanent shortage of labour may be partly due to the traditional sex division in Hadendowa society, with women excluded from taking part in herding or agricultural activities. It increases the strain on the male labour resources of the household and makes participation in agriculture even more difficult. However, some families may be in a better position as far as labour is concerned, and they prefer to keep their animals all the year round near the Gash Delta. But the regulations of the scheme do not allow the presence of animals within or on the scheme boundaries from sowing time until the harvest. Therefore, the coordination of herding and agricultural activities is a heavy drain on the labour resources of these families as their pastures could be 50 miles or more away from the Delta.

So the Hadendowa are confronted with labour shortage in combining the two occupations. This is in part because cash crop farming is more demanding in labour and partly because the agricultural schedule conflicts with their herding arrangements. Consequently they have given priority in the allocation of available labour resources to the pastoral sector; absenteeism has become one of the main problems facing the administration, as over two-thirds of the tenancies are allocated to the Hadendowa. Cultivation has to be delayed frequently until the end of September or early October, instead of starting in the middle of September, because the majority of the tenants are absent. Such circumstances have reduced the productivity of the scheme because the seeds must be sown with the minimal delay before the soils get dry. Importantly, climatic conditions play a major part in the rate of absenteeism. When there is a good rainy season over the region as a whole, most of the Hadendowa tenants prefer to remain on the hills where they find adequate grazing and sufficient rain cultivation of food crops, so there is a labour shortage in the scheme and agricultural plans are disrupted. On the other hand, during years of poor rains, which coincide with low floods of the Gash River, there is pressure on the scheme area from both human and animal populations with a land shortage; the authorities can neither meet the high demand for cultivation plots, nor protect the crop from the large number of animals rushing towards the Gash Delta. Generally, animals constitute a constant threat to the cultivation and according to the Gash Delta Agricultural Corporation's annual report of 1972 about 30 per cent of the crop is damaged annually by the herds.

Nevertheless, the size of individual tenancy in the scheme is not big enough to establish profitable farming, and therefore there are no economic incentives for giving priority to agricultural production. Although the minimum size of individual tenancy is set by the administration at five feddans, it is difficult to attain this minimum owing either to inadequate irrigation works beforehand or to the low level of the flood. The average individual tenancy in the scheme today varies from three to four and half feddans only. As a result of limited tenancies and inadequate labour, yields are remarkably low. An economic study of productivity in the scheme (Ahmed, 1970: 295) suggested that the tenant would not maintain a profit with less than about ten feddans and 30 per cent of the labour requirements from within his household. The majority of the households cannot participate fully or partly in agriculture due to constant labour shortage. Therefore, it is difficult for them under the present circumstances to make a profit from castor production. Moreover, the uncertainty of the flood precludes the increase in the size of the tenancies. But in spite of the fluctuations and decline in the size of average tenancies, tribal leaders and rich people still manage to maintain profitable tenancies averaging about thirty feddans. Further, tribal leaders cultivate even larger areas because of their powerful position in the administrative organization of the scheme. The total area registered to the prominant tribal leaders in 1970 was 2,452 feddans with an average of about 130 feddans for each. However, these areas were reduced in 1971 as part of government policy to undermine the native administration and the influence of tribal leaders. These tribal leaders have accumulated considerable profits from agriculture, because they can obtain plots large enough to establish profitable farming, and because they can afford to hire labour. Therefore they have succeeded in making use of the opportunities created by commercial agriculture and at the same time maintaining their animal wealth. They use part of their income from cultivation to invest more in the pastoral sector. They are not faced with the problem of labour shortage in combining both pastoralism and agricultural production, as they can hire agricultural labour as well as herders.

At the present, there are more than 16,000 registered tenants of whom only 5,000 or about 30 per cent attend their tenancies regularly. The flow of large numbers of West Africans and riverains has taken over the cultivation on the basis of crop-sharing. The main wave of West African migrants came with the beginning of canalization in the Gash Delta in 1923. Their number at the early period was estimated to be about 700. The agricultural authorities have been faced with the problem of labour shortage created by the Hadendowa absenteeism. So a policy has been adopted to secure a continuous labour supply from West Africans. Their settlements have been made permanent by providing them with a constant water supply through pipe systems. As a result, large communities of West Africans have developed with a continuously growing population which at the present time may be about 36,000.

In conclusion, there is a set of complex and interrelated factors influencing the Hadendowa to prefer animal husbandry to agricultural production in the Gash Delta. Inevitably, decisions concerning labour allocation between pastoralism and agricultural production depend largely on economic incentives. However, the peculiarity of the Gash Scheme, its dependence on flush irrigation from unpredictable floods as well as other technical, administrative and ecological shortcomings, supports the choice for the continuity of pastoralism.

REFERENCES

Abdel Rahman H. Ahmed (1970) *Castor in the Economy of the Gash Delta.*
Burckhardt, J.L. (1819) *Travels in Nubia*, Association for Promoting the Discovery of the Interior Parts of Africa, London.

22 The impact of development projects on population redistribution to Gedaref Town in Eastern Sudan

Mahgoub O. Gaafar and
K.V. Ramachandran

Introduction

With a rather high growth rate of population (estimated as about 2.2 per cent per annum during 1955–73), Sudan is still a sparsely-populated country (with a density per sq km of less than 6 in 1973). This low overall density masks the wide variations between the different parts of the country. For example, the Northern province has a density of less than 2 and there are vast tracts in the country uninhabited, while at the same time Khartoum province has 52 persons per sq km. Some councils have much higher densities. Thus one of the enigmas of Sudan is the existence of vast empty spaces and overcrowded towns, cities and even some rural areas. At the same time, the tendency of the past and indication of recent periods has not been to fill up the empty spaces but rather for population to move towards the already congested areas, thus depopulating the low density areas. This has created further imbalances in population distribution, aggravating the already-existing situation.

Climate, ecological factors and natural endowments have been some of the causes for population mobility, but development efforts prior to and especially since independence have accentuated the attractiveness or otherwise of areas. For example, construction of rail, road and water transportation, establishment of irrigation and agricultural projects, industries, commerce and trade and siting of educational, cultural and administrative centres all engendered movement of people from the less developed to the more developed and developing areas. Side by side with this, the diseconomy in providing educational, health, electricity, water, sewerage and other facilities in the low density areas resulted in further depopulation, and a vicious circle was created.

The tempo of movement accelerated in consonance with developmental efforts. For example, Table 22.1 indicates that whereas in 1955/56 (except in Northern province) more than 90 per cent of those enumerated in a province were born in that province, in 1973 several provinces indicated a substantial number of persons born elsewhere residing in their confines, with Khartoum having a third of its residents born elsewhere and Blue Nile and Kassala nearly a fifth. On the whole, in 1955–56 only 4 per cent of those born in a province were enumerated outside that province, while in 1973 it was more than 10 per cent. It is well-known that after

Table 22.1. *Percentage of population born and enumerated in the same province of Sudan by sex, 1955–56 and 1973*

Year		Bahr El Ghazal	Blue Nile	Darfur	Equatoria	Kassala	Khartoum	Kordofan	Northern	Red Sea	Upper Nile
1955–6	M	98.2	97.0	92.6	98.6	97.7	89.7	95.7	85.0	—	98.7
	F	98.5	97.7	96.6	99.2	97.8	90.9	96.9	90.9	—	99.1
1973	M	97.6	79.5	93.9	86.4	81.8	59.1	93.4	94.6	83.4	89.3
	F	98.1	85.7	94.3	89.1	85.6	70.0	95.4	95.9	87.2	91.8

Source: Tables 5.1 and 5.3 from Analytical Report, Sudan 1973 census, Khartoum, 1980.

independence in 1956, the government initiated several socio-economic development projects and improved transportation and communication. Also the bias
towards industries, commerce and trade and large-scale agricultural schemes and
the consequent neglect of the vast hinterland resulted in an exodus to the attractive
areas from the distressed areas.

It is thus obvious that there has been an increasing tempo of inter-provincial
movement, which has resulted in imbalances in population growth and settlement
patterns. For example, whereas Blue Nile, Khartoum and Kassala grew at high
rates (around 3 per cent per year), Kordofan, Northern province and Bahr El
Ghazal grew at low rates (around 1.5 per cent) and Equatoria and Upper Nile
showed decreases. In other words, the eastern and central regions showed
tremendous growth, the north and west had little growth and the south stagnated
or declined.

There is a distinct tendency for population to concentrate into the east-central
part of the country. The Lorenz curve indicates a less even population distribution
and the Gini coefficient increased from 0.31 in 1955–56 to 0.39 in 1973. The centre
of population which was calculated as lying around 12°28 latitude and 30°40
longitude in 1955–56 shifted to 12°77 latitude and 30°46 longitude in 1973 – a
slight north-east shift from around Abu Kershola to slightly west of Er Rahad on
the rail line.

Table 22.2 indicates unevenness in socio-economic conditions, with Khartoum, Blue Nile and Kassala coming out ahead of most other provinces. The only
exception is Northern province which, in spite of being not far from Kassala and
Blue Nile in development, has environmental limitations stimulating out-
migration of its population. As a matter of fact, people from the Northern province
constitute a large proportion of migrants to the Three Towns of Khartoum,
Khartoum North and Omdurman and to the agricultural schemes in Kassala. Also
a sizeable proportion of Sudanese emigrants originate from Northern province.

Table 22.3 confirms these observations with data about magnitude of migration
between provinces. For example, Blue Nile, Kassala and Khartoum gained
substantial numbers and Bahr El Ghazal, Darfur and Northern province lost
numbers. The other provinces indicated only marginal gains or losses. In all,

Table 22.2. *Selected socio-economic indicators – Sudan by province, 1973*

Province	% of literate females aged 10+ years	Doctor/dentist per 100,000 population	Accessibility index†	Urban percentage
Bahr El Ghazal	1.7	2.0	1.9	9.1
Blue Nile	24.3	4.5	5.8	14.3
Darfur	7.3	2.9	1.2	9.1
Equatoria	18.7	2.7	3.1	18.4
Kassala*	26.2	8.8	5.0	26.0
Khartoum	44.8	70.0	10.2	71.6
Kordofan	10.8	4.4	2.5	12.8
Northern	31.1	10.3	2.5	19.5
Upper Nile	4.7	2.0	1.1	4.6

† Road mileage per 1,000 square miles of area
* Kassala includes Red Sea
Source: Democratic Republic of Sudan (Department of Statistics): Second Population Census 1973, vol. 1; (Ministry of Health): 1976 Annual Health Statistics Report; and (Ministry of culture and information): *Sudan Facts and Figures.*

Table 22.3. *Net life-time inter-provincial migration, 1973 (settled population only)*

Age	0–14		15–54		55 and over	
Sex	M	F	M	F	M	F
Bahr El Ghazal	−1,641	−1,050	−11,401	−3,684	−977	−331
Blue Nile	26,486	25,170	80,391	54,456	14,329	8,363
Darfur	−9,139	−8,341	−109,832	−42,662	−13,962	−7,644
Equatoria	1,026	1,091	5,507	1,376	312	−56
Kassala	4,663	5,203	38,718	23,924	7,813	4,146
Khartoum	23,490	22,524	160,748	74,176	7,331	5,624
Kordofan	−36,927	−36,639	−89,278	−62,264	−4,242	−3,916
Northern	−21,054	−20,488	−102,181	−62,105	−14,113	−7,554
Red Sea	3,624	4,102	18,077	7,750	400	−123
Upper Nile	9,893	7,628	8,730	9,038	3,109	1,486

Source: Democratic Republic of Sudan (Census and Statistics Dept.), Second Population Census, 1973 Population Dynamics (Analytical Report), vol. II, Table 5.4, Khartoum, 1980.

around 1,400,000 persons in 1973 were recorded as residing in a province other than that of their birth.

These figures are for the settled population only. In addition, in the Sudan there are sizeable numbers of temporary migrant workers in the agricultural schemes who leave their homes and settle in the agricultural schemes for a considerable part of the year. Then there are nomads who move from place to place looking for pastures for their herds. Yet another facet of migration in Sudan is the influx of foreigners either on their way to Mecca for the pilgrimage or from neighbouring countries due to disturbed political and economic conditions.

Table 22.4. *Migration selectivity by age*

Age	% Migrants	% Non-migrants	Selectivity %
0–4	8.4	17.9	− 53
5–9	9.5	18.0	− 47
10–14	7.4	11.1	− 33
15–19	8.9	8.4	6
20–29	25.5	15.5	65
30–39	18.5	12.7	46
40–49	10.5	7.8	35
50+	11.3	8.6	31
	100.0	100.0	

Source: Republic of Sudan (Census and Statistics Dept.), Second Population Census 1973, Population Dynamics (Analytical Report), vol. II, Table 5.11, Khartoum 1980.

Table 22.3 also clearly shows the age-sex selectivity of migrants. As expected of inter-provincial migration involving long distances and a change in way of life and environment, there were more males than females in the streams, with sex ratio approaching 150 males per 100 females, especially to Khartoum. There were also substantial numbers of young adults among migrants, with 75 per cent reported in the age group 15–54. Part of the age selectivity might have actually been blurred by the long time interval between migration and the census enumeration in 1973. Even with this, the selectivity is obvious and is made more clear in Table 22.4, with closer age interval data. Whereas among migrants there were proportionately very few children as compared with non-migrants, there was a bulge in the young adult ages among migrants. The selectivity indices are negative at young ages and high and positive at young adult ages indicating the dearth of children among migrants and the preponderance of adults.

So far we have considered only inter-provincial movements. But there are large movements within provinces from one council to another. As a matter of fact, it is surmised that most of the inter-provincial migration may be actually specific to a few councils where developmental activities are pronounced. Unfortunately, because of coding and other problems, it is difficult to study migration between councils. However, an idea of the part played by migration can be had by comparing population growth or densities of councils over time. For instance, councils like Kassala, Gedaref (North and South), Rumbek, El Fasher, Darfur (South and West), Kosti, Medina, Managil, Mialiq, Hassaheissa, Sennar and Rufa Shukriya had high densities and high growth of population, implying in-migration. But in Tokar, Shendi, Aweil, Gogrial, Yirol, Dar Massalit, El Dueim, Hosh, Mahareiba, El Roseires, Abu Hagar, Singa, Dar Badariya, East Kordofan, North and South Jebels, Dar Hamid and Yei the growth was low even though the density remained high, probably indicating out-migration or reduced in-migration. In several others both the density and the growth rate remained low.

The high density and high growth rate in Gedaref and Sennar have been explained by the intensification of the mechanized agricultural schemes and the opening of opportunities for agro-based enterprises needing a large contingent of unskilled labour. The failure of the Gash and Baraka (Tokar) *Khors*, the decline in soil fertility and the inability of the cotton variety grown in that area to compete with the cotton grown in Gezira contributed to the decline of their population and the influx to the neighbouring Gedaref area.

The population of Sudan is increasingly depleted in the north and west and is concentrated in the east-central part of the country, comprising Khartoum, Blue Nile and Kassala. Whereas Khartoum, as the capital of the country has the administrative, recreational, educational, health and other infrastructure in addition to industries, trade and commerce concentrated within its confines, Blue Nile and Kassala have the majority of the organized large-scale agricultural schemes attracting migrants from areas in the north and west where climate and other factors have hindered progress and where there is a potential reservoir of manpower.

Thus it is clear that in the Sudan there is a sizeable internal movement directed towards the developed and developing areas in the east-central part of the country and away from the depressed areas in the west and north. The economic situation in the south also is equally poor, but because of transportation and other constraints there has been not much movement. Moreover, during most of the intercensal period 1955–73 there was an unsettled condition in the south and most of the movement from the south was to neighbouring countries rather than to the north. After the Addis Ababa accord (1972) there was a huge return movement to the south mostly to the towns and urban areas in general.

There are no comprehensive data about the socio-economic characteristics of the migrants nor do we know the reasons for their movements; only small-scale surveys have collected such important information. It is also only on indirect evidence that we can generalize about consequences of migration to sending and receiving areas; a few surveys have studied migrants to urban areas and the agricultural schemes but very few have studied the origin areas.

In this paper we shall report on the findings of a small-scale case study of one of the important receiving areas – Gedaref. This area is expected to assume great importance in view of the potentiality of the agricultural schemes.

Gedaref town – a profile

Gedaref area is one of the most important agricultural and commercial centres of Sudan (see Fig. 6.1, p. 75). Since it lies between the rivers Atbara and Rahad, is blessed with ample rainfall (around 600 mm annually) and has a fertile soil, the land is arable. The recognition of the potentiality of the area to feed the colonial army and the hinterland resulted in the introduction of mechanized agriculture in Gedaref around 1943. The major crop grown is dura, the staple food in the country, demand for which, both inside the country and neighbouring oil-rich Gulf countries, has created a good market for the produce.

For a period, Gedaref town served as a trade centre between Ethiopia and Sudan and a rail line was constructed to export dura, but now the line is not functioning. However, rail and roads link the area with Khartoum and with Port Sudan as well as with other important areas, like New Halfa in the north and Gezira in Blue Nile province. Moreover, the area lies in the path of the pilgrims to Mecca from the west. Since agricultural operations even today are labour-intensive and food production has assumed very great importance in view of the huge demands locally and internationally, a large labour force was needed to produce, transport and market the commodity. Thus the Gedaref area grew very fast. Between 1955 and 1966 the population of Gedaref town grew at 9.4 per cent per year, from 18,000 to 45,000. Between 1966 and 1973 the growth rate declined to 5.6 per cent and the population rose to 66,000. These high growth rates are clearly due to a huge influx consequent on the success of the mechanized agricultural schemes.

According to the 1964–66 survey, lifetime in-migrants to Gedaref accounted for 30.9 per cent of the total population and were predominantly males (sex ratio 140). More than 90 per cent of in-migrants came directly from their place of birth. Kassala and Northern provinces contributed 22 per cent of the in-migrants, and another fifth came from the western provinces of Darfur and Kordofan. The sex ratio of direct migrants was 137 as against the 172 of step-migrants. Direct migrants are usually followed by wives and children when the initial migrant settles down in a place after ascertaining the suitability of the location, whereas the step-migrant with no fixed destination comes more or less alone and continues to live alone.

As against 52 per cent of migrants in age group 18–37, non-migrants had only around 25 per cent in that age group. The sex ratios of migrants (aged 12 years and above) increased with age initially and declined at later ages, while those of non-migrants decreased with age. Non-migrants had very low sex ratios in the younger adult age group 18–37.

Almost half of the labour force in the town was made up of farmers, farm labourers or traders. Since physical ability to carry out the arduous agricultural operations was important and educational qualification or other skills were not necessary, most of these were illiterate. Thus even though the area attracted young male adults from other places, its own better educated natives were moving out to other towns or outside the country for job opportunities commensurate with their academic qualifications. Thus there was a dilution of the educational level of the people of the town, despite better facilities. For example, there was a decrease in the proportion of population aged seven years and above with no schooling and an increase in those with sub grade-education.

In 1973 two-fifths of the male population of the town were under 15 and about half were aged 15–44 years. On the other hand, among females, children under 15 years constituted the largest group. Between 1966 and 1973 there was a fall in the proportion of boys and a corresponding increase in the proportion of men, but among females there was an opposite tendency. There was also a steady increase in the sex ratio of the population from 108 in 1955–56 to 110 in 1966 and finally to 119 in 1973. The corresponding sex ratios at adult ages were 104, 109 and 151.

In addition to receiving migrants from other provinces of the country, Gedaref received pilgrims on the route to Mecca from West Africa, and the proximity and unsettled conditions in neighbouring countries like Ethiopia and Zaire also contributed to the attraction of sizeable numbers of foreigners. About one in nine of its population was reported as foreign-born in 1973. Since nationality is often difficult to determine, and there were advantages in misreporting nationality, it is suspected that perhaps there were some foreigners who were either not reported or were reported as Sudanese.

Thus we note that the town grew by internal and international migration. Since the potentiality of the area is great, still further growth in population can be anticipated.

The survey

Since the available data on Gedaref presented earlier pertain to periods before 1973 and do not cover reasons for migration, contacts of migrants with origin areas and other important aspects, a small case study was carried out.

In view of financial and time constraints, the sample selected for the survey was very small. From the World Fertility Survey (undertaken in 1980) segments, two were selected for our survey. Hence it is to be clearly understood that it cannot be claimed that the results would have much predictive value. Perhaps the findings could be used for diagnostic purposes and as a preliminary for further large-scale representative sample surveys.

The total number of households covered was 201, i.e. 1.25 per cent of the estimated number of households in the town, and included 1,175 persons. Four questions were addressed to all – age, sex, relationship to head of household and place of birth. For persons aged ten years and above, additional information was collected on last place of residence, residence status, ability to read and write, years of schooling, marital status, present occupation and tribe. For the migrants, detailed questions were asked on duration of residence, reasons for migration, who influenced the move, time spent seeking work, age at first migratory move, place to which first migrated, occupation at first place, number of migratory moves, property at home and who takes care of them, dependents in place of origin and their relationship, number of visits to place of origin, intention to return to origin area and reasons for returning.

Good cooperation was obtained from the respondents, and rapport between the respondents and the interviewers was excellent. However, due to ignorance, the quality of the responses might not be very good. All the same, since the enumerators belonged to the area and knew the people well, it is expected that the findings might more or less depict the true situation. The administration of the town gave full support and cooperation to the survey, and this facilitated data collection enormously.

The findings

Out of the 1,175 persons enumerated there were 647 males, giving a sex ratio of 122. Migrants constituted 41 per cent and they had a much bigger sex ratio of 141. Whereas among the total population around a third were children under 10, among the migrants they constituted only one in ten. On the other hand, only a third were aged 25 and above in the total population, but among migrants they were nearly 60 per cent. Among children the sex ratio was 116 as against only 87 for migrants. However, at adult ages (25 years and above) the migrants had a sex ratio of 143 as against 105 for non-migrants. Thus it is very clear that even in 1980 when the survey was carried out, the town had a substantial migrant population and male young adults constituted a sizeable segment of it.

Around two-fifths of migrants came from Kassala and more than a quarter from the Northern province. The neighbouring provinces contributed around another fifth and those born abroad were about 2.5 per cent. The sex ratio of the migrants from Kassala was 146 and was close to the sex ratio of 154 observed for those from the Northern province. However, those from other neighbouring provinces had a very high sex ratio of 178. The lower sex ratios of migrants from Kassala and Northern provinces are explicable by the fact that in the case of Kassala most of the migrants are from adjacent councils and it is not very difficult for these migrants to bring their family. In the case of those from Northern province, these are the longest duration migrants to the area and they are the pioneers who came at the inception of the scheme, bought land, ran the commerce and trade and hence are in a much better position to bring their families. They have more or less settled in the area, as we shall see later. Persons from the neighbouring provinces come to the town alone, and since most of them are in the town for a shorter time and hold less lucrative positions, they cannot afford to bring their families with them.

Thus we see that distance is an important factor in the determination of the quantum and characteristics of migrants, excluding the migrants from the Northern province, who, having arrived in the town earlier, are in an advantageous position.

Some 79 per cent of migrants to the town came from rural areas and only 16 per cent came from urban areas. Considering the fact that the total population of Sudan is estimated to be 75 per cent rural and 25 per cent urban, there is a slight over-representation of rural dwellers among the migrants, but the predominance of agricultural operations in and around the town makes natural such selection among migrants.

Although a majority of the migrants were from northern tribes, it is not in contradiction with the finding that most of the migrants were born in Kassala province, because most of these persons were children born to northern tribes who had come earlier to the province. As mentioned earlier, people from the north are the most mobile among the population of the country and Kassala province with its potential arable lands offered them the opportunity to settle down.

About 31 per cent of males and 46 per cent of females migrated to the town during 1970–80 and 30 per cent of males and 25 per cent of females had been in the town for more than 20 years. Whereas among those who had lived there less than 10 years there were proportionately more females, there was a significant male preponderance among earlier migrants, especially among young people (aged 10–44 years). On the whole, duration of stay in Gedaref was shorter for females than males, marriage and family migration being subsequent to male-dominated labour migration. It is interesting to note that migrants of less than 20 years' duration were more numerous than those of longer duration, but when we keep in mind that migration to Gedaref started in the late forties consequent on the establishment of mechanized agriculture and assumed immense proportions only in the mid and late fifties and especially after independence, this is reasonable. Moreover, the longer-duration migrants are subjected to the attrition of mortality and return migration, depleting their numbers very fast.

There was a marked improvement in literacy and also in the educational level of the population of the town. As against more than 50 per cent of males aged seven years and above with no schooling during 1955–73, the 1980 survey indicated only around 15 per cent with no schooling for those aged 10 years and above. Migrants had a more than three-fold majority among the non-schooled. For females, from the high three-quarters with no schooling in the past, the recent figure showed a fall to around a third. There was also a significant increase in those with sub-grade education especially for females. However, there continued to be an apparent stagnation in higher education among males due to an influx of less-educated migrants and an outflow of better-educated young natives.

There seems to be some improvement in the quality of migrants. For example, among migrants of less than 10 years' duration (recent migrants) only 12 per cent of males and 33 per cent of females had no schooling, as against 35 per cent for males and 72 per cent for females among longer-duration migrants. At every level of education among both males and females, the proportion was much higher among recent than earlier migrants. At the same time, there seems to be some acceleration of out-migration of better educated natives.

Another important observation from the survey was regarding the adjustment and mixing of migrants and non-migrants. For example, there were more married males than females among migrants. But an opposite tendency was noted among non-migrants and there was a balance by sex in the total married population, indicating some marriage between migrant males and native females. This socialization among the groups is a good augury for the town.

Thus we note a continuing influx of young male adults to Gedaref alongside some out-migration of Gedaref-born better-educated young persons. On the whole, the town continued to grow at high rates, perhaps around 5 per cent per year – slightly less than the rate observed for the period 1966–73.

Reasons for migration to Gedaref

Why do a large group of less-educated people move into Gedaref town? As we described earlier, Gedaref town serves the agricultural schemes in and around the area and since agricultural operations even today are labour-intensive, requiring physical rather than academic qualifications, and there are several adjoining areas in Kassala and even in other provinces with surplus population looking for opportunities for fruitful employment, the rush to the town is explicable. To confirm the conclusion, a question on the reason for migration to the town was addressed to all migrants.

As expected, most of the males (60.3 per cent) indicated economic reasons – to work in agricultural schemes as labourers, to acquire land and to obtain more cash income. On the other hand, most of the females (77.4 per cent) stated social reasons – to join the husband or household head, marriage, etc. Children were either joining the parents or coming for the better educational facilities, whereas older persons came for health or social reasons (for example, to stay with children and grandchildren).

Looking at the data in another way, we note that 81 per cent of heads of household moved for economic reasons, whereas 75 per cent of other members moved for social reasons. Again, most of the married males stated economic factors while most married females gave social factors for the move. It is interesting to point out that more short duration (less than 10 years) migrants stated social reasons, and this confirms our observation that recent migrants are either family type or family members joining the earlier migrants in contrast with the initial and early stages of organization of the agricultural schemes attracting the pioneer single male adults. In recent years many youngsters who came to the town obviously looking for work stated their reason for coming as joining their relatives. For example, 45 per cent of male and 54 per cent of female migrants stated that their move was influenced by friends and relatives in Gedaref. Most of the females, of course came to join their husband or family. A large proportion of males apparently came looking for jobs, but this was blurred by the fact that they came at the invitation of friends and relatives. A sizeable proportion (41 per cent) of males stated that they moved on their own initiative, but most of these were the pioneer long-duration migrants, males coming on their own.

Interestingly, 84 per cent of male and 95 per cent of female migrants moved directly from their birthplace to Gedaref. Since a sizeable number of migrants are from Kassala province with very little intervening opportunities, and persons from Northern province constituting a sizeable proportion who moved in the initial years of the establishment of the area, it is not surprising to find a majority of migrants coming directly to the area without spending time in other places *en route*. The rather difficult economic conditions in Kassala and Northern province make the situation in Gedaref very attractive to prospective migrants, and people moved in to profit from the opportunity. The influx from the nearby Gash and Baraka (because of their failure) added to the growth of the town.

Some consequences of migration to Gedaref

Migration affects both the sending and receiving areas and has an impact on the individual, his family and the community (of origin and destination).

As seen earlier, migration is selective by age and sex. While it is conceded that Gedaref gained the manpower needed for carrying out the strenuous agricultural operations, the plight of the origin areas was severe: 'heavy migration from the Northern province, for instance, has greatly disrupted demographic and economic conditions. As a result of out-migration, the population of this province is at present mostly composed of children, old people and adult females, all of whom contribute very little to economic production' (El-Bushra, 1975). This may be true of other out-migration areas as well, because of age-sex selectivity.

A majority of migrants (57 per cent) stated that they never visited their home areas and only 25 per cent had visited their home areas more than twice during the previous year. One reason for such infrequent visits would be the fact that a large proportion of migrants stated that their families were with them (only 11 per cent stated that they have dependants at origin areas). On the other hand, 82 per cent stated that they have no intention to go back to their origin areas. This implies that migrants have become reconciled to their new environment and have more or less cut off their roots. As stated by Khogali (1982), 'migration brought about separation of families and weakening and disruption of kinship ties . . .'.

Although the migrants stated that they have very few dependants left behind in their home areas, and many indicated no intention to return to those areas, still those who possessed land, cattle and other immovable properties in areas of origin usually entrusted such possessions to friends and relatives who were generally old men and women left behind in the depressed areas. Generally such lands do not get the attention required, and deterioration of their quality normally results in low productivity. Revitalization of such lands would be both time-consuming and costly, if not impossible.

Again, it is sad to note that, contrary to the Sudanese family solidarity, whereby even distant relatives are taken care of and helped when in need, migrants to Gedaref seem to be callous and to have cut off their roots from their origins and had no intention even to go back to these places. Perhaps the difficult conditions of life faced by them and their selfish motive to benefit from their sweat might be responsible for this change in the traditional hospitality.

Some policy implications

The government is very much aware of the large-scale migration and consequent imbalances in population distribution in the country and the vicious circle thus generated. Answering the United Nations Enquiry on Population, the government indicated that it perceived the spatial distribution of population to be extremely unacceptable and wished to promote policies to decelerate migration. It was felt that radical intervention was called for to alter the rural settlement patterns and adjust rural configuration (U.N., 1979: 131–2).

In Sudan, previous development plans and the colonial era encouraged the development of urban areas and big cities and also concentrated on the large-scale agricultural schemes in Gezira, Kashm El Girba and other projects which contributed to export commodities. In other words, the focus was on promoting national income growth rather than on social objectives of equity and justice. Rural areas were neglected and the stagnation of these areas coupled with some semblance of better life in urban centres and organized agricultural schemes attracted flocks of migrants. This resulted in further neglect of sending areas – both by the out-migration and the government – with concomitant congestion and other problems in receiving areas. This created a vicious circle, and still further exodus took place from the hinterland to the already overcrowded urban, developed and fast developing areas.

The government, as noted earlier, has realized the importance of balanced regional development for overall national development. In their *Six Year Plan of Economic and Social Development 1977/78–1982/83*, it was spelt out that the objectives among other things are 'devoting more attention to rural development and advancement of various retarded areas, encouraging local population to contribute more actively towards raising living standards in such areas. . . .' (Democratic Republic of Sudan, 1977).

One of the cornerstones of this planning is 'to distribute benefits of development as equitably as possible among various income groups and regions'. Towards achieving these objectives the government has envisaged policies 'which encourage development of rural areas particularly the traditional sector and provision of civic amenities such as schools, dispensaries, post offices and electric supply in backward regions combined with projects to create regional employment . . . to reduce the rate of rural migration'.

The creation of smaller administrative units, the decentralization of power and authority and financial and other assistance to backward areas, all have contributed to some improvement in the migration situation. However, much more will be needed to stem the tide. Agriculture, rural-based industries, handicrafts and education relevant to the needs of the people in the rural areas would all assuage the situation. Labour-intensive endeavours like road building, small irrigation schemes, poultry farming, etc., would generate employment and livelihood for a vast segment of the population, and would keep them in their areas instead of itching to move to the already over-crowded places.

It is not easy to persuade people not to migrate and stay in their homes especially when for a very long time such migration has been observed by people to be the only panacea for their problems. Since government is interested in turning the tide, it is imperative that their plans and policies should keep these in view. Again, mere platitudes would not help. What would be needed is action, and immediately.

REFERENCES

Democratic Republic of Sudan, Ministry of Culture and Information (1979) *Sudan Facts and Figures*. Khartoum.

Democratic Republic of Sudan, Ministry of Health (1976) *Annual Health Statistics Report*. Khartoum.

Democratic Republic of Sudan, Ministry of National Planning (1977) *Six-Year Plan of Economic and Social Development 1977/78–1982/83*. Vol. 1, Khartoum.

Democratic Republic of Sudan, Department of Statistics (1977) *Second Population Census 1973*, vol. 1: *Socio-economic characteristics*. Khartoum.

Democratic Republic of Sudan, Department of Statistics (1980) *Second Population Census 1973*, vol. 2: *Population dynamics*, Khartoum.

El-Bushra, E.S. (1975) The Sudan, in R. Jones (ed.), *Essays in World Urbanisation*. London, George Philip, pp. 380–84.

Khogali, M.M. (1982) Western Sudanese migrants to Khashm el-Girba agricultural region, in J.I. Clarke and L.A. Kosiński (eds.) *Redistribution of Population in Africa*. London, Heinemann, pp. 166–75.

United Nations (1979) *World Population Trends and Policies*, Vol. 2, New York.

23 The growth of Juba in southern Sudan

L.R. Mills

The Southern Sudan refers to that part of the country in general to the south of the Bahr El Ghazal and the tenth parallel. The external limits to this area were not finally delimited until the second decade of this century when the Lado Enclave was taken over from Belgian administration in 1910 and much of what is now eastern Equatoria was transferred from Uganda in 1914. Originally two provinces, the south was subdivided into three in 1945 and remained as such for the next thirty years. In 1972, following 17 years of civil war, a peace agreement brought the three provinces together as a semi-autonomous region within the Republic. Juba was declared the regional capital and centre of an administration and civil service with a range of a dozen or so ministries. Four years later the provinces were each split into two in the vanguard of a national programme of decentralization. As a result there is being built up today a vast hierarchy of administration ranging from the regional capital through six provinces and their capitals to more than fifty council areas.

In the context of population redistribution, it is argued here that recent population movements in the Southern Sudan have not been the product of development projects or of more underlying economic factors, but rather a result of the political history of the area and its consequences. Prior to independence (1956), development projects were few, localized and had little overall effect on population distribution. For almost two decades after independence any moves towards development came to a complete halt as a long-drawn-out civil war effected major changes in population patterns, with more than a million people fleeing into hiding or crossing to neighbouring countries as refugees. Following the Addis Ababa Peace Agreement (1972), the move back of many of these people was described by the United Nations High Commission on Refugees (U.N.H.C.R.) as the largest return movement in the history of Africa. Since then, in a process of relief, rehabilitation and development, the resources of the region have been overwhelmingly channelled into creating an administration and its concomitant employment. This trend has been largely concentrated in existing centres and has continued a rate of urbanization largely unprecedented in the Sudan. The whole process and its attendant problems are highlighted in the development and growth of Juba during the last decade. The current trends and situation in that town will be examined in some detail as a background to the implications of future urban growth in the region as a whole.

The south in 1955–56

At the time of independence in 1956 and the first national census, the three southern provinces had a population of 2.8 million people scattered over an area of 650,000 sq km. By any standards, densities were extremely low: few districts supported more than an average of five persons per sq km. The population was almost entirely reliant on subsistence agriculture with very few concentrations of population. Indeed, it could be said that no urban centre existed at that time. Even defining 'urban' in the 1955–56 census as any settlement above 5,000 persons, the total urban population of the south as a whole did not exceed 50,000 people. Juba was the largest settlement in the south with hardly more than 10,000 inhabitants, and no centre could be considered urban in function.

In the south as a whole the population was highly mobile (even more so than in the northern provinces) but over relatively short distances. More than 70 per cent of the population were enumerated in localities other than those of their birth. However, less than 4 per cent were found outside their province of birth. This relatively small amount of inter-provincial migration may be regarded to some extent as a product of the large size of most of the administrative units. With individual provinces larger than a number of African states, a move to another province could involve journeys of considerable distance. Other factors tending to reduce inter-provincial movement include the diversity of language and culture as well as the lack of a well developed transport network. All these factors applied especially to movements between the southern provinces and the rest of the country. In the southern provinces in 1955–56 only one per cent of the population had been born outside the south. For this area as a whole, movement, though small, tended to be outwards and in the first census a net migration loss of 9,000 people was recorded: some 16,000 people born in the south were recorded in the northern provinces, while 7,000 from the north had moved south. This outward movement from the south was overwhelmingly from Bahr El Ghazal and Upper Nile and was in two main directions. Initially there were relatively short-distance moves across the border into three provinces adjacent to the south. Secondly, a more localized and long-distance movement took people to Khartoum province. Seven out of ten out-migrants from the south went to the three neighbouring provinces of the north (Darfur, Kordofan and Blue Nile) and the remaining three out of ten made the longer journey to Khartoum province.

Movement into the south in 1955–56 was almost entirely confined to Upper Nile which received six out of seven of the in-migrants. On balance the movement within the country showed the south as having a net migration loss. This was heaviest in Bahr El Ghazal (8,000). In Equatoria there was a net loss of 2,000, while Upper Nile registered a small net gain of 1,000. The overall pattern is shown in Figure 23.1.

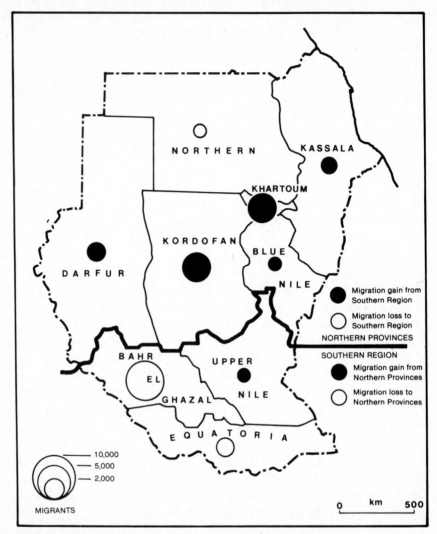

Fig. 23.1 Net migration in the Sudan between Northern provinces and the Southern Region, 1955–6

The impact of the civil war

In August 1955 a mutiny of the Equatorial Corps in Torit sparked off a civil war which was to last seventeen years. Fighting was sporadic and varied from place to place but the effects on population numbers and distribution were dramatic. By the time of the Addis Ababa Peace Agreement in 1972 it is estimated that the *de facto* population of the southern provinces as a whole was smaller than it had been twenty years earlier. When the 2.8 million were enumerated in 1955–56 for the south with an annual rate of natural increase exceeding the national figure of 3.3 per cent, a 1972 population of more than 4.5 million could have been expected under more normal circumstances. As it was, if the 1973 census figures are used as a basis for calculation, the ceasefire population in March 1972 must have been in the order of 2.6 million. This apparent drop in the region's total numbers may be explained by a variety of factors that would include a combination of out-migration, a higher death rate, lower birth rate as well as a likely underestimate in the census totals. Certainly the years of strife would have reduced rates of natural increase. Apart from the heavy toll of fighting, the lack of medical facilities would hasten a rise in death rates. The splitting of families and the general political and social instability would have a commensurate effect on reducing births. More dramatic, however, was out-migration in the form of an exodus of refugees to neighbouring countries. It has been estimated that, at the time of the Peace Agreement, approaching a quarter of a million people (some 10 per cent of the *de jure* population) were living in the five countries bordering the Southern Region.

Thus there are substantial and adequate reasons to explain a 1972 population similar to if not smaller than that recorded in 1955–56. Even a year later, in 1973, after a substantial influx of returning refugees, the growth rates at the provincial level gave negative growth figures for two of the region's three provinces. While the northern provinces as a whole had increased at an average of 2.7 per cent per annum since 1955–56, the southern provinces showed a growth rate of 0.3 per cent. This overall figure was derived from a 2.0 per cent annual increase in Bahr El Ghazal, but −0.6 per cent in Upper Nile and −1.0 per cent in Equatoria. However, subsequent work in this field suggests that the situation may not have been quite so grave. The 1973 census gave a regional total of 2,969,000 persons. Such a figure included a 5 per cent compensation for estimated under-enumeration. Even so, the census count, apart from not being able to include refugees still outside the country, did omit considerable numbers of displaced persons still in hiding within the region. It is thought that at the time of the census at least 175,000 people had not returned to the region and a probable 200,000 still had to emerge from hiding. Thus a more realistic estimate of the region's population would be in the order of 3.1 million.

Whether 2.6, 2.9 or 3.1 million, the fact remains that the population at the end of the civil disturbances was spread very thinly on the ground. Moreover, because of the civil war, the distribution patterns had changed and in some cases permanently. The out-migration of refugees is the most obvious case and certainly the easiest movement to measure. On a wider scale was that of the displaced persons within the region. Accurate data are difficult to determine. At the end of the war, when repatriation and relief were being discussed, estimates varied and were often no more than guesses; figures as high as 2.5 million were talked of. Indeed the initial estimate of the Commission on Relief, Resettlement and Repatriation for persons displaced within the Sudan was put at two million. When the Government set out its aid requirements after the ceasefire, a figure of 327,000 was given. At the time of the Peace Agreement, according to the U.N.H.C.R. approaching 177,000 people from the south were registered as refugees in surrounding countries. A further 25,000 people were also thought to be refugees but outside the control of the international agencies. This would give a total of 202,000 southern Sudanese abroad, although the figure was later revised to 219,400 distributed as follows:

Uganda	86,000
Zaire	67,000
Central African Republic	30,900
Ethiopia	35,000
Kenya	500
	219,400

Far more difficult to estimate was the number of displaced persons within the country. In April 1972 a figure of 800,000 had been arrived at, although some thought it conservative. In any case, within eighteen months of the Addis Ababa Agreement, the President of the High Executive Council was able to report that 1,190,000 individuals, refugees and returnees, had passed through the hands of the Resettlement Commission. Such a figure represented over one-third of the total population of the southern Sudan. The resettlement of these people did not reproduce the distribution and settlement patterns existing at the beginning of the civil war. Overall, the resettlement and subsequent attempts to provide a livelihood have had a major effect on population concentration in the decade 1972–82 and this has taken place largely in existing centres and particularly in the towns.

The situation in 1973

By the time of the second national census in 1973, the urban population (including all settlements of 5,000 inhabitants or more) of the south had risen from less than 50,000 to almost 300,000. As a proportion of the total population of the Southern Region the increase had been from less than 2 per cent in 1955–56 to more than 10 per cent. This six-fold increase in the urban proportion of the southern population compares with a doubling in the northern provinces (from 10.8 to 20.5 per cent). The urban population was found in 15 settlements (Fig. 23.2), eight in Equatoria accounting for almost 20 per cent of that province's population, six in Bahr El Ghazal representing 9 per cent of its population, and only one urban settlement in Upper Nile, namely Malakal, and this accounted for less than 5 per cent. If, however, a more usual lower limit of 20,000 inhabitants is taken for an urban settlement then only the three provincial capitals would be listed in 1973, which together accounted for a population approaching 150,000. Juba continued to be the largest settlement in the south with 57,000 people, Wau was of a similar size with 53,000, while Malakal had 37,000 inhabitants.

Whatever definition of 'urban' is used, the fact remains that while the population of the southern Sudan as a whole remained static or even decreased in

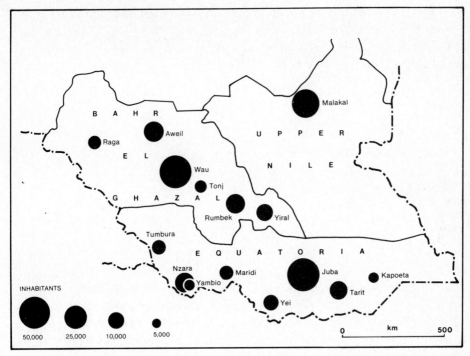

Fig. 23.2 Settlements with more than 5,000 inhabitants in the Southern Region of the Sudan, 1973.

the eighteen years between 1955 and 1973, the population of the towns increased remarkably. A substantial proportion of this increase undoubtedly occurred in the twelve months between the Peace Agreement of March 1972 and the census of April 1973. The growth of the towns during the war was in no way constant. For most of the time any large settlement (and particularly garrison towns such as Juba or Wau) provided a place of refuge from the sporadic fighting that took place in the countryside. Soon after the 1955–56 census (when the population had been put at 10,600) Juba was severely burned during fighting in July 1956 and over half the population fled, albeit temporarily. In the following years this movement was reversed with people seeking shelter from insecure conditions in neighbouring areas. By 1964 the town's population had almost doubled to 19,500. Following the October Revolution in 1964 army activity increased and after incidents in Juba in July 1965 many of the inhabitants fled. Beshir (1975: 76) quotes a figure of 7,000 for the population in 1965. Again this exodus was only temporary and was followed by a rapid influx to the town. The same author quotes a figure of 69,000 for 1969. Though undoubtedly an exaggeration, it does reflect the remarkable fluctuation in the town's population during the civil war.

At the time of the ceasefire, and even up to the 1973 census, the towns were large concentrations of people, in relative terms, but in very few respects did they display any marked urban characteristics. In the south, two industrial groups

Table 23.1. *The urban economically-active of the Southern Region and Northern provinces by industry, 1973*

Industry	Southern Region	Northern provinces
Agriculture, hunting, forestry and fishing	34.8	21.3
Mining and quarrying	0.0	0.2
Manufacturing	6.4	12.5
Electricity, gas and water	0.8	2.7
Construction	5.9	5.1
Wholesale and retail trade, restaurants and hotels	7.8	15.1
Transport	4.4	11.5
Finance, insurance and real estate	0.0	0.6
Community, social and personal services	39.9	31.0
Total	100.0	100.0

Note: Urban = centres with 5,000 or more people
Source: Democratic Republic of the Sudan, Department of Statistics, *Estimates of the Population and Socio-Economic Characteristics of the Sudan during 1973–1985*, Khartoum, April 1976, Table 15.

accounted for three-quarters of all urban economic activity (Table 23.1): the service sector and agricultural workers. Service activities accounted for 40 per cent of the economically active and comprised activities ranging from public administration, community services and defence. In 1973 the latter category of protective service and defence workers accounted for most of this group. Indeed, those of the protective service alone comprised the third largest group of occupations in the modern sector of the region, after that of unclassified manual labourers and agricultural and animal husbandry workers (Mills, 1975: 73). For the urban areas in 1973, it is thought that this category accounted for at least 30 per cent of all paid employment.

The second largest industrial group was that of agricultural workers (35 per cent), reflecting both the basis of the regional economy and the largely rural nature of the settlements classified as urban. The proportions of economically active in manufacturing (6.4 per cent) or trade (7.8 per cent) were approximately half those in the rest of the country while the proportion in transport was approximately one-third. Thus, in the early days after the Peace Agreement, paid employment in the towns largely reflected that of the region as a whole: public administration and defence together with agriculture.

In terms of occupations in 1973, a more detailed analysis is possible, which also permits an examination of the situation in Juba as the most urbanized settlement in the region. Using the major International Standard Classification of Occupations (I.S.C.O.) groupings, a similar pattern is seen in Juba (Table 23.2) save that the proportion of workers in agriculture was small (less than 5 per cent) while the service occupations accounted for more than 40 per cent of the employment. Again most of the occupations in this category were in the protective services. This figure compares with 32 per cent for all the urban centres in the South, 23 per cent in the rest of the country and only 16 per cent in the Three Towns of Khartoum, Khartoum North and Omdurman. The next highest group (12 per cent) in Juba

Table 23.2. *Percentage distribution of the urban economically-active of the Southern Region and Juba town compared with the Northern provinces and Khartoum by occupation group, 1973*

Occupation group	Southern Region	Juba Town	Northern provinces urban	Khartoum (1974)
Professional, technical and related workers	5.8	11.5	6.2	8.9
Administrative and managerial workers	0.6	0.4	1.0	1.3
Clerical and related workers	3.2	6.2	5.9	14.8
Sales workers	6.8	7.7	13.4	12.7
Service workers	31.5	41.2	23.3	16.1
Agriculture, animal husbandry and forestry workers, fishermen and hunters	32.4	4.3	13.2	2.9
Production and related workers, transport equipment operators and labourers	19.7	28.7	37.0	43.3
Total	100.0	100.0	100.0	100.0

Sources: Data for Southern Region and Northern Provinces from Democratic Republic of Sudan, Department of Statistics, *Estimates of the Population and Socio-Economic Characteristics of the Sudan during 1973–1985*, Khartoum, April 1976; those of Juba from L.R. Mills, *Notes for the Study of the Manpower Situation in the Southern Region*, Paper presented at the Workshop on The Southern Region's Development Training Needs, Juba, 1975; those of Khartoum adapted from UNDP/1LO, *Comprehensive Employment Strategy Mission, Sudan: The Socio-Economic Survey in the Three Towns 1974*, Geneva, 1976, Table 26.

was that of 'professional and technical workers', which was almost entirely composed of medical personnel and teachers. Production workers formed a much smaller group than in other urban centres as did sales workers.

The situation reflected by the 1973 census cannot be considered as a particularly accurate or long-term picture of the state of the economy or employment within the towns. It does, nevertheless, illustrate the state of flux and dramatic changes taking place in the urban areas. A year earlier fighting ceased. The Addis Ababa Agreement had been formulated into the Regional Self-Government Act for the Southern region and provision made for the establishment of legislative and executive organs with a wide range of functions and powers within the region. A People's Assembly was charged with the preservation of public order, internal security, efficient administration and the development of the region in cultural, economic and social matters. In Chapter IV of this act the areas of jurisdiction are enlarged in a list of 20 fields of activity. The first two on the list are probably the most important: 'the promotion and utilization of Regional financial resources for the development and administration of the Southern Region' and the organization of the machinery for Regional and Local Administration. Certainly these two functions have played the most important role in the context of recent population redistribution. Largely of necessity, it is the latter aspect of building up a regional network of administration that has played the most dominant role during the past ten years in creating employment and in subsequent population migration and concentration.

By 1973 the transition from military control to civilian leadership had taken place. Government and administrative activity was concentrated on resettlement, relief and rehabilitation for what turned out to be more than two million refugees and returnees. The logistics of transferring large numbers of people from their place of refuge to a new home required the construction of a large number of resettlement camps. Throughout the region, 44 reception centres were built to accommodate returning people from both abroad and within the country. These centres were generally situated in the main towns and, as such, they formed an important stimulus to the growth of the urban populations. In Juba, for example, it is thought that the population doubled with the arrival of refugees and returnees between the ceasefire and the 1973 census. Moreover, this post-war influx continued well into 1974. It is thought that up to 400,000 persons (Mills, 1975: 28) were still to return at the time of the census, and as with earlier arrivals many were to make for the towns.

The situation since 1973

Following the Peace Agreement, the Central Government made significant budgetary provisions to establish a Southern administration. This comprised 12.1 million Sudanese pounds (L.S.) to cover the regional recurrent budget and balance the provincial councils' budget as well as L.S. 1.4 million for a regional development budget. This ratio of 9:1 with regard to the recurrent and development budgets stayed much the same during the following ten years. In terms of creating employment, suffice it to say that up to two-thirds of the recurrent budget has been allocated to personnel services. Moreover, over the years, actual expenditure (as opposed to the amount allocated) has been considerably greater in the payment of salaries than in the provision of services and equipment or in the area of development. In the first five years of regional administration, for example, actual expenditure in Chapter I (i.e. personnel) varied between 60 and 90 per cent of the amounts budgeted, in Chapters II and III (covering services and equipment) the figures varied between 25 and 50 per cent while only 18 per cent of the sums allocated for development were spent (Ater, 1979). Thus, by looking at finance alone one sees how development in the Southern region since the civil war has been orientated towards building up a civil service and an administrative infrastructure. By 1976, the Regional Government alone paid more than one-quarter of all persons in employment within the region and almost two-thirds of all skilled workers. Of a civil service of almost 60,000 people, some 59 per cent were employed by the Ministry of Regional Administration, Police and Prisons (Mills, 1975: 116–18), mostly in the towns and particularly in Juba. These current trends in employment, in-migration and urbanization in general and their implications for the future, though extreme in Juba, do provide a basis for considering the needs and problems of the towns in the region as a whole.

During the period 1972–82 the population of Juba increased fourfold to approximately 110,000. Well over 80 per cent of the people over the age of 12 are in-migrants. By any standards this is high and has resulted in a mixed heterogeneous society comprising more than 45 tribes, although almost all (85 per cent) are from the Southern region. The overwhelming primary reason for coming to Juba has been to look for employment, and to a remarkable extent during the past ten years this has been provided. During the period 1973–79, for example, while the town as a whole grew at an annual rate of nearly 7 per cent, employment increased at a rate of 5.3 per cent. This figure is relatively high and reflects the low levels of employment at the end of the civil war and secondly the tremendous increase in employment which came with the establishment of a regional government and civil service centred on the town. In 1979, of the 21,000 in paid employment, over 80 per cent were on the payroll of the regional or central governments. Less than 15 per cent of jobs were to be found in the private sector.

The overwhelming effect that creating an administration centred on Juba has had on changing the status and function of the town is clearly borne out by the differential growth of varying categories of employment in recent years. Figures available for 1973 and 1979 (Table 23.3) reveal that during the six years the employed labour force grew from 15,500 to more than 21,000, an overall growth of 37 per cent. The 'production, transport and labouring' group increased by exactly the same amount and still forms a quarter of the workforce. This growth, parallel to the rate of employment as a whole, is a reflection of this group largely comprising unskilled labour and the ease and speed at which newly created jobs can be filled. The largely unskilled 'agricultural, animal husbandry, fisheries' group, though small, also grew at a similar overall rate (38 per cent). In the category of service occupations, growth was only 11 per cent over the six-year period. To a large degree this can be explained by the relatively stable size of the police force and army in the town. The group of sales workers in 1979 was almost the same as in 1973. This apparent lack of growth was produced by considerable numbers in this sector being made redundant in 1979 when various trading activities related to foodstuffs and brewing were closed down or curtailed by the authorities following an outbreak of cholera within the region. Professional and technical workers increased by 56 per cent over the six years but total numbers were not large: 1,645 in 1973 and 2,560 in 1979. This is the most skilled of occupation groups and growth has suffered markedly because of the lack of skilled, qualified personnel. The most spectacular growth, since 1972, has been in the cadre of administrative jobs. Indeed, the 'administrative and managerial' category increased by more than 1,200 per cent and 'clerical and related' by 330 per cent. Today 'clerks' and related workers account for almost 20 per cent of the total Juba labour force. These high growth rates are almost entirely the product of the town's new role as the administrative capital of the south. The trend is clear: Juba is emerging as an administrative and service centre with an extremely small, if any, productive base.

Despite the relatively high annual increase in the rate of employment, it has not

Table 23.3. *Occupation groups and employment status of the economically-active population of Juba in 1973 and 1979*

Occupation group	1973		1979		Percentage change 1973–79
	Number	% of total	Number	% of total	
Professional and technical workers	1,645	10.6	2,560	12.1	+56
Administrative and managerial workers	56	0.4	739	3.5	+1,220
Clerical and related workers	879	5.7	3,791	17.9	+331
Sales workers	1,097	7.1	1,083	5.1	−0.01
Service workers	5,878	38.0	6,499	30.6	+11
Agricultural, animal husbandry, forestry, fishing and hunting workers	607	3.9	840	4.0	+38
Production and related workers: transport equipment operators and labourers	4,098	26.5	5,613	26.6	+37
Not classified by occupation	1,207	7.8	49	0.2	—
Total	15,467	100	21,174	100	+37

					Percentage change per annum
Population of Juba	56,723		84,000		+6.8
Total economically active	19,613		28,300		+6.3
Total employed	15,467		21,100		+5.3
Unemployed (seeking employment)	4,146		7,200		+9.7
Unemployed as percentage of economically active		21		26	+3.6
Unemployed as percentage of total population		7.3		8.6	+2.8

Source: L.R. Mills, *People of Juba: Demographic and Socio-Economic Characteristics of the Capital of the Southern Sudan*, University of Juba Population and Manpower Unit Research Paper No. 3, 1981, Table 6-6.

kept pace with the numbers seeking jobs. Juba is the main centre in the south for those seeking paid employment and the rate of in-migration is increasing. By 1979, 26 per cent of the economically-active in the town were unemployed but seeking work. In the previous six years this category had increased at an annual rate of 9.7 per cent, i.e. more than 4 per cent faster than the filling of jobs. The main reason for such a high unemployment rate is not the lack of jobs but rather the critical shortage of people adequately qualified to fill vacant posts. The figures for the region illustrate this well. In 1976–77, four years after the establishment of the Regional government, the personnel budget was in the order of L.S. 10 million. As the introduction to the budget points out, the budget would have been higher, but, in recognition of the fact that personnel were not available to fill the posts, the proposals of individual ministries were cut by 10 per cent. The reduction could have been greater. A year earlier a total of 57,000 posts had been budgeted for and by the end of the year 20 per cent remained vacant. Even this figure does not portray the critical nature of the problem. Of the 57,000 posts, over 81 per cent were for the unclassified category of unskilled labour. Vacancies in that group generally reflect unutilized budgets rather than a shortage of labour, and budgets are frequently under-utilized because of the lack of trained manpower. In 1976–77 almost half of all posts in the 'administrative and professional' and the 'sub-professional and technical' grades remained empty awaiting qualified incumbents. Such a situation has not slowed down in-migration. The knowledge of vacant posts on a wide scale has swelled the influx of many who would be unqualified to hold them. Thus today the situation in Juba is well exemplified by three basic annual growth rates relating to the period 1973–79:

Growth of Juba's population   6.8 per cent
Growth of employment   5.3 per cent
Growth of unemployment   9.7 per cent

These trends must be borne in mind when examining and explaining the present-day urban environment in Juba, and in particular the state of housing and the provision of services. In no way has the development of the latter been able to cater for the influx during the last ten years or during the years of civil war.

In 1979 Juba comprised some 22,000 buildings and at least 18,000 of these were the traditional mud-walled, thatched-roofed *tukls* (Mills, 1981). Less than 15 per cent of all housing can be considered as of 'permanent' construction. Several *tukls* or other living quarters are usually found clustered together within a fence to form a compound. These may accommodate up to 25–30 people, although most tend to have between six and twelve occupants. In 1979 the overall average for all types of housing was 10.8 persons per compound, compared with 8.2 persons in the next largest settlement in eastern Equatoria Province (Fully, 1981). Of more consequence is the number of people in each living quarter. In 1979 this figure was 3.0 and as such expressed serious overcrowding. Very few buildings in Juba have been built with the permission of or on plots allocated by the authorities. Between 1972 and 1975, for instance, it was estimated that only 170 plots were allocated yet more than 2,000 compounds were established (Mamtaz *et al.*, 1977: 14). This growth has largely been confined to fourth-class areas within the town or the 'uncontrolled' areas developing outside the town's boundary and outside the prospect of any services.

In the provision of basic services in Juba, there is a sharp distinction between areas comprising what the authorities term the first three classes of housing, and a category of fourth-class and uncontrolled housing. The former reflect and still rely largely on the pre-independence infrastructure while the latter have little or no service support from the authorities. Suffice it to say that today at least three-quarters of the population live outside the first three categories of housing.

In 1979 only 17 per cent of the people of Juba had water piped direct to their homes. For a further 23 per cent water was delivered to the door, usually hand-carried, occasionally by lorry or by a growing fleet of donkey-drawn containers. Almost two-thirds of all households had to fetch their own water and generally from public standpipes. Of all the services, water is the major problem and especially in the fourth-class and uncontrolled areas. Cuts in supply and low pressure are experienced in all quarters, necessitating a number of journeys each day for the majority who have no piped supply. Long walks to alternative sources are the mode. In a 1977 housing survey (Mamtaz *et al.*, 1977) it was calculated that almost 60 per cent of all households were more than ten minutes' walking time from the nearest supply. With the provision of electricity the situation is similar but by no means so crucial. In 1979 less than 14 per cent of the population benefited from this amenity in their homes. As regards sewage disposal, most people in Juba do not have access to toilet facilities. Less than one-quarter of the inhabitants have a toilet within their compound.

Over the years the provision of basic services has not kept pace with the rapid in-movement of migrants. The extension of the water and electricity networks has not kept up with the expansion in population numbers and the concomitant spread in the *de facto* built-up area of the town. Figures for the years 1977 to 1979 illustrate this well. In 1977, for example, 26 per cent of all households had piped water. By 1978 this figure had dropped to 24 per cent and to 17 per cent in 1979. Similarly, the provision of electricity by household dropped from 26 per cent to 14 per cent.

Conclusion

This situation in Juba must be viewed against the causes of its rapid growth. The tremendous expansion in administrative employment and a concurrent concentration of people with increasing unemployment is being repeated in other centres within the region and particularly as newly-created provincial capitals are developed. The data available for Juba clearly outline the current trends *vis-à-vis* growth, employment and the overall urban environment in terms of housing and the provision of services. These must be viewed against the projections of future urban growth within the region. According to U.N. figures, the urban proportion of the region's population will increase from 15 per cent to more than 35 per cent by the year 2000. Such figures envisage Juba as having as population of almost half a million inhabitants (Bucht, 1980) by that time.

REFERENCES

Ater, I.M. (1979) Region financial resources and their allocations, paper presented at the Conference on Development Problems of the Southern Region, Juba.
Beshir, M.O. (1975) *The Southern Sudan: From Conflict to Peace*, Khartoum.
Bucht, B. (1980) *Sudan Population Projections, 1980–2000*, Social Statistics Support Programme Preview Paper No. 2, U.N. Population Division.
Fully, P. A. (1981) *People of Tarit: Migrants and Migration to the Capital of Eastern Equatoria Province*, University of Juba College of Social and Economic Studies, Year III Fieldwork Report.

Mamtaz, B. *et al.* (1977) *Juba Low Cost Housing Study*, Development Planning Unit, Bartlett School of Architecture and Planning, University College, London.

Mills, L.R. (1975) *Population and Manpower in the Southern Sudan*, I.L.O.

Mills, L.R. (1981) *People of Juba: Demographic and Socio-Economic Characteristics of the Capital of the Southern Sudan*, University of Juba Population and Manpower Unit Research Paper No. 3.

Index

absentee landlords, 86
Abuja, Nigeria, 13, 16, 198,
    202–4
Addis Ababa Agreement (1972),
    71, 301, 310, 312–17
administrative reform, 9, 16, 17;
    Nigeria, 200–4; Sudan, 310,
    317–19
African Development Bank, 215
Ajaokuta, Nigeria, 200
Ajoda new town, Nigeria, 198
amlak land, 278
Angola, out-migration, 69, 74,
    167, 169
apartheid, 176–93
Arusha conference on refugees
    (1979), 69
Arusha Declaration (1967),
    Tanzania, 125
Asosa Hoha settlement scheme,
    Ethiopia, 108
asylum states for refugees, 11,
    68–83
Awash Valley Authority
    (A.V.A.), Ethiopia, 89, 92–3

Bacita new town, Nigeria, 198
Bakolari Dam and Irrigation
    Project, Nigeria, 201, 204
Bangkok seminar (1979), 21, 27
Bantustans, 10, 176–93
Baraka scheme, Sudan, 301, 307
Barotseland, 168, 172
Barotseland Development Centre
    (est. 1947), 171
Benin, Nigeria, 201
betterment villages, 184–91
bilharzia, 33
Black Homelands, 10, 176–93
Bothashoek closer-settlement,
    South Africa, 185–91
Botswana, 71, 73–6, 81
British South Africa Company,
    168
Bumbugu Land Planning Area,
    Ghana, 212–13
Burundi, 76–8

Camp Five, Kenana, Sudan, 265,
    268, 270
camps: concentration, 157;
    labour, 275; refugee, 72, 108,
    318; youth, 13
Canada, absence of African
    refugees, 72–3
capitalism: and development
    projects, 31, 33, 39, 227, 265;
    and population movements,
    41–52; and wage labour, 56–7,
    61–2, 64
cash needs, stimulation of, 55–7
castor cultivation, 282–3, 292–5
cattle rearing: density, 10;
    disease, 169, 171; Sudan,
    272–3, 277–96; Uganda, 118–
    20; *see also* nomadic
    pastoralists
censuses, 12, 17, 142; Ghana,
    207; Mozambique, 153; South
    Africa, 179; Sudan, 220, 227,
    230, 231, 261, 313, 314;
    Tanzania, 141, 142, 145, 148,
    149; Uganda, 118
charcoal burners, 97
Chilalo Agricultural
    Development Unit
    (C.A.D.U.), Ethiopia, 92–3
Chilembe Communal Village,
    Mozambique, 157
Chokwé, Mozambique, 154
cities: capital cities relocated, 13,
    141, 198, 201–3; creation of,
    17, 310; distribution of, 5;
    growth of, 244, 297–323;
    primacy of major cities, 9, 11,
    58, 244; *see also* urbanization
civil wars: Ethiopia, 84;
    Mozambique, 155–8; Sudan,
    68, 234, 276, 310, 312–15,
    318; Zaire, 68
class stratification in
    development projects, 35, 39,
    40
closer-settlements, 184–91
colonial rule: anti-colonial

movements, 68, 69, 76, 81,
    155–8, 176, *see also* civil wars;
    and development strategy, 9,
    10, 153–4, 157, 163, 168–71,
    194–5, 211; and wage labour,
    53–8
commercial agriculture, 5, 9, 10,
    30, 32, 33; Ethiopia, 94–7;
    Mozambique, 153–5; Nigeria,
    199; South Africa, 180; Sudan,
    55–7, 80, 219, 245–50, 265–82,
    291–6; Tanzania, 78, 141; *see
    also* mechanization and
    modernization of agriculture
compensation for development
    project land, 267, 278
concentration camps, 157
contraceptive behaviour, 35, 234
co-operative settlement schemes:
    Ethiopia, 108; Mozambique,
    153–62
cotton cultivation, 30, 41, 55–6,
    272–3, 282–3, 292, 301

D.D.T. side-effects, 36, 215
Dedoro-Tankara Land Planning
    Committee, Ghana, 211–12
deforestation, 35, 130, *see also*
    soil erosion
delinquency, 198
density of population, 2–3, 5, 9;
    Ethiopia, 84–6; Ghana, 207–
    11; Mozambique, 153; Sudan,
    227–9, 234, 254, 259, 261,
    297, 300–1, 311; Uganda, 115,
    117, 118; and water supply,
    254, 259
depression (1931), 59
development gap, 276, 280, *see
    also* regional disparities
development projects:
    classification of, 22–3, 141;
    consequences of, 26–7, 30–40,
    141–52, 197–8, 297–309;
    determinants of, 26; Ethiopia,
    84–111; Ghana, 206–18;
    indicators of development, 20;